T0278290

WOMEN'S STUDIES QUARTERLY

VOLUME 50   NUMBERS 3 & 4   FALL/WINTER 2022

An educational project of the Feminist Press at the City University of New York, the College of Staten Island, City University of New York, Kingsborough Community College, City University of New York, and Borough of Manhattan Community College, City University of New York, with support from the Center for the Study of Women and Society and the Center for the Humanities at the Graduate Center, City University of New York

EDITORS
Red Washburn, Kingsborough Community College and The Graduate Center, CUNY
Brianne Waychoff, Borough of Manhattan Community College

EDITORIAL DIRECTORS
Dána-Ain Davis and Kendra Sullivan

GUEST EDITORS
Heather Rellihan, Anne Arundel Community College
Jennifer C. Nash, Duke University
Charlene A. Carruthers, Northwestern University

POETRY EDITORS
Julie R. Enszer, Cheryl Clarke, and JP Howard

PROSE EDITORS
Keisha-Gaye Anderson, Vi Khi Nao, and Lauren Cherelle

VISUAL ARTS EDITOR
Mel Michelle Lewis

EDITORIAL ASSISTANTS
Googie Karrass
Kayla Reece

EDITORS EMERITAE
Natalie Havlin 2017–2020 ▪ Jillian M. Báez 2017–2020 ▪ Matt Brim 2014–2017
Cynthia Chris 2014–2017 ▪ Amy Herzog 2011–2014 ▪ Joe Rollins 2011–2014
Victoria Pitts-Taylor 2008–2011 ▪ Talia Schaffer 2008–2011 ▪ Cindi Katz 2004–2008
Nancy K. Miller 2004–2008 ▪ Diane Hope 2000–2004 ▪ Janet Zandy 1995–2000
Nancy Porter 1982–1992 ▪ Florence Howe 1972–1982; 1993–1994

The Feminist Press at the City University of New York

EXECUTIVE DIRECTOR & PUBLISHER
Margot Atwell

ART DIRECTOR
Drew Stevens

SENIOR EDITOR
Lauren Rosemary Hook

SENIOR SALES & MARKETING MANAGER
Jisu Kim

ASSISTANT EDITOR
Nick Whitney

WSQ: Women's Studies Quarterly, a peer-reviewed, theme-based journal, is published by the Feminist Press at the City University of New York.

COVER ART
Inter Space by Heather Harvey

WEBSITE
feministpress.org/wsq
womensstudiesquarterly.com

EDITORIAL CORRESPONDENCE
WSQ: Women's Studies Quarterly, The Feminist Press at the City University of New York, The Graduate Center, 365 Fifth Avenue, Suite 5406, New York, NY 10016; wsqeditorial@gmail.com.

PRINT SUBSCRIPTIONS
Subscribers in the United States: Individuals—$60 for 1 year; $150 for 3 years. Institutions—$85 for 1 year; $225 for 3 years. Subscribers outside the United States: Add $40 per year for delivery. To subscribe or change an address, contact *WSQ* Customer Service, The Feminist Press at the City University of New York, The Graduate Center, 365 Fifth Avenue, Suite 5406, New York, NY 10016; 212-817-7915; info@feministpress.org.

FORTHCOMING ISSUES
State/Power, Christina B. Hanhardt, University of Maryland, and Dayo F. Gore, Georgetown University
Nonbinary, JV Fuqua, Queens College, Marquis Bey, Northwestern University, and Red Washburn, Kingsborough Community College and The Graduate Center, CUNY

RIGHTS & PERMISSIONS
Fred Courtright, The Permissions Company, 570-839-7477; permdude@eclipse.net.

SUBMISSION INFORMATION
For the most up-to-date guidelines, calls for papers, and information concerning forthcoming issues, write to wsqeditors@gmail.com or visit feministpress.org/wsq or womensstudiesquarterly.com.

ADVERTISING
For information on display-ad sizes, rates, exchanges, and schedules, please write to *WSQ* Marketing, The Feminist Press at the City University of New York, The Graduate Center, 365 Fifth Avenue, Suite 5406, New York, NY 10016; 212-817-7918; sales@feministpress.org.

ELECTRONIC ACCESS AND SUBSCRIPTIONS
Access to electronic databases containing backlist issues of *WSQ* may be purchased through JSTOR at www.jstor.org. Access to electronic databases containing current issues of *WSQ* may be purchased through Project MUSE at muse.jhu.edu, muse@muse.jhu.edu; and ProQuest at www.il.proquest.com, info@il.proquest.com. Individual electronic subscriptions for *WSQ* may also be purchased through Project MUSE.

Compilation copyright © 2022 by the Feminist Press at the City University of New York. Unless otherwise noted, copyright in the individual essays is held in the name of their authors.

ISSN: 0732-1562   ISBN: 978-1-952177-23-1 $25.00

EDITORIAL BOARD

Allia Abdullah-Matta, LaGuardia Community College
Linda Martín Alcoff, Hunter College and The Graduate Center, CUNY
Maria Rice Bellamy, College of Staten Island, CUNY
TJ Boisseau, Purdue University
Margot Bouman, The New School
Justin Brown, The Graduate Center, CUNY
Colette Cann, University of San Francisco
Sarah Chinn, Hunter College
Alyson Cole, The Graduate Center, CUNY
Tara L. Conley, Montclair State University
Paisley Currah, Brooklyn College
Dána-Ain Davis, Queens College and The Graduate Center, CUNY
Shelly Eversley, Baruch College CUNY
Jerilyn Fisher, Hostos Community College
Namulundah Florence, Brooklyn College
JV Fuqua, Queens College
Claudia Sofia Garriga-López, California State University
Katie Gentile, John Jay College
Gayatri Gopinath, New York University
Terri Gordon-Zolov, The New School
Christina Hanhardt, University of Maryland
Mobina Hashmi, Brooklyn College
Heather Hewett, SUNY New Paltz
Jackie Hidalgo, Williams College
Gabrielle Hosein, University of the West Indies
Hsiao-Lan Hu, University of Detroit Mercy
Jade C. Huell, California State University, Northridge
Ren-yo Hwang, Mount Holyoke College
Crystal (Jack) Jackson, Texas Christian University
Cristina Khan, SUNY Stony Brook University
Kyoo Lee, John Jay College and The Graduate Center, CUNY
Lore/tta LeMaster, Arizona State University
Mel Michelle Lewis, American Rivers Organization
Heather Love, University of Pennsylvania
Karmen MacKendrick, Le Moyne College
Roopali Mukherjee, Queens College
Soniya Munshi, Borough of Manhattan Community College
Amber Jamilla Musser, George Washington University
Premilla Nadasen, Barnard College
Sarah Soanirina Ohmer, Lehman College
Jackie Orr, The Maxwell School of Syracuse University
Rupal Oza, Hunter College and The Graduate Center, CUNY
Mary Phillips, Lehman College
Heather Rellihan, Anne Arundel Community College
Matt Richardson, UC Santa Barbara
Jennifer Rudolph, Connecticut College
Carolina Rupprecht, The Graduate Center, CUNY

L. Ayu Saraswati, University of Hawai'i
Gunja SenGupta, Brooklyn College
Barbara Shaw, Allegheny College
Lili Shi, Kingsborough Community College
Robyn Spencer, Lehman College
Saadia Toor, College of Staten Island
Laura Westengard, New York City College of Technology, CUNY
Kimberly Williams, Mount Royal University
Kimberly Williams Brown, Vassar College
Karen Winkler, Psychotherapist

Dedication

This issue is dedicated to Dr. Brianne Waychoff, a brilliant professor, scholar, writer, performer, artist, activist, editor, and all-around interdisciplinary powerhouse, feminist rock star, cat worshipper, social changemaker, and kind, generous, and compassionate person.

Dr. Brianne Waychoff
joined our feminist ancestors
on July 25, 2022.

Contents

Editors' Note

Red Washburn and Brianne Waychoff

We write this note during a moment of political urgency, just days after *Roe v. Wade* was overturned in the United States on Pride weekend. This decision ends federal protection of abortion, an important right of reproductive freedom and bodily autonomy, after approximately fifty years, alongside other ongoing attacks on LGBTQ and BIPOC rights, gun control, and other forms of hate violence.

We imagine *50!* as a tribute to Feminist Press, the journal *WSQ* itself, and its founder Florence Howe, who passed in September 2020, as well as a celebration of fifty years of interdisciplinary scholarship, including in women's, gender, and sexuality studies, Black, Latinx, and Asian American studies, LGBTQ studies, among many others. We imagine it as honoring the feminist work at City University of New York—namely, the Center for the Study of Women in Society, the Women's and Gender Studies Program at Brooklyn College, and the Women's, Gender, and Sexuality Studies Department (formerly Program) at Hunter College, all of which are approximately five decades old. We also imagine it as a commemoration of activism, especially Stonewall. We want this issue to chart this history as a form of recognition of our intellectual ancestors and colleagues. We also want to promote the future of transdisciplinary feminist knowledge and activist projects, just as much as we want to archive and celebrate it. However, we also imagine this issue as a form of academic resistance and activist promise for a new world. The rollback of abortion rights is yet another clarion call to keep doing the work, dance, dance, revolution–style. It is our greatest hope to keep thinking, reading, and writing for social change. We want a future for the field, and we want freedom for all people in the world. *50!* invites us to

WSQ: Women's Studies Quarterly 50: 3 & 4 (Fall/Winter 2022) © 2022 by Red Washburn and Brianne Waychoff. All rights reserved.

use history to imagine our wildest feminist utopias and Muñozian queer dreams not yet here.

We are thrilled to see this issue finally come to fruition. When we submitted our proposal to become coeditors of this journal in February 2020, this was one issue we knew we wanted to do. At that time, we had no inkling that our world would be irrevocably changed by the COVID-19 pandemic and our own personal losses. We were looking forward to lively celebrations of all the landmark anniversaries that were occurring, or about to occur. Our overarching goal for our three-year editorship was to create an intellectual genealogy and commemoration of these fiftieth anniversaries. When we came on board, there were some issue themes already under consideration, which we moved into production. This is the first issue that we have seen through its genesis.

Another editorial goal we had was to broaden collaboration and access by involving other campuses in our intellectual work with *WSQ*, and to bring more colleagues to the conversation and allow information to be available in the service of public intellectualism, feminist community, and social democracy. We have expanded *WSQ*'s editorial board to make it more diverse and interdisciplinary. Additionally, with one year remaining in our editorship, we have secured funding for editorial assistants after our departure, thus making the journal a bit more sustainable. Thank you to Dána-Ain Davis at the Center for the Study of Women and Society and Kendra Sullivan at the Center for Humanities for coming on board as interim editorial directors to oversee this funding and operations as *WSQ* transitions to new editors.

We want to thank the *WSQ* team and editorial board. We want to extend a huge thank-you to the guest editors, Heather Rellihan, Jennifer C. Nash, and Charlene A. Carruthers, all of whom did a wonderful job curating and editing this issue. We are very grateful for their work and vision. We want to thank our poetry editors, Cheryl Clarke, Julie R. Enszer, and JP Howard; prose editors Keisha-Gaye Anderson, Lauren Cherelle, and Vi Khi Nao; and visual art editor Mel Michelle Lewis. In particular, we want to extend a tremendous thank-you, thank-you, thank-you to the editorial assistants, Googie Karrass and Kayla Reece, both of whom worked tirelessly on communicating with the scholars, writers, and artists to make this issue happen. In addition, we want to extend a very big thank-you to Dána-Ain Davis, Eileen Liang, and Jennifer Bae for providing *WSQ* with internships in feminist publishing for graduate students in women's and gender studies at the City University of New York. Our partnership has significantly enriched the quality of the journal for our feminist communities across CUNY and beyond. We are greatly indebted to the Feminist Press for all its help with scheduling, copyediting, and distributing our issues, especially to executive director Margot Atwell, senior editor Lauren Rosemary Hook, and assistant editor Nick Whitney. We cannot thank you enough for your help and support. We also wish to thank Kendra Sullivan and Sampson Starkweather for collaborating with us and building a new home for the journal, including aiding with publicity, funding staff, and assisting with institutional matters. We acknowledge the support we have received from the National Women's Studies Association, namely from President Kaye Wise Whitehead, as well as the Community of Literary Magazines and Presses. Lastly, we tip our hats at each other for doing this work during a challenging time.

Red Washburn
Kingsborough Community
  College and the Graduate Center
Director of Women's, Gender,
  and Sexuality Studies
Professor of English and Women's,
  Gender, and Sexuality Studies
City University of New York

Brianne Waychoff
Borough of Manhattan
  Community College
Associate Professor of Speech
  Communications and Theatre Arts
Gender and Women's Studies
  Program
City University of New York

Fifty Years Is an Achievement: Reflections at the Intersection of Personal and Collective Memory

Heather Rellihan

In the fall of 1972, the inaugural issue of the *Women's Studies Newsletter* (*WSN*), the precursor to *Women's Studies Quarterly* (*WSQ*), announced itself as "the clearinghouse on women's studies" and marked its intention to serve as a "forum throughout the country for the women's studies movement—in higher education, continuing education, secondary and elementary schools, and in community liberation centers" ("Front Matter," 1). This issue, *50!*, marks a half century of critical interventions in education, knowledge production, and social justice activism. In the last five decades, *WSQ* has cultivated rich conversations within and around women's/gender/ sexuality studies (WGSS), charting the growth of an academic discipline and an intellectual movement in the academy and the community.

This issue is a celebration, and honoring fifty years of interventions into knowledge production necessitates that we ground our celebration in critical analysis, both of the field and of the traditional tropes of commemoration. We began our work on this issue by asking questions about the processes of collective memory-making, thinking critically about the ways in which an issue like *50!* could participate in, or challenge, master narratives about the field and about feminist publishing. We were also attentive to the economy of commemoration: thinking about whose rememberings travel and in what ways. And so, as we honor the history, contributions, and perseverance of *WSQ* in the following pages, we also ask questions about how we can trouble traditional tropes of commemoration by grounding our explorations of collective memory in feminist and queer analysis. Therefore, we mark the significance of *WSQ*'s contributions alongside and through intentional self-reflexivity, attentive to the ways in which commemoration can reproduce master narratives, and with the goal of using feminist and queer

WSQ: Women's Studies Quarterly 50: 3 & 4 (Fall/Winter 2022) © 2022 by Heather Rellihan. All rights reserved.

lenses to reorient our stories in ways that help us recognize our investments in particular kinds of telling.

Working on this anniversary issue has been particularly meaningful to me because of the close relationship between *WSQ* and the growth of WGSS in higher education. I was part of the first cohort in the PhD program in Women's Studies at the University of Maryland, a program described in this issue by L. Ayu Saraswati and Barbara L. Shaw in their essay, "Women's Studies and Its Institutionalization as an Interdisciplinary Field: Past, Present, and Future." I didn't start graduate school in women's studies, though. Like many students, I found women's studies when I wasn't looking for it. As a student in an English MA program, I took a feminist theory course, and it changed the trajectory of my education and my career by shifting my academic focus to women's studies—the course changed my life. What I remember the most from that course was not the readings on the syllabus, impactful though they were. It was the pedagogy, the strategic ways in which the professor, Katie King, cultivated deep and critical thinking through particular teaching practices. I had never experienced a classroom like that before. It was utterly transforming, scary at times but exhilarating. In that classroom, I learned what I now know to be key hallmarks of feminist pedagogy: I was invited to use my own experiences as a text for the course, and I was challenged to make visible my own assumptions, to trace back my beliefs and think critically about what I understood to be true. Not until that class did I recognize the ways in which power shaped knowledge production, or how my own ways of knowing were constructed and constrained. In the story I tell myself about my life, that class was a beginning. I went on to pursue a degree in women's studies, but that feminist theory course marks two other important milestones. It made me recognize how education could be liberatory, and the study of pedagogy has preoccupied my reading and writing ever since. It also made me see teaching as a form of activism. And so the history of *WSQ*, and the larger WGSS movement that it expresses, is meaningful to me because it is also my story.

While I'm a few years shy of fifty, reflecting on five decades of *WSQ* makes me think about how my life and the lives of so many others were shaped by WGSS education and activism, how the conversations in and through feminist publications and classrooms shaped the possibilities for my own life and career, as they have for so many others. Thinking about my own origin story—my early days as a feminist scholar in that feminist theory course—sent me off in search of the earliest issues of *WSQ*, when

WSQ was the *Women's Studies Newsletter* for a few years. Looking at those early days of the journal, I was struck by the excitement that came through those first pages, and the sense of earnestness and gravity. Also, I found myself surprised at how attentive the early issues were to education *outside* the academy. I had expected that women's studies would be defined by higher education, but the very first essay in 1972, "In Elementary Schools: A Case Study—The Woodward School" by Andrea Ostrum set the stage for many pieces that followed. The second issue included "Closeup: High School Feminist Literature Course" by Judy Small (1972) and "Creative Intervention in the Pre-School" by Phyllis Taube MacEwan, as well as voices from students. "Sixth Grader Speaks Out" recounts the story of a French teacher asking the girls to stay after class to clean up since they were "future housewives" and a handwritten note from East Hill Elementary School asks Feminist Press to send them information on "nonsexist books to order for [their] library" (Wolff 1972, 5). A comprehensive view of education continued throughout the trajectory of *WSN* with reports on elementary and high school education rivaling the space accorded to colleges and universities. There is also attention paid to public pedagogy, and education outside or alongside formal schooling.

The early focus of *WSQ/WSN* seemed to reflect back to me the things I had found in my feminist theory course and the things that have been the most meaningful for me in my career. I found myself getting excited reading about early feminist interventions in pedagogy, breaking into a smile, for example, when I saw a piece written by one of my mentors, Deborah Rosenfelt, which described "group-oriented" courses where "[i]ndividual competition for grades is de-emphasized" and "replaced by . . . some form of cooperative participation in both learning and teaching" (1974, 11). Rosenfelt emphasized how women's studies courses highlight the affective experience of learning, the liberatory potential of the classroom, and the responsibility to use education to make social change (11–12). While the field of WGSS has changed, evolved, and shifted since 1974 when those words were written, my classroom practices still center around those same foundational interventions, the things I first experienced in my feminist theory course. As I read about the feminist classroom practices in the 1970s, I found myself wondering whether today it is easier or harder to implement liberatory practices into our classrooms, easier or harder to challenge the disciplinary and disciplining structures of the neoliberal academy . . . or maybe, I thought, it is just different.

What also struck me as I read through the early issues was the overt and intentional framing of education as activism, as necessary to social change. Up until my feminist theory course, I had never thought about education as activism; education had never been presented to me in that language, and my own schooling was almost completely divorced from a focus on social justice. So, thinking about education as a path to liberation was an epiphany for me, an "aha!" moment, and it inspired my decision to teach at a community college. Community colleges serve the least privileged students within the postsecondary system. Community colleges educate around 40 percent of all undergraduates, but more students from the lowest socioeconomic quartile (Carnevale and Strohl 2011). These institutions also disproportionately enroll more Hispanic, Black, and Native American students, as well as students whose parents did not attend college ("Fast Facts" 2022; Ma and Baum 2016, 9). Because community colleges are the least prestigious schools within the higher education system, they are less able to push back against a neoliberal agenda, and WGSS programs at community colleges are especially precarious within this paradigm. As education becomes increasingly defined by job placement rather than democratic citizenship and social change, the WGSS classroom becomes more critical, particularly for community college students: "As students historically underserved by higher education, and from social classes historically exploited through capitalism, community college students have the most to gain from resisting this narrative, and the most to lose if they don't" (Rellihan and Carminati 2020, xxiii). For me, *what* I teach, *how* I teach it, and *where* I teach are all expressions of my feminist politics.

In her essay in this fiftieth anniversary issue, "Field Materialities: Building Women's and Gender Studies One Page at a Time," Agatha Beins points to the value of the *Women's Studies Newsletter* in its focus on field materialities, the administrative and service work that have created and sustained women's studies departments. While articulating that much was gained in the transition from *WSN* to *WSQ* in terms of enriching women's and gender studies scholarship, she also points to what was lost: a space for thinking and strategizing collectively about our "seemingly endless, repetitive, labor-intensive, oft-thwarted struggles to align institutional praxis with our political commitments." She rightly points out that "a twenty-first century *WSN* could serve as a guide for navigating the thorny process of simultaneously assimilating into and resisting higher education's status quo." Perhaps the reflection that emerges out of celebratory moments like *50!*

will encourage us to strengthen our networks of resilience. Like Beins, as I thought about the initial goals of *WSQ/WSN*, I, too, wondered what has been lost since those early issues. As I noted above, the early issues afforded significant space to K–12, but that attention faded, and WGSS in higher education soon became the focus. I wondered about the effect on education if the field of WGSS were as attentive to K–12 and public pedagogy as it is to higher education, if it focused as much on community colleges as on PhD programs. It is my hope that essays included in this issue, like Shereen Essof and Patricia Ardón's essay, "Alquimia: The Alchemy of Cross-Pollination in Movement Learning," will highlight the continuing power of our interventions in education, both inside and outside the academy, while reinforcing the link between the knowledge networks created by feminist publishing and the liberatory potential of critical pedagogy.

In her 1982 essay, "The First Ten Years Are the Easiest," Florence Howe reflected on the achievements of a decade of *WSQ/WSN*. "Our achievements are not to be minimized," she argued, for "[i]t is more difficult to sustain than to start an institution; it is more difficult still to build when roots are shallow and the structures tall" (1). Her words resonate four decades later. Fifty years of *WSQ* is an achievement. The structures are still tall, yes, but our roots are deeper.

Heather Rellihan is a professor of gender and sexuality studies and chair of Interdisciplinary Studies at Anne Arundel Community College (AACC). She also serves as codirector of the Curriculum Transformation Project at AACC. She is coeditor of *Introduction to Women's, Gender, and Sexuality Studies: Interdisciplinary and Intersectional Approaches* and *Theory and Praxis: Women's and Gender Studies at Community College*. She can be reached at hrellihan@aacc.edu.

Works Cited

Carnevale, Anthony P., and Jeff Strohl. 2011. "Our Economically Polarized College System: Separate and Unequal." *Chronicle of Higher Education*, September 25, 2011. www.chronicle.com/article/Our-Economically-Polarized/129094/.

Howe, Florence. 1982. "The First Ten Years Are the Easiest." *Women's Studies Quarterly* 10: 1–16. http://www.jstor.org/stable/40003345.

"Fast Facts 2022." 2022. American Association of Community Colleges. https://www.aacc.nche.edu/research-trends/fast-facts/.

"Front Matter." 1972. *Women's Studies Newsletter* 1, no. 1: 1. http://www.jstor.org/stable/40041818.

Ma, Jennifer, and Sandy Baum. 2016. *Trends in Community Colleges: Enrollment, Prices, Student Debt, and Completion.* College Board. trends.collegeboard. org/sites/default/files/trends-in-community-colleges-research-brief.pdf.

MacEwan, Phyllis Taube. 1972. "Creative Intervention in the Pre-School." *Women's Studies Newsletter* 1, no. 2: 5. http://www.jstor.org/stable/ 40041828.

Ostrum, Andrea E. 1972. "In Elementary Schools: A Case Study: The Woodward School." *Women's Studies Newsletter* 1, no. 1: 2. http://www.jstor. org/stable/40041819.

Rellihan, Heather, and Genevieve Carminati. 2020. "Introduction." In *Theory and Praxis: Women's and Gender Studies at Community Colleges*, edited by Genevieve Carminati and Heather Rellihan, i–xxxix. Arlington, VA: Gival Press.

Rosenfelt, Deborah Silverton. 1974. "New Overview of Women's Studies Courses." *Women's Studies Newsletter* 2, no. 1: 1–12. http://www.jstor.org/ stable/40041874.

Small, Judy. 1972. "Closeup: High School Feminist Literature Course." *Women's Studies Newsletter* 1, no. 2: 2. http://www.jstor.org/stable/40041825.

Wolff, Judith Starr. 1972. "Sixth Grader Speaks Out." *Women's Studies Newsletter* 1, no. 2: 5. http://www.jstor.org/stable/40041829.

Commemoration, Pedagogy, and Action

Charlene A. Carruthers

On April 2, 2022, nearly four hundred people gathered to commemorate the life of Black feminist scholar, activist, and educator bell hooks (née Gloria Jean Watkins) in her hometown of Hopkinsville, Kentucky. hooks died at the age of sixty-nine of renal failure in her home on December 15, 2021. She was a prolific writer and incisive cultural critic. The commemoration generated a space for collective mourning and celebration of a poet who published more than forty books. Commemorators shared memories about their experiences and remarked on her cultural and intellectual legacy. Images of hooks alongside quotes from her works, interviews, and speeches spread widely across social media channels. I joined the chorus as a mourner whose own thinking is shaped by her calls for love, communion, and radicalism in education.

The duality of celebration and mourning is characteristic of feminist pedagogy that draws from archives of struggles for liberation throughout the modern era. Archives are geographies of the past, the ongoing, and the future. They exist withing many places, including formal academic and government institutions, community centers, churches, civic organizations, and our homes. Scholars, artists, and movement workers pull from archives to make sense of their own experiences and ideas. Drawing from these archives as a feminist Black studies scholar and educator means that I traverse various histories of enslavement, genocide, and war. It also means that I cross through insurrection, mass mobilization, and institution-building amid white supremacist and patriarchal terror. This crossing back and forth, in between, and through is not linear. One song, class session, or text can cover the events and emotional toll of several hours or several hundreds of years.

WSQ: Women's Studies Quarterly 50: 3 & 4 (Fall/Winter 2022) © 2022 by Charlene A. Carruthers.
All rights reserved.

The impetus for *WSQ*'s creation, the journal's contributions to intellectual thought and political action and future, is undeniably dependent on its contributors and editorial team's commitment to transgressive education. hooks makes this charge clear in *Teaching to Transgress: Education as the Practice of Freedom*. For hooks, transgressive education calls educators to do even more than what is often considered critical or feminist pedagogy. Unlike critical and feminist pedagogies, well-being matters in transgressive pedagogy. This approach to education can and should be pleasurable. hooks explains that "the pleasure of teaching is an act of resistance" (1994, 10). This resistance counters "the overwhelming boredom, uninterest, and apathy that so often characterize the way professors and students feel about teaching" (10). What becomes possible if everyone who is committed to feminist education organizes collectively to change how education is shaped and experienced? There is much to be learned from many sites of education, be it inside of an academic institution or in a community organizing setting.

hooks urges us to connect the ideas learned in the academy with those learned outside of the academy. Doing so inevitably leaves educators who are also committed to anticolonial, feminist, and anticapitalist praxis vulnerable. Consequently, committing to transgressive education is a choice one has to make repeatedly, all the while weighing the risks and rewards of doing so. The emotional journey as an educator can contribute to our collective freedom. hooks writes that "to educate as a practice of freedom is a way of teaching that anyone can learn" (1994, 13). It is not limited to people who are primarily trained and located in the academy. However, the opportunity to learn how to educate as a practice of freedom is not readily available to everyone. As laws are introduced and passed in state legislatures to restrict the use of materials and ideas that examine racism, white supremacy, and the mere presence of LGBTQIA+ people in the United States, access to the archives or content needed to engage students is increasingly threatened and restricted. Still, as Black educators have consistently engaged, under the threat of criminalization and violence, in what education historian Jarvis Givens (2021) calls fugitive pedagogies, I am confident that transgressive pedagogy will survive this current historical conjuncture.

It will survive through storytelling, shared experiences, and curious researchers who ask questions and consult archives. Commemoration does not require a special journal issue—it can happen in our everyday lives. Commemoration allows us to connect and honor people we have never met, and places we have never touched. The next fifty years of feminist pedagogy, inside and outside of the academy, has an archive to consult that those who built the earliest political education, consciousness raising, and academic programs did not. We can look to scores of texts and visual and audio materials that provide road maps to feminist pedagogy in coursework and community organizing. These materials are not neatly packaged in a single archive of feminist syllabi, curricula, and guidebooks. However, they are not unattainable. They exist. We should all commit to building a culture in which sharing of information is encouraged and rewarded, as opposed to the frequent celebration of and reinforcement of individual exceptionalism.

Charlene A. Carruthers (she/her) is a writer, filmmaker, and Black studies PhD student at Northwestern University. A practitioner of telling more complete stories, her work interrogates historical conjunctures of Black freedom-making post-emancipation and decolonial revolution, Black governance, and Black feminist abolitionist geographies. She is author of *Unapologetic: A Black, Queer and Feminist Mandate for Radical Movements*. She can be reached at charlenecarruthers@northwestern.edu.

Works Cited

Givens, Jarvis R. 2021. *Fugitive Pedagogy: Carter G. Woodson and the Art of Black Teaching.* Cambridge, MA: Harvard University Press.

hooks, bell. 1994. *Teaching to Transgress: Education as the Practice of Freedom.* New York: Routledge.

Feminist Commemoration

Jennifer C. Nash

It is the time of anniversaries. *WSQ* celebrates its fiftieth anniversary at the same time that *Signs* and *Feminist Studies*—two other landmark journals in the field of gender and sexuality studies—prepare their anniversary issues. Academic feminism has moved to a period of commemoration, retrospection, and celebration. Feminist commemoration is often fraught, filled with celebrations of and anxieties about all that the institutionalization of academic feminism has achieved. If the stories we tell—to channel Clare Hemmings—often center on our field's precarity, the existence and durability of a slew of feminist journals, including *WSQ*, is evidence of the labor of generations of feminist scholars. Those scholars worked to ensure that the precarity that marked earlier feminist publishing projects (see Kitchen Table Press's history, for example) was replaced by the capacity of feminist publications to endure, to live on.

And yet, a celebration of all that we have accomplished always requires reckoning with the uneasy relationship academic feminism has to the professional and the institutional. These commemorations require that we reckon with how an "outsider" intellectual project has become, squarely, part of the academy, with its own genre conventions, conferences, journals, and forms of academic disciplining. To be clear, I lament none of this; instead, I name it to dispense with the romance that academic feminism is an outsider field. My own interest in feminist commemoration always swirls around how we anxiously mark the power we have accrued (including fifty years of *WSQ*) and the power that we have desired, including our desires for (at least) fifty more years of *WSQ*, even as we recognize that moments of commemoration and of looking back also include the sense that we do not know what the future will hold, what form(s) this—or any—feminist journal will take

WSQ: Women's Studies Quarterly 50: 3 & 4 (Fall/Winter 2022) © 2022 by Jennifer C. Nash. All rights reserved.

in the future. It is the fact that the future remains open that I think makes commemoration rich, exciting, edgy.

As we remember, celebrate, champion, and mark the desire for a future, it is important—to me, at least—to name and recognize that as a Black feminist, commemoration always requires bringing our dead with us: naming, remembering, marking, and celebrating the names and contributions of the scholars whose intellectual labor made possible the spaces that we stand and write in. We "take our dead with us to the various battles we must wage in their names—and in our names," as José Esteban Muñoz (1999, 74) reminded us, with a sense of the radical potential of mourning and celebration. We "take our dead with us" to remind ourselves that the space that we write in was forged with labor and love, in struggle, by myriad scholars, activists, thinkers, and writers who wanted one thing: for the work to continue. Here we are: writing, thinking, theorizing, dreaming.

Jennifer C. Nash is Jean Fox O'Barr Professor of Gender, Sexuality, and Feminist Studies at Duke University. She is the author of *The Black Body in Ecstasy: Reading Race, Reading Pornography*; *Black Feminism Reimagined: After Intersectionality*; and *Birthing Black Mothers*, all published by Duke University Press. She has published articles in journals, including *Signs*, *Social Text*, *Meridians*, *Feminist Studies*, *Feminist Review*, and *GLQ*. She can be reached at jennifer.nash@duke.edu.

Works Cited

Muñoz, José Esteban. 1999. *Disidentifications: Queers of Color and the Performance of Politics*. Minneapolis: University of Minnesota Press.

The Essays

Heather Rellihan, Charlene A. Carruthers, and Jennifer C. Nash

We intentionally begin this celebratory issue with Shirley Geok-lin Lim's 2011 interview with the late Florence Howe, founder of the Feminist Press. In "A Woman's Work: Editing and Narrating Memoirs at the Feminist Press" Lim captures then eighty-year-old Howe's insights about writing her memoir and finally telling *her own* story after a career of encouraging other women to tell their stories. Howe's reflections provide a context for understanding fifty years of feminist publishing, while also creating a window into Howe's sense of self as someone who never thought of herself as a "writing writer" and did not see "any other way to live meaningfully than to do work that touches people's lives in a meaningful way."

In her essay "Field Materialities: Building Women's and Gender Studies One Page at a Time," Agatha Beins examines the early issues of the *Women's Studies Newsletter* (*WSN*), the precursor publication that became *Women's Studies Quarterly* (*WSQ*), and notes how *WSN* provided a key site for discussion and information sharing around administrative and service duties. Noting that such labor is as essential as it is undervalued, Beins argues that when *WSQ* shifted to a focus on scholarship, the field lost an opportunity to share strategies and work collectively to subvert oppressive structures within the academy. Beins speculates on what a modern-day *WSN* might do for the field.

M. Bałut Fondakowski's piece, "Aunt Lute Books on Controlling the Narrative . . . Or Not," recounts an interview with Joan Pinkvoss, the cofounder of Aunt Lute Books. Pinkvoss's work building a grassroots, community-based, feminist press and publishing "risky" books like Gloria E. Anzaldúa's *Borderlands / La Frontera: The New Mestiza*, frames

WSQ: Women's Studies Quarterly **50**: 3 & 4 (Fall/Winter 2022) © 2022 by Heather Rellihan, Charlene A. Carruthers, and Jennifer C. Nash. All rights reserved.

Fondakowski's argument that Aunt Lute and other similar presses are "critical to decolonizing the [publishing] industry."

The focus of Clara Montague's essay, "'You're International, Not American': Academic Feminist Autobiographics and the Political Grammar of Nation," centers on two edited collections from the Feminist Press: *Changing Lives: Life Stories of Asian Pioneers in Women's Studies* (1995) and *The Politics of Women's Studies: Testimony from 30 Founding Mothers* (2000). Through a comparison informed by transnational feminist analysis, Montague examines metanarratives around academic feminism to demonstrate how "[discursive framings] can show how the nation works as an analytic category."

Aaron Hammes's "The Sex and Work of Sex Work in a Quarter Century of *Women's Studies Quarterly*" examines six articles focused on sex work that were published in *WSQ* in different historical moments. Hammes looks to three modes of representing prostitution in the journal: as a form of violence and trauma, as ethnographic and economic analysis, and as a form of labor. The article offers a strong critique of anti-prostitution feminism, criticizing the "virulence with which anti-prostitution feminists decry and defame sex-working people."

In "What Can Feminist Work Be?: A Conversation with *WSQ* Authors Kathi Weeks and Heather Berg," Samantha Pinto interviews Kathi Weeks and Heather Berg, two scholars who "pose radical, counterintuitive, and sensitive challenges to both Marxist feminist traditions and cultures of feminist theorizing about freedom, labor, and capitalism. They are both scholars who imagine horizons of thinking, writing, being, and acting beyond what is currently imaginable." Weeks and Berg reflect on their desires to publish in *WSQ* and the lives and travels of their respective articles after publication in *WSQ*.

"Feminist Citational Praxis and Problems of Practice," coauthored by Lori Wright, Neisha Wiley, Elizabeth VanWassenhove, Brandelyn Tosolt, Rae Loftis, and Meg L. Hensley, offers a powerful critique of conventional citational practices. The authors develop "feminist citational praxis" rooted in the idea of the feminist killjoy and offer a model of collaborative writing as one form of feminist writing otherwise.

Lolita Copacabana's "SCUM as Trans-form" treats the *SCUM Manifesto* as "occup[ying] a position that is both fascinating and disturbing—like so many manifestos of the male avant-garde tradition that came before it." Thinking with the manifesto as an essential form that centers rather than marginalizes rage, Copacabana considers how texts like *SCUM* allow us to say: "Get up, get up . . . Come on, come on, come on. No time to lose."

"Women's Studies and Its Institutionalization as an Interdisciplinary Field: Past, Present, and Future," coauthored by L. Ayu Saraswati and Barbara L. Shaw, closely engages with the history of the University of Maryland's Women, Gender, and, Sexuality Studies PhD program. The authors interview three faculty members involved in the formation of the doctoral program and draw on their insights to pose crucial questions of the institutional project of academic feminism like, "Can W/G/S/F departments be the conscience of the university, or are we only going to be conscious about our place in the institution and thus limit our ability to affect significant changes? . . . Are we serving the movement, or are we only serving our academic selves?"

Shereen Essof and Patricia Ardón's "Alquimia: The Alchemy of Cross-Pollination in Movement Learning" looks at the feminist pedagogical practices of the Alquimia Feminist Leadership Schools. They argue that these schools create "safe spaces" and practice a form of pedagogy that "transform[s] aspects of power that marginalize, demean, and threaten women and their communities while catalyzing imagination and action for long-term social justice and change agendas."

Marie-Lise Drapeau-Bisson analyzes public commemorations in her essay, "Movement Renewal and Attachments to the Past: The Commemorative Reception of the Feminist Novel *L'Euguélionne* in Québec." Drapeau-Bisson deploys concepts like *commemorative reception* and looks at alternative archives to examine the legacy of the 1976 Québec feminist novel *L'Euguélionne*, which was "lauded for encapsulating the zeitgeist of Québec's political mobilizations of the 1970s."

In their essay "Mourning Sarah Hegazi: Grief and the Cultivation of Queer Arabness," Sophie Chamas and Sabiha Allouche explore the practice of collective mourning by analyzing the social media response to the suicide of Sarah Hegazi, an Egyptian queer feminist who was arrested for brandishing a rainbow flag at a 2017 Mashrou' Leila concert in Cairo. Chamas and Allouche position the "abundance of social media posts, blogs, articles, Twitter and Instagram hashtags, and vigils" that surfaced in response to Hegazi's death as a "politics of countermemorialization that challenged nationalist commemorative practices and the politics they serve" and as a site for theorizing "the potentiality of queer Arabness as both a mode of making sense of and being in the world that can subvert, on the one hand, nationalisms, and on the other hand the pathologization and individualization of queer suicide."

Wendy Mallette explores feminist and queer collective memory in her essay, "Beverly Smith's 'Notes on This Mess': The Affective Politics of the Lesbian Feminist Killjoy in Queer Progress Narratives." By looking at the feminist magazine *Conditions*' 1979 special issue, "Five—The Black Women's Issue," and placing one of its pieces, Beverly Smith's "The Wedding," in conversation with Lisa Duggan and Nan Hunter's 1995 *Sex Wars*, Mallette is able to examine "the affective, temporal, and redemptive politics surrounding lesbian feminism within the stories that feminist and queer studies tell about their pasts and futures." Looking at concepts like the "figural negativity" of the lesbian feminist killjoy, how progress narratives can make use of "a division between good and bad subjects," and the relationship between negativity and desire, Mallette asks questions about what the lesbian feminist killjoy can teach us about our attachments to stories we tell about the field.

PART I. **FEMINIST PUBLISHING/*WSQ***

A Woman's Work: Editing and Narrating Memoirs at the Feminist Press

Interview with Florence Howe, New York, June 2011

Florence Howe and Shirley Geok-lin Lim

I had been calling on Florence Howe at least once a year each time I was in New York visiting my son and our friends. We met often at her West End condo, lunched in her favorite restaurant a few streets away, and talked about books. Still, I was astonished when she asked me to blurb her forthcoming memoir, *A Life in Motion*;[1] she was a star in the publishing firmament, and I felt inadequate. Of course, I said yes, and I read the preprint copy closely with fascination, gulping down huge histories of U.S. and international feminist activism in which Florence was a preeminent actor and also held a stage-front seat to the broad spectrum of civil rights movements from the early 1960s to the early twenty-first century, when due to increasing health problems she retired from her executive position at the Feminist Press and as professor at the City University of New York.[2]

In June 2011, I spent several hours recording an interview with her, focusing on how she positioned herself as a memoirist, in distinction from her work as acquisition editor, for a series of memoirs she had imagined, established, nurtured, and successfully shaped as "cross-cultural."[3] Florence's interview was one of four I had completed that I intended to include in a collection of interviews with women writers and scholars, titled "Women of a Certain Age."

Unfortunately, I retired from the University of California, Santa Barbara, shortly after and spent much of the next six years or so abroad, in conferences, lecturing, and on short- and long-term teaching residencies as visiting professor in various international universities (e.g., National University of Singapore and City University of Hong Kong). The projected collection was abandoned, and Florence's interview has remained unpublished.

More than a decade later, I offer this exchange, in which her voice carries

***WSQ: Women's Studies Quarterly* 50**: 3 & 4 (Fall/Winter 2022) © 2022 by Florence Howe and Shirley Geok-lin Lim. All rights reserved.

insights into her complex psychology as the indefatigable feminist activist who believed in recovering the writings of women, making visible and substantial the writings of new feminists and younger women, and pushing the circle of the center to include the writings of marginalized women, be they subordinated by class, race, language, region, or sexual identities. The major irony of the exchange clarifies that the brilliant editor and feminist visionary did not arrive at her confidence in her own position as a woman writer till she was in her eighties, and even then, that confident writerly identity was still in formation. Hers is indeed the voice of a woman of a certain age.

Shirley Geok-lin Lim: What are some major differences between the work of editing that you have done for so many decades and writing your own memoir?

Florence Howe: There is no simple difference. They are like day and night. Probably the greatest difference for me lay in writing my memoir. It turns out, even though I had not written my own book, I was pretty smart about people who were going to write their own memoirs. I knew poetry meant the opposite of prose, but I knew every poet could be a prose writer. I told Meena Alexander that she could actually do it.[4] In my view being a good editor depends on how much reading of good literature the editor has done. My main training was in the magnificent works I had studied in British literature, from *Beowulf* on, and the fact that I was such an avid reader when I was a child certainly helped. There is no substitute for reading, when you hear the sounds of good sentences in varied styles like Emerson, Jane Austen, and Virginia Wolfe, all quite different kinds of writers. The English sentence is an infinitely malleable instrument and very complex, and potentially capable of extra length and extra brevity.

SL: Can you develop on this thought?

FH: When you talk about editing, you have to distinguish between macroediting and other kinds of editing. *Macro* means considering and understanding where the book is coming from and how it is going there. The other kind has to do with hearing the sounds of English sentences, and this kind of editing is what most editors do. I like talking to people about what their plots would be. For example, Meena, whom I had approached, said she had never written prose, but I told her that anyone who has written poetry could write prose. It does not matter. But a memoir has to have a plot. I knew for Meena it would be about finding her tongue. Not her mother tongue, because she'd lost her native tongue. That is the basic theme of her book. So, she chose to write in French because that was the school language. That became her tongue early in life. She could never write in her native language, even in Sudan where she grew up. In all the hours of editing other people's memoirs and rewriting oceans of poetry, I get to understand how a whole book should move. But none of the editing work prepared me for writing my own memoir, except peripherally.

SL: Why is that so?

FH: Because I waited too long to write my memoir. I should have written it when I was sixty or seventy, but not eighty. If I were to go back to retrieve the odd bits I wrote when I was sixty, I know I would have written a very different memoir than the one I did.

SL: Is the issue an effect of aging?

FH: Partly aging, but partly the effect of Jack and Tillie Olsen on me. They were the first to hear me out and to say, "Where do you think you got your strength from?" They asked questions. For example, my views of my parents softened dramatically in the last twenty years of my life. I was much harsher, more antagonistic, and had more anger, especially regarding my mother.

SL: To return to the question of the age of the memoirist at the actual moment of writing, many of the memoirs you have published and mentored through the Feminist Press were written by younger women, some as young as in their forties. Do you intuit or have thoughts on differences, if any, between the life stories young women write and women past their sixties and seventies produce?

FH: My aim there as Feminist Press acquisition editor was very specific. I wanted to catch women's consciousness at the moment that they were part of these movements of social change in the sixties and seventies, during the civil rights anti-war movements. I was aware that women whose consciousness has changed, invariably, in some way or other, become agents of change for others. I knew consciousness was catching and one did not have to be in a specific consciousness-raising group in order to raise the consciousness of others. I knew that to change, women would eventually be change agents themselves. Instead of writing my own memoir, I set about to find people who would write memoirs that would illuminate this idea of changing consciousness for Feminist Press.

I thought one memoir would not do much. The instigating act for this was, at the end of the sixties, that my friends said, "You were a token woman in the [civil rights] movement. Write your own memoir."[5] I thought, how could I do something more significant than writing my own memoir? So, I hit upon this idea in the eighties to have a series of memoirs by women on how their consciousness was changed by feminism. One was Meena. The other was Toni McNaron, who had grown up in the Birmingham, Alabama, area and who had witnessed police attacks on Black picnicking families in Arkansas when she was not even a teenager.[6]

SL: What took you so long to write your own memoir, even if you wanted to do your series?

FH: For a couple of reasons. One was under the influence of the lack of a creative bone. I was timid about writing, even though I had written and learned so much. I assumed that such writing was of a different order. But I never wrote anything just for the sake of writing it. I never thought of myself as a *writing* writer. I wrote on assignment, so to speak.

SL: So, did you then, and even now, hold the distinction between assigned writing and writing just for pleasure or for oneself?

FH: To read, yes, I did. In some sense, I still do, because I write in my journal maybe five days week, and I write it for myself because no one gets it to read. For the past few months after my memoir was published, I have begun writing blogs. The blogs are public, and I am still having a difficult time figuring what topics would interest others

SL: Do you have still that view of yourself as a writer now?

FH: In part. I am aware that it took me two full years to write the memoir, and it wasn't till I was eighty to have these full years.

SL: You really wrote your memoir in two years?

FH: Well, I had bits and pieces. What I had, which I kept, were some clear portraits of my grandparents and parents. I had quite a lot written down and a lot in my head. If I were to go through all the papers and find all the old versions, some things would be there but vastly different.

SL: Would it be fair to say that although technically one would say your memoir took two years, in fact you had been writing bits of it over a much longer time?

FH: Yes, I wrote a good solid piece in a week at Hedgebrook in January 1997. Then I went to Bellagio in October of the same year and wrote 150 pages, beginning all over again. One of the puzzles to me was how to move forward; I never got very far, because I started at the beginning all over again. Then around the year 2000, I went to Hawai'i for two or three weeks and did nothing. I brought the full files with me: the correspondence between myself and a Black lover in the 1960s, and I wrote a section of a chapter on that affair; and the husband I was divorcing; and another man I would eventually marry (I was never involved with the three men at the same time). None of this was in the memoir. I spent these weeks and realized there was really no place in the memoir for these narratives.

SL: Am I understanding you correctly, that your sense of your value as a person lies in your world as an activist, both in the feminist civil rights movement and women's studies movement and in the establishment and success of the Press? Isn't this a particularly male-gendered and westernized thing, that other than the work one did, to see any notion of value of a subject is to be measured in terms of achievement?

FH: No, because as a woman one would expect that my value would be measured in terms of my marriage and a family. I don't see any other way to live meaningfully than to do work that touches people's lives in a meaningful way. It's not my achievement, but a contribution. But I am not alone in making the Press. I was the only one to stay with the Press, and you can attribute it to my stubbornness that it survived. But many saw women's studies as a driving force for curriculum change, and hundreds worked on that change. I was fortunate to be in secure positions to do what others hadn't done or to do what others couldn't or struggled to do. When Tillie Olsen handed me *Life in the Iron Mills,*[7] my whole world was affected. I could move from *Iron Mills* to *Women Writing in India,*[8] *Women Writing Africa,*[9] and other publications that would not have been possible without that first gift from Tillie Olsen.

SL: How does one know what belongs in a memoir? You've written this section. It sounds important to me!

FH: How? It was off the track of what I thought I needed to do at age eighty in the memoir. I had two important stories to tell, and everything else had to go.

SL: Besides the history of the Feminist Press?

FH: The history of the Feminist Press and the women's studies movement was the point of writing this memoir.

SL: This was a decision you made, or was that made for you?

FH: Why should anyone care about this book? Why should anyone care about me? What have I done for the world that anyone should be interested in me? I would say I made two contributions. Early recognition of the importance of the curriculum for the shaping of women's consciousness, for example, women's studies in history and literature. But not only that. At the exact same moment, I was in the group that founded the Feminist Press, and unlike other editors, I stayed with it for thirty years, and this was because Tillie Olsen gave me *Life in the Iron Mills* three months after the Press was founded.

SL: That's what you call the "backstory."

FH: I was the person on hand, to be at the halfway point, at age forty. I should have come to this awareness; I should see clearly what I was blind to several years ago: that cultural forces prevented women from positions in living in a male-dominated world, and somehow seeing either their history or understanding what they had written in the past—that in the past more women had understood the restrictions. These were narratives, themes, and structures that they arrived at autonomously.

SL: But your memoir has more than these years covered.

FH: I recognized at once: there was a hidden curriculum too messy to deal with in this void in women's consciousness, and that I stayed as the executive of the Press, were two stories that were too big, so that central story had to go. That was what happened. There was much more in the early version of my life—that to make room for what I thought was important, which a single memoir ought to have, it all would have been too crammed. I could have published a double memoir, but it was not possible. Every time I had a little time, I had to start at the beginning. Then there were several times when I could carve two or three weeks at Feminist Press and tried.

SL: Why did you not succeed?

FH: Well, up to the middle of the eighties, memoirs were mostly by white men decrying the end of the civil rights movement. To them, the movement did not include feminism, and I complained about it.

SL: You've talked about why it took you so long to write your memoir, *A Life in Motion*. Would you tell me again how long your memoir took: from moment of conception; when, where and how; to final draft sent for copy-editing; and why the time span?

FH: I'll tell you two stories. When the Hedgebrook people asked me to come out for a week and be a big sister for younger women who were having problems publishing with feminist publishers or working in feminist publishing, being responsible for feminist houses—they wanted me to mentor them. I agreed because the schedule was such that every day, all day until dinner, I was free to do my own thing. After dinner, I was to mentor, some from Canada and the U.S., and we talked mainly about fundraising, etcetera.

During the day, I began writing about my life, with the idea that someday when I was free enough, I would turn it into a book. I don't remember what I wrote: my grandparents, etcetera, some of which did appear in the book. This was around 1997. The book finally appeared in 2011, fourteen years later.

The second story occurred when I got the Bellagio Award in October 1997 to write a book about women's studies, and I mailed to Bellagio a big box of materials on women's studies, and in the process of packing the box, I began to look for cassettes of talks I had given on women's studies. I could not find the cassettes. Instead, I found the tapes I had made of my mother when I was Distinguished Professor at the College of Wooster in Ohio in January 1980.

I throw the tapes into my luggage. Before I go away, I say goodbye to my mother, who is in a nursing home in the Bronx. She doesn't know me, she doesn't speak, and I know she doesn't know whether I am there or not there, although I visit her once or twice a week. She has no voice. So I am in Bellagio, I unpack, breakfast, return to my room, and instead of unpacking my box of women's studies materials, I put my mother's tape on and listen to her strong, unmistakable voice for four hours. That's how long that tape runs. I begin then writing my memoir. I had no intention of writing the memoir. I never wrote any more of the 150 pages that I wrote in Bellagio. I wrote it a second time, a third time, etcetera.

SL: Is there something about the recursive process, that that was how you arrived at the memoir you finally wrote?

FH: Looking back at the published memoir, I think the first two chapters that I wrote and rewrote are the most polished. Most succinct. The structure is the most aesthetically pleasing, and the chapters are short, as though I kept peeling and peeling, down to the essence of those two chapters. I was embarrassed, after a week at Bellagio, that I was writing a memoir and not the women's studies book, and I mentioned this to the director, a young man, and he surprised me by saying, "Who cares? You can do whatever you wish." I felt it was strange. I did not feel relieved, I had to do a seminar, my project says a book on women's studies, and here I am working for three weeks on the memoir. I decided to do half the seminar on women's studies and half on the memoir. At the end, I confessed that I was very conflicted and could not sort it out. The male novelist at Bellagio said there was no conflict: "Your life story was also the story of women's studies." And the two were connected. My life story was part of the story of women's studies.

I've read your memoir, *Among the White Moon Faces,* closely and in fact there is more than one memoir between the covers.[10] It is about Asian American literature *and* your University of California, Santa Barbara, days. I always take myself as a culture-conscious person (if that's the right English expression), willing to get a glimpse of the ethnic heritage of different ethnicities and how this has influenced their lives.

SL: I note that, with the two stories concerning the moment when you conceived of your writing a memoir, you were rejecting the self-location of yourself as a writer who writes on assignment—that is, not a creative writer. At Hedgebrook, you wrote without an assignment in mind, and particularly in Bellagio; in fact, you were breaking the contract to write your assigned topic, a history of women's studies, in order to write a memoir of yourself and your mother (which of course you later rewrote.) That is, in terms of your personal psychology, it appears you emerged, although pretty late to my mind (in 1997 you were sixty-eight), as a creative writer when you transgressed against the assignment, and you confess to feeling guilt over that transgression.

FH: What I did while I was at Bellagio is, I took two days off from writing the memoir to write a lecture on women's studies, which I was supposed to give the following week in Poland. Two days out of thirty, writing for an assignment.

SL: Would you say the assigned writing is very different in voice- and style-structure from the writing of the memoir?

FH: In one sense there is no difference because writing is telling stories. If you believe writing is telling stories, then you would say there is no difference. I could say that, not only that but you need facts in both cases.

SL: The question of fact has been a thorny issue with recent memoir writing. With your facts (obviously, in women's studies writing, which is interdisciplinary), you operate with the rules of scholarship—that is, research, accuracy, verifiability, etcetera. Are you saying these same rules appear in memoir writing?

FH: Well, where possible. It is not always possible.

SL: Then, when not possible, what happens?

FH: You need to say it is not verifiable. This is what you think but there is no way to get it straight. Either everybody is dead and there are no sources, or if there are sources, they are not verifiable. For example, my father always said he was a citizen. Yet my mother said, long after he was dead, he was brought to the U.S. as a baby, and as far as I know, he never became a U.S. citizen when he grew up. As far as I know, he never voted. But he had a Social Security card, he drove a taxi—but I had no way of knowing whether he was a U.S. citizen. I suspect if I was to do the research, I would find a lot of things I said in the memoir may not be true. What I had to go on was my mother's memory.

SL: Did you trust it growing up, and did you trust it when you were writing the memoir?

FH: My mother never talked about the past. She talked about this only one time, when I interviewed her in 1980, by which time he had killed himself. As for women's studies, I could verify almost anything.

SL: Meaning: you have maintained an archive?

FH: Yes, I managed the archives of the development of Women's Studies programs all over the country.

SL: Gosh, when did you start maintaining this archive?

FH: In the sixties.

SL: And how long did you maintain it for?

FH: Till I stopped maintaining it, probably in the mid-eighties to late eighties.

SL: Has anyone picked it up?

FH: No, not that I know. All the files are now at Brown University in boxes that have not been touched in ten years.

SL: For your memoir, did you refer to, reread those archival materials?

FH: No. The particular aspects of women's studies that I was most concerned with in the memoir had to do with internal developments. I knew I could not cover everything, so I took it for granted the development of U.S.

women's studies was flourishing and was well covered. I spent the bulk of my women's studies time in the memoir on the work I did with Marilyn Chamberlain, spreading the information about women's studies in general around the world. Much of the women's studies focus comes in the three United Nations conferences, Copenhagen, Nairobi, and Beijing, where approximately sixty women's studies leaders from sixty different countries reported on the status of women's studies in their countries: twenty, twenty-five each time, and other conferences in which another twenty reported. In Costa Rica, we had eighty-plus countries. All the reports were published in *Women's Studies Quarterly,*[11] and they were sent around the world, so it was clear it was not a U.S. phenomenon but an international one.

SL: In the backstory, which may in fact be read as separate, albeit parallel, life stories to the larger stories of feminist movements and women's studies and the Feminist Press, your memoir talks about characters that are almost universally present in all memoirs—family figures and tragedies; growing-up trajectories, including education and social mobility; sexuality; and so forth. To focus a little on these more conventional life story elements: your mother features quite a bit, and for a feminist daughter and model, I read that daughter-mother relationship as both very troubled and yet painfully needy on the part of the daughter. Did you find it difficult to negotiate a feminist voice in narrating this daughterly ambivalence? For much of feminist writing, mothers are either to be idealized or hated, and your mother perhaps does both.

FH: I don't think I idealized her, but I do set her up to be, philosophically, what I had to overcome. Her life was not only very hard, but it was unsatisfying to her. Looking back at her life, I can now see what I could not see when I was younger, that she was so stuck in her life that when I complained that something was unfair—and it was unfair—her response was, life was unfair and to get used to it. Her view was that life was unfair to her, as well it was. She wanted to be a teacher, but her father said no. She wanted to be a business woman but had bad luck. Her getting married instantly made the business career impossible. She wasn't to get divorced, something you didn't do in a Jewish household in those days. Before she could do anything, she got pregnant again. I understood her as a woman who was stuck. And I came to this understanding while I was writing the memoir. The only way I could get what I wanted to be, who I wanted to be, I had to omit giving her her mission.

SL: Lie by omission?

FH: Yes, to lie by omission. I'd say I was going to the library and I would go visit one of my rich classmates whom I had gotten to know while I was in middle school.

SL: From what you've said, one may gather that the act of writing the memoir was also an act of discovering one's past and understanding the mysteries or coming to knowledge of what we were ignorant of. Am I concluding correctly?

FH: Yes.

SL: Would you address that more?

FH: Many writers report writing themselves into vision. Writing themselves into understanding something they thought they could not understand.

SL: One of the truisms regarding writing is that it is invention. Is there any relationship between writing as invention and writing as this "discovery" to an understanding that has not been received earlier?

FH: I think that is a fair way of putting it. There is no way I could go back to ask her these questions. If you asked her later on, as I often did even before her Alzheimer's, she would always say, "My life was wonderful. I had a wonderful husband and children." She would never admit that anything ever went wrong with her life. That is so bizarre, and it was impossible for me to accept. After she was dead, I found among her papers that she had actually taken a writing course while she was in Florida before she got really sick. She was in her late seventies or eighties, and I have a piece that she wrote, and it is really about a different person. How wonderful and strong her husband was, how much she loved her children, what a happy life together. Not a syllable about my father's mental illness and suicide and my brother's gambling and suicide. It was pure fiction and not good fiction at that. All I could think was, how pitiful. If I make that life pitiful, I am not doing her any favors. She was present and did real damage. But on the other hand, some of her meanness taught me to be stoic and to survive. She was stoic. I am sure I got that stoicism from her. I never cried. I refused to cry publicly.

SL: Do you think the length (536 pages) is a flaw in your memoir?

FH: Yes.

SL: And why so?

FH: It has too much in it. People who have read it and critiqued it in emails or print have said the following: the rage in it, that I am immersed in it, because the details are so convincing and important. On the other hand, a critic has said there are too many details.

SL: Why do you choose to believe one and not the other?

FH: I believe both of them. For the women's studies reader, the materials are great. For the general reader, they would prefer the family life, husbands, etcetera. It is a book for several kinds of readers. The reason that the structure is so unusual is that I wanted the readers to be able to move around. No one has to read the book in sequence.

SL: I have to say, I was fascinated by the husband stories, but I was almost equally fascinated by the social mobility story, which was not only that of education and becoming a highly esteemed academic woman but, beneath it all, the story of class change, from a working-class Jewish immigrant Brooklyn life to what appears as a successfully transformed, highly esteemed professional.

FH: If I wanted to be embarrassed, I would be most embarrassed about the years I went to Goucher College, beginning in the 1960s. I had two shames to cover up. One was my background, because my speech said nothing about me, and I said nothing about my family in New York. And my beautiful British husband, who was also a working-class British, was my third husband. I was recovering from two divorces. I kept a low profile until the moment I joined my students' picket line.

SL: Do you think that such systematics of social shame still govern private and public behavior and interior states among enlightened, educated Americans today?

FH: Yes. Especially, it is harder for some people, like African Americans or Asians. But it is still going on, this feeling about working-class people.

SL: More precisely?

FH: Contempt, expressed in amazement: "How could you have gotten to Harvard with your terrible speech?" My third husband's father spoke with a flat Liverpool accent that was hardly understandable, his mother spoke middle-class English, and he retooled himself into upper-class English. In England, the speech differential is more extreme than it is here.

SL: So here you are at eighty-two, having published your first real book, when you already had a collection of selected essays that appeared in 1984, and you have edited and coedited very important anthologies like *No More Masks!, Tradition and the Talents of Women,* and seven years later, *The Politics of Women's Studies* in 2000.[12] What advice would you give to women in their sixties, seventies, and eighties who are contemplating writing their first book, a memoir?

FH: Just do it.

SL: You're not going to get away with that! What problems may they anticipate? What books could they read to help them through their challenges of narrative strategies, finding their voice, and all the other technical and stylistic issues facing such a creative nonassigned writing project, besides your memoir?

FH: They should read a lot of other memoirs. I confess that while I was editing a memoir, I found it impossible to read others' memoirs. I opened up Kate Simon's book, *Bronx Primitive.*[13] *Bronx Primitive* and Kate Simon was another reason for thinking I did not have a creative bone in my body and that I could never write a memoir. I was with her when she died. The night before she died, I helped her put in the final changes of the galleys of her last memoir.[14] She trusted me to make the changes, and she trusted my ears to decide what should be changed and what not. So, when I started my memoir, I decided to read memoirs and I read *Bronx Primitive.* It is one of the most elegant memoirs ever written by anybody. In the five years I knew her, we had dinner once or twice a week, and I asked her how she wrote the memoir. She said, "I went to the library and I read the newspapers of the period." I asked her what else, "Did you have journals, and did you have notes?" And she said, "No, but I have a strong memory of places and streets," and that is one of the strong elements of her work. After all, she was a travel writer. After I put down *Bronx Primitive*, I said, "I could do that," and I never read another memoir. When I say, you should read memoirs, I always add a modifier: only if it is helpful to you. If they disturb you, if they lead you to think you can't write, drop it. I didn't read much of anything, except newspapers and magazines.

SL: But, of course, you had already read and very closely edited a number of memoirs in the immediate years before your own.

FH: Right, a dozen memoirs. I add one more note: some people think that being in a writing group is very helpful, with other people who are writing memoirs and reading sections aloud to the group. I can imagine that as very useful, but probably only if the group is pretty much on the same level, so there is little chance to get scared. I never had that opportunity and I am sorry I didn't.

Florence Howe (1929–2020) cofounded the Feminist Press in 1970. She became closely involved in the women's movement after her participation in the civil rights and anti-war movements in the 1960s. A founding mother of the women's studies movement during the 1970s and 1980s, she served as a professor of English at Goucher College and the College at Old Westbury, SUNY.

Shirley Geok-lin Lim won the Commonwealth Poetry Prize in 1980, the first for a woman and an Asian; placed second for the Asia Week short story competition and won two American Book awards for coediting *The Forbidden Stitch* and *Among the White Moon Faces*. She has published eleven poetry collections and three short story collections, three novels, *The Shirley Lim Collection*, and two critical studies, as well as edited/coedited numerous literary and critical anthologies. She received the Multi-Ethnic Literature of the United States and Feminist Press Lifetime Achievement awards, and University of California Santa Barbara Faculty Research Lecture Award. Learn more at lim.english.ucsb.edu.

Notes

1. Florence Howe, *A Life in Motion* (New York: Feminist Press, 2011).
2. For an introduction to Florence Howe's contributions to women's studies, see Marilyn J. Boxer, "Women's Studies as Women's History," *Women's Studies Quarterly* 30, no. 3/4 (Fall–Winter, 2002): 42–51, https://www.jstor.org/stable/40003241.

3. See the *Cross-Cultural Memoir Series*, Feminist Press.

4. Meena Alexander, *Fault Lines* (New York: Feminist Press, 1993).

5. With her fourth husband, Paul Lauter, Florence Howe was active in the anti–Vietnam War and socialist movements.

6. Toni McNaron, *I Dwell in Possibility: A Memoir* (New York: Feminist Press, 1992).

7. Rebecca Harding Davis, *Life in the Iron Mills* (1861, *Atlantic Monthly*; repr., New York: Feminist Press, 1985).

8. Susie Tharu and K. Lalita, eds., *Women Writing in India*, 2 vols. (New York: Feminist Press, 1991–93).

9. *Women Writing Africa*, 4 vols. (New York: Feminist Press, 2002–5).

10. Shirley Geok-lin Lim, *Among the White Moon Faces: An Asian American Memoir of Homelands* (New York: Feminist Press, 1996).

11. The United Nations organized four world conferences on women. *WSQ* (*Women's Studies Quarterly*) reported on all four. These took place in Mexico City in 1975, Copenhagen in 1980, Nairobi in 1985, and Beijing in 1995. https://www.unwomen.org/en/how-we-work/intergovernmental-support/world-conferences-on-women.

12. Florence Howe and Ellen Bass, eds., *No More Masks!: An Anthology of Poems by Women* (New York: Anchor Press, 1973); Florence Howe, ed., *Tradition and the Talents of Women* (Urbana: University of Illinois Press, 1991); Florence Howe, ed., *The Politics of Women's Studies: Testimony from 30 Founding Mothers* (New York: Feminist Press, 2000).

13. Kate Simon, *Bronx Primitive: Portraits in a Childhood* (New York: Viking Press, 1982).

14. Kate Simon, *Etchings in an Hourglass* (New York: Harper & Row, 1990).

Field Materialities: Building Women's and Gender Studies One Page at a Time

Agatha Beins

Abstract: Before becoming *Women's Studies Quarterly* in 1981, the *Women's Studies Newsletter* (*WSN*) chronicled the institutionalization of women's and gender studies (WGS) through the 1970s. It maps the field's early years and the range of creative, practical strategies educators, administrators, and students used to find space for a feminist education within a hostile institution. In this article, I explore the value of a publication like *WSN* and argue for its reincarnation in a twenty-first-century form by drawing on my experience as a WGS faculty member. Such a resource could offer practical tools for the quotidian, material field-building practices necessary to sustain and expand WGS, as well as for resisting the neoliberal status quo in higher education. **Keywords:** women's and gender studies; *Women's Studies Newsletter*; higher education; neoliberalism; labor; periodicals; archives

"I had NO IDEA that *WSQ* started as *Women's Studies Newsletter*," I wrote with surprise to Julie Enszer in summer 2021 after reading issues of the newsletter for the first time. Although I have taught and written about feminist newsletters and newspapers published in the 1970s and about the institutionalization of women's and gender studies (WGS), the *Women's Studies Newsletter* (*WSN*) had never surfaced during my time in archives, libraries, and classrooms. How had I missed it? As a compendium of articles, essays, resources, and reviews from WGS practitioners about their feminist ideals and daily labors, it maps the field's early years and the range of creative, practical strategies employed to find space within a hostile institution. Political energy, strength, vulnerability, and exhaustion live in its pages, too, reminding readers of the risks people took to administrate and teach in this nascent

WSQ: Women's Studies Quarterly 50: 3 & 4 (Fall/Winter 2022)
© 2022 by Agatha Beins. All rights reserved.

field. In doing so, the newsletter makes our past visible and usable (Kolmar 2012, 226), showing how WGS emerged through a multifarious, messy, and contingent array of efforts, successes, and setbacks. Because *WSN* holds such a useful archive, my earlier question bears elaboration: where in our histories of U.S. feminism and WGS is the *WSN*? Moreover, the process of institutionalizing WGS is not complete, so we can also ask, where/what is our *WSN* for the contemporary moment?

Here I consider the value of *WSN* both as an archive and as a way to construct a more usable present for those of us in higher education. On the one hand, in my experience, many of the obstacles to institutionalizing WGS in the 1970s still exist today, so we can learn from the innovative practices and radical dreams in *WSN*'s pages. I struggle to implement my feminist pedagogies at a university that keeps increasing faculty workload and the number of students in our courses. WGS programs still have to fight for resources and prove their academic validity. And, although much has changed in higher education in the past fifty years, we still need to demand radical, structural institutional transformation. On the other hand, the newsletter extends an invitation to explore how we narrate, record, and circulate twenty-first-century field-building practices in WGS. Taking a cue from *WSN*'s editorial vision and praxis, we can be more intentional about archiving, centralizing, and making accessible our administrative labor. Reincarnating *WSN* in a new format could support this important institutional work, offering practical tools for the quotidian, material field-building practices necessary to sustain and expand WGS. To elaborate this argument, I start with an overview of the field through the pages of *WSN* and then I offer two examples from my own institutional experience to illustrate the value of foregrounding our administrative labor as an important and ongoing part of WGS field building.

The *WSN* emerged in fall 1972 through a collaboration between KNOW, Inc., and the Modern Language Association's Commission on Women.[1] Thus, a community-focused feminist news distribution service and a formal academic professional organization formed the newsletter's roots ("About the Clearinghouse" 1972, 1). In the first issue, two letter-size, double-sided sheets contain three pages of content, and a mostly blank final page leaves space to affix an address label and postage so that when folded in half it would be easy to mail. In form and content, it would not be mistaken for a scholarly, peer-reviewed journal like *Feminist Studies*, which also published its first issue that year. *WSN*'s four pages of letter paper contrast with *Feminist*

Studies' 119 pages of thicker, sturdier paper stock. The editorials explaining each periodical's purpose further reinforce their distinctions. Rather than "encouraging analytic responses to feminist issues and analyses that open new areas of feminist research and critique," as *Feminist Studies* outlines ("Statement of Purpose" 1972), *WSN* editors aim to create "a forum throughout the country for the women's studies movement—in higher education, continuing education, secondary and elementary schools, and in community liberation centers." They continue, "We hope students, faculty, and movement women will write about their work. We look forward to articles about the major issues of the women's studies movement, and want especially to print reports about the development and directions of women's studies programs" ("Why a Newsletter" 1972, 1). From the outset, the newsletter served primarily as a site for nonscholarly writing about WGS: news briefs outlining the state of the field in different locations, reports about events and women's studies programs on different campuses, reading lists and bibliographies, descriptions of lesson plans and courses, and, for several years, information and updates about the National Women's Studies Association (NWSA). Its material field-building focus reflects what was happening on the ground and in the moment as faculty, staff, administrators, and students created a literal place for women's studies. As a result, the newsletter can be read as a kind of "how to" (or, at times, "how not to") and shows the varied formations women's studies took in different institutions, cities, and regions.

During the 1980s, *WSN* shifts in scope and genre, becoming less like a newsletter and more like a journal, a change signified in 1981 with the name *Women's Studies Quarterly* (*WSQ*). Over the next decades, contributions became longer and more conventionally scholarly, and identifying as "a peer-reviewed interdisciplinary journal" marks the overall editorial vision as distinct from the newsletter's ("About *WSQ*" 2022). Nonetheless, issues still contain a mix of writing styles and genres, as exemplified in the Fall/Winter 2021 special issue exploring *Solidão*. This transformation, in some ways, parallels the growth of WGS. Since the 1970s, the field has developed a rich, robust, stable intellectual presence through publications, conferences, and degree programs, so as a site of scholarly knowledge production, WGS needs periodicals like *WSQ*. Yet we lack a forum dedicated to sharing our institutional wisdom about and our experience, challenges, and successes in administrative labor, so I learn tips and tricks for navigating bureaucracy somewhat haphazardly, depending on which colleagues I might email or what might surface unexpectedly in a conversation or on WMST-L, a WGS listserv. Having struggled with the frustrations of working in an institution that often devalues and impedes feminist labor practices, I long for a place where we can record, think through, and share these material dimensions of our academic work.

My analysis of higher education relies on some broad generalizations and labels that belie the complexity of WGS, the *WSN*, and our daily labor but that I use to avoid repeating long lists of descriptors. "Academic," "intellectual," and "scholarly" help me refer to knowledge production practices that tend to result in academic capital for tenure and promotion: original "rigorous" research, peer-reviewed publications, and lectures and presentations about one's scholarship. In contrast, "material" and "field building" describe the administrative and service duties that, if recognized by institutions as work at all, are rarely given value commensurate with the time and attention they require. Advising and mentoring students and colleagues, completing program assessments, and attending faculty and committee meetings are just a few examples. Such a binary erases the creative, intellectual wisdom that material labor requires and cultivates, and our research, writing, revising, and presenting have material dimensions that affect where and how we convey ideas to others. This divide, however, reflects the conventions of higher education that rely on a distinction between "service" and "research/ scholarship" for describing faculty workloads and evaluating faculty performance. Further, as I discuss in this article, my concern that scholarly work overshadows material work and stands in for WGS itself leads me to disarticulate the two.

WSN's early years foreground this materiality, or the tangible things (resources, money, staff, reading lists) and labor (meetings, lesson plans, curriculum building) that were critical to establishing women's studies as a site of knowledge production. These topics appear in a variety of forms in *WSN*, two of which were "Closeups" and "Grass Roots," recurring features that offered fine-grained snapshots of WGS at local and regional scales. Closeups appeared through 1978, highlighting women's studies on specific campuses. Most often written by faculty, these pieces discussed what was salient, exciting, or challenging for the program at that particular moment. In the second issue, for example, Nancy Porter describes the origins of Portland State University's women's studies program: in 1970, they started with a lecture series and then proceeded to ask "department heads for permission to teach under an omnibus course number a variety of women's studies courses" to gauge faculty interest and propose a women's studies certificate.

Porter also explains their funding strategies and the obstacles they faced, such as slow administrative machinery (it took over eighteen months for the certificate to be approved) and department heads concerned that women's studies would deplete their own unit's faculty time and resources (1972, 6). Focusing on one of the first women's studies programs, at San Diego State University, Marilyn Boxer lists details like their "faculty allocation," which is "6.8 positions (plus .6 for administration)" and their $2,000 for "supplies and service expenses" out of the approximately $115,000 annual budget (1978, 21). Other Closeups offer student perspectives, lists of specific courses taught, relationships with other disciplines and departments, and efforts to infuse material labor with feminist values, such as including students in faculty meetings at the University of Hawai'i, Manoa (Ladd et al. 1973, 9). These reports reveal a program's architecture and the daily, nitty-gritty, bureaucratic, repetitive labors that support the existence of spaces where we do our academic work.

The Grass Roots series (appearing 1975–77) paints women's studies in slightly broader brushstrokes. Contributing editors selected a city or region, offered a sociopolitical overview of that place, and situated women's studies through its presence in academic and community spaces. Betty Burnett cites a low response rate from institutions and organizations in Southern Missouri yet includes six different universities, the public school system, and the Springfield YWCA in her report (1976). The piece about Chicago, which was a hub of women's liberation activism, spans one and one-half pages and mentions sixteen institutions—including four-year and community colleges—that offer courses about women and are in various stages of formalizing women's studies programs and curricula (Davidson 1976). Roosevelt University, for instance, does not have a minor or major, but each semester various departments offer eight to ten courses on women (5), and Chicago State University organizes a Women and Work series of lectures and workshops open to the general public (6). Creating a collage of courses, programs, events, and infrastructures, Grass Roots articles highlight the varied forms women's studies took in different schools and community spaces. Because a range of variables have affected how women's studies manifested at different sites, this series further illustrates the manifold, unpredictable, and often nonlinear paths toward institutionalization, a characteristic that still pertains to the field despite its current intellectual flourishing and visibility in higher education.

In 1975, *WSN* starts chronicling a critical dimension of women's studies not specific to a program or campus but to the paraprofessional infrastructure that supports a field. An easy-to-miss paragraph in the "To Our Readers" section notes that the previous issue of *WSN* had spurred women to organize a conference to "give full consideration to the possibility of establishing a national women's studies organization" and invites interested parties to contact Sybil Weir, coordinator of the women's studies program at San Jose State, for more information (1975, 2). From this came a wave of organizing that culminated in forming the National Women's Studies Association in 1977. There was a March 1976 preconference in Philadelphia (Greene and Reuben 1976), a Continuations Committee that met during the Berkshire Conference later that year (Weir 1976), and the national conference held the following January in San Jose. In the Winter/Spring 1977 issue, Florence Howe reports on the latter, where over five hundred attendees gathered to debate and vote on the organization's constitution, constituency, form, and structure (1977b). And the editorial in that issue tells readers that "the *Women's Studies Newsletter* [has] become the official disseminator of news and information" for NWSA, committing to "printing the news and views of the Association's formal structures and individual members" (Howe 1977a, 2). An "NWSA News" section (sometimes called "NWSA News and Views") becomes a regular feature of *WSN* through fall 1982, so for five years, five to ten pages per issue offer a glimpse into the inner workings of the association: NWSA committee and caucus meeting reports, updates from regional women's studies associations, conference information and registration forms, and articles taking a more analytical or reflective approach to the work of NWSA. In line with the newsletter's vision and purpose, this content lays bare how, why, and with what resources NWSA operated. Readers learn about the Coordinating Council's structure and process, which involved a rotating chair, a commitment to consensus building, and reserving meeting time for "criticism and self-criticism," which was a common practice in the women's liberation movement at that time (Wahlstrom and Greene 1977, 6). The daily materialities of developing and sustaining this academic organization surface, as well: a small note reports that Frank's Appliances, a business in Ft. Worth, Texas, donated a Codaphone 1400 so that now the association had an answering machine ("National Office" 1981, 83). And the first set of "NWSA Newsbriefs" thanks Jan Meriweather and Chris Bose, "two women who volunteered time over the summer transition period, when we had no office to and from which mail might flow" (McNaron 1977, 9).

Also notable is the number of pieces in *WSN* about teaching; some describe teaching within an area of study like Black women writers (Smith 1974), others focus on a particular course (Schniedewind 1978), and others explore pedagogy more broadly (Johnson 1973). Since feminist pedagogy—theorizing and practicing it—has been integral to my WGS education and is a priority in the program where I teach, these contributions reflected familiar terrain. However, the attention to women's studies in public schools was unexpected. From reviews of textbooks (Arlow and Froschl 1975), to a Closeup of a sixth-grade class (Fralley 1973), to pedagogy essays about teaching women's history in elementary classes (Hughes 1980), to including public school teachers in NWSA's national conference (Elwell and Lather 1980), the newsletter showed a number of concerted efforts to integrate a feminist education in sites beyond college campuses. Consistent with the newsletter's approach to depicting WGS, these pieces often attended to the material dimensions of educating students, such as when Ann Carver mentions working with colleagues from sociology and history to develop a lesson plan for her women's literature class (1979, 25).

This all too brief sketch of *WSN*, WGS, and NWSA is, of course, partial. I hope it at least illuminates the richness of our field's archives and the types of labor and material resources that have carved many paths toward institutionalizing WGS, one of which leads to me, now, sitting at my cluttered desk, drafting this article—with some job security (at this moment) provided by a tenured faculty position and with an overabundance of books and articles I am eager to read for my research and syllabi. I outline this history also because it raises some epistemological provocations about the tacit metanarratives that guide and order our feminist stories (Hemmings 2011). Analyses that construct and deconstruct a process of historicizing WGS, tend to center intellectual knowledge production (Orr, Braithwaite, and Lichtenstein 2012; Kennedy and Beins 2005b; Wiegman 2001b). When present, material practices are often situated through the academia/activism and theory/practice binaries wherein the latter term in each pair signifies what occurs in the nonacademic "real world," in distinction to the work we do in our teaching or scholarship (Orr 2012).

To explore one effect of this narrative paradigm, I analyze a course I regularly teach: Foundations for Scholarly Inquiry in Women's Studies, which is one of three required courses for the MA program in Multicultural Women's and Gender Studies (MWGS) at Texas Woman's University. Although the readings I assign come from a motley range of books and journals, my theoretical approach has been heavily influenced by texts like the

Fall 1997 special issue of *differences* (vol. 9, no. 3) and *Women's Studies on Its Own* (Wiegman 2001b), as well as my experience coediting *Women's Studies for the Future* with Liz Kennedy (2005b). These publications grapple with the apparently successful institutionalization of WGS through topics such as the subject of the field, curriculum development, WGS's engagement with "difference" and "diversity," and the role of activism, and they do so in a way that foregrounds epistemological and intellectual dimensions of our institutional presence and practices. The existential conundrum WGS faces in "The Impossibility of Women's Studies" (Brown 1997), for instance, doesn't result from a reduction in funding or faculty lines, the amount of time funneled into service work, or loss of space on campus. Prompted instead by the slipperiness of "the intellectual premises of women's studies now" (80), Wendy Brown wonders how we can ethically and responsibly create undergraduate and graduate programs if we have trouble articulating what the field is. My Foundations class syllabus has reflected Brown's assumptions through questions that center "intellectual premises":

> What is women's studies? What is the difference between feminist scholarship and women's studies scholarship? Is women's studies related to the subject being studied, the way it is studied, who is studying it, where research is published, or some combination of the four? Is it enough to merely call one's scholarship "feminist" to be a part of women's studies?

The word "scholarship" appears three times in four sentences, implying that the "foundations" of WGS mainly involve producing and circulating ideas. This focus is important, but when knowledge production becomes the only or primary signifier of WGS's presence and vitality in higher education, it can lead to metanarratives that marginalize material labor, such as in the way Liz and I organized *Women's Studies for the Future*—and thus WGS— through primarily epistemological and ontological tensions. We begin the "activism" section by citing "questions of the relationships of theory to practice and activism to scholarship" and some scholars' concerns that WGS no longer addresses "'real problems' faced by 'real women'" (Kennedy and Beins 2005a, 17). Therefore, the two chapters in this section that attend to material field-building labor (Balén 2005; Parada-Ampudia 2005) may be read only as examples of the struggle to align feminist theories and practices and not for the way that program administration is both an important part of WGS and a site where activism occurs.

It makes sense to highlight the field's scholarly and epistemological contributions, both of which have helped cement WGS's presence in higher education. PhD programs have increased from twelve to twenty-one in the past decade (Kitch and Fonow 2012; NWSA n.d.), and over nine hundred WGS programs exist worldwide ("Women's/Gender Studies Programs," n.d.). I also encounter traces of WGS thinking, such as interdisciplinarity (Jacob 2015), intersectionality (Bartlett 2017), and feminist pedagogy (Accardi 2016), far beyond the boundaries of the field, even if only nominally at times. Yet without commensurate attention to material field-building labor, we construct a skewed map of WGS. The daily experiences of faculty, students, staff, and administrators vary widely across time and location, as does the status and security of individual WGS programs. Amid continued resistance to the field's content and purported political agenda that we experience from our own institutions, elected officials, and the general public, neoliberalization leads administrators to run universities more like businesses and potentially devalue programs like WGS that are not perceived as fiscally profitable or quantifiably productive for the university (Williams 2019). Therefore, a well-established, respected, thriving body of scholarship does not necessarily correlate with a well-established, respected, thriving material presence. In parallel, a field's strong and perhaps even taken-for-granted presence at the national scale does not mean that each individual program can presume its institutional stability and future.

My Foundations class further amplifies a scholarship-centric version of WGS in its contemporary form by producing a linear chronology around academic labor. When we learn about WGS in the 1970s, we read pieces discussing the material work required to construct, wrest, and slip into institutional spaces, acquire resources, initiate conferences and gatherings, and build curricula (Howe 2000). Later years, though, brought a more stable and vibrant array of programs and degrees, national and regional professional organizations, and internationally renowned scholarly journals, and we explore this more recent past through topics like the field's epistemological and ontological core and the political facets of knowledge production. Concomitantly, course readings presume that we do intellectual work within the relatively static infrastructures that WGS founders established decades ago. Wiegman hints at this narrative formula, framing *Women's Studies on Its Own* through the field's anxieties that "academic feminism [has] betrayed its radical political roots, substituting abstraction for action, legitimacy for risk" (2001a, 3). Moreover, if our activist past consists of "visionary labor," whereas "a commitment to critique . . . today seems to animate Women's

Studies as a political project" (2001a, 2), it implies a shift in our modes of field formation from "labor" with its tangible connotations (even if visionary) to theoretical "critique." Relegating material field-building work to the past not only erases its continued necessity but also turns its presence into white noise, a background hum no longer needing the active intentional feminist designs that characterized WGS forty years ago. We do it, but it is not the work that has value. It is not the work that is worth recording in our archives or writing about in scholarly or popular publications. Rather, it is the meeting/program assessment/form creation/budget allocation/course scheduling/etc., we have to do so that we can do the work that matters and builds the field, namely academic knowledge production.

In addition to expanding and nuancing the range of labor that shapes our narratives about WGS, a contemporary *WSN* could be meaningful in constructing a more usable present for the field. I elaborate this claim through a wave of structural reorganization at Texas Woman's University that debunks the correlation between intellectual and material stability and the linear narrative of progress in which WGS has steadily grown and become more deeply embedded in higher education at local and national scales. In July 2020, about one month before the start of the fall semester, MWGS faculty learned about two major changes: the College of Arts and Sciences (CAS) removed one of our full-time, tenure-track lines, so for the indefinite future we have four instead of five faculty. CAS also decided to change our status from a department to a program and merge us with another department, citing budget exigencies and our small size as the main reasons for this downsizing. Myriad nuances that fall beyond the scope of this article shaped what happened, and it bears noting that MWGS was not unique: during the 2020–21 academic year, other CAS departments and programs were grouped into "divisions" and "schools." Moreover, I am not impugning a particular person or office at my institution. I do not believe anyone took delight in these changes, which occurred within a broader context of pandemic-exacerbated neoliberalism. Rather, this example shows nonlinearity in institutionalization, a facet of field building that becomes apparent through a material framework and at the scale of an individual program. Additionally, MWGS's epistemological presence on campus—and within the field of WGS—I hope remains strong. I celebrate my colleagues' active and rich scholarly work, and we are one of the few WGS programs that offers PhD, MA, and (as of fall 2022) BA degrees. In fall 2021, we also received approval to expand the MA program so that students can complete the degree entirely online. Therefore, the apparent strengthening and growth of our academic-intellectual offerings have occurred while our material presence, administrative support, and access to resources have shrunk.

When reading the *Women's Studies Newsletter*, I began wondering, if it still existed, how might it have affected our experience of this process, and could we have shared our negotiations to assist others? A colleague summarized what we experienced in the "NWSA Data Project on Higher Education Cuts," a crowdsourced spreadsheet compiling changes to WGS programs and women's centers during the COVID-19 era.[2] We need this data, but I am not sure if or how anyone is using it. It also lacks a narrative or analytical context, and the most recent dated entry is from October 2020, so we do not know how programs have fared since these budget cuts, furloughs, hiring freezes, and other austerity measures were implemented. NWSA in many ways seems like a logical host for a new version of *WSN*. Yet taking on such a forum would require additional material and intellectual labor along with support from institutional and individual members, and my point is not to give this task to NWSA. Instead, I emphasize the vacancy *WSN* left and that our present becomes less usable when we lack a forum that reliably and consistently houses and shares this type of information.

Although information about material field building in WGS does exist, our media landscape is decentralized in a way that may prevent us from constructing usable pasts and presents, a phenomenon Howe observed in a 1980 *WSN* editorial when listing the growing range of newsletters from WGS programs, organizations, and communities (1980, 2). WMST-L, a transnational women's studies listserv, occasionally includes messages related to field-building topics, but in recent years, announcements about conferences, jobs, and publications and queries about teaching resources seem to predominate. In addition to the aforementioned spreadsheet, NWSA's website offers a list of WGS PhD programs and resources for WGS program administrators and women's center directors. Its annual conference also enables program administrators to convene, and I have attended— and organized—sessions that address material labor practices in the field. Recent journal special issues further elaborate and analyze the impact of material-structural forces on our academic lives, focusing on the WGS PhD (Meyer and Tambe 2018) and academia's neoliberal, exclusionary, and gatekeeping practices (Nash and Owens 2015; Maldonado and Guenther 2019). Lastly, publications such as *Chronicle of Higher Education* and *Inside Higher Ed* often discuss bureaucracies and administrative issues in academia, albeit without much specific attention to WGS. I am grateful for these forums, but it can be overwhelming and time-consuming to keep track of them all. Nor do they provide what *WSN* did: regular coverage of daily field-building labor in WGS at local, regional, and national scales.

WSN thus made visible what is often unseen and marginalized, which includes our seemingly endless, repetitive, laborious, oft-thwarted struggles to align institutional praxis with our political commitments. In addition to centralizing this information, a twenty-first-century *WSN* could serve as a guide for navigating the thorny process of simultaneously assimilating into higher education and resisting it's status quo. The early decades of *WSN* opened up the field *in* process and *as* a process, clarifying that material labor practices are political. In her article about administrating a women's studies program at the University of South Florida, Juanita Williams describes a "paradox" in the job search process: administrators demand that we hire applicants with "the highest possible academic credentials," yet strong teachers and scholars have varied skill sets and training that does not necessarily include such credentialing. How does one hire in a feminist way, knowing that the institution could exploit hierarchies of power by appointing an instructor without a PhD "to the lowest faculty ranks," if the hire were even approved in the first place (1974, 12)? Accounts of being caught between conventional academic standards and feminist ideals about who has expertise, knowledge, and authority filled the pages of *WSN*, a tension that continues to permeate our academic lives and highlights the challenges of infusing material field-building practices with a feminist social justice ethic when hierarchical norms are so entrenched. Feminist approaches to administration, such as using a consensus model in decision-making, can also be time-intensive and thus discouraged within neoliberal paradigms of productivity.[3] Furthermore, a significant proportion of service work in higher education is often hidden, unremunerated, undervalued, and disproportionately shouldered by people already minoritized, so taking on this additional labor can exacerbate someone's already precarious position in academia (Duncan 2014; Maldonado and Guenther 2019).

In contrast to the relative success of institutionalizing academic feminist thought, pushing back against the violence of university policies, procedures, and hierarchies feels Sisyphean (Ahmed 2012, 26). For example, despite the work my colleagues and I do to keep the course caps low, for 100 percent online asynchronous classes, they rose from thirty-five to fifty between 2019 and 2021. The neoliberal market logic that extracts

labor—especially that of graduate student and contingent instructors—
bulldozes our feminist arguments about a student-centric pedagogy and
humane faculty and student workloads. The *Feminist Studies* special issue
"Doctoral Degrees in W/G/S/F Studies: Taking Stock" also explores the
gaps between feminist theories and practices in material-administrative
realms (and beyond), focusing primarily on the way graduate education
and WGS programs could better support PhD students (Meyer and Tambe
2018). In one article, Kristina Gupta analyzes several WGS PhD programs
based on their doctoral student handbooks and makes concrete recommendations related to student grievance procedures and parental leave
policies, among others (2018, 419). These "best practices" overlap with
my own feminist commitments, and I wish my university would consider
implementing them, but academia's stubborn logics and infrastructures
continually thwart our efforts to practice material field building in line with
our values. Reviving and updating *WSN* will not eradicate all of academia's
hierarchies, narrow definitions of excellence, and racist, sexist, classist gatekeeping practices, but it could give us a wider array of starting points and
tools for doing so in our administrative labor.

Certainly we must continue recognizing, celebrating, creating, challenging, and pushing the edges of women's, gender, sexuality, and feminist
studies scholarship. Our research and its circulation in academic journals,
books, and conferences keeps the field living, growing, and breathing.
Thus my interest in a contemporary version of the *WSN* is not intended
to divert attention from our intellectual work, nor is it a request to return
to the 1970s. The academic terrain in the 2020s is not what we experienced several decades ago; field-building practices and modes of sharing
those practices must adjust. Moreover, I resist the romanticized, nostalgic narrative of decline, apocalypse, or loss that imagines the 1970s as
the acme of revolutionary feminist fervor and recent decades as mired
in theoretical abstraction (Hemmings 2011). Lastly, do not let my argument become inescapably centripetal, pulling our attention only toward
the micro-scale machinations of field building. Instead, I want a reconfigu-
ration of *WSN* because institutionalization contains both intellectual and
material dimensions, and attending to both allows us to more accurately
assess and more fully know the scope of our field. Reducing WGS to the
former not only diminishes the field's expanse and complexity but also side-
lines the academic machine's constant hunger for and disciplining of our
bodies *in* and *as* material labor. We are perpetually building women's and

gender studies and, in this work, need to actively resist academia's norms. A contemporary *WSN* can nourish and revitalize these disruptive practices, as we learn from others to make our own work more effective and efficient. Just as important, it could reconnect us with the revolutionary sparks that WGS ignites by pushing back against sexism, racism, homophobia, classism, and ableism in higher education. Having been groundbreaking in our impact on teaching, learning, and knowing, WGS is in an ideal position to "engage the full range of feminist knowledge to more richly inform our institutional practices" (Balén 2005, 273). Material field building constitutes a powerful site where we can rupture the institutional status quo, and has the potential to mobilize our epistemological and practical wisdom to create a more usable present.

Acknowledgments

Much gratitude to Julie R. Enszer and Ashley Glassburn for their wisdom and idea-sparking insights as I worked on this article, as well as for the generative feedback from the special issue's editors.

Agatha Beins is an associate professor of multicultural women's and gender studies at Texas Woman's University and editor of the journal *Films for the Feminist Classroom*. Her research and teaching encompass the intersections of art and activism, feminist print cultures, the politics of archiving, and institutionalizing women's and gender studies. She can be reached at abeins@twu.edu.

Notes

1. The *WSN* is available online through CUNY Academic Works: https://academicworks.cuny.edu/wsq/index.6.html.
2. See "NWSA Data Project on Higher Education Cuts" on the organization's "Resources" page at https://www.nwsa.org/page/resources. The spreadsheet is posted at https://docs.google.com/spreadsheets/d/1fhzyp6jUZSa4fKDNlGrKYCLDqNVZ7M_nVrP9oHh1G54/edit#gid=0.
3. See, for example, the "Institutional Pedagogies" section in Wiegman (2001b).

Works Cited

"About the Clearinghouse on Women's Studies." 1972. *WSN* 1, no. 1 (Fall): 1.
"About *WSQ*." 2022. Feminist Press (website). https://www.feministpress.org/wsq.

Accardi, Maria T. 2016. "Feminist Pedagogy: Changing Lives, Libraries, and the World." *Choice* 54, no. 2: 150.

Ahmed, Sara. 2012. *On Being Included: Racism and Diversity in Institutional Life.* Durham, NC: Duke University Press.

Arlow, Phyllis, and Merle Froschl. 1975. "Women in High School English Literature." *WSN* 3, no. 3/4 (Summer): 18–22.

Balén, Julia [Jules]. 2005. "Practicing What We Teach." In Kennedy and Beins 2005, 272–84.

Bartlett, Tom. 2017. "When a Theory Goes Viral." *Chronicle of Higher Education*, May 21, 2017. https://www.chronicle.com/article/when-a-theory-goes-viral/.

Boxer, Marilyn J. 1978. "Closeup: Women's Studies Department at San Diego." *WSN* 6, no. 2 (Spring): 20–23.

Brown, Wendy. 1997. "The Impossibility of Women's Studies." *differences* 9, no. 3: 79–91.

Burnett, Betty. 1976. "Grass Roots Women's Studies: Southern Missouri." *WSN* 4, no. 2 (Spring): 1, 12.

Carver, Ann C. 1979. "Applying Feminist Approaches to Learning and Research: A Practical Curriculum Model." *WSN* 7, no. 2 (Spring): 24–26.

Davidson, Cathy N. 1976. "Grass Roots Women's Studies: Chicago." *WSN* 4, no. 3 (Summer): 5–6.

Duncan, Patti. 2014. "Hot Commodities, Cheap Labor: Women of Color in the Academy." *Frontiers* 35, no. 3: 39–63.

Elwell, Sue, and Patti Lather. 1980. "Scholarships for Teachers at the NWSA Convention." *WSN* 8, no. 3 (Summer): 12–13.

Fralley, Jacqueline M. 1973. "Closeup: An Elementary School Classroom." *WSN* 1, no. 3 (Spring): 5.

Greene, Elsa, and Elaine Reuben. 1976. "Planning a National Women's Studies Association." *WSN* 4, no. 2 (Spring): 1, 10–11.

Gupta, Kristina. 2018. "The Structural Vulnerability of Doctoral Students: A Political and Ethical Issue for Doctoral Programs in Women's/Gender/Sexuality/Feminist Studies." *Feminist Studies* 44, no. 2: 409–23.

Hemmings, Clare. 2011. *Why Stories Matter: The Political Grammar of Feminist Theory.* Durham, NC: Duke University Press.

Howe, Florence. 1977a. "Editorial." *WSN* 5, no. 1/2 (Winter/Spring): 2.

———. 1977b. "What Happened at the Convention?" *WSN* 5, no. 1/2 (Winter/Spring): 3–4.

———. 1980. "Goodbye, Women's Studies Newsletter—Hello, Women's Studies Quarterly!" *WSN* 8, no. 4 (Fall/Winter): 2.

Howe, Florence, ed. 2000. *The Politics of Women's Studies: Testimony from 30 Founding Mothers.* New York: Feminist Press.

Hughes, Sandra. 1980. "Teaching about Women's Lives to Elementary School Children." *WSN* 8, no. 2 (Spring): 3–5.

Jacob, W. James. 2015. "Interdisciplinary Trends in Higher Education." *Palgrave Communications* 1 (January). https://doi.org/10.1057/palcomms.2015.1.

Johnson, Laurie Olsen. 1973. "A New Inservice Training Model: SF Conference/ Course on School Sexism." *WSN* 1, no. 4 (Summer): 1, 10.

Kennedy, Elizabeth Lapovsky, and Agatha Beins. "Introduction." 2005a. In Kennedy and Beins 2005, 1–28.

Kennedy, Elizabeth Lapovsky, and Agatha Beins, eds. 2005b. *Women's Studies for the Future: Foundations, Interrogations, Politics.* New Brunswick, NJ: Rutgers University Press.

Kitch, Sally L., and Mary Margaret Fonow. 2012. "Analyzing Women's Studies Dissertations: Methodologies, Epistemologies, and Field Formation." *Signs* 38, no. 1 (September): 99–126.

Kolmar, Wendy. 2012. "History." In Orr, Braithwaite, and Lichtenstein, 225–39.

Ladd, Doris M., Dorothy Stein, Marilyn Harman, Judith Gething, Anne Kauka, Mirella Belshe, Donna Haraway, and Joan Abramson. 1973. "Closeup: Hawaii's Women's Studies Program." *WSN* 1, no. 4 (Summer): 8–9.

Maldonado, Marta Maria, and Katja M. Guenther, eds. 2019. "Critical Mobilities in the Neoliberal University." Special issue, *Feminist Formations* 31, no. 1 (Spring).

McNaron, Toni. 1977. "Elected by the Coordinating Council." *WSN* 5, no. 4 (Fall): 8–9.

Meyer, Leisa, and Ashwini Tambe, eds. 2018. "Doctoral Degrees in W/G/S/F Studies: Taking Stock." Special issue, *Feminist Studies* 44, no. 2.

Nash, Jennifer C., and Emily A. Owens, eds. 2015. "Institutional Feelings: Practicing Women's Studies in the Corporate University." Special Issue, *Feminist Formations* 27, no. 3 (Winter).

"National Office Gets Answering Machine." 1981. *WSN* 9, no. 4 (Winter): 38.

NWSA. n.d. "Ph.D. Program List." National Women's Studies Association. Accessed September 3, 2021. https://www.nwsa.org/page/PhDProgramList.

Orr, Catherine M. 2012. "Activism." In Orr, Braithwaite, and Lichtenstein, 85–101.

Orr, Catherine M., Ann Braithwaite, and Diane Lichtenstein, eds. 2012. *Rethinking Women's and Gender Studies.* New York: Routledge.

Parada-Ampudia, Lorenia. 2005. "The Institutionalization of Women's and Gender Studies in Mexico: Achievements and Challenges." In Kennedy and Beins, 262–71.

Porter, Nancy. 1972. "Closeup: Portland State University's Program." *WSN* 1, no. 2 (Winter): 6.

Schniedewind, Nancy. 1978. "Closeup on Women's Studies Courses: Women's Image: An Interdisciplinary Introductory Course." *WSN* 6, no. 1 (Winter): 25–26.

Smith, Barbara. 1974. "Teaching about Black Women Writers." *WSN* 2, no. 2 (Spring): 2.

"Statement of Purpose." 1972. *Feminist Studies* 1, no. 1 (Summer).

"To Our Readers." 1975. *WSN* 3, no. 3/4 (Summer/Fall): 2.

Wahlstrom, Billie, and Elsa Greene. 1977. "What Went on in Milwaukee." *WSN* 5, no. 3 (Summer): 6–7.

Weir, Sybil. 1976. "Planning Continues for the National Founding Convention." *WSN* 4, no. 3 (Summer): 1–2, 11.

"Why a Newsletter?" 1972. *WSN* 1, no. 1 (Fall): 1.

Wiegman, Robyn. 2001a. "Introduction: On Location." In Wiegman 2001, 1–44.

———. 2001b. *Women's Studies on Its Own: A Next Wave Reader in Institutional Change.* Durham, NC: Duke University Press.

Williams, Cobretti D. 2019. "The Personal Is Apolitical: Neoliberalism and Academic Capitalism in U.S. Women's Studies Programs." *Women's Studies International Forum* 74 (May/June): 1–8.

Williams, Juanita H. 1974. "Administering a Women's Studies Program." *WSN* 2, no. 3 (Summer): 5, 11–12.

"Women's/Gender Studies Programs & Research Centers." n.d. Joan Korenman, Gender and Women's Studies, University of Maryland, Baltimore County. Accessed September 7, 2021. https://userpages.umbc.edu/~korenman/wmst/programs.html.

Aunt Lute Books on Controlling the Narrative . . . Or Not

M. Bałut Fondakowski

Joan Pinkvoss, the cofounder of Aunt Lute Books, isn't really looking forward to this interview.[1] She's not keen on journalists, because too often they take stories and words out of context. But, as the 2019 recipient of the San Francisco Arts Commission's Artist Legacy Award, which acknowledges the impact of an artistic leader who has served a San Francisco–based organization consistently for twenty-five years or more, she said yes to my request. I was on assignment for a local magazine, and Pinkvoss knew the free media attention would be good for Aunt Lute Books, the small press she cofounded with Barb Wieser in Iowa City in 1982. Aunt Lute Books, which publishes on average three or four books per year, defines itself as a "radical feminist press publishing literature by those who have been traditionally underrepresented in or excluded by the literary canon" (Aunt Lute Books 2018a).

The conversation feels awkward at first, so to break the ice, I tell her that I first read Gloria E. Anzaldúa's *Borderlands/La Frontera: The New Mestiza* in 1996 in a class at Mills College,[2] but it was not until we sat down at the table in the Aunt Lute offices in the renovated brick building at 2180 Bryant Street that I realized Aunt Lute Books is its publisher. Certainly, few readers commit to memory the publishers of the books they love. But I now feel woefully unprepared for an interview with someone whose life's work is so essential to my—and many of my generation's—intellectual formation. Pinkvoss smiles as she watches me realize this. I ask what it was like to publish the book.

"We kind of created this book together," Pinkvoss begins. "It was very mutual[ly] respect[ful] and caring." Although Anzaldúa passed away in 2004, her shared sentiments toward Pinkvoss, "whose understanding,

WSQ: Women's Studies Quarterly 50: 3 & 4 (Fall/Winter 2022) © 2022 by M. Bałut Fondakowski.
All rights reserved.

caring, and balanced mix of pressure and gentle nudging not only helped me bring this creature to life, but helped me create it" (Anzaldúa 1999), live on in print in the work itself. To this day, *Borderlands,* Anzaldúa's groundbreaking semi-autobiographical work that remaps our understanding of what a border is, remains one of Aunt Lute's most in-demand books, though it took years for the book to find its readership and place in the canon. "When [Anzaldúa] was at UC Santa Cruz, she wanted to be recognized by academia," Pinkvoss says of the early years after the book's publication. "Now, finally she is being recognized by academics how she always wanted, because there are Chicanas in academia who can bring forward what her intentions always were."[3] Working with Anzaldúa, whom Pinkvoss always refers to fondly as "Gloria," is one of Pinkvoss's fondest, most foundational memories of Aunt Lute Books: "It is the best book in the world to be out there ... [Anzaldúa] invites everyone in ... anyone who views themselves in a borderland situation ... she invites them in." First published in 1987, the book is now in its fifth edition.

Despite graduating from the Iowa Writers' Workshop in the early '70s, Pinkvoss, now nearly eighty years old, knew from the start she did not want to be a writer: "I would almost get sick when I sat down to write," she says. But she never stopped loving the printed word, and she left the workshop with a particular affection for writing with "more rawness ... than the polished voice that had gotten into the workshop." Pinkvoss managed to pay her way through graduate school as a computer programmer, saving up enough money to travel to Switzerland to teach literature while she figured out what she was going to do for the rest of her life. When she left Iowa City, Pinkvoss "was one of the few lesbians in town—there were no Out groups and no discussion," but when she finally returned to the States, the Iowa City she once knew was pulsing with change.

"It was the '70s, and there was a burgeoning women's movement and lesbian movement," Pinkvoss recounts. "I had a chance to think about how I wanted to be involved. I always knew it was going to be the printed word, but how do you make a living?" Pinkvoss remembers when the publishers of the underground newspaper *Ain't I a Woman,* which was being circulated at the time, "wanted to do a self-help book on women's health." Their idea was to "include a picture of a speculum and mirror to show women how they could see themselves." Of course, "no one would publish it." What this made clear to Pinkvoss, and many of the mostly lesbians she regularly met with at the Women's Center in Iowa City, including Aunt Lute's cofounder,

Weiser, was that, "politically . . . if women were going to control what gets said, then they had to have control of the means of how it would get said." In other words, "if you didn't control the press, then you weren't going to be printed."

But, you need a little money to get started. And though a lot has changed since the 1970s, what it means to be grassroots and community-driven has not. With the Women's Center as a stable meeting place, the ten or so women driving the effort came up with a plan to raise the money to buy their first printer. At the time, Weiser was working in the Action Studies Department at the University of Iowa, the goal of which was to create learning opportunities outside the classroom. Well-known writer and activist Robin Morgan was a big voice in the women's movement, so Weiser invited Morgan to keynote a paid event through Action Studies. When Morgan accepted, the hope was that she would donate her honorarium to support the fledgling Aunt Lute Press. Of course, she did. "That's when we got the money to buy the equipment," Pinkvoss says, "at first printing on an offset printer."

But Pinkvoss and Weiser did not hit the ground running on establishing Aunt Lute. There were still multiple concerns: ongoing financing for the press, learning offset printing, and, most importantly, determining which voices to print. Pinkvoss observed, as did many others in the women's movement at the time, that "people [were] being left out . . . women of color weren't being heard in the same way" as the white women who were controlling the narratives of the movement. So while Pinkvoss took on a couple of jobs—including one at University Printing Services to learn offset printing and another as an electrician[4]—which solved the problems of money and skills needed—the third and primary concern was not so simple. Particularly because Pinkvoss, Weiser, and others in their group were white. "All you saw were feminist presses and every single one of them was run by middle-class white women . . . my realization," Pinkvoss continues, "was that in order to center the voices of women of color and lesbians, it had to be a very different kind of setup . . . it had to be grassroots, because 'we' could not decide what voices needed to rise to the top."

Intersectionality and solidarity are ways of living and doing activism that address injustices broadly and inclusively. The concept is encapsulated in the title of Fannie Lou Hamer's famous speech "Nobody's Free until Everybody's Free" (Brooks and Houck 2011, 134), delivered in 1971 at the founding of the National Women's Political Caucus in Washington, DC. But such an orientation does not appear out of nowhere. It is developed by the culture around us—the shows we watch, the leaders we listen to, and the books we read—and it requires vigilance to maintain. What that looked like for Pinkvoss at the time was "simple in a way, as—and I think lesbians were somewhat of a spearhead in this—when it became clear that women weren't very free, to buy that freedom it meant buying it for everyone." Based in a different part of the country than Pinkvoss, Cheryl Clarke shares a similar sentiment in the afterword to the 2014 edition of her 1986 poetic work, *Living as a Lesbian*: "During the 1980s, the era of *Living as a Lesbian*, lesbians of all colors read, wrote, and acted on our faith in ourselves to develop a culture of black lesbian-feminist politics and practice. We were activists on behalf of the Central American struggle, the anti-Apartheid struggle, and against the turn to the right of U.S. politics" (Clarke 2014, 128).

The lesbian and women of color writers from the '70s, '80s, and early '90s who were brought into print against all odds by Pinkvoss at Aunt Lute, as well as the publishers at Kitchen Table, Firebrand, and other presses,[5] called a generation of young women of color, white women, straight women, lesbians, and Queers to center "black lesbian-feminist politics and practice" in our intellectual and activist development. Searching for my own way to answer that call, I found a gig right out of college writing for *Sappho's Isle*—The Tri-State Lesbian Newspaper. It was unpaid, and I was not a good writer, so the stint was short-lived. But I did learn how much I longed to be in community with other Queers who were as invested in radically inclusive ideas as I was. So in 1997, after completing an MFA at Mills College, I launched *anteup*, a journal for Queer women poets and Queer woman–identified poets. The journal only released two print editions and a third online (the dot-com era had just started revving up), but in looking back at the journals now, it is easy to identify the radical feminist press influence and the centering of the very "black lesbian-feminist politics and practice" that Clarke writes about.

Given what I know about how hard it is to keep even a small journal in print, building Aunt Lute as a grassroots press dedicated to radical, multicultural women's writing—and keeping it that way for forty years—could not have been easy. Throughout the interview, Pinkvoss reminds me that she does not represent every opinion at the press, an attitude that captures the essence of Aunt Lute's collective, community-based publishing process. From the very first books Aunt Lute ever printed—a book of lesbian plays Pinkvoss cannot remember the name of, a couple of trade manuals for women carpenters and mechanics called "Against the Grain" and "Greasy

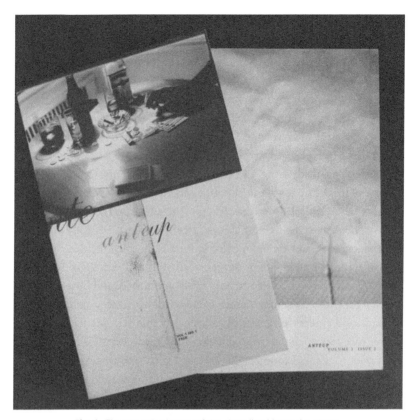

Fig. 1. The two print issues of the short-lived journal *anteup*.
Photo courtesy of the author.

Thumb," and Dodici Azpadu's *Saturday Night in the Prime of Life* and *Goat Song*—Aunt Lute has remained a grassroots press for writers who "just can't get it published someplace else," Pinkvoss says.

What that looks like in practice is serving writers who speak from within, to, and for the communities they represent. A good example of the cooperative nature of the press is when the Women of South Asian Descent (WOSAD) Collective approached Aunt Lute Books to compile writings by South Asian Women (Aunt Lute Books 2018b). The group, formed by students at UC Berkeley, were looking to make more widely available works that presented the perspectives of South Asian women. The result was *Our Feet Walk the Sky*, the first "comprehensive work to focus on South Asian American and South Asian immigrant women in the U.S." (Women of South Asian Descent Collective 2018). Another example is the book *Graffiti* (Dhawan, Laskar, and Thompson 2019). The writers of POC United

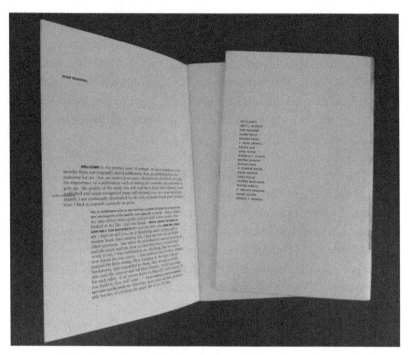

Fig. 2. Introduction, *anteup* volume 1, issue 1; list of contributors of *anteup* volume 1, issue 2. Photo courtesy of the author.

approached Aunt Lute Books with the anthology project, focused on creating "a literary safe space of creative play far removed from the white gaze."[6] For Pinkvoss, these books are a "good example of what we're trying to think about—finding people from communities who want to curate something, literarily speaking."

The practice of "finding" writers in this particular cultural moment—to be, in practice, grassroots—has not changed in the decades Aunt Lute Books has been around. It requires "collective input around the work [you're] going to put out," Pinkvoss says. "There's a lot of input from a lot of different people, and it wouldn't have succeeded if any one of us had decided they wanted to control the output." Editorially speaking, this means staying open to submissions that are reviewed by multiple members of an intentionally diverse Aunt Lute team, and a lot of the time, "you go into community yourself," to listen to and meet writers, which is exactly how Pinkvoss came to know, and eventually publish, Anzaldúa's work.

"In Iowa City [in the '80s] there was a group called Women Against Racism, which grew out of the Women's Center. They put on a couple of national conferences, and all these amazing women came: Cherríe Moraga, Nellie Wong, Winona LaDuke, Mona [Melanie] Kaye/Kantrowitz, Angela Davis," Pinkvoss says. It was "amazing what they put together. And that's where I heard Gloria read her poetry and was just blown away . . ." Referring to both the formation of Aunt Lute Books and meeting Anzaldúa, Pinkvoss adds, "—which shows how critical it is to have those kinds of spaces where people can meet and talk."

Like anything that is nearly half a century old, Aunt Lute Books has a storied history. Although founded in 1982 in Iowa City, it quickly became clear to Pinkvoss and Weiser "that we couldn't get these voices out unless we had a larger megaphone." Pinkvoss knew that "people pay attention to New York City and San Francisco," so in 1986, leaning on the connections she had made in the Bay Area while learning the electrician's trade, she and Weiser put a plan in place to move the press. But as life would have it, when the time came, Weiser's adventurous spirit led her in a different direction. Pinkvoss headed West on her own.[7]

Earlier, before the move, Pinkvoss had met Sherry Thomas, the owner of Spinsters Ink. Thomas "needed more people in her milieu who knew something about publishing and business, so we started talking and decided to put the two presses together." The merger was beneficial for a time, but a few years in, it became clear that Pinkvoss and Thomas had very different editorial intentions. So Pinkvoss and Thomas agreed to split the presses once again, and Pinkvoss created the nonprofit Aunt Lute, taking all the titles by women of color into the new Aunt Lute catalog. The move, which happened at the close of the 1980s, doubled down on the press's founding principles, adopting as its official mission to be an intentional, multicultural press.

The transition into nonprofit status opened the press up to new potential funding streams, which became particularly critical in the '90s when distribution companies were folding and the publishing industry started to crash. Pinkvoss remembers when they first started looking for grant support during that period: "Jim Sitter was running CLMP [the Council for Literary Magazines and Presses]" and, along with the head of the literature section at National Endowment for the Arts, gathered "people from nine different organizations—Aunt Lute Books, Poets & Writers, Copper Canyon Press, Milkweed, Graywolf—and they traveled us around to different arts organizations to explain why you had to support literature" with philanthropic contributions. That group of presses were the first ambassadors educating funders on the need for nonprofit support of literary presses, funders who

Fig. 3. The founding group of Aunt Lute Books when it became an official nonprofit with the mission to be a multicultural press. Interns and staff in San Francisco, 1991. Joan Pinkvoss, *top right*. Photo courtesy of Joan Pinkvoss.

could not quite wrap their minds around it: "You sell books, what do you need grants for?"

Well, to support the publication of culturally risky books, which is what Aunt Lute had been doing for years already. One of those books, *Why Can't Sharon Kowalski Come Home*, published jointly by Aunt Lute and Spinsters Ink in the late '80s, was about a lesbian couple in a life-altering automobile accident that laid bare the homophobia in the health-care system. The book's aim was to help gays and lesbians prepare themselves for the unimaginable possibility that they could be torn from their chosen families by the courts and blocked from making major medical decisions for their partners. As Pinkvoss explains, "That was a risky book because we could have been sued, but if you didn't take the risk then you weren't going to get the job done." Another one of those risky books was *Borderlands*.

"Aunt Lute had already decided to move to San Francisco in the summer of '86," Pinkvoss says, "and I knew enough to tell Gloria that we were making the move." Anzaldúa lived in Oakland, California, and Pinkvoss knew their proximity would make it possible to work together, though at the time, there was no frame of reference for a book like *Borderlands*: "Gloria and I did this book together, and it was quite a struggle to get her to let go of her material. She always was rewriting it; she was never done." In that classic grassroots style, when the book finally *was* done, Pinkvoss literally walked it into the New York offices of *Library Journal*: "Almost anybody who bought books read *Library Journal* reviews, whether you were a bookstore or library. Some women were running it at the time, so I went to talk to one of the editors. It was very hard to get an appointment. She said she'd give me five minutes, but when I came in, we talked for an hour. She was great. They chose it as one of their best books of 1987. The only small press book in the list." That review turned out to be crucial for gaining mass recognition of the importance of the book. "[Working with Anzaldúa] helped shape my knowledge that this is what I wanted to be doing for the rest of the time," Pinkvoss says.

The interview has gone on for much longer than either Pinkvoss or I intended, which is a good thing. But it is time to pack up. "I have this old picture," Pinkvoss says, and rummages around for a moment in the back office. She returns and places a photo on the table between us, a group of women on a couch in front of a mess of book boxes. I capture a photo of it with my phone. "I really didn't think I was going to enjoy this," Pinkvoss says of the interview; I never doubted it for a second. But I do have one last question, and it is about the future. What we read matters, and there is a

Fig. 4. In the old Aunt Lute offices on Mississippi Street, San Francisco, 1991.
Photo courtesy of Joan Pinkvoss.

lot more that goes into what we read than getting a book from a library or bookstore and sitting down with it. There is no direct path from writer to reader. There is curation at every level: editors, agents, publishers, distributors, sellers, libraries—even in self-publishing, since algorithms interfere. And curation is always conditional, with revenue often the primary concern. So I ask Pinkvoss what it means for her now, in comparison with the early days, to intentionally serve writers and communities of color.

"A tremendous consideration for Aunt Lute," and for her, Pinkvoss says, is: "how do you not put a white voice over a woman writer of color? How do you make space for those voices in a way that you can still be editing but not interfering in their voice?" At least part of the answer lies in always keeping that question close: "And if we talk about going on into the future, how that's beginning to look—and how everybody at Aunt Lute likes to talk about it now—is how we can still serve these voices without being gatekeepers."

Aunt Lute Press is too small to support every historically underrepresented and excluded writer. But their enduring catalog and their persistence in an ecosystem of small, grassroots presses doing the hard work of lifting up the voices of systematically marginalized people is critical to decolonizing the industry. That is what grassroots is and how it works. "I was [always] perfectly willing to think that Aunt Lute would close down if people didn't need it anymore and that would be okay with me," Pinkvoss says. "I don't think I have any attachment to it being around," she says. But after a pause, in which I imagine Pinkvoss may have been remembering the beginning of this interview,[8] when she told me why she does not like journalists, she adds, "except that . . . there still is a little bit about that thing of who controls the narrative."

M. Bałut Fondakowski is a Queer poet, novelist, and nonfiction writer and editor. Her work has been featured in *San Francisco Magazine*, the GIA Reader, and the *San Francisco Chronicle*, and she is currently working on a nonfiction manuscript that expands upon the role of radical Queer presses in movement building. She writes regularly at the Substack *Unfit to Print* and can be reached at mfondakowski@gmail.com.

Notes

1. In late 2019 on assignment for a regional magazine, I sat down for an interview with Aunt Lute Books (https://www.auntlute.com) cofounder Joan Pinkvoss, who had recently received the San Francisco Arts Commission's Artist Legacy Award (San Francisco Arts Commission n.d.). Due

to a change in California law regarding freelance work and a subsequent upheaval at the magazine, the article was neither accepted nor rejected for publication. This piece is based on that interview, which took place at the Aunt Lute Books offices. My inability to find a home for the piece until this publication is exemplary of the continued challenges women experience in telling our stories. As a point of note, in March 2022 I sat down with Pinkvoss for a follow-up interview to update the piece given the changes that the pandemic and world events have had on issues of equity, representation, and narrative. Pinkvoss and I were both very much looking forward to it this time around.

2. After a costly lawsuit battle between the college and alumni and trustees in 2021, Mills College merged with Northeastern University (Burbank 2022; Ramos 2021). The merger enables Mills to operate as Mills College at Northeastern University, but women's studies, ethnic studies, and other majors that defined study at Mills will no longer be offered—including the MFA in poetry, which was the degree I was working toward when I read Anzaldúa's *Borderlands/La Frontera: The New Mestiza.*

3. Use of the term *Chicanas*, as opposed to Chicanx or Chican@, is intentional, as this is the term Anzaldúa herself used in reference to herself and others of her time.

4. Although with Morgan's help they raised the money to purchase the offset printer, there was still a matter of where to put it. Pinkvoss explains, "So we went and talked to this guy who had a double garage, and he wanted to rent out part of it," which he was willing to do in exchange for the plumbing and electricity work that the garage needed. Pinkvoss volunteered herself to learn the trade, and because the Iowa union was not yet accepting women, she traveled to the Bay Area to work with Wonder Women Electric before returning to Iowa City to earn her Journeyman's and then Master's licenses. The relationships and connections Pinkvoss made during the time she spent in the Bay Area learning the electrician's trade would lay the groundwork for Aunt Lute Books's eventual move to California.

5. Kitchen Table: Women of Color Press published works by Audre Lorde and Barbara Smith, as well as the popular *This Bridge Called My Back: Writings by Radical Women of Color*, which recently celebrated forty years in print with the 2021 release of *This Bridge Called My Back, Fortieth Anniversary Edition*. Firebrand Books was the original publisher of Clarke's *Living as a Lesbian* and was also the publisher of works by Lorde, Jewelle Gomez, and Alison Bechdel.

6. From the POC United website: "To create our inaugural anthology, we joined forces with poet and novelist Devi S. Laskar. We gave the

contributors a special challenge: to write in a way that centers neither 'whiteness' nor 'anti-whiteness' and that is not limited by their struggle, their oppression, or how their characters will be received by the white imagination. The results are joyous and mind-expanding. Through poetry, short stories, and essays, the works in *Graffiti* expose lives that move in unexpected ways, rendering characters who don't fit cultural tropes. *Graffiti* shows what writers of color do when we are invited to scribble, scrawl, romanticize, and speculate without being politicized or exoticized" (POC United n.d.).

7. Weiser and Pinkvoss remain good friends to this day.
8. The author gratefully acknowledges Joan Pinkvoss for taking the time to share some of her own, and Aunt Lute's, story.

Works Cited

Anzaldúa, Gloria. 1999. *Borderlands/La Frontera*. 2nd ed. San Francisco, CA: Aunt Lute Books.

Aunt Lute Books. 2018a. https://www.auntlute.com.

———. 2018b. "WOSAD." https://www.auntlute.com/wosad.

Brooks, Maegan Parker, and Davis W. Houck, eds. 2011. *The Speeches of Fannie Lou Hamer: To Tell It Like It Is*. Jackson: University Press of Mississippi.

Burbank, Keith. 2022. "Mills College's Women's Studies Major Appears to Be on the Chopping Block." *Bay City News*, February 2, 2022. https://www.ktvu.com/news/mills-colleges-womens-studies-major-appears-to-be-on-the-chopping-block.

Clarke, Cheryl. 2014. *Living as a Lesbian*. New York: A Midsummer Night's Press & Sinister Wisdom.

Dhawan, Pallavi, Devi S. Laskar, and Tamika Thompson, eds. 2019. *Graffiti*. San Francisco: Aunt Lute Books.

POC United: Story-Telling from the POV of POC. n.d. "About." https://pocunited.com/.

Ramos, John. 2021. "Trustees, Alumni Suing to Prevent Merger of Historic Mills College in Oakland." *CBS Bay Area*, July 7, 2021. https://sanfrancisco.cbslocal.com/2021/07/07/trustees-alumni-suing-lawsuit-prevent-merger-northeastern-university-historic-mills-college-in-oakland/.

San Francisco Arts Commission. n.d. "Artist Legacy Grant (ALG)." https://www.sfartscommission.org/content/artistic-legacy-grant-alg-1.

"You're International, Not American": Academic Feminist Autobiographics and the Political Grammar of Nation

Clara Montague

Abstract: Over the last fifty years, the field of women's studies has grown from a few classes created by academic feminist activists into a global intellectual and political movement. Though the field has always been international, historiographies of its institutionalization have largely limited their focus to the Global North, an elision that reinforces unequal power dynamics among countries. This article analyzes the political grammars of nation in two edited collections from the Feminist Press in order to examine how metanarratives about women's studies have been produced and reinscribed through self-representational writing. **Keywords:** political grammar; transnational feminism; autobiographics; women's studies; Feminist Press

Introduction

In the fifty years since *Women's Studies Quarterly* began publication in 1972, the academic field for which it envisioned itself as a clearinghouse has undergone tremendous growth in the United States and around the world. At present, in addition to cross-border consortia and many collaborative, multi-institutional projects, there are at least nine hundred degree programs and research centers located in more than seventy countries (Korenman n.d.). Despite this global proliferation and the significant impact of transnational feminist thought, histories of women's studies at colleges and universities have largely limited their focus to North America, Western Europe, and Australia.[1] As one remedy, scholars such as Leela Fernandes have argued for a better balance between cross-border research and in-depth, locally specific analyses (2013). This article follows in the tradition of critically renarrativizing feminism, a practice Clare Hemmings has

WSQ: Women's Studies Quarterly 50: 3 & 4 (Fall/Winter 2022) © 2022 by Clara Montague. All rights reserved.

termed "recitation," in order to paint a more accurate portrait of the field's past and present (2011, 180–90). Through this comparison of differently situated autobiographics, I seek to document how scholars conceptualized themselves and their collective labor during a critical period of internationalization and institutionalization for women's studies.[2]

This article examines two edited collections published by the Feminist Press roughly halfway between its founding and the present day: *Changing Lives: Life Stories of Asian Pioneers in Women's Studies* in 1995 (jointly published by Kali for Women in India) and *The Politics of Women's Studies: Testimony from 30 Founding Mothers* in 2000. In addition to their shared publisher, these texts have important similarities in terms of time period, genre, and structure, with each comprised of autobiographic essays written by influential academic feminists during an especially important phase in the history of women's studies.[3] These examples of self-representational writing are useful for understanding how feminism has unfolded both within and outside higher education, because such accounts document the personal and political by featuring their authors' own experiences as well as shared stories of institutional and cultural change. The juxtaposition of multiple essays from different scholars loosely united by geography also offers an opportunity to observe trends in the field more broadly than would be possible by focusing on one author or location. Furthermore, comparing collections from Asia and North America allows us to consider how academic feminists across geographical sites have understood and represented their own positionings as intellectual and political subjects.

To analyze *Changing Lives* and *The Politics of Women's Studies*, I employ a transnational feminist framework by looking at how the authors refer to their own and other countries as well as the relationships among them. This approach draws on a body of scholarship that has critically interrogated the category of "the nation" as well as forces such as neoliberalism that continue to structure asymmetrical power relations across borders (Burton 2003; Grewal and Kaplan 1994; Mohanty 2003; Swarr and Nagar 2010). As Ashwini Tambe has argued, key facets of transnational feminist scholarship include "theorizing multidirectional connections between locales" and examining "the mobility of people, goods, and ideas" (2010, 3). Furthermore, this perspective helps to decenter the U.S. and Europe by exposing ongoing power disparities among nations, including past and present manifestations of colonialism. Understanding nuances in the discourse of transnationalism is particularly important in our present moment, in which women's studies scholars are critically reevaluating the role of cross-border exchanges in the history of feminist movements.[4] Therefore, this article combines transnational feminist theory with autobiographic analysis as a way of integrating diverse rhetorical approaches grounded in the authors' specific sociopolitical contexts. Both *Changing Lives* and *The Politics of Women's Studies* involve scholars reflecting on their personal and professional life trajectories as well as their experiences of field formation and social movements. Memoirs grant access to the intrasubjective and interpersonal dynamics that shape the conception, enactment, and narrativization of academic feminism, thus comprising a rich repository of knowledge that can offer guidance as we seek to challenge systems of inequality that continue to structure the production and dissemination of knowledge.

Literature and Methods

My analysis of how the nation appears in edited collections of autobiographic writing by academic feminists departs somewhat from traditional considerations of memoir, a genre typically conceptualized as book-length monographs that follow a single person through their life. I broaden this definition using feminist scholarship about women's knowledge production and literary cultures in order to argue that other kinds of self-representational texts—such as front matter, author sketches, and scholarly articles—can also provide valuable first-person data about women's studies transnationally. I also use Leigh Gilmore's concept of "autobiographics," a reading practice that places "emphasis on writing itself as constitutive of autobiographical identity [and] discursive contradictions in the representation of identity (rather than unity)" (1999, 42).[5] Autobiographics envision more than straightforward representations of individuals, instead examining how *processes* of self-narration can usefully deconstruct both personal and political subjectivities. Thus, Gilmore's method of autobiographic analysis has relevance not only to the study of women's self-representational writing but also to individual and collective stories of *how* women are studied. When applied to academic feminism, the framework of autobiographics foregrounds the significance of intersectionality, debates about naming, and the evidence of experience—all central themes in women's studies scholarship and praxis.

In the course of gathering texts about academic feminism around the world for my dissertation, I became aware of some recurring themes in this body of literature, specifically that many texts are coauthored, include autobiographic elements, or both. Often, when the author(s) speak about international collaborations or movement across borders, they do so based directly on their own lives. This commonality is unsurprising in itself given the self-reflexivity characteristic of women's studies scholarship. However, thinking through the lens of what Clare Hemmings calls "political grammar" led me to consider what insights might be gained by critically analyzing texts that speak from the first person. *Why Stories Matter* (2011) presents a methodology for unpacking metanarratives about feminist progress, loss, and return, as well as telling different stories through practices of citation, recitation, deauthorization, and disidentification. Though Hemmings focuses on academic journals, the book hypothesizes that similar metanarratives circulate through textbooks, monographs, edited collections, and memoirs—all genres invested in constructing specific histories of the field (19–21). Grammar is conventionally thought of in a prescriptivist sense, whereby writers follow a predetermined set of rules in order to express themselves "correctly" and thus achieve intelligibility. By contrast, Hemmings descriptively emphasizes the functionality of language, seeking to explain how combinations of words and ideas work together in order to produce meanings that can vary with context. Following the thread of autobiographics requires conceptualizing grammar not just as a set of rules but rather the framework through which we speak ourselves into being by taking up the linguistic and cultural roles of scholar and subject. As a result, scholars attuned to the analytic potential of autobiographics may consider how grammar can either reinforce or undermine the constructions of subjectivity articulated through various modes of textual self-creation, thus enabling a more robust consideration of identities and relationships.

Like *Why Stories Matter*, this article focuses solely on English-language sources because of a practical need to manage the project's scope. Though this undoubtedly limits my ability to make comprehensive claims about women's studies as a global phenomenon, Hemmings astutely observes that many texts appear in ostensibly Western sources through translation and other forms of collaborative or multiply sited production: "Feminist theory is certainly bound up in global power relations, particularly when we consider the various ways in which a presumed opposition between Western gender equality and non-Western patriarchal cultures is mobilized in temporal and spatial modes, but it also occupies a position of reflexive non-innocence that can break open those relations" (2). Limiting what is often understood as the women's studies canon to English-language sources necessarily reproduces linguistic hegemony, but it would be a vast over-simplification to assume that feminist perspectives from non-Anglophone countries cannot also be traced through this body of literature. Understanding how colleagues from different parts of the world strategically navigate global systems of speech, writing, and institutionalization can help us to critique our own processes and sustain connections across borders. By examining "the nation" in *The Politics of Women's Studies* and *Changing Lives*, I will document the different political grammars used in feminist autobiographics from the 1990s. By studying the political grammars used to recount academic feminist history, I hope we can better understand how power is organized, reproduced, and perhaps challenged.

Citation Grammar: Credentializing and Contextualizing

Despite their formal similarities and overlapping publication histories, the authors and editors of these two collections clearly conceptualize themselves and the field of women's studies very differently, particularly with respect to nation. In my analysis, I identify *credentializing* and *contextualizing* as two forms of political grammar that describe how scholars cite other countries. Credentializing grammar consists of brief references that denote the fact of an exchange, movement, or collaboration for the purpose of marking the author's prestige or expertise. By contrast, scholars use contextualizing grammar to describe how historical and present relationships among nations structure their lives and work. Both forms of citation are commonplace in women's' studies scholarship, and multiple modes of political grammar can be present within a single text, particularly one with multiple contributors.[6] Neither mode is superior, but authors make strategic decisions about which to use based on factors such as the text's purpose or intended audience. At the same time, credentializing and contextualizing grammars illustrate ongoing disparities among women's studies scholars based within different institutions and parts of the world.

Everywhere from author biographies and activity summaries to grant proposals and websites, individual scholars and collective projects alike reference connections across national borders as a way of credentializing their work.[7] This grammar appears constantly in all kinds of "narrative vitae" and, in my reading, illustrates two compelling insights about the institutionalization and internationalization of academic feminism. First, scholars often refer to other places as a way of marking their own affiliation, authenticity, or credibility. Typically occurring alongside other markers that convey status within the global economy generally and the higher education sector in particular, credentializing political grammar lends importance to the author or subject. Through these references, transnational exchanges become assimilated into the neoliberal university's systems of accounting for value and marketability. Furthermore, the way credentializing grammar leaves certain nations (un)marked can tell us a great deal about how power operates across borders. Together, the examples from *Changing Lives* and *The Politics of Women's Studies* that I discuss here illustrate how citation practices can alternately resist or reinscribe hegemonic discourses and political economies of higher education.

The juxtaposition of these two texts reveals important points about the narrativization of transnational academic feminism because of their continuities as well as the grammatical and discursive differences between them. Both are landmark collections of autobiographical essays by founders of women's studies, each of which is prefaced by a brief sketch of the author. Early on in my review of transnational academic feminist texts, *Changing Lives* and *The Politics of Women's Studies* emerged as companion pieces because of the similarities in their structures and genealogies. Given that both books were put out by the Feminist Press, Florence Howe unsurprisingly played an important role in their production, providing the foreword to *Changing Lives* and editing *The Politics of Women's Studies* in addition to writing its opening autobiographical essay. However, despite their overlaps in form, time period, and authorship, these two collections are also very different, particularly with respect to how they employ citational grammar to describe the transnational landscape of academic feminism. Taken together, these collective autobiographics illustrate how the nation functions in various ways for women's studies practitioners around the world.

Changing Lives: Life Stories of Asian Pioneers in Women's Studies
In her foreword to this collection, Florence Howe describes the encounter that led to *Changing Lives*. She recalls that this collaboration began in 1990 when a "small group of Philippine women" visited the Feminist Press. They told Howe about their plans for a book about "the story of women's studies in Asia," but initially, she was reluctant to get involved:

"Oh no," I said, trying to keep the conversation light, "I'm very flattered, but you can't have an American imperialist publisher." "No, no," Lucia Pavia Ticzon replied, speaking for the group, "We've thought about it, and we've decided that you're *international*, not American." We went round this conversation several times, until I could no longer manage the joking tone in the midst of tears. They were in earnest about The Feminist Press as an international institution. "Why don't you publish it yourselves?" I took a deep breath. "Why not establish a publishing arm?—you do everything else." They explained that they had no time for publishing now, and no expertise. Perhaps in the future. But the offer held. I said I'd be delighted to *co-publish*, but I thought they ought to have an Asian publisher, and I suggested Kali for Women in India." (xiii–xiv, emphasis original)

Eventually, this shared publishing arrangement with Kali for Women was indeed where *Changing Lives* ended up.[8] The Committee on Women's Studies in Asia was formed to oversee the project, and the book first came out with Kali for Women in 1994 under the title *Women's Studies, Women's Lives: Theory and Practice in South and Southeast Asia* before it was then published as *Changing Lives* by the Feminist Press the following year. Because of its joint publication and range of contributors, *Changing Lives* represents a significant accomplishment for transnational academic feminism—each essay offers a nuanced portrait of women's studies in the individual life of the author as well as academic feminism across different national contexts.[9]

Despite its significance, however, Howe's description of the book's conception also raises questions about the process by which it was created as well as the dynamics among its stakeholders. The narrative presented in her foreword suggests a developmentalist logic whereby Howe felt compelled to help these colleagues because they lacked access to the institutional resources required of mainstream publishing. However, this framing narrows consideration of the long-standing colonial relationship between the United States and the Philippines to a joke—that is, a rhetorical move intended to "keep the conversation light" (1995, xiii). Left unspoken are the material and epistemic hierarchies, past and present, that structured Ticzon's request in the first place. This elision limits Howe's discussion of her Filipina collaborators to a credentializing gesture that internationalizes the Feminist Press. In Howe's recounting of her exchange with Ticzon, "imperial" gets subsumed by "international," and as a result, the tears shed by her colleagues are noticed but not addressed. We as readers seem meant to sympathize with their plight but not ask any further about those emotions or the complex systems that produced them. Autobiographics that are limited to credentializing grammar thus tell us that an exchange happened, but not much else. Informed readers may deduce some of the histories underlying such a narrativization, but on its own, this form of political grammar cannot substantively critique or effectively intervene in hegemonic processes of knowledge production and dissemination.

The credentializing grammar that predominates Howe's narrative about the origins of *Changing Lives* diverges from the autobiographic essays by Asian academic feminists it contains. Each essay in the collection is worthy of further consideration, particularly for scholars interested in the women's movements and educational politics of their respective countries. In this article, I focus on the chapter by Aurora Javate De Dios, which stands in stark contrast with Howe's omission of the historical relationship between the United States and the Philippines.[10] In recounting her own life as well as the Filipina feminist movement within and beyond higher education, De Dios writes extensively about the effects of both U.S. and Spanish imperialism. She explores how the Philippines' independence movement and protests against militarism served as important incubators for feminist activism throughout the twentieth century (35–37). While also critiquing martial law and patriarchal violence in Filipino society, De Dios highlights how U.S. development aid as well as World Bank and International Monetary Fund policies in fact reinforced these problems, propping up the Marcos regime in the name of economic progress and industrialization.

Since the 1970s, feminist groups like MAKIBAKA and GABRIELA have organized resistance to the commodification of Filipina women around U.S. military bases, while working abroad, and via sex tourism (39). In addition to leading scholarly research on these subjects, academic feminists in the Philippines have emphasized how using local languages in their work enacts the potential of women's studies as a popular education project, "narrowing the great cultural divide between the English-speaking elite and the masses" (42), while also contesting misperceptions of women's studies as inherently "too western" (47). Reading De Dios's account of the global forces that have structured her own experiences as well as the shared history of Filipina women's studies, I was struck by the dissonance between how this autobiographic essay and Howe's foreword describe the relationship between the United States and the Philippines. Though each scholar positions their national identification by referring to other countries, De Dios contextualizes and offers an explicit critique of the power dynamics between these two nations. She further offers recommendations for how to build the field of women's studies in ways that work to dismantle long-standing global hierarchies. For example, De Dios's emphasis on conducting women's studies in a plurality of local and indigenous languages requires a concurrent decentering of English as well as Spanish given their colonial legacy. Her conceptualization of transnational academic feminism insists that women's studies scholars from more privileged countries address our complicity with systems of linguistic hegemony, global finance, labor exploitation, and neocolonialism. Credentializing grammar can only offer a narrow window into the nature of cross-border exchanges; contextualization is necessary for autobiographic accounts to articulate insights about the politics of location that illuminate a path forward.

The Politics of Women's Studies

From our present vantage point, having benefited from an additional twenty-five years of theorizing about transnational feminist collaborations, it feels a bit easy to critique Howe's foreword to *Changing Lives* for neglecting to address the global politics that structured the book's publication.[11] Moreover, interpreting this text as a predecessor to another edited volume from the Feminist Press, *The Politics of Women's Studies: Testimony from 30 Founding Mothers*, reveals how the elision of nation has been a structural problem in U.S. women's studies overall rather than a shortcoming of any one scholar or publisher. Though it came out only five years later, *The Politics of Women's Studies* makes no mention of *Changing Lives*, nor does it explicitly contextualize its subjects or contents in terms of place. Whereas each author in *Changing Lives* gets labeled by their home country, the authors' nationalities in *The Politics of Women's Studies* go unmarked precisely because they are all presumed to be from the United States—a false universalization that extends to the scope of this collection as a whole.[12] As a publisher, Howe would likely have considered this text's intended audience as based in the United States and framed its significance accordingly. Despite the impacts of globalization and the internationalization of higher education, it seems that the United States continued to see itself unproblematically as the center of academic feminism at least through the year 2000.

In her preface to *The Politics of Women's Studies*, Howe cites the "initiating moment that inspired this volume" as occurring in 1995 when, at lunch with an unnamed "founding mother," Howe realized that time was running short to gather stories about the field's inception (xi–xii). Howe's reflection on the necessity of preserving and sharing autobiographics by women's studies founders resonates deeply with my own scholarly investments in telling the story of academic feminism, particularly at our present historical juncture a half-century into the field's institutionalization, when the window of opportunity to gather these first-person narratives about the field's proliferation has closed even further. That said, maternal and sororal metaphors construct a limited narrative about feminism that can reduce our understanding of its diverse actors and influences.[13] Indeed, this collection's subtitle, *Testimony from 30 Founding Mothers*, suggests that women's studies began with the academic feminists whose personal and professional stories are contained therein, obscuring the ways in which women's studies has always been a diversely sited project.

In not mentioning the Committee on Women's Studies in Asia in her description of how this latter Feminist Press book originated, Howe obscures an important part of the genealogy for this text—and the field as a whole. Thus, the credentializing political grammar employed in Howe's preface to *Changing Lives* is symptomatic of the power imbalance underlying the relationship with her Filipina colleagues as well as between the United States and the Philippines more generally. Even though she locates the inception of the idea for *The Politics of Women's Studies* immediately after *Changing Lives* was published, Howe does not reference the earlier book within this text. Because the latter collection centers entirely on the United States without acknowledging its own standpoint, *The Politics of Women's Studies* misses an opportunity to theorize the field in a more complete, transnational way. In my reading, the juxtaposition of these two texts constitutes an opportunity for the field to reflect on how we might renarrativize women's studies in ways that center rather than obscure the field's transnational history as well as connections across borders in the present and future.

One notable discussion of cross-border projects in *The Politics of Women's Studies* occurs in Mariam K. Chamberlin's essay, "There Were Godmothers, Too," which addresses her work at the Ford Foundation. A major funder of academic feminist collaborations, especially between the 1970s and 1990s, Ford saw supporting women's studies programs and research endeavors as a strategy for addressing sexism within higher education as well as carrying out international development. Chamberlain notes that her "jurisdiction at the Ford Foundation was largely confined to the United States. We were active to a lesser extent in Canada and Western Europe, but programs else-where in the world—the developing countries and Eastern Europe—were the province of the International Division of the foundation, which did not have women's studies on its radar" (362). This compartmentalization of gender and international issues broke down by the 1990s, when Ford sought to build links between women's studies and area studies as a way of simultaneously "engendering" and "internationalizing" curricula at U.S. colleges and universities.[14] As Chamberlain describes, Ford's agenda for supporting academic feminism abroad was to "develop" other nations by promoting postsecondary education and employment for women, espe-cially in Asia and the former Soviet Union. Though key to the growth and institutionalization of women's studies, the political grammar of develop-ment often used by the financial backers of such endeavors necessarily relies on a unidirectional conception of how feminism moves across borders, one in which power and knowledge remain primarily located in the Global North. While this discourse can be strategically useful in terms of securing material and logistical resources from governments and NGOs, develop-ment grammar relies on progress narratives as well as imbrication with the logics of colonialism and academic capitalism in ways that make it difficult for collaborative women's studies projects to survive those systems with their political aspirations intact.[15]

Though each author represented in this collection is unique, and their essays reflect a diverse range of personal, political, and epistemic orienta-tions, the commonalities in how they approach citation grammar illustrate themes that run throughout U.S. women's studies, which can be compared with work by academic feminists from Asia. Overall, the references to other countries in *The Politics of Women's Studies* are far less robust, appearing primarily in the opening autobiographical sketches about each scholar. The U.S. academic feminists who describe their lives and work in this book mostly employ citation as a credentializing gesture—bringing up Fulbright grants, travel for research and fieldwork, consulting, and academic exper-tise in postcolonial or area studies. There are a few instances where scholars touch on transnational family legacies, identity formation, or activist proj-ects, but on the whole, these autobiographic narratives about U.S. women's studies exhibit far less depth and self-reflexivity than those crafted by the academic feminist contributors to *Changing Lives*. This example of creden-tializing grammar shows how U.S. women's studies has felt less compelled to consider the ways in which national identifications and global forces have shaped its research agenda, institutionalization, and sense of self. Academic feminists in Asia have not had the same luxury, and though it is important not to valorize their work solely on this basis, the difference offers a reminder that women's studies scholars must consider the politics of location in remembering and renarrativizing the field.

Conclusion

Creating and sustaining equitable partnerships across difference has often been a shared aspiration for academic feminists, but achieving equity is always easier said than done. Nonetheless, examining political grammars of nation used by women's studies practitioners can provide valuable insights for current and future transnational academic feminist projects. Autobiographics from the 1990s and 2000s, in particular, illustrate both scholars' lived experiences of and theorizing about their cross-border relationships during a major period of international growth for the field. Indeed, what scholars say about themselves and their work matters because, by their very nature, autobiographic texts reveal how we conceptualize ourselves and others in relation to systems of power. The purpose of analyzing political grammar is not to judge autobiographic representations of women's studies or rank them by authenticity, but rather to recognize how complexly we are embedded within language, institutions, and nations. Contemporary academic feminist practitioners can use this opportunity to reflect on how we carry out and describe our own work as women's studies continues on its trajectory of international and institutional growth.

In retelling the history of the Feminist Press, and the field of women's studies more broadly, our work will be well served by sustaining critical attention to political grammars of nation. The mere mention of another country tells us nothing more than the fact of a relationship or exchange, but the way such citations are discursively framed can show how the nation works as an analytic category. My aim in analyzing these various grammars is not to definitively declare that some collaborations were sufficient while others were not—feminist ideals of equity and solidarity have always been in progress. However, building on this field's unique capacity for self-reflection, we might learn from the past in order to chart a path forward in which academic feminism can survive, and perhaps even thrive, despite the challenges facing women's studies, the higher education sector, and society as a whole.

Clara Montague is a lecturer in gender, women's, and sexuality studies at Grinnell College. She is also a doctoral candidate at the University of Maryland completing her dissertation on the transnational history of women's studies. Clara can be reached at montague@grinnell.edu.

Notes

1. For a contrasting example telling the history of women's studies across different locations, see Montague and Tambe (2020). This chapter compares the unique histories of academic feminism in South Korea, Turkey, and the United States in order to analyze similarities and differences across national contexts, with the goal of renarrativizing women's studies through a transnational lens.

2. Higher education researchers often use the concept of *internationalization* to describe how colleges and universities have responded to and been transformed by the shifts brought about by globalization since the 1990s (Altbach and Knight 2007). My use of this term is also informed by feminist scholars who employ it in order to foreground the political economy of cross-border exchanges (Joseph, Ramamurthy, and Weinbaum 2005).

3. In this article, I focus on edited collections from this time period because of its particular importance to the history of women's studies in higher education. The field grew considerably in the 1990s, with new degree programs established in more than thirty countries alongside expanded international partnerships. Also around that time, many scholars who helped found women's studies in the 1970s began to reflect more formally on and document their work, which led directly to collections like *Changing Lives* and *The Politics of Women's Studies*. Juxtaposing these two particular texts helps to paint a more complete picture of academic feminism during this decade, but future research might usefully investigate the political grammar of nation in autobiographic writing from other time periods, including the present.

4. Transnational feminism has been the topic of several recent National Women's Studies Association conferences, including in 2019 and 2020. Academic feminists have sought greater inclusion of people and ideas from diverse national backgrounds while also critiquing their omission in both the past and present. Simultaneously, women's studies scholars have traced the ways in which feminism has in fact always been transnational by more fully describing historical cross-border exchanges. For examples, see Tambe and Thayer (2021).

5. Autobiographics departs from autobiography, which has traditionally been understood as a self-authored and relatively comprehensive account of one person's life. By contrast, autobiographics include a wider set of writing and reading practices and emphasizes how these texts constitute a narrative

subject. This shift brings a more diverse set of texts into the purview of literary examination in addition to reframing the relationship between author and text.

6. The politics of citation remains an important debate in academic feminism, gaining recent visibility, for example, through the #CiteBlackWomen campaign founded by Christen A. Smith (2017).

7. My critique of credentializing political grammar overlaps with scholarship that examines how feminists in the Global North have deployed images of Third World women in order to legitimize their work, such as Agatha Beins's study of second wave publications (2015).

8. The Kali for Women version of this book came out in 1994 as *Women's Studies, Women's Lives: Theory and Practice in South and Southeast Asia.* Its contributors and content are the same as the Feminist Press version, with the exception of Florence Howe's foreword. Though the text includes essays from academic feminists based in countries usually categorized as East, South, and Southeast Asia, the Kali for Women version's subtitle may reflect the specific geographic focus of this press.

9. Florence Howe's foreword is followed by the book's introduction, cowritten by Malavika Karlekar (who also contributes a chapter on India) as well as Barbara Lazarus (another member of the Committee on Women's Studies in Asia and a provost at Carnegie Mellon University at the time). Other contributors to this volume are listed here in order and with their home countries as specified in the table of contents—Aline K. Wong (Singapore), Aurora Javate De Dios (Philippines), Cho Hyoung (Korea), Fanny M. Cheung (Hong Kong), Fareeha Zafar (Pakistan), Konta Intan Damanik (Indonesia), Li Xiojiang (China), Liang Jun (China), Noemi Alindogan-Medina (Philippines), Nora Lan-hung Chiang (Huang) (Taiwan), Thanh-Dam Truong (Vietnam), and Yasuko Muramatsu (Japan).

10. Aurora Javate De Dios is now professor of international relations, migration, and gender studies as well as senior project director of the Women and Gender Institute at Miriam College in Quezon City, Philippines.

11. Howe's own chapter in *The Politics of Women's Studies,* "Learning from Teaching," offers a fascinating discussion of the early days of the Feminist Press as well as her experiences teaching undergraduate courses in literature, composition, and women's studies during the 1970s. Readers of this special issue may be interested in Howe's work with the Modern Language Association as well as her founding of the Feminist Press while at Goucher College in Baltimore and its transition to SUNY. Florence Howe did discuss the significance of *Changing Lives* during a 1994 address at the Centre for Women's Development Studies in India (1997) as well as an address to

the Latin American Studies Association (1999), both of which were later published by WSQ.

12. In the table of contents for *The Politics of Women's Studies*, each author's institutional affiliation is included after their name, but there is no mention of national identities or locations as in *Changing Lives*. In addition to Florence Howe, the contributors are listed here in order: Nancy Hoffman, Sheila Tobias, Jean Walton, Nancy Topping Bazin, Barbara W. Gerber, Annis Pratt, Josephine Donovan, Inez Martinez, Mimi Reisel Gladstein, Kathryn Kish Sklar, Gloria Bowles, Margaret Strobel, Mary Anne Ferguson, Electra Arenal, Barbara Smith, Nellie Y. McKay, Beverly Guy-Sheftall, Marilyn Boxer, Elizabeth Lopovsky Kennedy, Tucker Pamela Farley, Annette Kolodny, Myra Dinnerstein, Sue-Ellen Jacobs, Yolanda T. Moses, Johnnetta B. Cole, Nona Glazer, Nancy Porter, and Mariam K. Chamberlin. Of these, only one was affiliated with a non-U.S. institution (Kolodny at the University of British Colombia), and one was affiliated outside higher education (Chamberlin at the Ford Foundation).

13. The metaphor of mothers and daughters in both academic and nonacademic feminism has been richly described in Astrid Henry's *Not My Mother's Sister* (2004), which emphasizes the problems that result from overreliance on generational distinctions. Familial discourse has also been analyzed through critiques of the "global sisterhood" framework, which has particular relevance to feminist relationships across borders (Wu 2010).

14. This shift at the Ford Foundation, which had a significant impact on funding for transnational academic feminism, is well-documented in the archive of the University of Maryland's Curriculum Transformation Project (1989–2010), which resides with the special collections and university archives in College Park, Maryland. See also Lay, Monk, and Rosenfelt (2002).

15. Transnational feminist theory has included critiques of development within activism, academia, civil society, and government. See Saunders (2002).

Works Cited

Altbach, Philip G., and Jane Knight. 2007. "The Internationalization of Higher Education: Motivations and Realities." *Journal of Studies in International Education* 11, nos. 3/4: 290–305.

Beins, Agatha. 2015. "Radical Others: Women of Color and Revolutionary Feminism." *Feminist Studies* 41, no. 1: 150–83.

Burton, Antoinette, ed. 2003. *After the Imperial Turn: Thinking with and through the Nation*. Durham, NC: Duke University Press.

Committee for Women's Studies in Asia, eds. 1994. *Women's Studies, Women's Lives: Theory and Practice in South and Southeast Asia*. New Delhi: Kali for Women.

————. 1995. *Changing Lives: Life Stories of Asian Pioneers in Women's Studies.*
New York: Feminist Press.

Fernandes, Leela. 2013. *Transnational Feminism in the United States: Knowledge,
Ethics, Power.* New York: New York University Press.

Gilmore, Leigh. 1999. *Autobiographics: A Feminist Theory of Self-Representation.*
Ithaca, NY: Cornell University Press.

Grewal, Inderpal, and Caren Kaplan. 1994. *Scattered Hegemonies: Postmodernity
and Transnational Feminist Practices.* Minneapolis: University of Minnesota
Press.

Hemmings, Clare. 2011. *Why Stories Matter: The Political Grammar of Feminist
Theory.* Durham, NC: Duke University Press.

Henry, Astrid. 2004. *Not My Mother's Sister: Generational Conflict and Third Wave
Feminism.* Bloomington: Indiana University Press.

Howe, Florence. 1997. "'Promises to Keep': Trends in Women's Studies
Worldwide." *WSQ* 25, nos. 1/2: 404–21.

————. 1999. "Women's Education: Policy Implications for a New Century,"
WSQ 27, nos. 3/4: 169–84.

Howe, Florence, ed. 2000. *The Politics of Women's Studies: Testimony from 30
Founding Mothers.* New York: Feminist Press.

Joseph, Miranda, Priti Ramamurthy, and Alys Eve Weinbaum. 2005. "Toward
a New Feminist Internationalism." In *Women's Studies for the Future:
Foundations, Interrogations, Politics,* edited by Elizabeth Lapovsky Kennedy
and Agatha Beins, 207–28. New Brunswick, NJ: Rutgers University Press.

Korenman, Joan. n.d. "Women's/Gender Studies Programs & Research Centers."
University of Maryland, Baltimore County. https://userpages.umbc.
edu/~korenman/wmst/programs.html.

Lay, Mary M., Janice Monk, and Deborah S. Rosenfelt, eds. 2002. *Encompassing
Gender: Integrating International Studies and Women's Studies.* New York:
Feminist Press.

Mohanty, Chandra. 2003. *Feminism without Borders: Decolonizing Theory,
Practicing Solidarity.* Durham, NC: Duke University Press.

Montague, Clara, and Ashwini Tambe. 2020. "Women's Studies." In *A
Companion to Women's and Gender Studies,* edited by Nancy A. Naples,
25–39. Hoboken, NJ: Wiley Blackwell.

Saunders, Kriemild. 2002. *Feminist Post-development Thought: Rethinking
Modernity, Post-colonialism and Representation.* London: Zed Books.

Smith, Christen A. 2017. Cite Black Women Collective. https://www.
citeblackwomencollective.org.

Swarr, Amanda Lock, and Richa Nagar, eds. 2010. *Critical Transnational Feminist
Praxis.* Albany: SUNY Press.

Tambe, Ashwini. 2010. "Transnational Feminist Studies: A Brief Sketch." *New Global Studies* 4, no. 1: article 7.

Tambe, Ashwini, and Millie Thayer, eds. 2021. *Transnational Feminist Itineraries: Situating Theory and Activist Practice.* Durham, NC: Duke University Press.

Wu, Judy Tzu-Chun. 2010. "Rethinking Global Sisterhood: Peace Activism and Women's Orientalism." In *No Permanent Waves: Recasting Histories of U.S. Feminism,* edited by Nancy A. Hewitt, 193–220. New Brunswick, NJ: Rutgers University Press.

The Sex and Work of Sex Work in a Quarter Century of *Women's Studies Quarterly*

Aaron Hammes

Abstract: This investigation for *Women's Studies Quarterly*'s fiftieth anniversary examines the treatment of sex work over the second half of that history. Using six articles either focused on or directly considering sex work or prostitution, I constellate a sense of how the symbolism and connotation of sex work has shifted and transformed through three decades of publications in a prominent women's studies journal. These articles originate from economic, sociological, and activist perspectives and concentrate on everything from migrant ethnography to violence against women. Both the anti-prostitution and sex worker rights perspectives reveal their advocates' political commitments and are put in dialogue and opposition in light of different aims gathered under the mantle of feminism and women's studies. This critical review suggests the treatment of sex work as a political and economic litmus test for future prospects in women's studies and inclusive and intersectional feminisms. **Keywords:** prostitution; sex work; SWERF; intersectionality; labor rights; carceral feminism; neoliberalism

There are a few undeniable realities regarding sex work in North America that undergird any consideration—academic, political, cultural—thereof. Sex work comprises a variety of trades, of which prostitution, generally thought of as in-person, indoor or outdoor, full-service, single-contract sexual labor, constitutes a small percentage.[1] Sex work is highly sex-gendered work,[2] statistically dominated by Assigned Female At Birth (AFAB) cis women, but with an overrepresentation of transgender and gender-non-conforming people, as well as a not insignificant portion of cis men. Many trades under the umbrella of sex work are highly criminalized in North America, and thus the most marginalized sex workers are subject to a great

WSQ: Women's Studies Quarterly 50: 3 & 4 (Fall/Winter 2022) © 2022 by Aaron Hammes. All rights reserved.

deal of contact with the criminal legal system, as well as the potential for violence from clients and other actors (notably law enforcement) who are emboldened and empowered by the criminalization of the labor. But beyond that, *sex work* is deployed as a stand-in for everything from women's sexual oppression to queer liberation, human trafficking to expressions of labor power and bodily autonomy. The contrast between these deployments is striking and reflective of a few iterations of the use—the work, truly—of *sex work* in a preeminent academic journal devoted to women's studies, *Women's Studies Quarterly*.

The past twenty-five years of *WSQ* are perhaps marked more by the lack of attention to sexual labor than even its misuse, a manifestation of the ways in which feminism and institutional understandings of women's studies can invisibilize sex workers as bad actors or tragic consequences of patriarchy and objectification, including of oneself. This inquiry, however, concerns three distinct moments in sex work's emergence in the pages of *WSQ*, critically tracking not so much a smooth evolution or progression in thinking about sex work, but rather what each portrayal tells us about feminism—that is, how *WSQ* has theorized bodily autonomy, labor, and the criminalization of survival, and the many contradictory ways sex work has been (mis)appropriated regarding each.

The three modes of sex work discourse considered below begin with a 1999 special issue of *WSQ*, *Teaching about Violence against Women*, which features subsections including "Trafficking in Women's Bodies" and "Resistance Strategies," each of which situates "prostitution" alongside various forms of violence and trauma.[3] There is nary a dissenting view, other than the strawmen set up by a couple of the authors with whom I will engage more directly. This section rehearses now-classic, overbaked Sex Work Exclusive Radical Feminism (SWERF) logics that cannot envision versions of sex work that are uncoerced or anything other than employ of absolute last resort.

The second mode is drawn from a more ethnographic and economic analysis of sex work at the U.S.-Mexico border, found in a 2010 issue of *WSQ*. The contrast is palpable between a truly intersectional feminist approach (such as that espoused by anticarceral feminist formations like INCITE! and Critical Resistance, whose work is cited in a 2019 issue) that considers sex workers a (potentially) marginalized population within and across communities and one which locates it strictly among acts of gender-based violence.

The third mode, here reflected in *WSQ* issues from 2014 and 2019, reflects on a labor category that positions sex workers as not just laborers like any others but members of a varied and particularly sex-gendered set of waged and unwaged industries. Thus, *WSQ* has leapt from a fairly explicitly SWERF orientation that repeatedly relegates any and all sex work, irrespective of context, condition, or circumstance, to either victimhood or deviant criminality, to considering sex work in a diasporic, migrancy-focused frame, to finally a couple of articles that (re)consider sex work in contexts of emotional labor, financial mobility, and other criminalized work. Comparing these frames offers a glimpse into shifting narratives and tensions around who is a "good feminist," what work women are permitted to do, and how they are permitted to do it.

I. "Sex Work as Violence against Women"

The topography of the "Teaching about Violence against Women" issue is itself telling. The first, lengthiest section is populated with articles that tend to evacuate women's agency from the violence against them, rendering them a passive receptacle for oppression and harm. Furthermore, said violence is localized in specific—bad—men, failing in most instances to consider institutional, state, and corporate violences (let alone those perpetrated by other women or nonmen). The first subsection of the special issue is entitled "Trafficking in Women's Bodies," which reduces the category of "woman" to "non-man body," perhaps by design. However, by also situating articles regarding prostitution alongside those on labor and sex trafficking, any possibility of examining motivations for participating in sex work is foreclosed because they are measured in terms of interpersonal violence rather than the manufactured vulnerabilities that lead only some to enter the trades. In this framework, those who enter more or less voluntarily are either deluded or simply incorrect. It is almost as if Gayle Rubin's (2012) widely read and still influential decoupling of sex work and trafficking was written in response to such an issue.

Mona Eliasson's introduction to the issue opens with an accurate rendering of the contents in the form of a litany of presumed sources of harm, equivocated and oversimplified in the form of a list: "Men's violence against women—both hidden and visible—cannot be understood separately from gender, as many different forms of violence are directly tied to patriarchy: pornography, prostitution and trafficking, incest, rape, battering, and female sexual mutilation (FGM), all of which work to constrict or fore-close women's personal freedom and right to self-determination" (Eliasson 1999, 6).

The contents of Eliasson's list are meant to elicit disgust and revulsion, solidarity and resistance, an enumeration of obstacles to be abolished in the name of women's safety and freedom from violence. Further telling is Elias-son's qualification of not just violence against women but "men's violence against women," a singular, binaristic conduit for constant and unspeakable gendered harm. Even the punctuation around sex work belies an immutable truth: "prostitution and trafficking," twin, interchangeable oppressions strip-ping the occupant of either subject position of any agency, locus, or opinion on their situation, its permanence, and the prospects for its persistence. In such a list, prostitution is trafficking is prostitution, a syllogism that admits of mere semantic, rather than putative, distinctions, and no recognition of the effects of such a conflation. This strategic equivocation is very clear in its postulates regarding sex work, taking them to require little to no evidence or argumentation: "Prostitution can hardly be explained in terms of personal choice and individual preference" (1999, 6). Still, Eliasson does presume that prostitution needs to "be explained" in some fashion. As Melissa Gira Grant notes, sex work seems to be the only work that needs constantly to be explained and justified in order to be tolerated (Grant 2014, 39).

Kelly Holsopple's "Pimps, Tricks, and Feminists" and Carole Pateman's "What's Wrong with Prostitution?" are sandwiched between articles writ-ten about South and East Asian labor trafficking, and the phrase "sold into prostitution" recurs multiple times here. Holsopple's brief piece, a choir-preaching polemic whose ire is aimed at "proponents of prostitu-tion" (1999, 47) or, more specifically, feminists who "promote prostitution" (49), operates from a series of reductive definitions of sex work and sex workers, all motivated by a deeply carceral ethos of criminalizing bad men (all clients) and shaming and rescuing victimized women (all workers). The theme of passive, instrumentalized women—always and only women—and prostitution coded as pure evil wrought upon them persists throughout both pieces. Prostitution, in Holsopple's accounting, "is meant to destroy women," and "pimps and tricks inflict prostitution on women and children" (47). Holsopple activates a particular kind of sex panic, sensationalistic and lurid, which obscures the sorts of institutionalized violence wrought by criminalization and allows violent clients and managers to persist: prostitu-tion results in "broken bones, mutilation, dismemberment, or death" (48),

it "hurts and kills women and children" (51), and "it purposely dehuman-
izes women" (49). The author does not, however, explain why prostitution
would do that, and as she delves into the harms of "promoting" prostitution for purely passive "prostituted women" (47), she ends up referencing
precisely the brutalities of criminalization and the ways in which sex work
mirrors other forms of highly sex-gendered, classed, and racialized labor.

Holsopple notes, with no sense of irony at her own lascivious descriptions, that "prostitution is not just sex" (49), an almost uncanny echo of
the decades-old call by activists and allies for a fuller consideration of the
labor element of sex work. Her analysis is limited, though, by an inability
to see prostitution as anything other than violence, completely ignoring the
material conditions (pecuniary, affective, and status- or access-based) that
are diffuse across the sex trades and the workers therein. When Holsopple
suggests that "supporting prostitution as consensual sexual activity and
labor"—points not particularly up for debate for most workers—"will not
protect these feminists from being treated like prostitutes" (50), she fails to
ask an ensuing question: What if we saw to it that prostitutes were treated
better, so that "being treated like prostitutes" was never an automatic harm?
Another irony is lost on the author as she proclaims that "violence against
one group encourages violence against others" (51), and that "historically,
women have been used to implement customs of social and sexual control
over other women," which is as terse and clear a description of SWERF
thinking as one could conceive. Holsopple is not interested in reducing
the violence wrought by criminalization and stigma; she is instead in step
with "end demand," anti-prostitution thinking, prepossessed with erasing
the sex worker altogether.

Carole Pateman approaches her titular question, "What's Wrong with
Prostitution?," from a less polemical angle, setting up a series of straw figures
and a quite different set of "proponents of prostitution" from the phan-
toms of the preceding article. Pateman's analysis is ostensibly economic,
but is rooted in a similarly incredulous view that women (again, always
women) could possibly participate consensually (relative to any level of
consent in labor under capitalism) in employ that is so deeply objectionable
to her personally. Whereas Holsopple ends up making a muddled argument for decriminalization as harm reduction, some of Pateman's evidence
could—in a very different issue of *WSQ*—summate to an argument for sex
worker rights as class revolution. Unfortunately, Pateman's commitments
are revealed in the friction between her assertion that "one can argue for

trade union rights while calling for the abolition of capitalist wage labor" (1999, 54) and the rather reactionary avowal that "labor power is a political fiction" (59). How better than "labor power" does one describe the ability to attain self-sufficiency, extricate oneself from class hierarchies that openly reject them, or simply take advantage of an in-demand and often highly specialized skill set, as is the case for many sex-working people? These varieties of criminalized class mobility are also "fictions" for Pateman, whose conception of sex work belies a SWERFism that simply cannot comprehend consent in transactional sex.

For Pateman, it is decisive that "there is no desire or satisfaction on the part of the prostitute" (57), begging a series of corollary queries about the degree of either of those things in most waged (or, for that matter, unwaged) labor. Furthermore, and echoing the preceding article, the worker can only be thought of in instrumental terms: "'prostitutes' are subject to 'clients'" (the scare quotes drip with disdain), and sex work is coded as "the unilateral use of a woman's body by a man in exchange for money" (60). Pateman's argument "against" sex work hangs on a few of the same presuppositions as Holsopple's: there can be no agency for the worker, either as a worker or simply as a person involved in a transaction, and instead she is a stand-in for women's subjugation to men. Disappointingly, Pateman couches her anti-prostitution rhetoric in many of the same tired clichés of debasement and, to use Eliasson's term, "foreclosure" that have dogged attempts at destigmatization and sex worker organizing for generations. Pateman's ostensibly political-economic analysis is veiled by an inability or unwillingness to decouple a rather puritanical sense of what constitutes good or worthy sex or work from the sex-gendered, classed, and—wholly absent from this piece of hers—often racialized labor of sex work. For Pateman, full-service sex work (assumedly the only form that interests her here) constitutes the actual trade of one's body: "As prostitutes, women openly trade their bodies and, like workers (but unlike a wife), are paid in return" (54). There are echoes of Emma Goldman's incendiary essay, "The Traffic in Women," which essentially puts marriage and prostitution on a (near) spectrum of women exchanging sex for protection, shelter, and other forms of survival compensation (1990). This concept of "selling one's body" is not only a perverse reduction, but an ontological untruth: the body remains before, during, and after the work. Nonetheless, Pateman concludes that because "the services of the prostitute cannot be provided unless she is present" (59), then it must be the case that "when a prostitute contracts out use of her body she is thus selling *herself* in a very real sense" (61). This passivity is, again, almost shockingly out of step with the experiences of many if not most sex workers. The unasked questions in this branch of Pateman's labor-based arguments persist: What worker does not sell themselves in the way suggested here? Furthermore, how much other emotional, sex-gendered labor is inconceivable without the "presence" of the worker? Of course, it is not just that the worker is present, it is that her services are of a particular variety, such that these writers cannot understand any sex between ostensible men and women as other than necessarily "for" the former and "against" the latter; the presence of capital only adds the "contractarian" (66) inflection that Pateman sees as decisive in the power and agency imbalance.

It is this contractarianism that stands as the keystone of Pateman's answer to her titular question: "When women's bodies are on sale in the capitalist market . . . men gain public acknowledgment as women's sexual masters— that is what is wrong with prostitution" (62). This is perhaps the greatest tension in Pateman's sense of the work of sex work: it is a marker of "public access" to women's bodies, a "unilateral right" (60) of (bad) men, the sense that "anyone who needs a sexual service should have access to the market, whether male or female, young or old, black or white, ugly or beautiful, deformed or handicapped" (55). This is an unequivocally nasty list—at once ableist, binarily sex-gender reductive, ageist, racist, and superficial—that again misrepresents the transactional nature of sex work: a revocable agreement whose tenets are negotiated and renegotiated according to a metric of "bounded authenticity" (Bernstein 2007, 6) not unlike that of various other service professions. The picture of sex work painted by Holsopple and Pateman totally ignores the overarching and predominant cause of any offense against the above transactionality, the greatest obstacle to worker solidarity and organizing against the very violence that the two writers see as endemic to sex work: criminalization. It is criminalization that reinforces this presumed access, which disallows institutional and state protection of the working conditions of sex workers, the greatest danger to sex-working people and perhaps the one that lands these considerations, in a venue that understands itself as a "clearinghouse on Women's Studies," between FGM and incest. Pateman reiterates, betraying her disinterest in any of the many contrasting accounts sex workers have given of their work: "The prostitute is always at a singular disadvantage in the 'exchange' . . . there are no 'objective' criteria through which to judge whether the service has been satisfactorily performed" (61). The "disadvantage" is the criminalization and stigmatization of the workers' labor and presumed lifestyle, and as for the "objectiveness" of criteria, would Pateman make a similar argument about therapy, massage, studio art, or, indeed, the publication of an academic article—each an industry similarly lacking such empirical, measurable, and universal criteria?

Before pressing on to the next era in the representation of sex work in *WSQ*, one final peculiarity of the above examples is worthy of note. Mona Eliasson's editorial introduction unselfconsciously notes that "resistance to violence takes many forms but is easiest when fought collectively" (1999, 8), though it is rather apparent that this collectivity would not include the traitorous sex workers who identify neither as victims nor seek to exit the trades. Eliasson describes Pateman and Holsopple's orientation toward the workers themselves: "while these writers feel compassion and respect for individual prostitutes"—though there is no evidence for this claim in either of their articles—"they firmly condemn the trade's exploitation of women" (7). Sex workers are pure victims for these writers, and while Pateman tosses off the highly qualified note that "to argue there is something wrong with prostitution does not necessarily imply any adverse judgments on the women who engage in the work" (56), she argues throughout her piece that the worker is essentially reducible to the work: always available, always degraded, a signifier of polluted gender relations under free-market capitalism. For her part, Holsopple offers a positive prescription that is entirely in line with Kate D'Adamo's (cited in Bernstein 2018, 166) sense of addressing the sort of "manufactured vulnerabilities" that often lead to both trafficking and more potentially precarious sex-working situations: "Feminists should advocate and act to provide housing, education, and skills training for women" (Holsopple 1999, 51). Why this list is somehow mutually exclusive of making conditions safer for sex working people is mystifying.

II. Sex Work as Marginalizing Mystique

After the above special issue devoted a few articles to either prostitution or various forms of coerced sexual labor, sex work in *WSQ* was mostly limited to contexts of Mexico and South and Central America. The research is predominately ethnographic or sociological, as exemplified by both the title and content of Susanne Hofmann's (2010) "Corporeal Entrepreneurialism and Neoliberal Agency in the Sex Trade at the US-Mexican Border." Hofmann proceeds from a set of presumptions and concerns so entirely alien to the analyses above as to be nearly unrecognizable. Rather than approaching sex work from the metanarratives of abuse, sexual degradation, or symptom of gender imbalance, Hofmann deploys an economic analysis that accounts for the sex trade as "bodily entrepreneurialism" (2010, 233). It is a concept that shares at least one characteristic with its predecessors in *WSQ*, a nearly fetishistic concern with the worker's body in the sex trades, as if the labor in so very many other industries was not equally predicated on the labor power of one's movement, strength, and expertise—in short, the worker's body. More novel is Hofmann's ensuing theorization of "erotic capital," which she notes "can level existing social and economic inequalities and thus act as a catalyst to exit marginalized communities" (233).

This definition is complicated when read against a statement produced by Critical Resistance and INCITE! around the same time as Hoffman's research. These activist-scholars saw sex workers as "marginalized women" due to the intersectional impacts of criminalization and stigma: "The criminalization approach has brought many women into conflict with the law, particularly women of color, poor women, lesbians, sex workers, immigrant women, women with disabilities, and other marginalized women" (Critical Resistance and INCITE! 2019, 254). This brief statement was reprinted in the *WSQ* subsection "Classics Revisited," in an issue celebrating the fiftieth anniversary of Stonewall (a movement spearheaded by sex-working, queer, and trans people of color). The contrast between a truly intersectional feminist approach (such as that espoused by these anticarceral feminist formations) that considers sex workers a (potentially) marginalized population within and across communities and those that locate it strictly among acts of gender-based violence is palpable. Of course, sex work can at once represent a set of marginalized communities, and at the same time be a means to "exit" them.

Regardless, Hofmann's own orientation toward her sex-working subjects is one which could safely be called materialist and liberatory. She writes: "Demystifying sex work requires an understanding of sex workers as aspiring corporeal entrepreneurs who make use of their bodily and erotic capital, responding to neoliberal structural demands while creating opportunities for themselves" (234). There are a variety of terms and concepts here that would be entirely foreign to the limited analyses a decade earlier in the same publication venue. For the earlier authors, demystifying meant either "exposing" prostitution's betrayal of women's sexual availability and subservience or else revealing it as sexual violence against women. Pateman understands sex workers as corporeal, but she, like Holsopple, sees the trades as reducing sex workers to nothing but bodies. She certainly would not comprehend the concept of bodily or erotic labor as Hofmann accounts for it—labor power is fictional in her analysis—and the sex worker is at an insurmountable disadvantage in every transaction. Hofmann, for her part, is more interested in sex work as a "professional practice" (252), and one in which sex workers perform "strategizing and mind work . . . in pursuit of their profession" (235).

Hofmann's analysis is much more trenchant than that of her predecessors but remains somewhat limited by understanding sex work almost strictly as a means of working adjacent to, but unbounded by, neoliberal understandings of agency and labor—the workers are, ultimately, "unable to escape the global politics of neoliberalism" (252). The next pair of essays endeavors to reframe sex work according to broader conceptions of sex-gendered and criminalized labor, as well as the activist organizing structures that emerge in the persistent face of phobic publics.

III. Sex Work as Reproductive Labor

To summarize, in the pages of *WSQ* the preceding authors have "used" sex work as a foreclosure of women's choice; as violence, exploitation, and murder; as a symptom of limitless sexual availability of women; and as a manifestation of bodily entrepreneurialism, an (ultimately conscribed) response to neoliberal demands placed on marginalized peoples. Heather Berg situates sex work entirely differently from her predecessors: "I use 'reproductive labor' capaciously as connoting those forms of work, paid or otherwise, that produce not things but affects, bodies, desires, social systems, and so on. This includes labors as seemingly diverse as motherwork and massage, porn performance and food service, television production and volunteer community service" (Berg 2014, 164). This situating has the effect of broadening the scope of how to consider sex work, placing it within a constellation of labor rather than a sui generis species of activity. Ultimately, Berg's piece reflects on anti-prostitution and SWERF thinking, and at the same time considers what alternatives are available to marginalized groups whose voicelessness can feel institutionally foreclosed. This is almost the inverse approach of Pateman and Holsopple, who proceed in the face of what they see as growing legions of "proponents" of sex work. Berg notes, "The fervor of anti–sex work stigma makes the affective soldering of workers to work more obvious" (171), an echo of Melissa Gira Grant's (and others') theorizing of the inseparability (due to stigma, policing, and, yes, institutionalized misogyny) of the sex worker from their work. Berg's tact is to consider how SWERFism, embodied in her analysis by the particularly virulent Sheila Jeffreys, "ignores what is perhaps the most central assumption of anticapitalist thought—work _is_ subordination" (171, author's emphasis). An analysis that declaims the sex trades as intolerably debased or degrading based on their bodily nature; the acts, images, or services assumedly protected within the bounds of amative coupling; or their gendered, raced, and classed stratification generally fails utterly to account for these same characteristics in much other labor. Berg offers a circuitry between the stigma and "end demand" that critics such as Jeffreys—not necessarily herself an anticapitalist thinker—trade in: "The dangers of a (re)productivist framework that, on the one hand, elevates some forms of reproductive labor to the status of dignified and ostensibly not exploitative work and, on the other, pathologizes others that fail to meet the criteria for social necessity. Here, prostitutes have failed to pay the social necessity debt; not only does this render them abject victims, it also negates the possibility of organizing for improved working conditions, better policies, or access to vital services" (171–72).

This standard also produces the kind of cognitive dissonance that propels Pateman to hold that one can be anticapitalist while supporting trade unions and at the same time that labor power is a political fiction; or Holsopple's call to advocate for better material conditions for women while ignoring the ways in which criminalization and censure have decimated these conditions for sex-working women. At the simplest level, if sex work is not work, then there can be no worker organizing. But even if the labor is acknowledged, the layers of "social necessity debt" reveal a respectability politics that need not be challenged very far to reveal the ways in which it was never about the work, just the sex. Berg pushes the sex-worker-labor-organizing-as-anticapitalist-mobilizing one step further, decrying "reformist" activism in a language invoking radical feminist thought from Rosa Luxemburg (1990) to bell hooks (hooks 2014, 23). Berg notes that such activism, while perhaps accomplishing some gains, "limited the radical potentiality" of sex worker organizing, as "exclusions affect workers who, lacking the class, regional, and racial capital necessary to choose work for reasons other than economic survival, fall short of the altruistic-care-worker-as-public-servant ideal" (172). Berg's considerations are motivated by a set of "foreclosures" wholly different from those of the special issue published fifteen years earlier. It is perhaps unremarkable that a truly intersectional analysis that proceeds from sex workers' most fundamental needs, as opposed to their inherent status as victims or potential sex-gender traitors, first emerges so "late" in the history of a prominent women's studies journal. More interesting is the massive leap from the scant references to the conflated "dangers" of sex trafficking and prostitution to a more nuanced consideration not only of sex work but also the harms of anti–sex work thinking and half-measure organizing. Out of neither resignation nor detachment,[4] Berg postulates that, at a certain point, sex workers' "failure" to convince the "gatekeepers" of feminism, labor organizing, or "the status quo" more broadly "that their existence is legitimate" may leave "positive estrangement" as the only out (173). Abstention from and refusal of a respectability politics that has never had room for the vast majority of sex-working people is a reasonable enough response, and Berg gestures toward a kind of mutual aid divorced of neoliberal precepts of "duty" and "refusing the fiction" that we are "holding capital accountable" within the current economy of "social necessity" (174–75).

Crystal Jackson's (2019) work in *WSQ* is even more explicitly concerned with organizing and mutual aid in the face of phobic publics, acknowledging the "economy" detailed in Berg while considering not just the anticapitalist but also the anticarceral potentiality of sex worker solidarity. Jackson's "Sex Workers Unite!" shares with Hofmann's and Berg's pieces the understanding of the state and its violence workers (police, the criminal legal system, and prisons with their industrial complexes) as holding a near-monopoly on labeling sex workers, as well as on adjudicating those labels. She writes: "Individuals who sell sex/ual services are subject to punitive laws that situate them as criminals or victims, necessitating contact from law enforcement" (170). Jackson is tracing a particular circuitry, from the laws of the state (faceless, nameless, detached from the individuals and groups to whom they apply), to the labels they create (in this instance, either "criminal" or "victim," or sometimes, confoundingly, both), and finally to the enforcers of those laws, who at the moment of contact produce the sex worker (Grant 2014, 4). Jackson's comment draws out the inherently limited narratives of victimhood and criminality, as well as a certain brand of carcerality supposedly necessitating both the construction of victimhood and contact with police.

The clearest sign of the altered state of play in this most recent *WSQ* article, however, is Jackson's enumeration of adversaries to sex worker well-being. While Hofmann broadly cited neoliberal markets and the "mystification" of sex work under poverty conditions, Berg pointed to SWERF logics and reformist activism as aggressors and impediments to sex worker safety and advancement. Jackson is the most direct about harmful laws, as well as mainstream and institutional feminisms as manufacturers of stigma and constructs—not unlike those deployed by the earlier writers detailed in this inquiry—which can understand sex work only as violence or a social problem to be solved. Using Elizabeth Bernstein's terminology, Jackson writes: "Today's carceral feminists situate the nation-state as the guarantor of gender equity and freedom from violence for women and girls" (2019, 172). The result of this situating for sex workers, about which Bernstein herself has written at length,[5] is, for one, "sexual labor and sex trafficking are conflated as a universal experience of violence" (172). Jackson is equally direct about the confluence of exclusion from access to labor organizing and mainstream feminist institutional support, as well as various forms of criminalization, in preventing sex workers from conventional means of improving workplace conditions. While five years earlier, Heather Berg was contextualizing sex work in terms of other, variably analogous forms of reproductive labor, Crystal Jackson points to struggles unique to sex-working people, and the resultant need for alternative organizing networks, or "peer socializing," which "forms social nodes that (a) fight stigma, (b) set the framework for support network building, and (c) affirm value in two categories: business and camaraderie intertwined, and emphasizing *value*, including the value of the person's safety and health, and the monetary value of the work itself" (176). Recall the sex work–phobic analyses of the "violence against women" issue: workers are wholly individualized conduits for bad men's sexual desires (always violent, always exploitative); any harms, whether physical, emotional, or ideological (that is, hampering mainstream—white, middle-class—feminist goals) are the result of the inherent violence and trauma of the work. The state and its laws, phobic publics and their representatives, and reductive assumptions regarding the workers and their work were entirely absent from those analyses. Jackson works within a different social justice paradigm, one which prioritizes the individual and improving conditions for those in the trades, rather than attempting to abolish their work with no consideration that this goal is, first, demonstrably impossible and, second, does not take into account the needs and voices of the workers themselves. While Holsopple may well use her own past experiences in the trade as the monolithic experience of all workers,[6] she remains unwilling to inquire as to how people get into sex work, and whether and how they would like to exit the trades. A statement such as the following in Jackson's work would be unintelligible to Eliasson, Pateman, or Holsopple: "Broadening what counts as harm reduction values the worker. Valuing the person's sense of self, wellness, and individual needs without demanding someone quit sex work if they want to be safe and happy" (180). The anti-prostitution line would see only one means of harm reduction: abolition. Even then, prominent anti-trafficking activists such as Nicholas Kristoff (2009) have openly advocated for sweatshops as positive alternatives for sex work, again demonstrating that it is strictly the sex, and not the work (if it even qualifies as work for this camp), which is objectionable. Furthermore, there is a real sense in which the SWERF analysis forecloses selfhood for sex workers, thus mooting any individual needs other than exiting the trades, which assumedly restores the worker's potential to rejoin womanhood. Safety is to be found only outside of any remunerated transactional sex, and happiness is, well, somewhat beside the point.

Jackson's analysis could be described, albeit in quite a different valence from Pateman's, as economic, concerned as it is with measures of human value resistant to neoliberal accounting. She notes, somewhat in line with Hofmann, that "increasing value and making more money is a social justice issue for sex workers" (181), which recognizes both that increasing value is an end separate from but intimately related to making more money, and that whereas both may or may not be social justice issues more broadly speaking, they certainly are for this population. Jackson argues that "valuing labor and valuing the person as a smart, agentic, complicated individual destroys the criminal-victim master status" (182). Yet, each of the anti-prostitution analyses fails women by one or more of the means by which Jackson seeks to "increase value," because the workers' labor holds no value for them and is in fact deleterious to the cause of women more generally. Jackson goes on to define the political reality (to invert Pateman's earlier phrase) of labor power: "Explicitly valuing labor means exposing the intersection of gender, class, and sex itself in capitalist society—an action that makes many anti-prostitution activists point to both sex workers' oppression and their false consciousness." The only "fictions" here are those of phobic publics and the state: sex workers must be oppressed because their labor power is an outgrowth of their (partial) secession from neoliberal markets and late capitalist possibilities. They neither sell their bodies nor participate, wittingly or not, in patriarchal hegemony; they are women (and nonbinary people, and femme and masc people, and men …) whose primary concerns are the same as any other laborer: safety, survival, and thriving. The only rescue necessary is rescue from the evils of either criminalization or capitalism, which are arguably one and the same.

IV. The Work of Sex Work and Its Feminist Discontents

Tracing the trajectory of treatments in *WSQ* raises questions regarding both the relative absence of such highly sex-gendered work and the nearly diametrically opposed presumptions about it. Sex work is reduced to "men's violence against women" or expanded to a potential harbinger of anticarceral and anticapitalist revolution. This opposition begs the question: What kind of feminisms are supported by neoliberal, carceral ideologies, and which ones (likely the same) purport to reduce violence against women by abolishing one of the forms of labor available to the most marginalized populations among them? More pointedly, who is served by the accounting of "social necessity debt," and how does this ledger consider women's value as workers, or people? More broadly, who is a good feminist, what counts as work, which workers are reducible to their bodies, and who gets to decide? One version of "the debate" gets played out in the academy, another in the statehouse, and a third in the streets. Which form it takes in *WSQ* may be a bellwether of future prospects for decriminalization, decarceration, destigmatization, and full consideration in feminist thought.

This inquiry traced sex work in wildly disparate iterations of its use over just a few articles, but in a journal digitally housed by the Feminist Press, feminism is a surprisingly background player in each. Pateman writes in reaction to a "radical change" in the way "recent feminist discussions" handled sex work (1999, 54), and Holsopple names feminists (given pride of place in her title) who "promote prostitution" as the enemy (1999, 49). The latter is so concerned with feminists who "imitate men" that she is willing to write off any woman whose experience in sex work is not defined by violence as unworthy of the mantle of feminism (1999, 50). Eliasson self-identifies as a "feminist psychologist" (10), but that appellation is called into question by the exclusivity of its object—what is your feminism worth if it is founded even in part on exclusion?

Interestingly, the terms "feminism" and "feminist" appear in neither Hoffman's article nor the piece by Critical Resistance and INCITE! (2019). The exclusion in Hoffman is interesting, as her stated aim of theorizing "women's agency" in the sex trade in "a larger neoliberal context" (233) cries out for anti-corporate feminism and a more overt analysis of how capitalism and free markets will not bring about equity and access for the groups they so effectively and efficiently marginalize. In the case of Critical Resistance and INCITE!, the elision may be more strategic, since these are groups founded by and working for women of color, cash-poor folks, disabled folks, survivors of state and gender-based violence—their feminism is in the very bones of the tenets of their statement. But capital-*F* Feminism has not always been an ally to these populations, and a bit of implicit (or explicit, for that matter) distance is itself a radical act.

Berg, on the other hand, is more than happy to name anticapitalist feminism (though the inclusion of the modifier implies that feminism is not de facto anticapitalist) as her ethos through the analysis of sex work as work. It is the materialist charge of (re)productive labor that animates the analysis, and Berg's subject position (at the time of writing) as a doctoral student in feminist studies seems to add a certain onus onto what feminism has to say and what it has to answer for regarding the treatment of sex-working people. Jackson initiates her thinking about mutual aid from older feminist concepts, taking perhaps the broadest, "big tent" version of feminism—one that seeks communitarian protection and care through capacious and compassionate definitions of "women" and "femmes." That sex work–inclusive feminisms—whether "promotional" or not!—are more radical and nuanced is perhaps not entirely surprising. But the virulence with which anti-prostitution feminists decry and defame sex-working people should stand as a hallmark of why it ought to be dead and buried in 2022.

Aaron Hammes holds a PhD in English from the CUNY Graduate Center. He has most recently taught courses in sex work studies, prison abolition, social deviance, and contemporary queer and trans literatures at John Jay College and Hunter College in Manhattan. Dr. Hammes has published on sex work, transgender postnormativity, and '70s crime film in *South Atlantic Review* and *Humanities Review*, among others. He is in the process of editing a manuscript on transgender minor literature, as well as a book on performativity and sex work, stemming in part from his organizing with the Support Ho(s)e collective in Chicago and New York City. He can be reached at ahammes@gradcenter.cuny.edu.

Notes

1. Estimates regarding data collection vary for a number of obvious reasons, but Gira Grant cites 11 percent (2014).

2. I use the term *sex-gendered* in the lineage of Gayle Rubin's (1984) "sex/ gender system" (35) and Paul B. Preciado's (2020) and Nicola Mai's (2019) deployments of "sex-gender" to complicate biological and cultural essentialisms regarding self-identity and phobic institutional presumptions and dictates regarding sex and gender.

3. I will move back and forth between the terms "prostitution" and "sex work," the former of which, more often than not, is used as a pejorative by anti-prostitution advocates.

4. Evidenced at least in part by her continued work on the subject, most recently in *Porn Work* (Berg 2021).

5. For an early depiction of carceral feminism, see Bernstein (2010). For an extended treatment of carceral feminism's commitment to anti-prostitution-as-anti-trafficking, see Bernstein (2018).

6. This was a tactic employed not infrequently by another anti-prostitution feminist, Andrea Dworkin.

Works Cited

Berg, Heather. 2014. "An Honest Day's Wage for a Dishonest Day's Work: (Re) Productivism and Refusal." *WSQ* 42 (1/2): 161–77.

———. 2021. *Porn Work: Sex, Labor, and Late Capitalism.* Chapel Hill, NC: University of North Carolina Press.

Bernstein, Elizabeth. 2007. *Temporarily Yours: Intimacy, Authenticity, and the Commerce of Sex.* Chicago: University of Chicago Press.

———. 2010. "Militarized Humanitarianism Meets Carceral Feminism: The Politics of Sex, Rights, and Freedom in Contemporary Antitrafficking Campaigns." *Signs: Journal of Women in Culture and Society* 36, no. 1: 45–71.

———. 2018. *Brokered Subjects: Sex, Trafficking, and the Politics of Freedom.* Chicago: University of Chicago Press.

Critical Resistance and INCITE! 2019. "Gender Violence and the Prison-Industrial Complex." *WSQ* 47, no. 3/4 (Fall): 253–58.

Eliasson, Mona. 1999. "Editorial." *WSQ* 27, no. 1/2 (Spring): 6–10.

Goldman, Emma, and Alix Kates Shulman. 1990. *The Traffic in Women and Other Essays on Feminism.* Ojai, CA: Times Change Press.

Grant, Melissa Gira. 2014. *Playing the Whore: The Work of Sex Work.* London: Verso.

Hofmann, Susanne. 2010. "Corporeal Entrepreneurialism and Neoliberal Agency in the Sex Trade at the US-Mexican Border." *WSQ* 38, no. 1/2: 233–56.

Holsopple, Kelly. 1999. "Pimps, Tricks, and Feminists." *WSQ* 27, no. 1/2 (Spring): 47–52.

hooks, bell. 2014. *Feminist Politics from Margin to Center*. New York: Routledge.

Jackson, Crystal A. 2019. "'Sex Workers Unite!': U.S. Sex Worker Support Networks in an Era of Criminalization." *WSQ* 47, no. 3/4: 169–88.

Kristof, Nicholas. 2009. "Where Sweatshops Are a Dream." *New York Times*, January 4, 2009. https://www.nytimes.com/2009/01/15/opinion/15kristof.html.

Pateman, Carole. 1999. "What's Wrong with Prostitution?" *WSQ* 27, no. 1/2 (Spring): 53–64.

Rubin, Gayle. 2012. *Deviations: A Gayle Rubin Reader*. Durham, NC: Duke University Press.

What Can Feminist Work Be?: A Conversation with *WSQ* Authors Kathi Weeks and Heather Berg

Samantha Pinto, Kathi Weeks, and Heather Berg

One of the calling cards of *WSQ* is the way it creates rich conversations within subfields of women's, gender, and sexuality studies. Through its special issue format, *WSQ* gives us a window into intra- and interdisciplinary thinking and makes reading each issue an event in the field, a recalibration, and often a turning point in established ways of thinking and doing feminist work. And it is this focus on feminist work that spurred me to stage a conversation between two scholars whose essays appear in *WSQ*'s archive and who think about the politics of feminist labor across generations, spheres, and critical landscapes. Kathi Weeks is the author of many articles and books on feminist theory, including 2011's *The Problem with Work*, a Marxist feminist critique of work, or paid labor, as a given political good. Heather Berg's 2021 *Porn Work* takes Weeks's call to critique work to the pornography industry, using ethnographic methods elucidating the complex feelings, "hacks," and limits of sexual labor to argue for an anticapitalist and antiwork feminism. In their respective *WSQ* articles, "Down with Love: Feminist Critique and the New Ideologies of Work" (2017) and "An Honest Day's Wage for a Dishonest Day's Work: (Re)Productivism and Refusal" (2014), Weeks and Berg extend these discussions, problematizing the ways we talk about feminist labor and the reproduction of feminism itself through labor—scholarly, reproductive, and otherwise. Weeks eschews the rhetoric and metaphorization of work as a labor of love or labor one loves, insisting that this seemingly anticapitalist turn pitches labor as a romance, a generic category and inequitable system that feminism has long critiqued. Berg dares to imagine the labor of social reproduction as a bad object or, at the very least, not just an assumed social good.

In their extended and extensive bodies of scholarship, Berg and Weeks

WSQ: Women's Studies Quarterly 50: 3 & 4 (Fall/Winter 2022) © 2022 by Samantha Pinto, Kathi Weeks, and Heather Berg. All rights reserved.

pose radical, counterintuitive, and sensitive challenges to both Marxist feminist traditions and cultures of feminist theorizing about freedom, labor, and capitalism. They are both scholars who imagine horizons of thinking, writing, being, and acting beyond what is currently imaginable. They are also scholars who, as you will see in the conversation below, are not afraid of change within their own work and in feminism. Whether deftly discussing the problems with "care" as a model of feminist labor or acknowledging the limits of their own previously published scholarship, Weeks and Berg take this conversation as a moment to be reflective, funny, vulnerable, optimistic, grateful, ethical, generous, and, of course, brilliant. They resist the lure of what Weeks refers to below as "models of the good subject" in favor of thinking about what academic, activist, and everyday "experimentation and rule breaking," in Berg's terms, might bring to feminist work that reaches beyond the individual and toward collective imaginative practices. Separately, together, and below, Weeks and Berg stage Marxist feminism as a vital meeting ground for critical race feminism, anticapitalist scholarship, and the many ways we want, feel, write, act, and work as feminists.

Samantha Pinto: Why did you "choose" *WSQ* for your articles on labor, language, sex, and sexuality?

Heather Berg: I was drawn to *WSQ*'s special issue format, and to Rosalind Petchesky and Meena Alexander's *Debt* special issue in particular. I love being able to think together about a term in this way. I wrote about the "social necessity debt," but it was important that that sit alongside work that was reckoning with debt in more concrete ways. Maybe the reverse is also true, where talking about the concreteness of debt lands differently alongside discussions of its symbolic force. Thinking alongside others interested in the politics of debt got me to ask new questions.

   Also, I'm always hoping to get sex worker theory into spaces where people who don't think they care about sexual labor might read it. Rather than study sex work, I want to think about what sex workers can teach about debt, care, refusal, and so on and make a case for why it should matter to those engaging feminist studies from other points of entry. Special issues invite that kind of engagement.

Kathi Weeks: I, too, was interested in *WSQ*'s special issue configuration and was delighted to work with the fabulous editors, Alyson Cole and Victoria

Hattam, on the topic of precarious work. The journal's format supports what I see as interdisciplinary feminist inquiry at its best: when we weigh in on the same problematic from different angles of vision and with diverse analytical approaches. The collection of pieces in the issue represents not only a wealth of scholarship on the topic, but can also, I think, enable a more critical and expansive understanding of the concept of precarity itself. Or at least that was the reaction I had to reading all the contributions in proximity to one another.

Incidentally, the issue editors organized a delightful launch event in New York, for which they invited authors and others to present short performative presentations—except I had to go on after the sword-swallower. Very tough act to follow.

SP: Both of you explore and expand a Marxist feminist tradition—expanding it through sexuality and through race, respectively, in your articles. Can you speak more about your work and feminism's relationship to its Marxist genealogies (what they mean to you; what they mean for the field; hidden, dismissed, undervalued routes through Marxist feminism, etcetera)?

KW: I'm happy to see that U.S. Marxist feminism is once again thriving after a bit of a lull in the period from the mid-1980s through the 1990s. Marxist feminism seems to feel even more relevant to many feminists today than in the 1970s, when that awful metaphor of the unhappy marriage was used to describe it and divorce proposed by some as the best solution to its many problems. There are of course still pockets of resistance to Marxist feminism among some Marxists, various orthodox reflexes that lash out at the theoretical innovations necessary to confront racial, colonial, settler, heteropatriarchal capitalism. But this remains a very small minority in my experience; most Marxists recognize at the very least that years of feminist studies of "women's work" under Fordism are now relevant to increasing numbers of workers under the conditions of post-Fordism—that feminist scholarship is no longer optional to Marxist theories of capitalism in the present conjuncture. As for the other side of the equation, feminists today have the opportunity to draw on an ever more vibrant and radically heterogeneous array of Marxist theories, including queer, Indigenous, post- and decolonial, Black, and transgender Marxisms, to name a few. My own work continues to be informed by autonomous Marxism's contributions to anti- and postwork political theory and by Althusserian mappings of subject construction in the context of complex structures. But that said, my approach to Marxism is pretty eclectic and tailored to the problem at hand rather than to any partisan commitment to a theoretical or political line.

One thing that might distinguish my approach to Marxism from that of some other feminist theorists, and I suspect this applies to Heather's work as well, is an emphasis on production and labor more than consumption and the market, waged and unwaged work more than the commodity form, and also the priority I place on struggles against regimes of work—what Marx called "forced work," together with exploitation, managerial rule, productivism, and what Heather calls "reproductivism"—more than private property ownership as the only or even primary target.

HB: My answer to this question follows Kathi's closely, not least because her work has been so formative for me. *The Problem with Work* spends just a few pages on sex work, but its critique of white, middle-class sex worker organizing's reliance on work ethic discourse made so much click for me. Like Kathi, I think '70s Marxist feminism has a lot to offer workers who must "struggle against both labor's misrecognition and devaluation on the one hand, and its metaphysics and moralism on the other" (Weeks 2011, 13). That affinity helps explain why Marxist feminists in the Wages for Housework school were sex worker–inclusive in ways other feminist radicals, including other anticapitalist feminists, couldn't be.

But the wife-whore continuum Wages for Housework elaborated—in one way or another, all intimacy is work—has its limits, even as its gestures to inclusion feel so refreshing next to many of the alternatives. Part of this is traceable to Wages for Housework's disengagement with gendered labor that is already paid, such as the domestic work Black, brown, and migrant people were doing for (bad) pay long before '70s Marxist feminists made the demand. Angela Davis's critique of that oversight is crucial for thinking about whether the demand for pay really will help get us to where we (anticapitalists) want to go. The other limitation is traceable to Wages for Housework's tendency to undertheorize paid sex's insurgent potential, where the difference between wives and sex workers might be that sex work doesn't reproduce the worker for capital in quite the same way. If it did, it would (like the nuclear family) be encouraged rather than reviled. I'm interested in the tension between these two things.

It's in thinking about sex work's antiwork potential, and the everydayness of sex worker refusal, that I find Autonomism most useful. As someone who thinks a lot about anticapitalist approaches to sex work, I'm fascinated by takes like Alexandra Kollontai's, which locates paid sex work as work refusal in the Soviet context. I'm interested in what it might look like to do a queer reappropriation of that line—what if sex work is antiwork, what if that's a good thing? There I find myself returning to Kathi's Autonomist critique of socialism's fetish for the good worker. I'm thinking about how demanding pay for sex, and using that pay to refuse other kinds of work, can be a (partial) means of struggling against the managerial rule Kathi mentions above, whether it comes from capitalist bosses or state socialist ones.

SP: Both of you explore the affect of work—the emotional experience of doing work; the self's relationship to labor; how various labor is received, consumed, perceived from outside of the worker in question; and perhaps most importantly, how women's labor and sexual-reproductive labor is narrativized. How, do you think, might this translate to the way we think about feminist work in particular—activist, academic, etcetera? What are the affects you note in the field, from the field, about the field that shape it or that you'd like to see challenged and reshaped?

HB: I'll focus my answer to this question in terms of how feminist academia has sometimes narrated itself in relationship to care work and care workers. So much of the feminist project around valuing care rests on appeals to the social necessity of care work. I'm interested in how this carries over across ideological boundaries—socialist feminists are just as likely to make appeals to the value of care as lean-in liberals. I don't think that the problem with care work is that consumers and agents of the capitalist state don't know it's socially necessary. The work wouldn't have such a long history of being violently compelled if people in power didn't know it has value. Care-working conditions are bad because the work is racialized and feminized, and so I think that appeals to care's value won't actually get the goods if what we want is better futures for workers. What they do do, though, is set up a dynamic in which workers have to frame appeals for their own rights in terms of how better conditions mean better services—"our teaching conditions are students' learning conditions."

Of course, this makes the work almost impossible to refuse—you can't wage a fight for better conditions based on the social necessity of a job and also refuse to do it. Wages for Housework famously makes a claim that "to say that we want money for housework is the first step toward refusing to do it," but I'm not totally convinced that most Wages for Housework feminists were ready to make good on the threat. Because I believe that those in power know exactly how much value care work has, I also think that credible threats of withdrawal are one of the best weapons we have. There's no space for this in a feminist discourse premised on appeals to social necessity.

Appeals to the social necessity of care make sense in the context of academia's fraught class politics. It's easy to read writing on care for evidence of whether the author sees themself as more likely to do or consume paid care, as part of a community that lives and dies by mutual aid or can expect to hire out when the time comes. Part of my own awareness around this came from listening to academic audiences engage Kathi's book. The question of who does dirty work in a postwork future always seemed to vex. I remember one interviewer saying it wouldn't possibly be him on garbage duty.

Obviously, it's crucial to ground these conversations in the reality that we'll all need care at some point. Disability studies gets at this exactly, and some of my favorite care theory comes from texts like Lakshmi Piepzna-Samarasinha's *Care Work*. But there's a difference between acknowledging interdependence, as the Care Collective's *Care Manifesto* urges, and ignoring the racialized class conflict that marks paid care work at the point of the exchange. Premilla Nadasen's recent "Rethinking Care Work" essay gets at this beautifully, returning us to the problem of racialized exploitation. I think a lot of feminist writing on care avoids racialized class conflict for the same reason other care consumers do—it's hard to sit with the reality that those laboring for you and your loved ones might hate it, and you. In answer to Sam's question about feminist affects I'd like to see shift, my hope is that more of the work of dealing with that anxiety can happen before it filters into the demands some feminists make in exchange for allyship.

Sex workers don't have to answer to social necessity's blackmail in quite the same way—they couldn't even if they wanted to—because the client doesn't carry the affective burdens attached to other consumers of care. Sex workers spend a lot of time pretending to care about clients on the clock, and many refuse to perform the same in their activism too. If we imagine how impossible it would be for the domestic workers invited to speak at academic panels to say that out loud, we see the ways sex workers have room to maneuver that other care workers usually don't. For me, sex work opens up the possibility of a care discourse that centers working people: sex work has value because its pay sustains workers and their communities. This gets us to the question of self-valorization, and I think sex workers have much to teach about marking the difference between care that sustains working people and care that sustains capital. Community care often does both, and this is a tension that earnest appeals to social value can't do justice to.

KW: I'd like to pick up on Heather's astute critical take on some of the feminist literature on care. I have serious trepidations about the affectively laden term *care* itself, some of which I think dovetail with Heather's key concerns. I should say right away that I don't think we should stop using the term—I wouldn't even know how to do that. But I think we should at least pay attention to some of its baggage that might get in the way of some of what we hope to accomplish when we deploy the term. One of my concerns bears on some—although by no means all—of the literature on care ethics. The ethic of care was intended as a counter-ethic to that industrial iteration of the Protestant work ethic that dignified factory employment and devalued unwaged household work as love not labor. But particularly in the context of postindustrial employment, much of which expects us to bring not just our hands but also our hearts to work, I think the ethic of care functions to expand the scope of the traditional work ethic so that it can include more forms of paid employment and also nonwaged household work, as well as serve to add weight to its prescription to devote ourselves single-mindedly to work and its discipline. As Heather notes, this makes it difficult to refuse work ("don't you care?" "you're uncaring!"). But as those admonitions suggest, it's also indexed to the individual in a way that diverts our gaze from the structures that organize, distribute, manage, and defend caring labor.

This brings me to my larger concern about the language of care: that it's so tightly tethered to the field of ethics, and with it to the figure of the individual, that it's ill-suited to the project of politics. Caring is both a practice and a feeling-state; it is something that subjects do and feel, and in this time and place, that means it's something that is performed by and resides in individuals. I think that's part of the power of the feminist claims that care is important and that we should care more and better: it hails us as individuals towards a certain ethical value orientation. Everyone does and should care; it shouldn't be the low-waged job assigned to just some. And the way the term couples a practice with a feeling-state also forces recognition of the impact of the practice on subjectivity and subjectivity on the practice, which is perhaps just another way of saying that it involves emotional labor. My problem here is that I think it's hard to separate care from the terrain of ethics and models of the good subject and attach it instead to politics and collective action aimed at structural change. Given the term's baggage, what I described as its tethering as an affect to the unit of the individual rather than the collective, the notion of a "politics of care" seems a bit of an oxymoron. Here's another way to frame my point that brings us back to Heather's argument: What if the inability to refuse care work is baked into the very category of care?

HB: I'm drawn to Kathi's point here about the oxymoron that is a "politics of care." I'll respond, briefly, by just saying that this is one of the things that makes invitations for a "caring society" feel like such a political dead end for me, especially when they are presented in the terms of liberalism rather than militant, anticapitalist world building. They seem to fight the other side using leverage that isn't at all symmetrical. Racial capitalism and the state structures that prop it up aren't caring. Those who benefit from this system, including white, middle-class liberals who consume undervalued care work, won't be gently moved to care otherwise.

SP: Your articles have had multiple lives beyond the pages of *WSQ*—whether as a Verso text or as foundational to an eventual book that is particularly about sex work, etcetera. Can you speak to the life and life cycle of your articles—how they were shaped, what they came out of, and how you think of them now in relationship to your work, past, present, and future?

KW: Just about all of my work over the course of my academic career, and this certainly includes the essay in *WSQ*, is constructed as a contribution to the future of Marxist feminist theory that draws from the Marxist feminist past for inspiration. Toward this end, I seem to deploy a standard approach. To dress up this political and intellectual reflex perhaps a bit more than it deserves, my "method" involves using some tendency from the 1970s—like standpoint theory, Wages for Housework, family abolitionism, and critiques of heteropatriarchal love and romance—and refashioning it so it can be brought to bear on some aspect of life under capitalism today. Talk about a one-trick pony! In my defense, or by way of accounting for this stubborn fixation, I am profoundly attracted to 1970s U.S. radical and Marxist feminist theory, which I continue to find generative for thinking about the present, even if it is also often frustrating and woefully deficient. And because of my foundational commitment to anticapitalist theory and practice, I remain convinced that Marxist feminist theory is worth both preserving as an archive and continually reinventing as a tool.

HB: My *WSQ* essay came from a seminar paper in my first semester of graduate school, and it relied on the archive of that course. My archive would look different if I wrote the essay today. Queer of color critique offers a lot more to the antireproductivist project I tried to stake out than the largely white queer archive I was working with at the time, for example. I wish that had been on my radar then, but the good news is that there is always more work to do.

I still stand by the general critique of reproductivism, though, and that has absolutely structured the writing I went on to do. My belief that workers matter more than consumers shaped my stubborn choice to ignore porn consumers and claims about what porn means for them in *Porn Work*. The claim that workers should demand good pay and conditions (and, well, everything) regardless of the social impact of their jobs structures my approach to my current project on left sex worker politics. And I'm still very much drawn to feminist politics that are resolutely antiwork.

SP: Building on the above question on the afterlives of feminist publication, as feminist scholars of labor, how do you make sense of various markets of and for feminist publication (like *WSQ*, but also any other media or mediums you want to talk about)? How have you seen feminist work and ideas about work change in feminist scholarship and activism?

HB: As precarity grows and the promises of good work break down for more and more people, I think feminists have gotten hungrier for antiwork critique. In terms of what this means for feminist activism, I can speak to the sex worker activism that's closest to home for me. In the years since my *WSQ* essay came out, sex worker activists have shifted pretty remarkably from "sex work is work" framings to "sex work is antiwork," now a common T-shirt slogan when we march. There's a growing awareness around the limits of respectability as a political strategy, where organizers see that framings of sex work as good work exclude 1) those whose experience is more complicated and 2) those who haven't actually achieved their political aims. There's more open conversation, for example, about how sex work is an everyday work resistance strategy for people with disabilities, where sex work isn't work like any other but is instead a hustle that makes living possible for those who can't or won't suffer through straight jobs. Organizers are still fighting for a legal remedy, but campaigns like Decrim NY foreground how criminalization harms everyone in sex trades regardless of their point of entry or experience of the work, rather than tactically ask for privacy for "consensual" workers who are imagined to be white, able-bodied, cis, and working indoors.

In terms of scholarship, L. H. Stallings's *Funk the Erotic*, Sophie Lewis's *Full Surrogacy Now*, and Saidiya Hartman's *Wayward Lives, Beautiful Experiments: Intimate Histories of Social Upheaval* are recent texts that engage antiwork politics in ranging and really exciting ways. I'm also excited about the turn in care scholarship to focus away from "valuing" commodified care and toward thinking about mutual aid that reproduces us against work rather than (or sometimes at the same time as) for it. Hil Malatino's *Trans Care*, Alexis Pauline Gumbs, China Martens, and Mai'a Williams's *Revolutionary Mothering*, and Dean Spade's *Mutual Aid* are some examples.

I think part of this comes from a shift in the feminist publication markets Sam's question gestures to. There's such an appetite for radical critique right now, not least because growing precarity makes it clear to more and more people that we'll need creative resources to survive "this crisis (and the next)," as the subtitle for Spade's book puts it. It's probably not an accident that many of the texts I named in this turn come from independent left publishers rather than academic presses. There's also so much exciting feminist theorizing coming out of left publications like *Spectre*, *Lux* magazine, *Endnotes*, *Invert*, and *Pinko*. I'm more and more feeling the sense that this generation of scholars is souring on the promise that job security will be forthcoming if they (we) toe the line. It's bad news that that security is elusive even for those who play by all the rules, but some possibilities are opening up even as others close. Thinkers are finding cracks and room to maneuver in academia's general breakdown. This will necessarily shape the work that comes out of feminist academic journals like *WSQ*, and I think we'll continue to see more experimentation and rule-breaking, even behind paywalls.

KW: Like Heather, I welcome the recent proliferation of venues where we can publish our work. In addition to the excellent journals Heather mentioned, I would note as well the importance of platforms like Patreon where growing numbers of younger scholars in particular, some of whom have been excluded from or precaritized within academia, can share, and at least begin to support, their writing and research.

As for how I've seen feminist ideas about work change, I've noticed, and been thankful for, a recent willingness to scale up our theoretical analyses of work, so that rather than focus only on the subjective and experiential register we can also take aim at larger structures and infrastructures. So for example, we can talk about waged work as a system of income allocation and governance rather than be confined to addressing only this or that job. Part of this opening has to do with the fact that capitalism is once again a legible and legitimate topic of inquiry, which is also the reason why I think Marxist feminism is enjoying something of a moment.

To mention another example of scaled-up feminist theories of work, I've been excited to see that family abolitionism is being revived in feminist theory and politics. A text that Heather mentioned, Sophie Lewis's *Full Surrogacy Now*, is a great example of this project. At least one way to understand family abolitionism is that it scales up the critical study of domestic labor so it can encompass its key structural locus, support system, and managerial regime, namely, the institution and ideology of the family. From the perspective of this version of an abolitionist account, the problem with the organization of domestic labor is not its so-called outsourcing, or even that its labors are divided by gender, race, class, and nation, but also the way that the family functions as such a reliable mechanism of this labor's privatization, and as such, an alibi for the shocking absence of social support for household-based childcare and eldercare, including even having enough time off waged work to devote to those labors.

I realize that family abolitionism has been deeply fraught for feminist scholars since the 1970s. It feels as if most feminist theorists have spent the past several decades trying their best to fend off charges of being antifamily. I'm not sure this will succeed in making it more palatable to the skeptics and critics among us, but I understand family abolitionism as a political project, not an ethical injunction. That is to say, it is a long-term collective effort to grasp in theory and transform in practice the institutional structures that delimit our possibilities for sociality and cooperation—to open them up to myriad options and to finally reject liberalism's privatization, which precludes significant support for household-based labor—rather than a call to change our individual desires and choices about whom we want to cohabitate with. The argument is about, once again, structures not individuals.

HB: As we close, I'm thinking about Kathi's invitation to think structurally rather than in terms of individuals and wondering what this might mean for how we talk about the everyday life of antiwork practice. In *Wayward Lives,* Saidiya Hartman talks about "the miracle of upheaval: small groups, people *by themselves,* and strangers threaten to become an ensemble, to incite *treason en masse*" (8, emphasis in original). I'm viscerally drawn to this, in part because, as a Marxist ethnographer, I'm always looking for the small ways everyday people refuse and thinking about how those might link up to bring "treason en masse" (or, to put it in John Holloway's terms, small cracks that might spread, once connected). But Kathi's rejoinder is making me reflect on the other, messier reasons I might be drawn to stories of everyday insurrection, not least that they make confronting current conditions feel a little less crushing. So, I'm thinking, too, about Sam's question regarding the work we do as feminists, and about how the stories we choose to tell (the telling being part of our jobs) are as much about what helps us keep showing up (to struggle, but also to work) as they are about structural analysis and long-range strategy. Part of what draws me to the Autonomist tradition is the political heft it assigns to everyday refusal. Kathi's book is to blame for my having learned about Autonomism in the first place, so I'm returning to the source to ask your thoughts on what to do with this tangle.

KW: I appreciate Heather's insistence on attending to the register of everyday life. And I certainly think that any structural(ish) analysis worth its salt rejects a dualistic conception of the categories of social totality and everyday existence, and grasps the relation between subjects and structures in terms of all of its nonfunctional and antagonistic potential. In other words, the kind of structurally focused analysis I want to affirm recognizes that, as Foucault put it, "it is a fact that people rise up." But, whether or not it takes place in a space we would call "everyday life," I also think that to be *political,* refusal must be collective. For that reason, I was inspired most by the examples of sex worker community building and political advocacy efforts that Heather discusses in her magnificent book, *Porn Work.* I continue to fear that the all too familiar figure of the individual, and methodological individualism more generally, not only but perhaps especially under neoliberalism, is a kind of black hole where politics—and for me that means thinking, acting, and wanting at a social level, as in the case of the ensemble-inciting treason referenced in the quote from Saidiya Hartman—is too easily undermined.

Samantha Pinto is professor of English and affiliated faculty of African and African Diaspora Studies, Women's and Gender Studies, and the Warfield Center for African American Studies at the University of Texas at Austin. She is the author of *Infamous Bodies* and *Difficult Diasporas*, the coeditor of *Writing Beyond the State*, and a coeditor of the *Black Feminism on the Edge* book series with Duke University Press. She can be reached at samantha.pinto@utexas.edu.

Kathi Weeks teaches in the Gender, Sexuality, and Feminist Studies program at Duke University. She is the author of *Constituting Feminist Subjects* and *The Problem with Work: Feminism, Marxism, Antiwork Politics and Postwork Imaginaries*, and a coeditor of *The Jameson Reader*. She can be reached at kweeks@duke.edu.

Heather Berg writes about sex, work, and social struggle. Her first book, *Porn Work*, explores workers' strategies for navigating—and subverting—precarity. Her writing appears in the journals *Feminist Studies*, *Signs*, *South Atlantic Quarterly*, *Critical Historical Studies*, and others. Heather is assistant professor of women, gender, and sexuality studies at Washington University in St. Louis. She can be reached at heatherberg@wustl.edu.

Works Cited

Hartman, Saidiya. 2019. *Wayward Lives, Beautiful Experiments: Intimate Histories of Social Upheaval.* New York: W. W. Norton & Company.

Weeks, Kathi. 2011. *The Problem with Work: Feminism, Marxism, Antiwork Politics, and Postwork Imaginaries.* Durham, NC: Duke University Press.

Feminist Citational Praxis and Problems of Practice

Lori Wright, Neisha Wiley, Elizabeth VanWassenhove, Brandelyn Tosolt, Rae Loftis, and Meg L. Hensley

Abstract: This article critiques current citational norms and advances feminist citational praxis. Through the process of writing a dissertation collaboratively, we developed our feminist citational praxis. We share the development of our praxis and highlight three problems of practice we have discovered. We reject normative citational rituals and encourage authors to center scholars and scholarship that are often silenced through academic citational exclusion. Intentionally citing Authors of Color, women, transgender, and nonbinary scholars as well as disabled authors/authors with disabilities is feminist citational praxis. We ground our feminist citational praxis within the feminist killjoy paradigm and encourage readers to develop their own feminist citational praxis. **Keywords:** feminist; citation; collaborative writing; praxis; killjoy

Academic writing relies on citation; appropriately crediting the source of information distinguishes legitimate scholarship from plagiarism. By definition, a cited work enters into the discourse of a discipline; an uncited work is excluded from that discourse. In this way, citation itself defines the boundaries of knowledge. Questions of whose work is included within these citation boundaries have been explored across disciplines (for example, see Baskaran 2021; Bolles 2013; Kumar and Karusala 2021; Mott and Cockayne 2017; Nakassis 2013). Novice researchers are socialized into a system of recognizing what counts as academic knowledge and what is excluded from that domain (Burgess, Cormack, and Reid 2021, 59; see also Nadasen 2019). Adherence to the norms of academic knowledge serves as evidence of the researcher belonging to the culture of academia. However, that adherence

WSQ: Women's Studies Quarterly 50: 3 & 4 (Fall/Winter 2022) © 2022 by Lori Wright, Neisha Wiley, Elizabeth VanWassenhove, Brandelyn Tosolt, Rae Loftis, and Meg L. Hensley. All rights reserved.

simultaneously functions to construct and maintain the boundaries around academic knowledge itself.

Current rituals of reflection and reproduction of what already exists hide and underutilize the voices and contributions of Authors of Color, authors with marginalized genders and gender identities, and disabled authors/ authors with disabilities. CisHeteroPatriarchy is a system that elevates power and privilege over people with marginalized genders, people of color, queer people, and people with disabilities.[1] Normative citational practices reinforce CisHeteroPatriarchy.

Feminist citational practices provide an opportunity to "flip the script" on CisHeteroPatriarchy. In *Feminism Is for Everybody*, bell hooks defines feminism as "a movement to end sexism, sexist exploitation, and oppression" (hooks 2015, 1). We utilize this definition of feminism to ground feminist citational practice, praxis, and rituals, as this definition aligns with our values, professional ethics, and scholarship. Further, we argue that any citational practices that do not fulfill hooks's definition are not feminist citational practices.

In the introduction to the Spring/Summer 2020 issue of *Women's Studies Quarterly*, editors Natalie Havlin and Jillian M. Báez highlight "past and ongoing struggles to build a radical politics of citation" (2020, 10). They frame their issue as addressing multiple aspects of feminist scholarship, including, "How might feminist scholars grapple with the power dynamics of whose work is recognized and built upon in order to transform our scholarship and political practices?" (10). In sharing our feminist citational praxis in this article, we, too, choose to address this question. In the same issue, Nadasen (2019) argues that tending to the "politics of citation" with care can "create scholarly space for nontraditional subjects that have the potential to overturn the racialized and gendered hierarchies in academia" (156–57). As we and other scholars continue this conversation, we collaboratively build a feminist citational ritual.

We attempt to further the conversation regarding feminist citational praxis as a stepping-stone toward future feminist citational rituals. We argue that any individual act of citation may or may not be feminist, but it is only through the intentional grounding of feminist practices in feminist theory that a feminist citational praxis emerges. As feminist citational practices lead to feminist citational praxes over time, a new feminist citational ritual emerges to challenge the citational rituals that have existed in academic culture and reinforced dominant narratives and voices across time. In this article, we explain and share our experience creating our own feminist citational praxis, including three main problems of practice that we encountered. As Sara Ahmed reminds us, "Feminism is at stake in how we generate knowledge; in how we write, in who we cite. I think of feminism as a building project: if our texts are worlds, they need to be made out of feminist materials" (2017, 14). The building blocks of these future feminist worlds are created through feminist citational rituals.

On CisHeteroPatriarchal Practices

CisHeteroPatriarchal citational practices are silencing practices that exclude and oppress marginalized voices and perspectives within the academy (Burgess, Cormack, and Reid 2021; Craven 2021; Duriesmith 2018). Greater authority is ascribed to written and published knowledge than experiential or oral knowledge (Burgess, Cormack, and Reid 2021; Craven 2021; Ymous et al. 2020). Privileging written knowledge effectively silences much Indigenous knowledge, which has traditionally been transmitted orally; privileging written and published knowledge excludes disabled voices/voices with disabilities, as the acts of writing and publishing have been constructed inaccessibly to many disabled people/people with disabilities. When the hierarchies of citation privilege written forms of knowledge over all other forms of knowledge, then the confines of knowledge become more restrictive. As Kimmerer (2013) describes, this practice "deprives us of the wealth of intergenerational knowledge provided by our communities" (quoted in Burgess, Cormack, and Reid 2021, 58).

The culture of the westernized academy and, by extension, academic writing, is meant to be a meritocracy in which the best arguments are the most read and built upon by future scholars (Zivony 2019). This meritocratic argument itself is inherently based in an ableist perspective in which "only the strongest survive." A series of obstacles and privileges differentially shape the pathways of every author, leading to inequality in who publishes, how they conceptualize what they publish, where they publish, and what they actually publish, as well as who reads that publication and who cites it. As is well documented in the literature, White authors, male-identified authors, and so-called able-bodied authors are cited at much higher rates than Authors of Color, authors with marginalized gender identities, and disabled authors/authors with disabilities (Chakravartty et al. 2018; Ymous et al. 2020).

Citation disparities are exacerbated by citational approaches that are color-evasive (Annamma, Jackson, and Morrison 2017),[2] those in which a citing author simply considers which pieces of prior knowledge are most valued within their discipline. Particularly in a context of well-documented silencing of Authors of Color, disabled authors/authors with disabilities, and authors with marginalized gender identities, invoking so-called fairness as a defense for citing without attention to who is being cited and who is being silenced, is based on a misunderstanding of fairness. Charlene Carruthers notes that we "cannot afford to treat 'the people' as an abstract concept . . . we have to be specific in order to understand who is present or missing" (Carruthers 2018, 98). Therefore, all ideas have a fair chance at being considered when authors deliberately cite those ideas that have been silenced.

Citational politics and the ways they are practiced can be inclusionary or exclusionary, but they are *never* neutral (Craven 2021; Rhodes 2021). Ignoring who authors the publications one cites is a political statement. Deliberately citing authors from one or more demographic groups or epistemological perspectives is a political statement (Nadasen 2019). Choosing not to consider the identity of the authors one cites is to choose to continue to elevate the messages, positions, and canons produced by White, male, cisgender, able-bodied, and English-speaking voices (Burgess, Cormack, and Reid 2021; Craven 2021; Mott and Cockayne 2017; Smith et al. 2021). Cite Black Women, created by Christen A. Smith in 2017, is an example of a formalized movement to push back against the erasure of marginalized voices, in this case specifically, Black women.

The Material Outcomes of Citation

Scholarly citation is often considered the currency of the academic realm, and it produces material outcomes for those being cited (Baskaran 2021; Kumar and Karusala 2021; Rhodes 2021). As Mott and Cockayne explain, "In addition to publication, citation is taken as an assumed proxy for measuring impact, relevance, and importance, with implications for hiring, promotion, tenure, and other aspects of performance evaluation" (2017, 2; see also Ahmed 2019; Baskaran 2021; Bolles 2013; Kumar and Karusala 2021). These material benefits are disproportionately accrued by scholars who are the beneficiaries of frequent citations, as "status or reputation depends, in part, on the frequency" of citation (Bolles 2013, 67), which further secures a scholar's position in academia (Baskaran 2021; Bolles 2013; Kumar and Karusala 2021; Mott and Cockayne 2017; Rhodes 2021; Rose 1993). This security creates a virtuous (or vicious) cycle.

Being cited also strengthens one's reputation as an authority in an academic discipline. When one is cited frequently, one is found on more reference pages. When a scholar mines the reference page of an article, that scholar is more likely to find the frequently cited author. Since scholars "are asked to follow the well-trodden paths of citation" (Ahmed 2019, 167), those scholars cited more frequently will continue to be cited more frequently as a means for emergent scholars to demonstrate their expertise in their academic discipline. In short, well-cited scholars have authority precisely because they are well cited (Mott and Cockayne 2017, 13).

Finally, having one's work cited means not only that one's work is being read, but that it is becoming integrated into the scholarly conversation: "Good habits in citation are about extending a line; you have to show how much you know of a field by citing those deemed to have shaped that field" (Ahmed 2019, 168). When a scholar lays out the line that came before them, they are marking their understanding of the canonical knowledge that led to today (Craven 2021). Similarly, being cited in someone else's future work extends your contributions into the line, marking your work as part of the disciplinary canon (Bolles 2013; Burgess, Cormack, and Reid 2021; Duriesmith 2018; Mott and Cockayne 2017; Rhodes 2021).

Our Feminist Citational Praxis and Problems of Practice

Five of us, two Black women (Lori and Neisha) and three White women (Beth, Rae, and Meg), coauthored a fully collaborative, autoethnographic dissertation sharing and examining our story of creating feminist sisterhood between Black women and White women. The sixth member of our collective (Brandelyn, a White woman) was the committee chair and the keystone of our collaborative work.

Three key decisions established our emergent feminist citational praxis. First, when we began writing the dissertation, we assigned a different color text to each author as a clear visual representation of what each author had written. Although this began as a form of accountability for a nontraditional dissertation, each color in a sense became the author's voice. We literally saw our and one another's words and thoughts in full color, and we were able to see who wrote them and who edited them. Our paragraphs became mixtures of colors as the editing process continued. Seeing the color distribution in the document let us know where we were in our collaborative process because sections were not complete until every color was present and intermixed. In addition, we used a distinct color for those ideas we captured that arose organically during our group discussions. The original dissertation was left in full color, with the seven colors representing the five individual authors, one dissertation chair, and a group voice. We made this decision in order to ensure that each individual idea was attributed to the individual voice from which it came. We did not realize it at the time, but this act of attributing individual ideas to individual authors created an internal example of our praxis.

Second, we became intentional about who we read, who we cited, and whose voices we amplified. We began our dissertation via a course on Women and Leadership taught by Brandelyn, in which the course texts and pedagogy centered Black feminists and feminisms. These texts served as the starting point for our scholarship, which further cemented Black feminists and feminisms as our sources of knowledge and points of reference. We had become hyperaware of the academic silencing of Women of Color in our readings and through shared personal stories. During a meeting early in our dissertation process, one of the coauthors offered the idea that we should refrain from citing White men and that we should instead center feminist Women of Color. Everyone enthusiastically agreed, further reinforcing our belief that we were embodying feminist theory. Our second emergent feminist citational praxis was to center the voices and texts of feminist women, prioritizing feminist Women of Color. At the time, this decision felt like an alignment between feminist theory and action research; we were putting our feminism into action.

We also made a conscious decision about how we, as authors, would be listed in the dissertation, to establish a norm for how we wanted to be cited from both the dissertation and any coauthored publications in the future. We resisted the norm of citing ourselves alphabetically because that would have placed the White women in our group before the Black women. Therefore, the third decision of our praxis was choosing to cite ourselves in reverse alphabetical order, meaning that when we are cited in text in most styles, Wright (Lori's last name) appears as a proxy for the whole group. When we are cited on a reference page, Wright and Wiley (Neisha's last name) appear first and second in the citation. Both of these choices are intended to increase the likelihood of the material benefits of citation coming first to Lori and Neisha.

As quickly as we established our feminist citational praxis, we discovered three problems of practice. First, by citing only women, we were ascribing gender based on traditional gender norms and also dismissing voices and experiences of transgender, gender-nonconforming, and gender-nonbinary folx.[3] Second, we recognized the necessity of citing cisgender men in some sections, in part due to the historical valuation of cisgender men's academic work over women's academic work, recognizing that men, especially White men, are often credited with work that is not theirs to own (Ahmed 2017; Edmonds 2019). Third, we decided that, regardless of the potential usefulness of particular literature or theories, there were authors we would not cite in our work; however, we also understood that the choice to include or exclude an author rested on our incomplete knowledge of that author.

Problem of Practice 1: Ascribing Gender and Gender Identity

In the interest of accountability, to ensure our citational prioritization of women, we created a spreadsheet listing every citation we used and including the presumed race and gender of the authors based upon publication names, photographs, and biographical data available online.

Our intentionality in tracking who we cited reinforced our commitment to centering the ideas expressed by feminist women, particularly feminist Women of Color. We did not form our ideas and then cite Women of Color to affirm our ideas and attempt to appear inclusive. Our citations indicated the work by which we were influenced, and tracking who we were citing became an accountability measure to ourselves, a way to ensure that we were remaining true to our intention of centering the voices and texts of feminist women and prioritizing feminist Women of Color.

Our practice of tracking citations, though revolutionary to us then, was problematic. It reinforced normative correlations between physical characteristics and perceived identities. Additionally, relying solely on authors to disclose their identities publicly required they be in positions both personally and professionally that allowed for safely identifying their identities without fear of retaliation or loss of resources. Finally, ascribing gender and gender identity based on author names and without demographic identifiers carries the risk of unintentionally excluding trans and gender-nonbinary authors.

Our citation tracking became a mechanism to notice which ideas we were privileging: "What you pay attention to grows" (brown 2017, 42). We perceive our feminist citational praxis as reflecting the care with which we engaged with these ideas and authors. Our intent is to be *care-full* (that is, full of care) in our work, simultaneously growing our own thinking alongside that of the authors we cite (Nash 2020; Tierney 2020). We recognize that the unintended outcomes of our citational practice contradict the aims of feminism in that they do not "end sexism, sexist exploitation, and oppression" (hooks 2015, 1). We are in search of a better process for citational analysis. We wonder: What practices have others utilized to center the voices and scholarship of authors with marginalized identities?

Problem of Practice 2: The Necessity of Occasionally Citing Men

Our excitement at citing only women dissipated when we realized the magnitude of the citation legacy that credited White men as founding theorists and leading scholars. In researching theories of social capital in relation to Black women faculty and staff retention in higher education, we became acutely aware that both the canons of social capital overall as well as specifically in relation to Black women faculty and staff retention in higher education were credited to men. Lori and Rae messaged about the challenge that emerged between feminist citational praxis and documenting the path already established by the academy:

> **Rae:** Y'all, I'm having a difficult time with social capital. I want to cite only women but the founding fathers of social capital theory are men. Can we discuss opening up to citing men? I'm down to put something in our methodology about intentionally citing women, with special attention to women of color, but that white men still have the most published agency in some of our topics?
>
> **Lori:** Rae, I feel you. Lots of info on the history of women in higher ed and also a lot of the retention research has been done by white men (Tinto, Pascarello, Terenezi, Astin, Bean, etc.). (Rae Loftis and Lori Wright, text messages, November 18, 2018)

Such conversations and subsequent research led to our decision to prioritize women, especially Women of Color, and to the composition of an explicit, written statement that acknowledges the historical exclusion and marginalization of Voices of Color within knowledge production and expresses our determination to do better. For too long, ideas have been unfairly attributed to White men, even when the ideas were articulated and developed by scholars with marginalized identities. We continue to wonder: How, when conducting in-depth explorations of established concepts, do other scholars balance the resulting overrepresentation of White male authors with their intention to promote the scholarship of authors with marginalized identities?

Problem of Practice 3: Not Fully Knowing Who You Cite

The poet Nikki Giovanni admonishes us: "Black groups digging on White philosophies ought to consider the source. Know who's playing the music before you dance" (quoted in Collins 2000, 112). Meg discovered that one of the sources in our dissertation was an avowed Nazi from the 1930s. She had been searching for a date for a citation Lori had used to establish the groundwork for our research methodology when she happened upon the reference's personal history. "Darlings," Meg messaged the group, "we've unknowingly cited a Nazi" (Meg Hensley, text message, January 10, 2019).

The methodology section of the dissertation that Lori had written and included the citation was some of her best and well-thought-out writing up to that point. After what seemed like a never-ending search to find a useful methodology to fit our unorthodox and unique dissertation, she had found a dissertation by a group of Black women struggling with the same challenges we faced. The methodology they referenced and cited spoke exactly to what we were searching for. When Meg alerted the group that this methodology was credited to a Nazi, the decision to find a different methodology was immediate. We were in complete agreement that we could not knowingly cite an avowed Nazi, but that did not mean that Lori did not feel disappointed and angry that so much of her contribution was erased. After all, another group of Black women had cited him, so what was the issue? Of course, this was a rhetorical and perhaps emotional question at best, because despite how many pages she had written, she knew, without hesitation, that the integrity of what we had committed to—deliberately choosing who and what we wanted to cite—was far more important than having a problematic citation removed.

Ultimately, the section was cut, and we developed a new methodology. This experience resulted in extra diligence when checking the basic backgrounds available on each of our sources in addition to researching their presumed gender and racial identities (our first problem of practice). As Shirley Rose states, "It is not enough to demonstrate familiarity with relevant related work. . . . One must also know when . . . not to acknowledge another's work" (1993, 30–31). Through this experience, we discovered one of our lines in the sand, when not to "acknowledge another's work": we always draw the line at Nazis.

Drawing a line is not a problem of practice; you have to draw a line. The questions are: Where do you draw a line, and do you have the information you need to draw the line? Nazis, of course, are not the only ones on the other side of our line. As the story above demonstrates, we not only unknowingly cited a Nazi, but we also only discovered accidentally that the author was a Nazi. Moving forward, we wanted to hold ourselves more accountable to our feminist citational ideals. We decided we needed an intentional practice to obtain a fuller understanding of the authors we were considering including in our work. Rae began to conduct internet searches of each author's name followed by the word "controversy." This practice did not identify any information that led to us excluding additional authors.

As with our practice of checking the racial and gender identities of authors we cite, we acknowledge the limitations of this practice. Checking online sources means relying on another form of citation. Particularly given the silencing of the survivors of all forms of abuse and oppression, we acknowledge that documentation on the internet reveals far fewer problematic authors than there are problematic authors to be revealed. We wonder: How do other scholars draw lines about who to cite and who not to cite? How do others balance their more inclusive citational practices, which might include public identification of author identities (such as disability and gender identity) with the potential for harm to authors with marginalized identities? How do we (individually and collectively) decide what would prevent an author from being included in our work, and how does that potentially interact with what Patton and Ward (2016) have identified as our culture of disposability?

Implications

Our feminist citational praxis grew out of three intentional decisions: to attribute individual contributions to individual authors within our collaborative group; to intentionally read and cite Authors of Color; and to cite ourselves in reverse alphabetical order to privilege the Black authors in our collaborative group. For us, these practices were liberatory because they opened up an expansive space to use our imagination (Burgess, Cormack, and Reid 2021, 60). We also discovered three problems of practice. First, by relying on CisHeteroPatriarchal paradigms, our citational practices reinforced problematic identity ascribing and inadvertently excluded trans and nonbinary authors. Second, our occasional citation of White men continued to reproduce the dominant narrative of CisHeteroPatriarchal knowledge production (Duriesmith 2018; Mott and Cockayne 2017). Third, we learned our own citation boundaries and responded by endeavoring for intentionality over accidentality in knowing as much about our sources as is readily available.

Feminist citational practices acknowledge the historical marginalization and silencing of Authors of Color, authors with marginalized genders and gender identities, and disabled authors/authors with disabilities in academia via the intentional crediting of their scholarship. As we consider the limits to who, how, and why we cite, we must also deeply evaluate our own relationship with the academy. Our group's practices of being intentional about who we read, who we cite, and whose voices we amplify form our feminist citational praxis. We recognize that our feminist citational praxis centers voices and ideas that have previously been overlooked or silenced, while at the same time, it remains inclusive of only those ideas deemed "acceptable" by processes such as peer review and individual gatekeepers such as dissertation chairs.

To practice feminist citation is to be what Sara Ahmed (2010) describes as a feminist killjoy. Several years later, Ahmed also wrote, "We become a problem when we describe a problem" (2017, 39). Through feminist citational praxis, we are called to, and are able to, describe and disrupt the problematic CisHeteroPatriarchal processes and outcomes of citation in academia (Ahmed 2019; Craven 2021, Duriesmith 2018; Mott and Cockayne 2017). Engaging in feminist citation practice is a divergence from academic norms and therefore can be criticized as disruptive to the academic community (Rose 1993). However, as Ahmed explains, in order to craft new knowledge, "we might have to cite differently: citation as how we can refuse to be erased" (2019, 212). Citational feminist practice allows us to center ourselves as valuable scholars and our knowledge as scholarship; to acknowledge a different risk, as risk of being a killjoy replaces risk of being erased; to write what needs writing; and to continue the line of scholarship in which we are situated.

Being a scholar is always risky. Sharing scholarship exposes all authors to judgment, to challenge, to argument, to being wrong. To share scholarship is to embrace the tension between producing the most complete and accurate work one can today, while knowing that eventually, even the most solid scholarship will become an artifact of a more incomplete time as the discipline and even the author themself evolves. Marginalized authors experience the same risks all authors experience, with the additional risk of being disciplined by the CisHeteroPatriarchal paradigms through exclusion and erasure. The six of us choose to risk being labeled killjoys because we know that even without being killjoys, we will still be erased. We are afraid, but we do it anyway (Lorde 1997).

We entered into our feminist praxis intentionally centering the voices and texts of Black feminists and Black feminisms. Our intentionality rested on our embrace of the Combahee River Collective's statement: "If Black women were free, it would mean that everyone else would have to be free since our freedom would necessitate the destruction of all the systems of oppression" (quoted in Taylor 2017, 22–23). Unfortunately, we failed to fully embody these words. hooks's definition of feminism—"a movement to end sexism, sexist exploitation, and oppression" (hooks 2015, 1)—was a statement we came back to repeatedly, and always to include all women of all racial identities. However, we did not use this same logic to recognize that no demographic group exists separate from disability. In doing so, we failed to engage the lens of critical disability studies (DisCrit). The limitations of our own conceptual lenses at the time artificially severed disability from racism and sexism.

We have learned many things since writing our dissertation, which has led to new awareness regarding our feminist citational praxis. We failed to recognize and acknowledge the varied disabilities in our own group. Reading DisCrit revealed how we were focused both on upholding ableism and on othering our own disabilities. We continue to excavate our own multiple identities and how these intersect with disability and our scholarly identities. We are also becoming aware of the difficulty of citation-counting in relation to disability because, as with the problems of practice we described above, this relies on making inferences. In the case of disability, such inferences are based on physical characteristics or rely on an author to disclose their disability publicly in an easily available or accessible format. Reflecting on our feminist citational praxis and emergent problems of practice has reinforced for us that feminist citational practice is "the map of a process, not the map of a territory" (Kim 2020, 8).

In addition, we are painfully aware that feminist citational rituals are a product of the system in which we currently live. We recognize in ourselves our own yearning for credibility, to be seen as legitimate creators of knowledge (Tierney 2020). Feminist citational ritual may be a better approach to citation than CisHeteroPatriarchal citational rituals, and yet we are reminded of Mariame Kaba's words: to live with "one foot in creative destruction and the other foot in the possibility of making new things" (Kaba 2021). It is our intent to forward our processes and contributions to help make new things: feminist citational rituals. At the same time, the world as it currently exists (we are thinking particularly of the commodification of imagination within capitalism) frames and restricts our imagination of feminist citational rituals.

We intend to contribute to "building another world entirely organized around Black women's brilliance, one that undoes violence and embraces an ethic of redress" (Nash 2020, 81). Our intentionality to cite women in our dissertation, prioritizing Authors of Color, was born out of Brandelyn's decision to center Black feminisms in the course from which our dissertation emerged. Centering Black feminisms and feminists provided us with our definition of feminism (hooks 2015), gave us the language and catalyzed a contradiction in which we could grapple with ourselves, and allowed us a better perspective of the roots of gender oppression. Scholars committed to feminist citational practice must intentionally engage with Black feminisms and feminists *throughout* their work, not as an afterthought or a token addition of Black women's scholarship to their reference list (Nash 2020). As Jennifer Nash (2020) tells us, Black feminisms are a rich canon of scholarship; authors who include Black feminisms should develop a citational practice that honors the richness of their legacy and engages meaningfully with the depth and breadth of the scholarship rather than securing a citational diversity quota.

Finally, since completing the dissertation, we have grown to recognize that the power in our collective voice is distinct from the power in our individual voices. We also recognize the extent to which each individual's perspective was shaped by interactions with other members of the group. What one person writes represents the thinking, conversations, and conflicts of multiple people. In this spirit, we produce a final voice in a single color that is the voice of the collective, not representative of the contributions of six individual scholars. We perceive this collective voice to be a break with CisHeteroPatriarchal norms of authorship, while we also concurrently state that by placing our names on this piece of work, we reinforce the idea that any person, even a collective of persons, can "own" an idea. We are mindful of Octavia Butler's words: "There's nothing new under the sun, but there are new suns" (Butler 2001). We hope that our move toward collective authorship is a move toward a new sun. Moving beyond the concept of ideas as property would be journeying to yet another new sun.

We hope that, together with other feminist scholars who are developing their own citational practices and praxes, we will build a new future through feminist citational rituals. We acknowledge that the new rituals we will build together will not be without problems of practice. As authors and scholars, we recognize that we are but six women in the long line of who has been, who is, and who is yet to be, and we are committed to being good ancestors while recognizing that our ancestors paved the way for us (Wilson 2020). Uplifting the voices of Authors of Color, authors with marginalized genders and gender identities, and disabled authors/authors with disabilities creates opportunities for future scholars to celebrate individualized perspectives and differences, rather than creating a false narrative of a "universal" human experience. It is every scholar's privilege and burden to carry our ancestors' words and ideas forward in a way that centers justice, joy, and healing in our respective disciplines, in our practices, and in our lives.

Lori Wright, EdD, is a Black, temporarily able-bodied female. Her work centers inclusive and equitable practices that support academic success and retention for historically excluded student populations at the University of Cincinnati. Contact her at lorilynn1027@gmail.com.

Neisha Wiley, EdD, is a Black, female, temporarily able-bodied licensed social worker with over twenty years of experience and a faculty member in the School of Social Work at Northern Kentucky University. Contact her at wiley.neisha@gmail.com.

Elizabeth VanWassenhove, EdD, is a White, disabled, queer ciswoman who works with teacher candidates at Northern Kentucky University. A Montessori-trained educator, she approaches her work preparing future teachers though Black feminism and anti-oppression. Contact her at elizabeth.vanwassenhove@gmail.com.

Brandelyn Tosolt, PhD, is a White, Disabled, ciswoman faculty member in the College of Education at Northern Kentucky University. Her work centers the margins, disrupts normative practices, and creates joyful, liberatory educational praxis. Contact her at brandelyntosolt@gmail.com.

Rae Loftis, EdD, is a White, Queer, temporarily able-bodied ciswoman who works in diversity, equity, and inclusion administration and student affairs at Eastern Kentucky University. She approaches anti-oppression through the lens of Black feminisms and Queer frameworks. Contact her at raeloftis@gmail.com.

Meg L. Hensley, EdD, is a White, disabled, queer ciswoman administrator in student affairs at Northern Kentucky University. She approaches her work and scholarship through a lens of Black feminism and anti-oppression. Contact her at meglhensley@gmail.com.

Notes

1. The term "CisHeteroPatriarchy" does not encompass all dominant identities within the term itself; however, we use it as such.
2. We explicitly reject the term "colorblind" as a way to describe this exclusionary practice of citation rituals. Using this term denies agency to Authors of Color and disabled authors/authors with disabilities.
3. We use the term "folx" as intentionally inclusive of all genders and nongenders. While the term "folks" is often viewed as gender-inclusive, the intentional use of "x" in folx is in alignment with trans- and gender-inclusive language.

Works Cited

Ahmed, Sara. 2010. "Killing Joy: Feminism and the History of Happiness." *Signs* 35, no. 3: 571–94.

———. 2017. *Living a Feminist Life.* Durham, NC: Duke University Press.

———. 2019. *What's the Use? On the Uses of Use.* Durham, NC: Duke University Press.

Annamma, Subini Ancy, Darrell D. Jackson, and Deb Morrison. 2017. "Conceptualizing Color-Evasiveness: Using Dis/Ability Critical Race Theory to Expand a Color-Blind Racial Ideology in Education and Society." *Race Ethnicity and Education* 20, no. 2: 147–62. https://doi.org/10.1080/13613324.2016.1248837.

Baskaran, Priya. 2021. "Taking Our Space: Service, Scholarship, and Radical Citation Practice." *Rutgers University Law Review* 73, no. 4: 101–22. https://ssrn.com/abstract=3862982.

Bolles, Lynn. 2013. "Telling the Story Straight: Black Feminist Intellectual Thought in Anthropology." *Transforming Anthropology* 21, no. 1: 57–71.

brown, adrienne maree. 2017. *Emergent Strategy: Shaping Change, Changing Worlds.* Chico, CA: AK Press.

Burgess, Hana, Donna Cormack, and Papaarangi Reid. 2021. "Calling Forth Our Pasts, Citing Our Futures: An Envisioning of a Kaupapa Māori Citational Practice." *MAI Journal* 10, no. 1: 57–67. https://doi.org/10.20507/MAIJournal.2021.10.1.8.

Butler, Octavia E. 2001. Notes/Unfinished Manuscript "Parable of the Trickster," mssOEB 1-9062. The Huntington Library.

Carruthers, Charlene A. 2018. *Unapologetic: A Black, Queer, and Feminist Mandate for Radical Movements*. Boston, MA: Beacon Press.

Chakravartty, Paula, Rachel Kuo, Victoria Grubbs, and Charlton McIlwain. 2018. "#CommunicationSoWhite." *Journal of Communication* 68, no. 2: 254–66. https://doi.org/10.1093/joc/jqy003.

Collins, Patricia H. 2000. *Black Feminist Thought: Knowledge, Consciousness, and the Politics of Empowerment*. 2nd ed. Abingdon, UK: Routledge.

Craven, Christa. 2021. "Teaching Antiracist Citational Politics as a Project of Transformation: Lessons from the Cite Black Women Movement for White Feminist Anthropologists." *Feminist Anthropology* 2, no. 1: 120–29. https://doi.org/10.1002/fea2.12036.

Duriesmith, David. 2018. "Negative Space and the Feminist Act of Citation: Strategic Silence and the Limits of Gendering an Unloving Discipline." In *Rethinking Silence, Voice and Agency in Contested Gendered Terrains*, edited by Jane L. Parpart and Swati Parashar, 66–77. London: Routledge.

Edmonds, Brittney M. 2019. "The Professional Is Political: On Citational Practice and the Persistent Problem of Academic Plunder." *Journal of Feminist Scholarship* 16 (Fall): 74–77.

Havlin, Natalie, and Jillian M. Báez. 2020. "Editors' Note." *WSQ: Women's Studies Quarterly* 48, nos. 1/2: 9–13.

hooks, bell. 2015. *Feminism Is for Everybody: Passionate Politics*. 2nd ed. New York: Routledge.

Kaba, Mariame. 2021. "Harm, Punishment, and Abolition with Mariame Kaba." By Prentis Hemphill. July 5, 2021. *Finding Our Way*. Podcast, MP3 audio, 57:13. https://www.findingourwaypodcast.com/individual-episodes/s2e12.

Kim, Annabel L. 2020. "The Politics of Citation." *Diacritics* 48, no. 3: 4–9.

Kumar, Neha, and Naveena Karusala. 2021. "Braving Citational Justice in Human-Computer Interaction." *CHI '21 Extended Abstracts of the 2021 CHI Conference on Human Factors in Computing Systems*, no. 11, 1–9. https://doi.org/10.1145/3411763.3450389.

Lorde, Audre. 1997. *The Collected Poems of Audre Lorde*. New York: W. W. Norton.

Mott, Carrie, and Daniel Cockayne. 2017. "Citation Matters: Mobilizing the Politics of Citation toward a Practice of 'Conscientious Engagement.'" *Gender, Place & Culture* 24, no. 7: 954–73. https://doi.org/10.1080/0966369X.2017.1339022.

Nadasen, Premilla. 2019. "Response to Sherwin and Piven's 'The Radical

Feminist Legacy of the National Welfare Rights Organization.'" *WSQ* 47, nos. 3/4: 155–63.

Nakassis, Constantine V. 2013. "Citation and Citationality." *Signs and Society* 1, no. 1: 51–78.

Nash, Jennifer C. 2020. "Citational Desires: On Black Feminism's Institutional Longings." *Diacritics* 48, no. 3: 76–91.

Patton, Lori D., and LaWanda W. Ward. 2016. "Missing Black Undergraduate Women and the Politics of Disposability: A Critical Race Feminist Perspective." *Journal of Negro Education* 85, no. 3: 330–49. muse.jhu.edu/article/802787.

Rhodes, Catherine R. 2021. "Citation: Direct and Indirect." In *The International Encyclopedia of Linguistic Anthropology*, edited by James Stanlaw. Hoboken, NJ: John Wiley & Sons. https://doi.org/10.1002/9781118786093.iela0051.

Rose, Shirley K. 1993. "Citation Rituals in Academic Cultures." *Issues in Writing* 6, no. 1: 24–37.

Smith, Christen A., Erica L. Williams, Imani A. Wadud, Whitney N. L. Pirtle, and the Cite Black Women Collective. 2021. "Cite Black Women: A Critical Praxis (A Statement)." *Feminist Anthropology* 2, no. 1: 10–17. https://doi.org/10.1002/fea2.12040.

Taylor, Keeanga-Yamahtta. 2017. *How We Get Free: Black Feminism and the Combahee River Collective.* Chicago, IL: Haymarket Books.

Tierney, Matt. 2020. "Dispossessed Citation and Mutual Aid." *Diacritics* 48, no. 3: 94–115.

Wilson, Jamia. 2020. "A Love Note to Our Literary Ancestors: Then and Now." *WSQ* 48, nos. 1/2: 307–10. https://doi.org/10.1353/wsq.2020.0002.

Ymous, Anon, Katta Spiel, Os Keyes, Rua M. Williams, Judith Good, Eva Hornecker, and Cynthia L. Bennett. 2020. "'I Am Just Terrified of My Future': Epistemic Violence in Disability Related Technology Research." *CHI '20 Extended Abstracts of the 2020 CHI Conference on Human Factors in Computing Systems.* https://doi.org/10.1145/3334480.3381828.

Zivony, Alon. 2019. "Academia Is Not a Meritocracy." *Nature Human Behaviour* 3: 1037. https://doi.org/10.1038/s41562-019-0735-y.

SCUM as Trans-form

Lolita Copacabana

The summer of 2020 is the first summer of the COVID-19 pandemic, and I spend it (in the Midwest, locked up, scared, confused, alert, anxious, sad, sometimes mad) working on a series of collages. I'm not a visual artist, but a writer, and before this unexpected move into graphic media, I've been writing from cut-ups, finding hidden poetry, or what seems like it, in the headlines of the magazines available for free on the generous, quiet streets of Iowa City. The world is ending and I'm broke, in a country that is merciless to its immigrants. But is that even what I am? I'm a graduate student six thousand miles away from the place where I was born—I have a visa that only allows me to work under very specific and very limited conditions. I've been away for three years now, and I'm still not sure if I'm entitled to use the word. As a matter of fact, I've been explicitly denied it.

The Ides of March enter, like a lion, and April is the cruelest month. Although during the day the streets of Iowa City, a college town, are indeed suburban, peaceful, and pretty quiet, my nights are not so tranquil. There are lockdowns all over the world, including Argentina—my home country— and even in some parts of the U.S., but Iowa is one of only seven states that has entirely foregone a shelter-in-place order: from under my heavy blankets and the brightly dotted Midwestern sky, party music never stops playing outside. I still get invitations to get-togethers, and people get offended when I decline. My mood swings—to say the least—and, after a particularly challenging and confusing day, I find myself working on a collage that looks like the cover of a book: *Todas las formas en las que estoy enojada*. I staple a few blank pages behind the collage cover and—for some reason, the first paragraph of Valerie Solanas's 1967 *SCUM Manifesto* ringing in my head—start

WSQ: Women's Studies Quarterly 50: 3 & 4 (Fall/Winter 2022) © 2022 by Lolita Copacabana. All rights reserved.

to quietly enumerate them. All the ways in which I'm angry. All the senses in which I am full of rage. All the forms taken by the fury inside me.

I start with a very detailed list of what the pandemic has stolen away from me. What it has imposed. What it restricts, what it implies. Fairly soon I've gone way past the virus, Solanas resounding more and more loudly inside of me. The list continues to grow, it seems to have a life of its own. Night comes, eventually, and, exhausted, I take a picture of my collage. I upload it onto Instagram, and, a couple of hours later, come to realize that the ways in which I'm angry are probably many, but also that I'm very evidently not alone.

IN AN ESSAY PUBLISHED IN 2019 in the literary journal *Full Stop*, Chavisa Woods compares Valerie Solanas's infamous status in social memory to the reputation of several male artist-felons, among them William Burroughs (who in 1951 shot his wife dead), Norman Mailer (who in 1960 stabbed his wife in the chest, nearly piercing her heart), Pablo Neruda (who matter-of-factly confessed to having raped a servant while visiting her country as a diplomat), Charles Bukowski (who kicked and punched his girlfriend during an interview about his writing and was said to have been abusive to several of his female partners), and the French Marxist philosopher Louis Althusser (who strangled his wife to death in an act of cold-blooded murder).

In an effort to re-signify Solanas's *SCUM Manifesto* for what it actually is—a masterwork of literary protest art that is, generally, wholly misread—Woods also takes the time to show how much of her work is actually a point-by-point rewrite of multiple texts by Sigmund Freud. Where Freud's renowned essays are rife with suggestions of female castration and hysterectomies as treatments for all sorts of psychological troubles suffered by women, says Woods, *SCUM* is infamous for suggesting that castration might improve the behavior of men. Solanas also replaces penis envy, Woods points out, not only with vagina envy, but "most often, with women's emotional openness, complexity and individuality as the focus of men's envy." And where Freud accuses the mother of being to blame for the "horrible fate" of a boy becoming homosexual, Solanas accuses the father of being to blame for the horrible fate of becoming a straight man.

While it's pretty obvious that Solanas wrote the *SCUM Manifesto* as a parody that, using the vernacular of her epoch, mocks popular, sexist, and heterocentric thinking about gender and sexuality of the time, upon reading it "everyone freaked out, because when we talk about men the same way men have talked about women for centuries, it reads as grotesque and insanely violent, un-compassionate, and shocking"—which was exactly the point of Solanas's intervention, says Woods.

"Valerie Solanas and the Limits of Speech" by Natalya Lusty argues that the *SCUM Manifesto* can be read within the context of feminist experimental writing concerned with radically refashioning the gendered nature of manifesto discourse. Lusty proposes that this reading of *SCUM* is pertinent not only because Solanas considered herself a writer first and foremost but also because the historical conditions in which she lived actually precipitated this highly idiosyncratic manifesto and its reconceptualization of revolutionary discourse, particularly the historically gendered assumptions of the manifesto's rhetoric and performative practice.

Highlighting the wit and strikingly provocative, satirical nature of Solanas's prose, "which literally jumps off the page as a hyper-performative verbal assault against patriarchy and capitalism," as well as the deeply trenchant and anarchist temper of the intervention, Lusty argues that SCUM revels in the rhetorical violence of the genre, and that the intoxicating psychosis that saturates the cruel and bitter criticism of this manifesto is, in many ways, a precondition for any self-respecting manifesto.

"We stand erect at the summit of the world," declares Filippo Tomasso Marinetti in his 1909 *Founding and Manifesto of Futurism*—deliberately macho-male, points out Lusty. And it is precisely the macho-male status of the genre that Solanas takes on, caricaturing and inverting the worst excesses of Marinetti's misogynistic proclamations. But while Marinetti's scream wins him a point, "Solanas' scream is rendered silent by virtue of its 'hysterical'—in both senses of the word—caricature of macho-male manifestic discourse." As an angry and wounded utterance, says Lusty, the *SCUM Manifesto* is neither a heroic nor indefensible text; while it responds to a primal sense of injury and alienation, in stretching the manifesto form toward the impossible limits of speech, it occupies a position that is both fascinating and disturbing—like so many manifestos of the male avant-garde tradition that came before it.

OF LATE, thanks to the influence of Gertrude Stein and Anne Boyer, I have often found myself making connections between the restrictions imposed on us by literary forms and those made by garments. I've spent much of the past year translating Boyer's *Garments Against Women* (a book that addresses the fact that available forms—like garments and literature—are made of the materials of history, from hours taken from the lives of women and children, but are mostly quite unsuited to the shape, motion, and variations in what they contain), as well as researching the subversive nature of poetic prose, a practice borrowed from Europe and brought to America by Stein, a consistently revolutionary agent.

Very much in the spirit of Boyer's book, the first line of Stein's poem "The Long Dress" ("What is the current that makes machinery, that makes it crackle, what is the current that presents a long line and a necessary waist"), a personal favorite, points to the existence of a historical current that determines and constricts forms, both in literature and in female clothing. In this poem Stein explores the origin and the arbitrary nature of tradition and the way in which, made compulsory, traditions become oppressive—particularly to women. The poem is composed of seven sentences, the first of which are questions, and in two cases, insistent ones ("what is the wind, what is it"). In the last two sentences, in the same way couplets behave at the end of a Shakespearean sonnet, the lyric voice arrives at a conclusion ("A line distinguishes it. A line just distinguishes it."). It's simple: a border, a frontier, an arbitrary division, a limit which, like the rest of the objects Stein writes about in *Tender Buttons*, is cultural, of a symbolic order, a product of patriarchy.

And it is in making these connections that when the summer's almost over and I'm back in Texas, my second home in the U.S., I feel inspired to produce a new series of collages—visual representations of what I understand Solanas's literary intervention to have actually been about. By making a parody of both the historically gendered assumptions of the manifesto's rhetoric and performative practice (as in the case of Marinetti), and the sexist, androcentric, and heterocentric thinking on gender and sexuality in her time (as in the case of Freud), Solanas's text transgressed gender expectations and mandates regarding her literary production (which, combined with her 1968 shooting of Andy Warhol, an event that projected her into the media spotlight in a way that greatly complicated its reception, condemned her intervention to the damnation of being misread, misinterpreted, and dismissed).

Dressed in what society deemed male-only garments (the rhetoric of modernist male avant-garde manifestos, represented in my collages by designer power suits), Solanas dared make a radical inversion of roles in which the violence of men—brutally disfigured in a subaltern position (something I represent, visually, by the constrictions of feminine clothing and the ludicrously theatrical presentations of female gender performance in *Vogue*'s September 2020 issue)—was meant to fire back at them.

Fig. 1. Lolita Copacabana. *Untitled*, 8.5 × 11 in. 2020. Image courtesy of the author.

Fig. 2. Lolita Copacabana. *Untitled*, 8.5 × 11 in. 2020. Image courtesy of the author.

Fig. 3. Lolita Copacabana. *Untitled*, 8.5 × 11 in. 2020. Image courtesy of the author.

Fig. 4. Lolita Copacabana. *Untitled*, 8.5 × 11 in. 2020. Image courtesy of the author.

AMERICAN FEMINIST SCHOLARS—such as Ann Rosalind Jones in "Writing the Body"—have criticized the positions of French feminists found in their discussions and celebration of the feminine, both in regard to their theoretical inconsistency and their political implications. According to Jones, the turn to *féminité* as a challenge to male-oriented thinking (as proposed by writers like Julia Kristeva, Luce Irigaray, Hélène Cixous, and Monique Wittig) implies that female subjectivity is derived from women's physiology and bodily instincts as they affect sexual experience and the unconscious, and because of this, both theoretical and practical problems arise in connection to them.

According to Jones, *féminité* and *écriture féminine* are problematic concepts, idealist and essentialist in nature. Because gender identity comes into being in response to patriarchal structures, and there is no essential stratum of sexuality unsaturated with social arrangements and symbolic systems, Jones understands French theorists to be "bound up in the very system they claim to undermine," with the result that these concepts thus become "fatal to constructive political action." Although Jones concedes that women's physiology has important meanings for women in various cultures, and that it's important for us to express those meanings rather than to submit to male definitions of sexuality, she doesn't see the female body as a good place from which to launch an attack on the forces that have alienated women from what their sexuality has become, fearing this would put them in an awkward position in relation to earlier theories about women's nature.

In her criticism, Jones cites materialist feminists who, according to her, are also suspicious of the logic through which *féminité* defines men as "phallic, solipsistic, aggressive, excessively rational—and then praises women, who, by nature of their contrasting sexuality, are other-oriented, empathetic, multi-imaginative." Rather than questioning the terms of such a definition (woman is man's opposite), says Jones, *féminité* as a celebration of women's difference from men maintains them. "By reversing the values assigned to each side of the polarity, it still leaves man as the determining referent, not departing from the male-female opposition, but participating in it," she argues. "What we need," says Jones, "is to move outside the male-centered, binary logic altogether."

Psychoanalytic theory is not, as Jones correctly points out, feminist dogma. Psychoanalysis as theory is, as a matter of fact, a much more straightforward instrument—through its clinical applications, for example—for the maintenance of a given social order. Indeed, psychoanalysis is a discipline that (much like, say, anthropology) was not devised as a theory to further social change—and as such is not intrinsically revolutionary but, on the contrary, was created in order to maintain a *very specific* social order. Contrary to many people's belief, though, this does not mean that, in a Foucauldian turn of events, and similarly to many other cultural devices—like syntax, or an AK-47—psychoanalysis cannot be made useful as a set of tools for feminist analysis or other revolutionary endeavors.

As a matter of fact, "as lens and a partial strategy," Jones ends up recognizing, despite her criticism, *féminité* and *l'écriture féminine* are "vital." Certainly, says Jones, "women need to shake off the mistaken and contemptuous attitudes toward their own sexuality that permeate Western . . . cultures and languages at their deepest levels, and working out self-representations that challenge phallocentric discourses is an important part of that ideological struggle." Conventional narrative techniques, as well as grammar and syntax, express the unified viewpoint and mastery of outer reality that men have claimed for themselves, and literary modes and language itself are still—if of course not the sole—important aspects of this transformation.

In this context, as we move toward the thinking and the broadening of women's discourse, we are confronted with conflicting forces and voices that create dilemmas for the woman writer, among them—as Christiane Rochefort points out—the limited availability of forms and themes, which often favor a literature of reaction, of standing against, a literature of outrage. As a literary intervention, it's easy to understand Solanas's *SCUM Manifesto* as just this kind of manifestation. An outraged "examination of the words, the syntax, the genres, the archaic and elitist attitudes toward language and representation that have limited women's self-knowledge and expression during long centuries of patriarchy."

By satirically clothing herself in masculine literary garments, Solanas both ridicules and highlights the phallocentric nature of Western culture as well as the androcentric discourses through which medical and literary disciplinarians have appropriated the world, dominating it through verbal mastery. Much in the fashion of French feminists, Solanas's intervention points out how symbolic discourse is another means through which men get away with objectifying the world, reducing it to their own terms, in ways that are unthinkable for others.

"If women have a role to play . . . it is only in assuming a negative function," says Kristeva, which is why they should "reject everything finite, definite, structured, loaded with meaning in the existing state of society.

Such an attitude places women on the side of the explosion of social codes: with revolutionary movements." In fact, "woman," to Kristeva, Cixous, and other feminist French theorists, represents not so much sex as an attitude, an approach, a means to engage—a subjective position that embodies "a resistance to conventional culture and language," a crucial consideration Jones also points out at the beginning of her article but, after a certain point, engrossed in her argument, simply appears to forget. Indeed, rather than formulating a new discourse, *SCUM* anarchically challenges some existing patriarchal discourses that stand—embracing the liberating potential of her (female and thus) marginal position, as Kristeva posits.

FEW PEOPLE ARE AWARE that Valerie Solanas's most notable intervention was not her only literary output, but that she is the author of two other,
lesser-known works. The first is "A Young Girls' Primer, or How to Attain
the Leisure Class," a nonfictional piece about panhandling and prostitution published in 1966 in the soft-porn magazine *Cavalier*. The other is the
1967 play *Up Your Ass, or, From the Cradle to the Boat, or, The Big Suck, or,
Up from the Slime*, about which she approached Andy Warhol that same
year, looking to obtain his support for a production. When she addressed
him outside his New York studio, The Factory, Warhol accepted her only
manuscript for revision, only to later claim that he had lost it. After refusing
to pay Solanas for the lost manuscript, Warhol jokingly offered her a job as
a typist and later paid her twenty-five dollars to appear in his film *I, a Man*.

In a 2013 paper, through performative writing and drawing on Hélène
Cixous's notion of *écriture féminine*, Desireé Rowe explores how the archival treatment of Solanas's "lost" manuscript of *Up Your Ass* marks her as an
abject body. In it, Rowe recounts the difficulties she faced when attempting to get a copy of the sole manuscript, which for decades had been kept
in the archives of the Andy Warhol Museum in Pittsburgh, Pennsylvania.
She tells the story of how the museum insisted that Rowe first make an
appointment and then show proof of her affiliation with an institution of
higher education, and how subsequently the museum demanded that she
pay eighty dollars an hour for every hour it took archivists to retrieve the
copy of *Up Your Ass*, as well as covering the cost of photocopying and mail-
ing. About how, after agreeing to all this, Rowe had to wait from four to eight
weeks for the Museum to contact her confirming the details and telling her
that, after payment, they would send her a copy of Solanas's script. How
none of this granted her permission to reproduce the script—not even to
quote it. How after learning about these restrictions, which she describes
as "complete bullshit," began the process of historical gatekeeping she had
to negotiate for the following two years of her life.

According to Cixous, *écriture féminine* is a space that can serve as a
springboard for subversive thought and is therefore a preliminary part
of the process of transformation of social and cultural structures. In this
space, writing can be subversive to the degree that it allows women to free
themselves from the self-admiring, self-stimulating, self-congratulatory
phallocentrism that is endemic to the "history of reason," says Rowe, who
subscribes to Cixous's notion that writing can offer a place of solace from
the continued violence that occurs against the bodies of women. For Cixous,

écriture féminine acts as a destabilizing force in texts, where the introduction of instability is radical and creative. The language in which women write has the potential to not only free their individual bodies from the confines of the masculinist discourse but to create a ripple effect in the system of discourse itself.

Alas, Solanas wanted her writing to be read and embodied, says Rowe, "not to disappear in a Warholian lightning trunk." In her exploration of Solanas as a radical feminist, Rowe makes a parallel between the disappearance of *Up Your Ass* and the erasure of the memory of Solanas herself. She says that by losing Solanas's performance text, Warhol perpetuated the scene that Cixous described and in which every woman who attempts to write for a larger public fears: "I am afraid. As a free writer? Worse still: a woman. Yes, I am afraid: afraid of solitude, of hatred and rejection, afraid of being *horribly burnt*"—Solanas, through the rejection of her script (and the subsequent loss) was "horribly burnt," says Rowe. The rejection and fragmentation of Solanas's text is a rejection of Solanas, she says. A rejection of her body and, to take it all a step further—a rejection of her body-as-text.

Fig. 5. Lolita Copacabana. *Untitled*, 8.5 x 11 in. 2022. Image courtesy of the author.

Fig. 6. Lolita Copacabana. *Untitled*, 8.5 × 11 in. 2022. Image courtesy of the author.

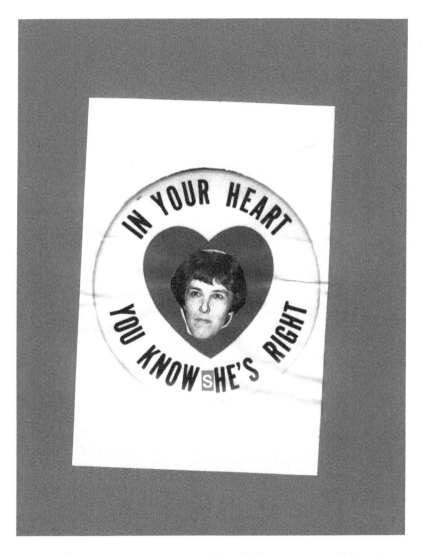

Fig. 7. Lolita Copacabana. *Untitled*, 8.5 × 11 in. 2022. Image courtesy of the author.

Fig. 8. Lolita Copacabana. *Untitled*, 8.5 × 11 in. 2022. Image courtesy of the author.

IN "THE BLEEDING EDGE: On the Necessity of Feminist Manifestos," Breanne Fahs addresses the curiously ubiquitous appearance of the term "manifesto" in our present day, and what appears to be its irksome proliferation in "all the wrong places"—from advertisements and billboards to start-up company slogans and self-help books. Presenting it as something symptomatic of what she deems a "corporate appropriation" of the word, Fahs speaks of this phenomenon as one that seriously undermines and dilutes the potential political impact and significance of this heavily charged genre.

In revising its history, Fahs situates the explosion of feminist manifestos in the period between 1967 and 1971—a period marked by rampant sexism, but also a time of consciousness-raising, collective organizing, and emerging feminist resistance—and links it with the validation of women's anger in the late 1960s, "a cultural zeitgeist moment that recognized women as, finally, fed up and truly *enraged*." According to Fahs, it was this that finally allowed women to push back against cultural dictates regarding politeness and respectability: second wave feminists honored a kind of "sweaty, frothing, high-stakes" feminist anger that translated into rants, scuffles, shouts, and locked arms, igniting a mood that permeated their writing, filling it with a kind of explosive anger that both brought forth many fruit and significantly differentiates from the many "likeable, friendly, and benign ones" we have come to know today.

Fahs's brief analysis of the manifesto's history also addresses the difficulties of creating coherent narratives about documents such as these, which are stubbornly stuck in a continuous present that bears no relevance to the past. Good manifestos know that others in the future will annihilate them too, she highlights. Manifestos are hotheaded, urgent, sweeping, radical, revolutionary thoughts that mark major breaks with traditionalism and its incremental, slow, steady change—their job being to inject, instead, forceful and dramatic claims. But manifestos are not merely performance art, Fahs warns her readers: at their core, "manifestos want to radically upend and subvert public consciousness around disempowerment, giving voice to those stripped of social and political power."

Indeed, the manifesto is a genre that "demands blood," where "words work like bombs," and where authority is performed for the benefit of the people. Its authors—who "often lack social and institutional power but insist on taking it anyway"—demand to be heard, says Fahs, and their readers—"who often feel at once seduced and perhaps assaulted by the text"—are absorbed in the writer's urgent and impatient language. For women, manifestos have, for over the past two hundred years, opened a door to authority, rage, and audiences, no matter how marginal their author. Therefore, to imagine the essential role of feminist manifestos is to situate an "angry, manic, authority-grabbing, insubordinate voice at the center of feminism rather than at it margins," says Fahs.

And this is precisely what I'll be thinking about in a couple of weeks, when the fall semester inaugurates and I'll smile warmly, already fondly, through Zoom, at Arianna Salas, a student in my Writing Fiction course on our first day of classes. A fiery young woman, she will stare at me wide-eyed, mouth slightly ajar, perhaps confused (am I being ironic?) when, after her brief personal introduction to the class—when she says that she has signed up because "she is very angry"—I'll tell her that both her and her anger are very welcome in the classroom. That I'm very much looking forward to their contributions.

I will, no doubt, be thinking about bell hooks and Audre Lorde, too. About hooks's philosophy of the classroom in *Teaching to Transgress*, whose lessons, as an educator, I always keep close to my heart. And about Lorde's keynote presentation at the National Women's Studies Association conference in Storrs, Connecticut, in 1981, on "The Uses of Anger," of course. I will be thinking about my collage at the very beginning of the pandemic and *Todas las formas en las que estoy enojada* and how Lorde, in her presentation, speaks of anger as being her response to racism, and how she had to fight against her fear of her own anger, remaining in silence, trying to ignore it, afraid of its weight, and how that fear had ultimately "taught her nothing." How Lorde speaks about every woman having "a well-stocked arsenal of anger," which could potentially be useful against the oppressions she faces— both personal and institutional—precisely the ones that have brought that anger into being. "Focused with precision," says Lorde, this anger can actually become "a powerful source of energy serving progress and change." "Anger is loaded with information and energy," I will think, as I smile invitingly at Arianna, whose expression will change from confusion to intrigue and perhaps mild excitement as we turn to meet another classmate. And my brain will continue to quote Lorde: "focused with precision, [anger] can become a powerful source of energy serving progress and change."

In her introduction to *Burn It Down*, Fahs speaks about a *feminism of againstness*, one that "values complaint, rage, tension, new forms of solidarity, and radical social change," arguing that we need a feminism "full of outbursts and ill-tempered," full of "fire in its belly." Fahs points out that the feminist manifesto reclaims language, takes back power, decides for itself what words can and cannot injure, allowing "for a real politics of the gutter to emerge" from what Valerie Solanas called "the garbage pail that men have made of the world." At its best, Fahs concludes, the feminist manifesto is "not only a weapon against patriarchy but a weapon against the worst aspects of feminist politics"—as it "refutes liberal tendencies of moderation and incremental, slow, 'wait and be patient' modes of reform." A dictum that seems very resonant indeed to Lorde's words, when she later says: "It is not the anger of other women that will destroy us but our refusal to stand still, to listen to its rhythms, to learn within it, to move beyond the manner of presentation to the substance, to tap that anger as an important source of empowerment."

THE FALL SEMESTER of 2020, the first to be completed during the pandemic, finds me writing about women and anger for a hybrid-genre literature course I'm taking for my second—now bilingual—MFA. I'm living in El Paso, Texas, and—although I love being able to dedicate my time to literature and teaching Creative Writing under the desert sun—I'm still broke, still not allowed to call myself an immigrant, still angry. Still on U.S. soil, too, despite ICE's brutal attempt over the summer to use the COVID crisis as an excuse to kick international students out of the country. Because of the virus, I have not been able to travel back to Argentina during the break, and due to visa restrictions, I am forbidden to produce income, which, combined with the health issues I have been dealing with, has left me completely bankrupt and on the edge of debt. Starting my fourth consecutive year living in America, this "nonresident alien" has to laugh when the elections start and—with the world watching, convulsed by nerves and expectations—an acquaintance from back home (whatever that means, at this stage) naively asks if I'm allowed to participate in them. I know somebody who spent over eleven years in this country as a student and educator, living on a meager wage and paying taxes without any possibility of their civic voice being heard, I answer back, as my eyes rest on yet another green and white Border Patrol truck making its way along the shore of the Rio Grande. Of course I can't vote. I don't even feel comfortable having this discussion on social media. I promised many things, including the fact that I had no intention of staying in this country, when I applied for my F-1 visa, I calmly remind myself.

I'm sitting on my newly installed kitchen counter—the one pandemic investment I made with my now necessary roommate to create more working space at home—when I hear Zoe Leonard's poem for the first time. I'm staring out a big window that faces the I-10, with Ciudad Juárez (Mexico) to my right, the Franklin Mountains to my left, and the mountains of New Mexico—and the setting sun—looking quite spectacular over on the horizon. The view is from the slope of Sunset Heights, the neighborhood where our apartment is located. I'm surrounded by papers, Adrienne Rich, Audre Lorde, and bell hooks, and for some reason—perhaps simply for inspiration, or perhaps because I'm burnt out—I'm watching for the *n*th time Martha Rosler's 1975 *Semiotics of the Kitchen* video performance. In it, a young Rosler recites alphabetically a list of kitchen instruments and appliances, with a mostly neutral facial expression, while she mimics, energetically and with a vague air of intended promotion or instructional exhibition, a proposed used for each the items she displays. The whole video is under seven minutes long and built around a single zoom-out at the end. Dead-pan comedy, New-York style, amidst what looks like a strange set, midway between an artist's loft and a television studio reminiscent of that of stars like Julia Child—also meant to evoke late-night commercials of the Ginsu knife variety, I presume—I stare at this strange woman doing strange things. I wonder about her odd composure. How the stabbing of her fork, her ice pick, and her knife seem to contain both a resigned, matter-of-fact calmness, and also the edges of a contained anger, the spasms of a confident internal force. I'm thinking vaguely about my best friend's favorite T-shirt, too—a simple white cotton garment with red block letters that spell "Kitchen table press"—when I open her email. It's barely a link, and the subject reads: "I Want a Dyke for President."

It's Leonard's poem. I hear it once, I hear it twice, and then I settle into playing the poem full blast in my headphones until I've almost memorized it. Later, I recite it with a little dance while I prepare dinner and then, over quinoa soup and leftover broccoli, tell my roommate all about it. How it was conceived as a response to Eileen Myles's 1992 presidential candidacy, which in turn was a reaction to a commencement address delivered by George H. Bush in Ann Arbor, Michigan, an address in which he'd attacked what he'd called "the notion of 'political correctness,'" saying that it had led to "inquisition, censorship and bullying" on some college campuses. I show them the digital version of a *New York Times* article from back then: Bush was alluding to a Brown University student who had been expelled for shouting racist slurs, and to two City College faculty members who had recently been rebuked for comments about racial superiority. I tell them about the case of a sophomore at Connecticut who had been ordered to move off campus after posting a sign on her dorm room that had made fun of "preppies," "bimbos," "men without chest hair," and "homos." I show them pictures of Eileen Myles: outdoors, with a big wide smile, crouched over a pile of dirt in ripped jeans, cheekily playing with the stick a distracted dog clenches in the left side of its jaw.

I tell my roommate about how in 1992 Myles, a poet, ran as an "openly female"—and openly gay—write-in candidate. I tell them how that year she wrote letters to everyone in her list asking for donations for mailings and buttons, how she declared she was opposed to the special treatment that this country reserved for white, upper-middle-class, heterosexual men and their spouses and children, how she said she was against special treatment for fundamentalist Christians and . . . fetuses. How she decided to use every event she was invited to participate in—from coffeeshop readings to panel discussions and memorials—as a campaign opportunity. All about her "An American Poem," too, the one in which the speaker is a secret Kennedy who's also a lesbian poet. About the letters she wrote to her supporters, and about the final one of them, in which she discusses fair trade, labor laws, and the Mall of America, where "millions of people seem to worship a cartoon dog." I read them the last paragraph of that moving letter, too—there, when Myles talks about the election booth and says it's dirty "like a peephole or a dressing room and a confession," and urges prospective voters to exercise their freedom by writing down her name in the empty white space that will appear before them, "empty as poetry," empty as their freedom of speech.

I want a dyke for president too, says my roommate, as they stretch their arms way back on our beautiful and sturdy beige Salvation Army flowered couch. It's the night before the final day of the elections, and I smile because, as opposed to me, they can (and will) actually vote. Although there's air conditioning in the desert, we have practically no heating in the apartment, and I hold my hot water bottle like a baby, close to my heart. Valerie Solanas for President of the USA, I murmur. What? My roommate asks. I said, *Valerie Solanas for President of the USA*. It's the name of a play, I say. Sara Stridsberg, a Swedish playwright, wrote it. I've been trying to get a hold of it, but it's only been translated into French, and the only available copies all seem to be over sixty dollars. My roommate gets that look on their face, the special glint in their eyes I'm already learning to love. Solanas was raped by her dad and her grandfather, you know? They know. She was a homeless person and a prostitute and a PhD student, too. They nod. Standing up quickly, they look like a deranged, over-caffeinated version of Elliot Page— saying, well *that's* a button I'd like to have.

We spend the rest of the evening frantically working on a new set of collages. By two a.m., the whole room is sticky, covered in multicolored confetti. Our bodies are stiff, and we're moderately drunk, our giggles excited, a little manic. My roommate stands in the middle of it all holding a pair of beanies and two heavy coats, an unnecessarily dramatic flashlight sticking out of their left pocket. An extra thick ring of silver duct tape hangs from their wrist as a bracelet. Come on, they say, behind that piercing glint, that excruciatingly teasing grin. They make a roll out of our fresh collages like a newspaper, like the cinnamon buns we got from the food pantry and saved for breakfast. Our bikes are waiting, they say. The sun will be out in just over three hours, and we must paint the town anew. Get up, get up, they say, waving their hands with impatience. Come on, come on, come on. No time to lose.

Lolita Copacabana is a writer, editor, and translator from Buenos Aires, Argentina. In 2017, the Hay Festival included them in *Bogotá 39*, a list of the best Latin American authors under forty. They have an MFA from the University of Iowa and are the author of *Buena Leche* and *Aleksandr Solzhenitsyn*. They live in El Paso, Texas. They can be reached at justlola@gmail.com.

Works Cited

Boyer, Anne. 2015. *Garments Against Women*. Boise, ID: Ahsahta Press.

Fahs, Breanne. 2020. *Burn It Down! Feminist Manifestos for the Revolution*. Brooklyn, NY: Verso.

hooks, bell. 1996. *Teaching to Transgress: Education as the Practice of Freedom*. New York: Routledge.

Jones, Ann Rosalind. 1981. "Writing the Body: Toward an Understanding of 'L'Ecriture Feminine.'" *Feminist Studies* 7, no. 2: 247–63. https://doi.org/10.2307/3177523.

Leonard, Zoe. 2017. *I Want a President*. Mexico City: Gato Negro Ediciones.

Lorde, Audre. 2007. "The Uses of Anger: Women Responding to Racism." In *Sister Outsider: Essays and Speeches*, 124–33. New York: Ten Speed Press.

Lusty, Natalya. 2009. "Valerie Solanas and the Limits of Speech." *Australian Literary Studies* 24, nos. 3/4: 144–54.

Marinetti, Filippo T. 2001. "The Founding and Manifesto of Futurism." In *Manifesto: A Century of Isms*, edited by Mary Ann Caws, 185–89. Lincoln: University of Nebraska Press.

Myles, Eileen. 2002. "An American Poem." Poetry Foundation. https://www.poetryfoundation.org/poems/53965/an-american-poem.

Kristeva, Julia. "1974. In *New French Feminisms: An Anthology*, edited by Elaine Marks and Isabelle De Courtivron, 166–67. New York: Schocken Books.

Rochefort, Christiane. 1975. In *New French Feminisms: An Anthology*, edited by Elaine Marks and Isabelle De Courtivron, 211–15. New York: Schocken Books.

Rosler, Martha. 2003. *Semiotics of the Kitchen*. Chicago, IL: Video Data Bank.

Rowe, Desirée D. 2013. "The (Dis)appearance of *Up Your Ass*: Valerie Solanas as Abject Revolutionary." *Rethinking History* 17, no. 1: 74–81.

Solanas, Valerie. 2004. *SCUM Manifesto*. London: Verso.

Stein, Gertrude. 1997. *Tender Buttons: Objects, Food, Rooms.* Mineola, NY: Dover Publications.

Stridsberg, Sara, and Jean-Baptiste Coursaud. 2010. *Valerie Jean Solanas va devenir Présidente de L'Amérique: Théâtre.* Paris: Stock.

Woods, Chavisa. 2019. "Hating Valerie Solanas (And Loving Violent Men)." *Full Stop*, May 21, 2019. www.full-stop.net/2019/05/21/features/chavisa-woods/solanas.

PART II. **EDUCATION**

Women's Studies and Its Institutionalization as an Interdisciplinary Field: Past, Present, and Future

L. Ayu Saraswati and Barbara L. Shaw

Abstract: To celebrate the fiftieth anniversary of *WSQ*, this article offers a snapshot of the history of women's studies (WS), one that establishes it as an interdisciplinary field alongside Black studies and ethnic studies. It also provides a roundtable among scholars who were integral to the formation of a PhD in WS program, strategies for small undergraduate departments and programs in an era of consolidation and elimination, and a call to reenvision the field's purpose. In addition to arguing for solidarity and collaboration between women's, gender, sexuality, and feminist (W/G/S/F), Black studies, and ethnic studies, it asks scholars-teachers to reimagine its curricula and research and writing practices as a method of un-disciplining. This is not a simple return to its roots though its history matters in addressing the pressing social justice concerns of the twenty-first century. **Keywords:** history of women's studies, Black studies, and ethnic studies; field formation; social movement roots; neoliberal challenges; future transformations

Anniversaries are often considered a time to celebrate and reflect. For this fiftieth anniversary of *WSQ*, we want to do both. We want to celebrate how far women's studies (WS) in the United States has come and reflect on the challenges that we have (yet to) overcome.[1] We thus offer a snapshot of the history of WS, one that establishes it as an interdisciplinary field alongside Black studies and ethnic studies programs specifically. We construct this history by consulting published materials and by interviewing three professors in WS (now women, gender, and sexuality studies—WGSS) at the University of Maryland (UMD), College Park, who were there during the formation of the WS PhD program. We focus on UMD because we hope to

WSQ: Women's Studies Quarterly 50: 3 & 4 (Fall/Winter 2022) © 2022 by L. Ayu Saraswati and Barbara L. Shaw.
All rights reserved.

zoom in on a WS department and PhD program whose formation is tied to race studies. UMD has also been one of the public institutions that has been at the vanguard of graduate education in WS in the United States. Moreover, UMD is where the coauthors received their PhDs (Saraswati received hers in WS; Shaw received hers in American Studies and a graduate certificate in WS). Reflecting on the history of the WS PhD at UMD functions as a lens through which we can better grasp the field's formation in higher education, and its role as a part of a larger story-memory of WS as a field.

To offer a fuller picture of the evolution of WS in academia, the article next addresses the struggles that Shaw and her colleagues are currently experiencing in sustaining an academic unit at a private small liberal arts college (SLAC). Shaw also offers strategies that respond to particular neoliberal challenges facing tuition-dependent undergraduate institutions. Shaw is currently the director of Interdisciplinary Studies, co-chair of Women's, Gender and Sexuality Studies (WGSS), and the interim coordinator of Black Studies at Allegheny College.

Looking closely at the earliest history of WS, the past formation of the WS PhD, and the present struggles of a small undergraduate program is meant to document the wide-ranging journey that WS has taken as a field and how its institutionalization is connected to and has diverged from that of Black studies and ethnic studies. These conversations are also offered to provide some preliminary thoughts about possible future directions that we may take if we are to continue to exist, grow, and thrive. If the past fifty years have allowed WS to shape academia, what can we do so that in the next fifty years it remains relevant and significant and can even revolutionize higher education to be more transgressive, progressive, and social justice–oriented? Black studies, ethnic studies, and WS have questioned how knowledge is produced and who has the power to tell these stories. In doing so, Black studies emerged as an interdisciplinary field unapologetically focused on the social constructions of racial formations and the power ascribed to race in the U.S. Interdisciplinarity and analyzing the interlocking systems of power that are reflected in gender, race, class, sexuality, nationality, and dis/ability have become the foundations of women's/gender/sexuality/feminist studies (W/G/S/F) and distinguishes the field. But as this article cautiously asks, will our theoretical approaches embedded in intersectionality and transnationalism discipline and deliver us to our death-by-institution?

Roots and Routes

In the last three to four decades, WS scholar-teacher-activists have questioned the field's objects of study, asking self-reflexively: "What is the subject of Women's Studies? How does Women's Studies negotiate the politics of alliance and the politics of difference? How can Women's Studies fulfill its promise of interdisciplinarity? What is the continuing place of activism in women's studies? And . . . how has feminist pedagogy responded to changing social conditions?" (Guy-Sheftall 2008, 103). These questions have led to multiple iterations of academic programs' names and curricular emphases (Bhatt 2020; Wiegman 2012). These are also the questions that guide our conversation in this article.

Acknowledging our diverse approaches, overall, the field has grown exponentially. According to Guy-Sheftall, there are more than nine hundred undergraduate W/G/S/F programs, over ten thousand courses (which often are full, with pressures to add more students), an international presence, and over twenty-two programs that offer W/G/S/F doctoral degrees (Guy-Sheftall 2020). Fifty years after its establishment in academia (e.g., through classes, programs, and departments, as well as academic journals such as *WSQ*), this data certainly is impressive and important. It is imperative, however, that we celebrate the field's growth while emphasizing that its formation has been articulated alongside other programs like Black studies and ethnic studies, which we will focus on in this article.

While the organization of the first WS program at San Diego State University in 1969–70 marks a significant milestone, it is not the beginning of the story, and as Clare Hemmings (2011) argues, how we tell our stories—whether it is about feminist theory or the beginnings of the field—matters. Acknowledging the tireless work of named and unnamed feminists, abolitionists, and labor and anti-war activists throughout the nineteenth and twentieth centuries, the institutional foundations of contemporary W/G/S/F academic units grew out of mid-twentieth century social movements. This narrative is well told in journals and books that have sought to build an archive and anchor the importance of WS in higher education (Ginsberg 2008; Guy-Sheftall 2020; Guy-Sheftall and Heath 1995; Howe and Bhule 2000; Messer-Davidow 2002; Wiegman 2002, 2012; Shane 2020). In *Women's Studies: A Retrospective*, Beverly Guy Sheftall (1995) carefully traces the history of WS by naming the civil rights movement and the emergence of Black studies in 1968–69 as pivotal for the field. And in turn, Noliwe Rooks's extensive research into the genesis of Black studies in *White Money/Black Power* points to two things that had an effect in laying the groundwork for the field: "First, during the period, students offered a profound critique of society's handling of racial exclusion, and second the broad participation of white and brown college students in demands for an end to elitist and Eurocentric higher education was widespread" (2006, 4). As Rooks explains, while the first is well told, the second disrupts oversimplified narratives of singular struggle. By 1968, a coalition of student groups culminated their organizing efforts with a five-month strike, demanding "equal access to public higher education, more faculty of color, and a new curriculum that would embrace the history and culture of all people including ethnic minorities" (Diaz n.d.). How things change is how they remain the same: all three of these interventions remain critical and important to transform higher education into the space it purports to be.

The emergence of Black studies at San Francisco State in 1968–69 was the spark that would ignite the exponential growth of Black studies, women's studies, and ethnic studies programs over the next decade. While this story captured national headlines, in the years preceding any program development, small groups of named pioneers and unnamed faculty (often adjunct and tenure-track) banded together to disrupt the "knowledge economy" of disciplines to offer individual classes on topics such as women and literature or Black history (Messer-Davidow 2002, 20). These were the foundations, and collectively the little-known stories show us how students and faculty worked in solidarity to demand changes to curricula and practices in higher education as well as to build grassroots programming. As Rachel Corbman explores in her work, WS field formations did not occur exclusively on college and university campuses. Conferences were places where scholar-student-activists actively engaged in contesting and broadening the contours of WS by "literally generat[ing] discourse" that attended to "racial politics and gender, sexuality, and LGBTQ+ identities" (Corbman 2019, 2–3). Key publications, such as Audre Lorde's *Sister Outsider* (1984) and Moraga and Anzaldúa's *This Bridge Called My Back* (1983) also emerged to shape the field.

Black studies, ethnic studies, and WS programs emerged alongside one another facing similar yet different institutional obstacles with their focus on race, gender, ethnicity, and class formations. Scholar-teacher-activists in each of these fields were warned their work was "only political," their contributions would be "ignor[ed] as an academic area of study," and their careers in higher education would suffer (Moses 2000, 319). Undeterred, faculty forged ahead, creating discrete fields of study. With specific reference to inaugural WS programs, Guy-Sheftall in her introduction to *Persistence Is Resistance: 50 Years of Gender, Women & Sexuality Studies* (Shane 2020) names the 1970s as a decade for growing stand-alone programs, and the 1980s as the decade of "'mainstreaming' Women's Studies throughout established curriculum" and the one during which "women of color began to critique both Women's Studies and gender focused curriculum for their relative lack of attention to questions of race, ethnicity, class and cultural difference" (Guy-Sheftall 2002). Forty years later, the many early critiques of WS remain critical to organizing its institutionalization (Blea 1992; Crenshaw 1989; Davis 1981; García 1997; Guy-Sheftall 2008; hooks 1981; Hull, Bell-Scott, and Smith 1993; James et al. 2009; Lorde 1984; Moraga and Anzaldúa 1983).

Establishing a Women's Studies PhD Program: Reflecting on Past Struggles

The growth of WS as a field and discipline within academia is reflected and cemented through the creation of W/G/S/F doctoral programs across the country. The University of Maryland, College Park, enrolled their first five WS PhD students in fall 2000; Saraswati was part of that first cohort. In this section, Saraswati invites three WS UMD professors, who were there to build the program, to reflect on their triumphs and struggles: Claire Moses, who at the time was the chair and graduate chair of the WS department, A. Lynn Bolles, and Ruth Enid Zambrana.[2] This conversation is intended to help us better understand the conditions that made it possible for such a doctoral program to be established at that historical juncture and to be established as intersectional, interdisciplinary, and (to a certain extent) international from its very inception.

> **Ayu Saraswati (AS):** First of all, I want to thank all of you for your willingness to reflect back on the history of the PhD program in WS at UMD. These reflections will help us contextualize the emergence of WS as a field, and as a(n) (inter-)discipline that is built in conversation with other programs, like race/ethnic studies programs, and with activism around these intersectional issues. To start our conversation, could you please share with us how the PhD in WS program at UMD was approved? Were there any challenges that you experienced?

Claire Moses (CM): By the time we proposed a PhD in WS, the ground-work had been carefully laid. The hardest battles were all fought years/decades before: the challenges of getting an initial certificate with a director and one department faculty; the challenges of getting the dean's approval for three tenure-track faculty; the challenges that our department faced in competition for the additional hiring of women and persons of color that were available to all departments in the entire university; the challenges of adding a graduate certificate to the under-graduate program; the challenge—once we had a core faculty tenured in the department of about six—of asking that we be recognized as a department (rather than a program); followed by the establishment of a BA, followed several years later by the MA and PhD.

Interestingly, the challenges were greatest for the earliest proposals. In contrast, the opposition to the PhD was quite limited. The university was obviously changing over the twenty years of our evolution—with more and more supporters, especially among administrators, over these years understanding and agreeing with feminist goals and understand-ing the connection to the study of women. It also helped that most of our new faculty were hired at the senior level and had high intellectual achievements. That our faculty were individually so well respected—their reputations were a real plus.

Remembering the challenges in the early years—through the time of the proposed BA—the most memorable opposition statement was "Women's studies? What will we have next: dog studies?" But by the time our proposal for a PhD went to the faculty Senate for approval, the number of feminist faculty affiliated with our department and the campus-wide respect for our department far outweighed the opposition.

AS: What you said is really important, Claire. It helps me frame the struggles that we're currently experiencing. Last year, we proposed to have a master's degree at our university, but it was rejected. They cited the pandemic and budget issues as the reason. But what you said made me realize that we first need to build solid institutional support to be able to do this.

What about you, Ruth? How do you remember the creation of our PhD program?

Ruth Enid Zambrana (REZ): I was hired in 1999 by Professor Claire

Moses. She was thrilled to have me help her present the PhD proposal ready for Senate approval. She shared with me the WS history of development, from being in a trailer as an office to moving to Woods Hall; the importance of developing scholars in the interdisciplinary field of WS to open new doors for women academics; unveiling key gender issues in the public discourse; introducing new and more inclusive ways of thinking, such as intersectionality and inclusion in history; and engaging in change and social justice for women and underrepresented minorities. She instructed me on all the nuances of our department's growth and the field of WS so I could support and assist in presenting the rationale for the PhD program in the Senate along with Bonnie [Thornton Dill] and others. It was a powerful performance by the faculty, and it was approved without much revision.

Lynn Bolles (LB): Getting the PhD approved was a collaboration among the women, and a few men, who were part of the WS certificate and morphed into the PhD-builders. I remember we had lots of meetings. At that time, it was with Clark (doesn't exist now) and Emory.

AS: I think what Lynn said about collaborating with other universities holds true even to today. The National Women's Studies Association (NWSA) holds a preconference for WS administrators, chairs, and directors so they can work together, as part of their annual conference. And last year, when I was chair of my department and we had experienced a bit of backlash when our BA program was recommended to be offered as part of an interdisciplinary studies major, I reached out to several WS departments, including UMD, to ask for advice. Everyone showed up and provided me with convincing data and strong support. We were able to ride out that storm.

I want to return to what Ruth mentioned earlier, that the program was imagined to be intersectional and interdisciplinary from the very beginning. Could you speak more about this?

REZ: Claire had a powerful vision of a field that would blend the humanities and the social sciences. . . . The curriculum drew both from the humanities and equally from the social sciences. The faculty was about 50 percent humanities scholars and 50 percent social scientists. . . . Bonnie [Thornton] Dill built on that force and infused the teaching and curriculum with intersectionality. Black feminist thought and social justice activism were also integrated into our intellectual community.

CM: The very early efforts to establish WS date to the early 1970s and were spearheaded by the few feminist faculty members who existed in a number of different departments. But it was their feminism and the model of recently established Black studies programs that inspired them. It was definitely intended to be interdisciplinary, but with a meaning that appears lost today. The mission of early WS was to transform the structure of the university and break the powerful department borders that secured the disciplines. Establishing a "program" that brought together faculty from multiple departments and creating a new whole was radical in its time; there really existed nothing like that at that time. Over time, much changed: the core grew and brought in its own faculty from multiple disciplines, and we never had control over hiring in the other departments and as a result, some WS-affiliated faculty left and were not replaced. The radical antidepartment structure reverted to the established practice as we ultimately became a department. For many years, however, our department was interdisciplinary only so far as it included faculty whose research derived from different disciplines. The true creation of interdisciplinarity can really be dated to the establishment of the PhD and its truly interdisciplinary curriculum, and our training them to merge multiple disciplines in the research of the individual students.

The evolution of intersectionality is different. First of all, none of us used the term "intersectional" for decades. There were articles included in the earliest feminist anthologies (e.g., *Liberation Now*) that were written by Black women in the Welfare Rights Movement and a Black women's reproductive rights group in New Rochelle, NY, that I was able to use—mostly with the intent of being inclusive of Black women's experiences (after all, I had been active in the civil rights movement in the 1960s—most feminists of my generation had been). And there was some good writing to explain the split between Black radical women and the white-dominated feminist movement. (It was more white-dominated in the 1970s, by the way, than in the 1960s: just look at the racial diversity of the founders of NOW in 1966.) Being "inclusive," however, was not quite the same thing as placing race (along with women) in the founding of WS. "Women" and sexism were the founding of WS—and even early theoretical articles on "double jeopardy" saw feminism and racism as two separate forms of oppression.

The first important article that was theoretical (rather than a description of a particular Black women's activism) was in the mid- to late 1970s: the Combahee River Collective article. The word "intersectional" was never used in that statement, but once the word came into existence, we could look back to it and see how the concept of intersectionality (although never named as such) was embedded there. Also, before the word "intersectional" was used, Bonnie [Thornton Dill] wrote an article calling for a new feminist activism and used the term "multiracial feminism." (Her earlier Center, which she had founded at Memphis State before coming to Maryland, was another example of her "multiracial feminism.") The word "intersectional," when it finally came into usage, always carried two meanings: the understanding of social construction of persons as a merging of multiple forms of identity that could not be separated out—in other words, intertwined rather than side-by-side oppressions. Bonnie Dill's term "multiracial feminism" was also absorbed into the new terminology, as "intersectional" was sometimes used for an activism that would address all forms of oppression in tandem with other social movements beyond the women's movement. (I cannot remember if intersectional was already used in the spate of articles and anthologies that flowed from the Anita Hill debacle—but the concept was certainly spelled out in all.) And by the late 1990s, the term "intersectional" was consistently used within WS scholarship (and beyond).

LB: Don't forget that we wanted to make a program that was interdisciplinary that reflected an international reality. We wanted graduate students to understand that WS and gender and women's studies was not a leftover-from-woman's-lib gesture but a more inclusive one.

REZ: That's right. Debby Rosenfelt also mounted a wonderful WS summer curriculum to teach women in the U.S. and internationally about WS and intersectionality and its applications within different disciplines. The faculty developed a sense of community commitment through the annual summer institute.

AS: I remember the summer institute! I loved being the graduate assistant for that program!

All of you mentioned the focus on race, and how it was crucial in establishing the PhD program. Congratulations, by the way, on the new department name! I feel the new name, the "Harriet Tubman Department of Women, Gender, and Sexuality Studies" truly reflects the long-time commitment of the department that focuses on the importance of race—the intersectionality of race and gender. Not many WS departments in the world offer a "Black women's studies" minor, but you have been offering that as a joint program with African American studies since 2005! On your website, the department states that this name change is driven by your department's desire to "live up to Tubman's legacy" and her "commitment to women's rights and universal suffrage," as well as to reflect your "ongoing practices of challenging racism and gender-based discrimination in our teaching, research, and service. And it marks our understanding that our role as educators is not only to award degrees and credentials but to facilitate individual and collective transformation." I really admire that. Congratulations!

One of the PhD program's four major fields is indeed called "Gender, Race, Racialization, and/or Diaspora Studies" (or, on the department's website, it is listed as "Race and Racialization, Ethnic and Diasporic Studies, Black Feminist Thought and Intersectionality"). This was my major field! I believe that the program's focus on race and racialization had a significant impact on me. I remember that when I applied to the program, I wrote that I wanted to study how the United Nations shapes the women's movement agenda in Indonesia. But then, after taking Bonnie's class, WMST 611: Power, Gender, and the Spectrum of Difference, I became intrigued by skin-whitening practices in Indonesia as a perfect site to analyze the intersectionality of race, gender, skin color, and beauty ideals. I ended up writing a dissertation and book on that topic. I feel that, had the WS program at UMD not been built in articulation with race and racial formation studies, I would not have shifted my focus to race, racialization, and racial formation in my research.

REZ: That makes sense. The department in developing the PhD program laid the foundation for its own birth, so to speak, in race and racial formation, history, and intersectionality, and with a strong humanities and social science interdisciplinary mix. . . . Bonnie was asked by Dr. Kirwan [president of UMD] to launch the Consortium on Race, Gender, and Ethnicity (CRGE) in 1999, and I joined her. Bonnie obtained funding for the CRGE Interdisciplinary Scholars Program (CRiSP), where many WS students were trained on intersectionality. I do not remember how many students were funded by CRGE, but it was between eight and ten.

LB: If anything, what made our program so attractive to those who applied was the faculty members who illustrated the importance of racial identity, which was embodied not as a part of personhood but as an intellectual challenge in the kinds of work we were doing.

AS: That's true.

If I can go back to what Claire mentioned earlier, I want to highlight how the evolutions of interdisciplinarity and intersectionality that help us understand the evolution of WS as a field chart the moments when both practices (interdisciplinarity and intersectionality) have become the tools both *to* discipline and to define it *as* a discipline. What I mean by this is that at UMD, as part of its PhD in WS curriculum, students are asked to write "the second-year interdisciplinary paper." Because all students have to write this interdisciplinary paper, interdisciplinarity becomes a tool to "discipline" WS students. Of course, for me, if it weren't because of this training, I would not have been an interdisciplinary scholar. I am grateful for this.

But I think Claire is right that interdisciplinarity has and can become another method to produce knowledge but has lost its power to further dismantle "the master's house." WS is on track to become a discipline that produces theories and scholars who are absorbed into the increasingly neoliberalized university and institution, rather than being a force that disrupts it and demands that the institution be more social justice–oriented. The methods and practices that were once imagined to revolutionize higher education may bring our feminist activist and social justice goals to an end. This worries me.

REZ: But we also need to remember that our department has also been engaged in a lot of movements and reshuffling, and in a process of anchoring its strengths to redefine itself. It is my expectation that WGSS will retain a commitment to interdisciplinarity and find its communal strengths across subdisciplines so as to define its unique positionality as a department and in the larger scholarly and social justice world of gender, women, and sexuality studies.

AS: What a wonderful and hopeful note to end our conversation! Thank you!

Building and Sustaining a Small Program in a Small Place

The roundtable conversation in the previous section provokes this question: How does the fear of W/G/S/F being absorbed into the administration of the neoliberal university play out in the present moment? In this section, Shaw explores this question by focusing on the recent challenges and practices of the WGSS program at her small liberal arts college (SLAC).

In 2009, when Shaw arrived as a visiting assistant professor at Allegheny College, WS had successfully turned a joint appointment into a line for the program, doing the hard, political work of solidifying its place on a small campus. It had become a major in the mid-1980s with a steering committee of dedicated feminist and queer faculty from across campus, and in the decade that Shaw has been there, the WS faculty line became a tenure-track position (and Shaw was awarded tenure), WS changed its name and curriculum to WGSS following a self-study, and most recently, it was named a department.

For all practical purposes, WGSS is successful—or at least successfully institutionalized—and the faculty and students maintain the field's social justice roots within their classrooms. As a small program at a small college, our struggles resemble the ones that Guy-Sheftall articulated in 2008: despite growth, "women's studies is still institutionally fragile . . . they also have inadequate budgets and very little control over their curriculum because they depend on departmental courses and joint appointments . . . [and] in recent years [have faced] a tremendous backlash and tightening of resources" (110). With and despite these structural constraints, WGSS at Allegheny College has built strong faculty affiliations and curricular connections across campus and continues to work collaboratively with students and alumni.

Allegheny College is a predominantly white institution (PWI), a rural private SLAC that is a part of the Great Lakes College Association (GLCA). Similar to many of the thirteen colleges in the consortium, it is tuition-dependent, with a relatively small but growing endowment that faces a series of financial challenges in the midst of a pandemic, political challenges to the worth of a liberal arts education, and demographic changes. Its central mission has been to make accessible a solid liberal arts education to first-generation and middle-income students regionally and nationally. While entering classes have varied over the years, roughly one-third of the student body is first-generation or low(er) income and receives substantial financial support through Pell Grants and college scholarships. Academically, every student is asked to major in a program in the humanities, social sciences, or sciences and minor in another division, as well as complete an independent senior thesis with a two-member faculty board. Interdivisional programs such as WGSS, Black studies, and community and justice studies—all programs that share some of their course offerings and live in between the humanities and social sciences—may be combined with any major or minor. While WGSS enrollments in both the major and minor have been up and down over the years and often correlate to the emergence of new programs, the minors have been consistently high (ranging from seventeen to forty-five). The same has not been true for Black studies and what was previously called LGBT studies (both minors).

Metrics are our inheritance from the neoliberalization of colleges and universities, and our academic program's existence is tied to "data-driven" administrative decisions. In an era defined by Trumpism that denigrates higher education and seeks to ban books (knowledge) and eliminate W/G/S/F studies, Black studies and critical race theory, and ethnic studies, administrative bodies are making calculations about what current middle school and high school students (and their parents or guardians) will want to pursue and pay for, while striving to maintain a robust liberal arts education. The NWSA's chairs meeting and preconference for chairs are some of its most crowded sessions, as we collectively address what is working for (small) programs to stay afloat, how W/G/S/F programs can get in front of consolidations and elimination, and how to be strategic within and not just struggle against administrative vision. All this casts the dye for the field to be disciplined (in the Foucauldian sense) *because* our existence and survival are inherently tied to what Dean Spade (2015) has named administrative violence.

Knowing that quantitative metrics matter, WGSS faculty at Allegheny College have strengthened their program in four substantive ways while providing students the curriculum and space to explore the revolutionary roots and routes within WGSS, queer studies, Black studies, trans studies, and disability studies. One way of doing this was to combine the WS and LGBT minor in 2014, with the respective steering committees agreeing that this would provide the best support for queer studies and its students on a small, rural campus. With few students enrolled in the LGBT minor across many years, it faced elimination. Now, many students, including students of color who want to study or self-identify as queer, gay, lesbian, bi/pansexual, nonbinary, genderqueer, and trans, have found homespace in WGSS, Black studies, and community and justice studies.

A second way the WGSS program at Allegheny has strengthened itself has been to embed its classes in distribution requirements and robustly enrolled programs (such as global health studies, environmental science and sustainability, and international studies). The third way has been by building shared required classes between Black studies and WGSS (e.g., Black Feminist Thought) and, hopefully soon, sharing their upper-level seminar requirement with social justice–oriented programs. And finally, WGSS at Allegheny has built solidarities, written grants, facilitated curricular institutes to share resources, and built a network with W/G/S/F programs throughout the GLCA.

With the downsizing of some institutions, as well as the retirement of many of the founding faculty, small programs in small places face similar struggles—as well as possibilities—as larger institutions (though on a different scale). Connections, evolutions, affiliations, and solidarities have the potential to keep small W/G/S/F departments and programs from being fully consolidated or eliminated and may strengthen their antiracist and social justice offerings. In doing research for this piece, we are profoundly struck by how some of our contemporary concerns—such as maintaining and growing tenure-track lines and curricular offerings, as well as retaining queer and trans faculty and faculty of color—echo those expressed by faculty working to secure WS forty to fifty years ago. In addition to sustained structural constraints, it seems what is missing in our contemporary moment is renewed student activism that can once again stand shoulder to shoulder with faculty to insist on the centrality of social justice programs *regardless of* enrollments and administrative metrics because W/G/S/F, Black studies, and ethnic studies are integral to a twenty-first-century liberal arts education (Cole 2004).

By Way of Conclusion: From Predicament to Prediction

Thus far, we have laid out some of the predicaments and past and present struggles revolving around the institutionalization of W/G/S/F within higher education. This conversation would not be complete without contemplating the possible futures of the field.

W/G/S/F has been built on interdisciplinarity and intersectionality. Conversations with the professors at the University of Maryland, College Park, provide us with history and evidence for how the WS doctoral program was created with these as foundations and with the goal of transforming the university structure and curricula. Since then, we have continued to expand and grow as a field in small and large institutions, even as we experience some challenges. We have been successful in teaching sought-after courses that are part of the broader university curriculum (sometimes fulfilling university foundation or distribution requirements) and, as faculty members, serving on undergraduate and graduate students' thesis or dissertation committees in other fields. Taken together, these are remarkable achievements, as they allow us to shape the kinds of work that students do and pursue after graduation, even when they do not major or minor in W/G/S/F.

However, we want to assert that although intersectionality, interdisciplinarity, and, later, transnationalism have defined the field, these interventions are no longer enough. We need more transformative and transgressive methods and theories that can revolutionize institutions of higher education. Thus far, we have been successful in producing works that employ different and multiple disciplinary methods, making them converse with each other—the "inter-" in *inter*disciplinary. This certainly deserves a celebration, as we are able to challenge traditional boundaries. However, it then creates new ways of disciplining our scholarship. Our interdisciplinary work begins to look a lot like that produced in traditional disciplines. Certainly, producing intellectual work that is legible and acceptable for promotion and tenure is necessary if we are to continue to exist in academia, and citing feminist, queer, trans, and disabled scholars and scholars of color is a critically important and political intervention in scholarship. It is also time that we return to how and why WS, Black studies, and ethnic studies were established in the first place, which was—as Moses, Rooks, and Guy-Sheftall have reminded us—to dismantle the master's house of disciplinary boundaries and university structure.

We also need to remember that the longer W/G/S/F is part of the institution, the more pressures we face to fulfill the parameters of "success" that the university has set for us. This often necessitates translating our success into quantifiable measures of the number of majors, the number of student semester hours or enrollments in classes, the percentage of students scoring tenure-track and other prestigious positions, and other administrative metrics. The stronger we feel the need to discipline ourselves and our students to measure up to the university standards of success, the more W/G/S/F evolves to be just another discipline within the neoliberal university. This is what is hurting us. We need to remember that the field is not simply striving to be departmentalized; it is part of a movement that is in solidarity with many other social movements (Wiegman 2012).

If we agree that we need to keep W/G/S/F tied to being an agent for social change, then, what needs to change? Certainly, we would like to frame this question as an invitation for *all of us* to come up with ideas, rather than a gateway to prescribing what to do. For us, the preliminary and first step involves poking at the disciplinary boundaries and thinking about other ways of doing and disseminating research. For instance, rather than doing interdisciplinary work by simply incorporating two or more different methods (e.g., interviews and archival research), can we transform each of the methods simultaneously? Can we conduct interviews by incorporating the body into the research? An example of this could be doing body mapping as a research method to transform our interview method (Coetzee et al. 2019; Dew et al. 2018; Lys et al. 2018; Jager et al. 2016).

Not only the method, but also the research product (textbook, anthology, academic article, etc.) itself needs to be transformed. Can we produce the kind of (non)writing that challenges academic conventions? For example, Løchlan Jain's work incorporates "visual arts as an ethnographic method of analysis and communication" (Jain 2020). His most recent book, *Things That Art: A Graphic Menagerie of Enchanting Curiosity* (2019), was published by the University of Toronto Press under the ethnoGRAPHIC series. The series focuses on publishing "ethnographic research in graphic novel form." It invites us to contemplate what our work can do when, rather than written in an academic language understood by only a few, it is represented through images that help us all make sense of the world. Similarly, we might consider other public forms of writing that reach broader audiences (e.g., blogs, online articles, memoirs, and policy memos).

It is urgent, crucial, and critical that we find alternative, progressive, and transgressive ways to do our teaching and disseminate research. We need to move away from the conventional ways of thinking, writing, doing research, and delivering course materials. As communication studies scholar Devika Chawla (2011) reminds us, we desperately need to disinherit the writing skills we have learned in academia, especially when they keep the knowledge that we produce powerless in the face of the status quo. We therefore need to produce knowledge that connects our theories and praxis while centering the politics of the everyday in a way that is impactful for the academic world, not only as separate from daily life but also as part of it. Podcasting, for example, has made some of these interventions, though it is not (yet) valued in the same ways as citational writing practices.

We would like to end this essay by reflecting on what Moses cautions us about the future of W/G/S/F:

> Among the strong departments with multiple faculty and graduate degree programs, I foresee a future in which the departments remain unchallenged. Among smaller programs, the threat is always there to dissolve these programs completely or to reorganize them into new entities along with other interdisciplinary programs. Even the latter worries me less, however, than the direction in WS scholarship that I see now and into the future. And that is a scholarship that is more and more a traditional discipline—with a discourse that is accessible only within the academic discipline. In other words, the strict borders of disciplinary departments that we once hoped to break down now encircle us as well. And worse, our disciplinary discourse cannot be understood outside the academy—sometimes not even among academics in other disciplines—and therefore no longer speaks to the needs of women. Pessimistically, I see a tragic split between the academic work of WS and feminist activism.

Moses's words are powerful reminders that although we have indeed accomplished much in the fifty-plus years that W/G/S/F has been institutionalized in academia, we need to mindfully and strategically shift the direction of our field if we are to remain a force in academia and also have strong ties to feminist, anti-racist, and other contemporary social movements. Can W/G/S/F departments be the conscience of the university, or are we only going to be conscious about our place in the institution and thus limit our ability to affect significant changes? It is important that we, as scholar-teacher-activists, ask ourselves daily: How are we serving the students without succumbing to and being exploited by the increasingly neoliberalized institution where we work? Are we serving the movement, or are we only serving our academic selves?

L. Ayu Saraswati is professor of women, gender, and sexuality studies at the University of Hawai'i at Mānoa. She is the author of *Pain Generation: Social Media, Feminist Activism, and the Neoliberal Selfie* and *Seeing Beauty, Sensing Race in Transnational Indonesia*. Her forthcoming book, *Scarred: A Feminist Journey through Pain*, is a mix of memoir and academic text. Her articles have appeared in *Feminist Studies*,

Meridians, Women's Studies International Forum, Gender, Work & Organization, Diogenes, Sexualities, and *Feminist Formations.* She can be reached at luhayu@gmail.com.

Barbara L. Shaw is associate professor of women's, gender, and sexuality studies at Allegheny College, is the co-chair of WGSS, coordinator of Black Studies, affiliated with Black Studies and Global Health Studies, and was awarded the Elliott Professorship for Interdisciplinary Studies in 2019. She coedited with L. Ayu Saraswati *Feminist & Queer Theory: An Intersectional and Transnational Reader* and coedited with L. Ayu Saraswati and Heather Rellihan *Introduction to Women's, Gender & Sexuality: Interdisciplinary & Intersectional* Approaches. Her current project is focused on gender, sexuality, race, health, and health policy. She can be reached at bshaw@allegheny.edu.

Notes

1. We use "women's studies (WS)" when referring to the early history of the field or programs that are named "women's studies." We recognize the naming variations since its early history and use women's/gender/sexuality/feminist studies (W/G/S/F) to capture the various iterations, acknowledging it may not represent all programs and departments. We also use "Black studies" and "ethnic studies" in recounting the early history of these fields, recognizing that they have similar but different community, intellectual, and institutional contexts that have also resulted in naming variations since the late 1960s.

2. We sent out questions via email, which they answered separately. In presenting the answers, we decided to reconstruct them as a roundtable conversation. To hold the integrity of their words, we sent the draft of this article to each of the three professors to make sure that we did not misquote or misrepresent them and to give them a chance to revise it as necessary.

Works Cited

Bhatt, Amy. 2020. "Women's-Gender-Sexuality-Feminist Studies: The Politics of Departmental Naming." In *Persistence Is Resistance: Celebrating 50 Years of the Gender, Women & Sexuality Studies,* edited by Julie Shayne. Seattle: University of Washington Press. https://uw.pressbooks.pub/happy50thws/.

Blea, Irene I. 1992. *La Chicana and the Intersection of Race, Class, and Gender.* Westport, CT: Praeger.

Bobo, Jacqueline, Cynthia Hudley, and Claudine Michel, eds. 2004. *The Black Studies Reader.* New York: Routledge.

Chawla, Devika. 2011. "Narratives on Longing, Being, and Knowing: Envisioning a Writing Epistemology." In *Liminal Traces: Storying, Performing, and Embodying Postcoloniality*, edited by Devika Chawla and Amardo Rodriguez, 97–111. Boston, MA: Sense Publishing.

Coetzee, Bronwyne, Rizwana Roomaney, Nicola Willis, and Ashraf Kagee. 2019. "Body Mapping in Research." In *Handbook of Research Methods in Health Social Sciences*, edited by Pranee Liamputtong, 1237–54. Springer Singapore.

Cole, Johnetta B. 2004. "Black Studies in Liberal Arts Education." In *The Black Studies Reader*, edited by Jacqueline Bobo, Cynthia Hudley, and Claudine Michel, 21–33. New York: Routledge.

Corbman, Rachel. 2019. *Conferencing on the Edge: A Queer History of Feminist Field Formation, 1969–1989*. PhD diss., Stony Brook University.

Crenshaw, Kimberlé. 1989. "Demarginalizing the Intersection of Race and Sex: A Black Feminist Critique of Antidiscrimination Doctrine, Feminist Theory and Antiracist Politics." *University of Chicago Legal Forum*, issue 1, article 8: 139–67.

Davis, Angela. 1981. *Women, Race & Class*. New York: Vintage.

Dew, Angela, Louisa Smith, Susan Collings, and Isabella Dillon Savage. 2018. "Complexity Embodied: Using Body Mapping to Understand Complex Support Needs." *Forum: Qualitative Research (FQS)* 19, no. 2. https://www.qualitative-research.net/index.php/fqs/article/view/2929/4196.

Diaz, Daniel. n.d. "The Ethnic Studies Movement: A Brief History." UCLA Center X: XChange Publications and Resources. Accessed June 5, 2022. https://centerx.gseis.ucla.edu/xchange/ethnic-studies-k-12/historical-timeline-for-ethnic-studies/.

García, Alma M. 1997. *Chicana Feminist Thought: The Basic Historical Writings*. New York: Routledge.

Ginsberg, Alice E. 2008. *The Evolution of American Women's Studies: Reflections on Triumphs, Controversies, and Change*. New York: Palgrave Macmillan.

Guy-Sheftall, Beverly. 2002. "Introduction: 50 Years of Women's Studies" in *Persistence Is Resistance: Celebrating 50 Years of Gender, Women & Sexuality Studies*, edited by Julie Shayne. Seattle: University of Washington Press. https://uw.pressbooks.pub/happy50thws/.

———. 2008. "Women's Studies: A View from the Margins." In *The Evolution of American Women's Studies: Reflections on Triumphs, Controversies, and Change*, edited by Alice E. Ginsberg, 103–16. New York: Palgrave Macmillan.

Guy-Sheftall, Beverly, and Susan Heath. 1995. *Women's Studies: A Retrospective: A Report to the Ford Foundation*. New York: Ford Foundation.

Hemmings, Clare. 2011. *Why Stories Matter: The Political Grammar of Feminist Theory*. Durham, NC: Duke University Press.

hooks, bell. 1981. *Ain't I a Woman: Black Women and Feminism*. Boston, MA: South End Press.

Howe, Florence, and Mari Jo Buhle, eds. 2000. *The Politics of Women's Studies: Testimony from 30 Founding Mothers*. New York: Feminist Press.

Hull, Akasha (Gloria T.), Patricia Bell-Scott, and Barbara Smith, eds. 1993. *All the Women Are White, All the Blacks Are Men, But Some of Us Are Brave: Black Women's Studies*. Old Westbury, NY: Feminist Press.

Jager, Adèle de, Anna Tewson, Bryn Ludlow, and Katherine Boydell. 2016. "Embodied Ways of Storying the Self: A Systematic Review of Body-Mapping." *Forum: Qualitative Research (FQS)* 17, no. 2. https://www.qualitative-research.net/index.php/fqs/article/view/2526.s.

Jain, Løchlann. 2022. "Commodity Violence: The Punctum of Data." *Visual Anthropology Review* 36, no. 2: 212–33.

———. 2019. *Things That Art: A Graphic Menagerie of Enchanting Curiosity*. Toronto: University of Toronto.

James, Stanlie M., Frances Smith Foster, and Beverly Guy-Sheftall, eds. 2009. *Still Brave: The Evolution of Black Women's Studies*. New York: Feminist Press.

Lorde, Audre. 1984. *Sister Outsider*. Trumansburg, NY: Crossing Press.

Lys, Candice, Dionne Gesink, Carol Strike, and June Larkin. 2018. "Body Mapping as a Youth Sexual Health Intervention and Data Collection Tool." *Qualitative Health Research* 28, no. 7: 1185–98.

Messer-Davidow, Ellen. 2002. *Disciplining Feminism: From Social Activism to Academic Discourse*. Durham, NC: Duke University Press.

Moraga, Cherríe, and Gloria Anzaldúa, eds. 1983. *This Bridge Called My Back: Writings by Radical Women of Color*. New York: Kitchen Table Women of Color Press.

Moses, Yolanda. 2000. "Linking Ethnic Studies to Women's Studies." In *The Politics of Women's Studies: Testimonies from 30 Founding Mothers*, edited by Florence Howe, 316–24. New York: Feminist Press.

Rooks, Noliwe. 2006. *White Money/Black Power: The Surprising History of African American Studies and the Crisis of Race in Higher Education*. Boston, MA: Beacon Press.

Shane, Julie, ed. 2020. *Persistence Is Resistance: Celebrating 50 Years of Gender, Women & Sexuality Studies*. Seattle, WA: University of Washington Libraries Pressbooks Publishing Platform.

Spade, Dean. 2015. *Normal Life: Administrative Violence, Critical Trans Politics, and the Limits of Law*. Revised and expanded ed. Durham, NC: Duke University Press.

University of Toronto Press. "ethnoGRAPHIC." http://www.utpteachingculture. com/related-series/.

Wiegman, Robyn. 2012. *Object Lessons*. Durham, NC: Duke University Press.

Wiegman, Robyn, ed. 2002. *Women's Studies on Its Own: A Next Wave Reader in Institutional Change*. Durham, NC: Duke University Press.

Alquimia: The Alchemy of Cross-Pollination in Movement Learning

Shereen Essof and Patricia Ardón

Abstract: We explore the meaning, significance, and specific practices of feminist pedagogy of the Alquimia Feminist Leadership Schools. In this paper we show how these schools, convened by Just Associates (JASS) in Mesoamerica and nurtured from the experience of JASS globally, contribute to strengthening movements and movement leaders (largely Indigenous and rural land defenders). We examine how Alquimia creates safe spaces and uses feminist popular education to challenge and transform aspects of power that marginalize, demean, and threaten women and their communities, while catalyzing imagination and action for long-term social justice and change agendas. **Keywords:** feminist pedagogy; popular education; movement building; epistemic communities; lifelong learning

Preamble

Knowledge is not a point of arrival. It is a point of departure—a point of departure for more learning. Popular education does not try to standardize consciousness or thinking, which we see as an important approach to abandon. It is not the classical partisan political training that so many receive. Knowledge is intended to provide critical tools, and we engage conceptual frameworks as tools to enable a reading of the present that can shed light on past experiences that can point to the future (Ardón 2021).

We are two women thinking about knowledge, learning, and movements—relationships that sit at the intersection of our work at Just Associates (JASS).[1] In this conversation are the echoes of the multiple knowledge processes and experiences of other colleagues in JASS and those of the women with whom we work. Shereen Essof, from Zimbabwe, is the executive director of JASS, and Patricia Ardón, from Guatemala, is the

WSQ: Women's Studies Quarterly 50: 3 & 4 (Fall/Winter 2022) © 2022 by Shereen Essof and Patricia Ardón.
All rights reserved.

regional director of JASS Mesoamerica. We each bring years of experience in feminist movement-building support and organizing, feminist pedagogy, popular education curriculum design, and facilitation. Our experience has been harvested from different locations constituting a constellation of feminist practice in academia, nongovernmental organizations (NGOs), as well as within and alongside social and women's movements.

Our shared starting point in this piece is the central question: What is the meaning and significance of feminist pedagogy and learning within movements? From there, we explore what constitutes feminist praxis and what is the rich vein of alliance building and cross-pollination of public feminisms and feminist scholarship that exists and is possible between and among a range of sites and locations as part of the movement project? Because we are "speaking" across contexts, and our mother tongues are different, we start with the recognition that we enter from different doorways, with implications for language, reference points, histories, and meaning-making. This, a cross-pollination in itself, is also what interests us. We have crafted this paper out of numerous conversations,[2] as well as through written reflections, to enable the greatest freedom of form and clarity of expression. We hope that the intertwining of our words and voices offers the same complexity of insight and inquiry we experienced in exploring the importance of pedagogical praxis and learning within movements.

Learning, Knowledge, and Movements

If we want to explore the relationship between learning, knowledge, and movements, we need to begin by acknowledging that each of these are highly political terms that should be looked at through the lens of geopolitics, history, and struggle. Decolonial, feminist, anti-racist, queer, and anarchist traditions demonstrate the exclusions and violence at the heart of the emergence and reproduction of racism and capitalism, as well as how these systems are all built upon alienation and separation that is deeply gendered (Fanon 1963; Foucault 1980; Holloway 2002; Mama 2001; Hill-Collins 1991; hooks 2003; Anzaldúa 2007; Lugones 2010; Tamale 2013). The violence against women occurs through relationships of "power over" (Miller 2006), which involves hierarchy and competition. Such violence is reproduced through a spatial logic of separation, division, and dispossession that is deeply authoritarian, given that it involves a view of the world that is reflective of the interests of those in power (Freire 1972).

Feminists demonstrate that these alienated relationships become embedded in our hearts, minds, and bodies (Lorde 2007; Hill-Collins 1991; Anzaldúa 2007). This alienation impoverishes our world, our relationships with each other, and ourselves. These alienated relationships create binaries such as teacher/student, man/woman, black/white, hetero/queer, rational/emotional, mind/body, and urban/rural, and these relationships reinforce received understandings of how power and privilege accrue as a result of our intersectional identities (Crenshaw 1991). This systemic inscription of people in relationships of power and privilege necessitates deep work on the part of movements to disrupt, dismantle, and heal the resulting social realities and decolonize our minds, imaginations, sense of self, and sense of possibility. This political commitment and work are both part of and necessary to our liberation.

Majority-world feminists in formal and informal learning spaces pay attention to movement learning, centering pedagogical approaches that support the deconstruction of power and privilege, and the unlearning of hegemonic relationships, as well as practices and recouping of knowledge in ways that weave new knowledge and more equitable, liberated ways of being.

Feminist Popular Education

Pioneered by Brazilian educator Paulo Freire, popular education is a people-oriented and -guided approach to education (Freire 1972). By centering participants' life experiences, this approach affirms the dignity of all participants and recognizes that everyone in the room is both a teacher and a learner in developing critical consciousness. This approach attempts to inspire people to look at their world from new perspectives, empower people to think for themselves, and enable them to create change. Critical consciousness fosters an in-depth understanding of the world and encourages collective action against oppressive elements in a struggle for human dignity and liberation.

Another unique feature of popular education is its use outside traditional formal education settings. By adapting to participants and their context, popular education may be used in the community, in people's homes, or even in outdoor settings, to name a few nontraditional sites. This approach meets people where they are at, both literally and with respect to their lived experiences. Feminist popular education (FPE) is the engine of JASS's movement-building work. In Mesoamerica, the Alquimia (alchemy)

Feminist Leadership School brings FPE to life as an approach and methodology in working with largely indigenous and rural land defenders. Behind the name is an intentional meaning that captures the essence of feminist pedagogy. The school is called "Alquimia" to give the sense that knowledge is constructed collectively by building on the wisdom and knowledge of all participants and facilitators. Some of the learning components, such as the school curriculum, are structured, but content is never imposed. Alquimia sees "participants as protagonists of the entire process, starting with the design and planning and leading to the organization of the training processes itself" (JASS n.d.).

Alquimia is called a "school" because it encourages a systematic and intentional education process. This is done in formal and informal ways with partners and allies to generate knowledge together. Participants see the school as "feminist" because it seeks to challenge, contribute, and transform the intersecting oppressions that women face in all spheres of their lives due to gender, race, class, ethnicity, age, environment, sexual orientations, nationality, and more. The alchemy of the school lies in the co-construction of process and the pooling and cross-pollination of intent and knowledge, across people and spaces, to pave the way for the transformation of women from spectators to actors in their lives (Boal 1979).

In this paper, we explore feminist movement pedagogy by looking at feminist popular education as represented by Alquimia through five frames: thinking about power; embracing multiplicity and complementary forms of knowledge; heart, mind, and body; conceptualizations of space; and communities of practice.

Thinking about Power

For Alquimia, the relationships between self and social transformation, the personal and political, and the individual and collective is critical when thinking about teaching and learning. The relationship between self- and social transformation starts with learning to question and challenge the explanations for why things are the way they are (Kilgore 1999). The sharing of experiences of power and inequality by an individual woman is a means to lay bare what is actually a systemic story of collective destabilization. The personal is fierce and becomes deeply political. Alquimia places value in knowing history as a way of destabilizing the power and hierarchy of knowledge and, as such, seeks to reclaim hidden histories. As Ardón

(2021) points out, "The history we learn at school is not always useful as it is a history of the dominant. We need to listen, create, and believe in our own stories, questioning and challenging ourselves, querying inherited knowledge, and legitimize perceptions and knowledge that flow from us and others, and the processes we promote."

Alquimia questions ways of doing and learning by provoking epistemological rupture, moving from magical consciousness to critical consciousness and change, placing a value on cognitive dissonance in the process. This commitment to unlearning is one of the main commitments in Alquimia. To unlearn what we have learned and learn a new way of being and living requires the development of "new eyes." The reading of history is essentially a critical exercise. Alquimia speaks of "unlearning" history as a way to shed preconceptions and find new ways of seeing the world. Unlearning has a political-epistemological meaning: getting rid of that which is asserted as rigid and immutable truth. History is not an immovable truth: "It is not for nothing that the indigenous people, for instance, do not trust the Kaxlanes or Ladinos, non-indigenous people, in Guatemala. They filter the information they get from them because it symbolizes historical domination, the domination exercised by the Spanish invaders during years of colonization. They trust the white God but shift him, tailor him to their own purposes and beliefs, a trait of resistance" (Ardón 2021).

There is a continual contestation between those who hold oppressive power and those who seek change. For Alquimia, this necessitates creating safe spaces to do this counterhegemonic work; it requires a leveling of power relations between "teachers" and "students" and an interrogation of systemic power. Alquimia uses a power analysis framework (JASS n.d.) to both make visible and address the interconnected systemic oppressions women face in their homes, families, communities, and organizations. This allows participants to see how power manifests and allows for the transformation of oppressive power relations by building positive forms of power at the individual and collective levels, helping to construct political identities of resistance and transformation.

Transformative power is mobilized to build movement, which is derived from building collective knowledge, vision, and strength that fuels people and movements to confront, engage, and ultimately change oppressive forms of power to advance a vision of care and repair for people and the planet. Power over and transformative power are not seen as two distinct arenas in Alquimia; they are present everywhere. Just as power over can be present in our own organizations and leadership, transformative power is possible in the cracks and opportunities for change that are found in the dominant structures of power.

Through a range of methodological approaches (We Rise 2016), transformative power is explored through five dimensions: power within, a person's sense of self-worth and self-knowledge; power to, the unique potential of every person to speak, take action, and shape her life and world; power with, the collective strength that comes with finding common ground and community with others; power with, expressed in alliances and solidarity that multiplies individual talents, knowledge, and resources through collaboration for a larger impact; and power for, the combined vision, values, and demands that orient shared and collective work and that inspire strategies and alternatives—the world we seek to create.

Embracing Multiple and Complementary Ways of Knowing

Cross-fertilization in Alquimia takes place through constituting a collective and embracing multiple and complimentary ways of knowing. Alquimia deliberately brings women together across identity divides, geographies, and issues to build bridges across differences and strengthen movements. Alquimia believes that there is a need to stretch ways of thinking and to break out of hegemonic silos. Some of the critical questions posed include: How do we see and respect each other? How do we find common ground? How do we come to trust each other?

For Alquimia it is important not to idolize marginality and to break the idea that marginality is the basis of unity. Marginality isolates, meaning you run the risk of not being able to see "the other." It can prevent you from connecting across struggles: "Marginality should not be an identity symbol. We can embrace our marginality because we are contesting oppression and defending ourselves. We can create a 'ghetto' within which we communicate with each other and from which we relate to those in power. We need to recognize this natural tendency and explore ways to move beyond this in order to forge alliances" (JASS n.d.).

In forging these alliances, Alquimia works with a range of partners and allies within movements, civil society organizations, research institutions, and universities to contribute "new" knowledge to further catalyze learning processes. Alquimia experiments with a range of approaches, including using participatory engagements and debates, dialogue, and negotiation, as well as reading and reflection, which all generate more complex analyses and understandings, and new personal and shared collective knowledge and agreements.

This political work requires methodologies that do not dichotomize but rather contribute to a deeper analysis that considers diverse perspectives and differentiated and complementary contributions. The engagements have to allow for recognizing difference and recuperating everyday and cultural practices as well as embracing multiple and complementary forms of knowledge, including the affective, embodied, oral, cognitive, and cultural.

If you create space for a wide range of actors and knowledge points as part of learning, there is an implicit understanding that this kind of cross-pollination will generate conflict. Feminists always argue that within a group that is deconstructing power, we need to integrate care and prepare for conflict, because it is an intensely demanding and emotional process (FRIDA 2016; JASS and FHGR 2017; UAFLA 2018). Dealing with conflict in a learning space without reproducing dominant ways of exercising power is critical in Alquimia's approach: "Conflicts always arise. We have to go slow and take time to learn from one another, and address how differences of identity, position and privilege can reproduce the very inequalities that divide women" (JASS n.d.). Addressed in this intentional way, conflict can become a deep source of learning and push us to a more inclusive and nuanced, perhaps more radical understanding of who we can be, how we can be with one another, and what can change beyond the limitations of dominant thought.

Heart, Mind, and Body

Given the historical trauma and pain that comes from oppression and violence, Alquimia values emotion and embodied experience as forms of knowledge. For Alquimia, "the whole question of care and collective care that many feminist organizations have adopted is transversal to all Alquimia processes precisely because it, the unlearning and questioning processes, awaken feelings and emotions, difficult and painful experiences" (JASS n.d.).

At its source, these painful feelings come from experiencing inequities and the multiple violences generated from structural inequalities. In a society that seeks to dehumanize women, feeling feelings and legitimizing them is not only a radical act but also the genesis for action, as well as a form of caring for ourselves, individually and collectively, in a system that does not.

Feminists have contributed to a more comprehensive dimension of experience, "Sentipensar," feeling-thinking (Moreas and de la Torre 2002), in which all levels of consciousness and unconsciousness are brought into play. In Alquimia, there is a commitment to reclaim the knowledge that exists outside the circumference of rational thought and break with what limits thinking and practice. As Ardón (2021) observes, "We need to consider how to create a movement that unites spirit and body and reclaims related social practices. On this level, it is important to break the resistance to a holistic and interconnected sense of ourselves before talking about alliances and movements."

This way of thinking allows Alquimistas (participants of Alquimia) to draw on more than the rational and combine poetry with science and music with silence. Caring for ourselves as whole beings—heart, mind, and body—is about acknowledging the dynamic interaction of these in our lives and pedagogies to ensure that creativity and joy become fundamental ingredients that contribute to how we think about learning and how we learn. The incorporation of artistic and playful expressions that generate contagious, passionate, playful, joyful, and liberating learning for women and men serves to reweave the social fabric by recouping our humanity and creating communities of care, trust, and solidarity.

Alquimia understands that the realization of deep transformations requires time, commitment, and the work of many: "We have to do it collectively. The challenge of doing it with joy, something that is apparently so simple, becomes something extremely transgressive, and very important" (JASS n.d.). These intangibles in the alchemy of movement learning work contribute immensely to creating the conditions for imagining and creating new realities and ways of being and how movements learn and move together.

Conceptualizations of Space

The spatial cross-pollination and the importance of teaching and learning can be explored in three ways through Alquimia. First, feminists take the creation of safe space seriously, and Alquimia promotes "political agreement" among participants that determine the construction as well as habitation of the space. Alquimia creates safe spaces for women to bring their whole selves by encouraging them to be, be together, express themselves, discover others, to interact, partake in levity, and build knowledge. Alquimia creates conditions that enable women to speak openly about their pain, dreams, and hopes by centering respect, compassion, and curiosity. Creating safe spaces enables women to recover and gain strength and find the tools to support and sustain them when they return to their communities.

Alquimia takes into account how women's multiple roles have the potential to impact their "membership" in Alquimia: "We need to create spaces that consider the intimate, private sphere, and its impact on women's participation (individual and collective care, safety, care of children). We need to strengthen individual and collective protection and engage with women at times that accommodate their needs. We consciously incorporate spontaneous and heart/mind/body elements in the conceptual and methodological work and try to build safe and loving spaces" (JASS n.d.). There is a tacit understanding that the learning space has to mitigate the replication of the violence and vulnerabilities perpetuated against women, and the backlash Alquimistas may experience when they are perceived to be engaging in learning or acts of transgression.

Second, Alquimia understands that the "school" is a "space" in which different knowledge processes and learning happen informally and formally. The former include virtual dialogues and *Escuelas vivas* or Live Schools, which happen in the moment of a current event or protest action—short, on the streets and in real time; leadership strengthening and movement accompaniment in response to specific training requests or specific needs of allies and movements. Regarding the latter, Alquimia, as a modular course lasting a year or more, combines formal (in situ) and experiential learning.

The Alquimia course has been formulated through cross-pollination— design, curriculum development, and methodology—with participants (largely indigenous and rural land defenders), supporting allies, and organizations, as well as JASS. It is adapted to accommodate shifting contexts and movement needs. The curriculum includes modules on power; alliances and addressing conflicts between women; the history of women's struggles (contextualized); FPE methods and techniques to scale up learning; women's strategic and collective leadership; self-care, bodies, protection, and safety; economic justice for women; and other topics that arise from the contextual needs of the participants.

Using the pedagogical approaches outlined above, courses have been conducted at a regional level since 2013, with the participation of indigenous and rural women activists and defenders from the Mesoamerican region stretching from Mexico to Panama. National courses have been carried out in Honduras from 2018 to 2021 and Guatemala from 2020 to 2021. Mexico implemented its first course in 2021. These courses have strengthened the strategic leadership capacity of women. At present, the political facilitator's course has been implemented to complement leadership strengthening and enrich capacities for training within the organizations and movements. In Honduras, the Alquimia school was accredited with the Women's Rights Centre and the Department of Social Work of the National University, and in Guatemala, with the Latin American Faculty of Social Sciences. "For many women being able to say: 'I am going to university' can invoke respect, and is different to saying: 'I am going to a feminist workshop.' which can provoke resistance amongst families and communities" (JASS n.d.). Whether in formal or informal learning spaces, the approach remains collaborative, ethical, systemic, intersectional, historical, dialectical, and holistic.

However, there is a third way Alquimia understands space in terms of how and why we learn. In this consideration, the "school" is not understood as just a physical place, a learning course, or a one-off event but conceived as a space for ever-evolving learning and knowledge production built from the activities developed in the different areas of movement work (Melero 2018; Cooper and Walters 2009). In this understanding, the movement is the ongoing site of sustained engagement and continuous learning. The actual work of strategy development or tactical actions like protests or blockades can be seen as critical sites where learning takes place in the day-to-day.

The School as the Movement

The idea of the school as "the movement" and an organizing principle has been echoed by other movements such as Abahlali baseMjondolo, the shack-dwellers' movement in Durban, South Africa; the Kurdish women's movement of Rojava (an autonomous region) in northeastern Syria; and the Piqueteros (picketers), a radical mobilization of unemployed workers in Argentina.

Abahlali baseMjondolo maintains that "everyone thinks" (Pithouse 2008, 37). Thinking results in understanding and in new knowledge. In November 2005, the University of Abahlali baseMjondolo was born, driven by the movement and supported by a range of movement allies, including media practitioners, academic activists, and legal practitioners. Abahlali has long recognized that it is the assertion that they think that they have a right to speak and be listened to that is most threatening to hegemony. As one of the leaders of Abahlali remarked in 2006, "They [power holders] come for us when we try to say what we think" (Abahlali baseMjondolo 2006).

The women of the revolutionary movement in Rojava believe that the ideological battle—the more significant battle—takes place in the classroom and is fought with pens (Espinosa 2020). Jineology, which informs their ideological orientation, stems from the umbrella word "Jin," meaning women, and derived from "Jiyan," meaning life (ECR 2020). It is an epistemological process promoting women's freedom. It challenges knowledge as a patriarchal concept and proposes itself as a method to explore questions collectively (Dirik 2015). The Institute for Educational Science, established as part of the revolution, is tasked with designing a new curriculum to reflect the self-administration's broader attempts at challenging the capitalist patriarchal regimes that precede and surround it.

The Piqueteros in Argentina argue along the same lines, that every person, woman, and man, has a voice and a vote, and everyone can express their opinion. It is not that no one knows anything, but rather that we all know something (Sitrin 2003, 477). For the Piqueteros, building community kitchens, organic gardens, bakeries, and popular libraries is a threat to the hegemonic order because "they are about new and other ways of thinking and gaining consciousness. The Piqueteros believe that the state is afraid of women who think, afraid of women with a conscience, and so they respond with violence. Yet they know that women are able to do many things through their work, their thoughts, and their ideas. This is learning. This is also a revolution" (Sitrin 2003, 477).

This understanding of the school as the movement is dynamic because not only is it emergent (Forte 2018), but it also combines and integrates multiple characteristics. It is context-specific, fluid, gendered, highly political, intersectional, embedded in the day-to-day, tacit, and not always recognized as a site of learning (Foley 1999). Despite being evolutionary and cumulative, it is nonlinear (Foley 1999). The emancipatory pedagogical practices start with the reality of knowing and recognizing the context, needs, interests, affections, intuitions, wisdom, and knowledge that participants, facilitators, and other resource people have in order to create synergies, mutual learning, and new knowledge that is critical, not just for survival but also for changing our worldly reality. In doing this, there is also a commitment to "generate theory from feminist praxis and to interrogate power, build solidarity and reciprocity in ways in which care for self, other and the earth/cosmos become central to our action both on the streets and in the bigger processes of transformation" (JASS n.d.). This understanding of learning means that learning occurs in multiple spaces, based on the needs of movement actors. It is transversal and involves multiple allies and contributors across sites who cross-fertilize it through supporting movement thinking, learning, strategy, and action, and herein lies the catalytic nature of alchemy in general.

To focus on learning and knowledge production in this way invites a recognition of movements as ongoing sites of imagination, creativity, engagement, and power building (Hope and Timmel 1984; Motta and Esteves 2014; Melero 2018) that support the construction and unleashing of liberatory/radical identities and relationships, resist subjugation, and invite transformation while at the same time serving as educational and knowledge-building spaces (Foley 1999, 2001; Choudry 2009, 2015; Delgado 2011a, 2011b; Cox 2014; Kapoor and Choudry 2010).

Further, this recognition allows for an expansion, but also a challenge, to received understandings of how, where, when, and why learning takes place and knowledge is produced (Feminist Africa 2008; Choudry 2009; Walters and Manicom 1996). It expresses a potency in the knowledges produced, which have the potential of influencing and completely transforming our world in several ways: from the creation of new frameworks for the analysis of socioeconomic and political realities; the redefinition of concepts and theoretical frames; participatory learning; the production of tools, curricula, and methodologies (Cox 2014; We Rise 2016), and technological access.

For Alquimia, learning and struggle are not solely about individual identity, access, recognition, or rights but also about how one thinks about teaching, learning, and perspectives of knowledge that have to do with the model and logic of life itself. This is rooted in commitments to solidarity and reciprocity in which care for self and other but also for the earth and cosmos are seen as central to processes of transformation—*buen vivir* (Salazar 2015).

Communities of Practice: Cross-Pollination and Social Transformation

As indicated, then, the school by its very nature must invest in the growing of deep political relationships of trust, of revolutionary love and comradeship, as central to community building. Furthermore, it must also invest in forging strategic alliances across a range of sites and actors, in catalyzing, strengthening, and advancing the goals of the movement project. While the idea of alliances is good, they are ultimately only acquired in practice. Alquimia sees joint actions as a way of better seeing "what elements and formations are involved and how each of them offer learning. . . . There are always emerging actors, the old and the new—young people too matter in the equation" (JASS n.d.).

This often involves experimentation, navigating synergies and conflicts, in how to create and develop expanded and shared political purpose out of difference, across sites and geographies, while crafting new pathways for social and political relationships with others, once removed from, but as key to, the school or the feminist political project. Whoever cares about creating change has to abandon the idea that they are going to change the world as an individual making great sacrifices. For Alquimia, the complexity of change and movements does not depend on individuals; it depends on an "us." There is a need to "recover a kind of pendulum thinking, the coming and going of people and ideas, to create a permanent spiral of learning, ideas forever evolving and being challenged" (Ardón 2021).

Escobar has termed these deliberate and cultivated relationships "meshworks," notable in that their ontologies are not fixed or rigid and that they represent the diversity of our world, resulting in especially fertile, fluid and adaptable, heterogenous, and overlapping interconnections that engage in both vertical and horizontal networking and are interlinked with other hierarchies and networks, and yet maintain their characteristic plurality without imposing uniformity (Escobar 2008). In this, we believe, lie the roots of communities of practice or epistemic communities (Okech 2020). Meshworks can encompass a broad range of people and practices, as well as the ongoing commitment, engagement, and solidarity with the movement by allies wherever they may be located, rooted in shared ideological principles and praxis in ways that feed, cross-pollinate, and catalyze shared feminist political goals across sites as part of a bigger transformatory vision for our world.

Shereen Essof is a Pan-African feminist, activist researcher, popular educator, and serves as the executive director of Just Associates (JASS), with twenty-plus years of work grounded in engagement with womxn in social movements, community-based organizations, and cultural collectives committed to building, organizing, and amplifying the voice of womxn. Shereen can be reached at shereen@justassociates.org.

Patricia Ardón is a feminist and social anthropologist, a cofounder of Just Associates (JASS), and the regional director of JASS Mesoamerica, with over thirty years' experience with grassroots movements throughout Central America. Ardón is a member of the Alquimia School and an advocate for women's rights and peace-building worldwide. Patricia can be reached at patricia.ardon@justassociates.org.

Notes

1. JASS (www.justassociates.org) is a feminist movement support organization dedicated to building the voice, visibility, and collective power of women for a just and sustainable world for all. We equip and strengthen the leadership and organizing capacity of women leaders and their organizations in Mesoamerica, Southeast Asia, and Southern Africa. We strengthen women's organizing strategies to transform the systems, structures, and beliefs that perpetuate inequality and violence in four areas of their lives: bodies, voice, resources, and safety. Founded in 2002, JASS was built on long-standing relationships of political trust and solidarity, grounded in shared ideas about how change happens—a learning community of activists, organizers, popular educators, and scholars connected by years of experience in common struggles for social justice and human rights.

2. We would like to thank Dr. Awino Okech for her invitation to develop this article. We would also like to acknowledge Alexa Bradley, programmes director at JASS, for contributing to the thinking.

Works Cited

Abahlali baseMjondolo. 2006. "University of Abahlali baseMjondolo." http://abahlali.org/university-of-abahlali-basemjondolo.

Anzaldúa, Gloria. 2007. *Borderlands/La Frontera: The New Mestiza*. 3rd ed. San Francisco, CA: Aunt Lute.

Ardón, Patricia. 2021. "About Feminist Popular Education." Feminist Hiking Collective. https://feministhikingcollective.org/semillas-blog/f/about-feminist-popular-education---conversation-wipatricia-ardon.

Boal, Augusto. 1979. *Theatre of the Oppressed*. London: Pluto Press.

Choudry, Aziz. 2009. "Learning in Social Action: Knowledge Production in Social Movements." *McGill Journal of Education* 44, no. 1 (Winter): 5–17. https://doi.org/10.7202/037769ar.

———. 2015. *Learning Activism: The Intellectual Life of Contemporary Social Movements*. Toronto: University of Toronto Press.

Cooper, Linda, and Shirley Walters. 2009. *Learning/Work: Turning Work and Lifelong Learning Inside Out*. Johannesburg: HSRC Press.

Cox, Laurence. 2014. "Movements Making Knowledge: A New Wave of Inspiration for Sociology?" *Sociology* 48, no. 5: 954–71. https://doi.org/10.1177/0038038514539063.

Crenshaw, Kimberlé. 1991. "Mapping the Margins: Intersectionality, Identity Politics, and Violence against Women of Color." *Stanford Law Review* 43, no. 6: 1241–99.

Delgado, Ricardo. 2011a. "Acción colectiva y educación popular: contribuciones para un conocimiento emancipatorio" [Collective action and popular education: contributions for emancipatory knowledge]. *Folios*, no. 33: 57–64. https://doi.org/10.17227/01234870.33folios53.60.

———. 2011b. "Educación para la ciudadanía desde la acción colectiva" [Education for citizenship through collective action]. *Magis. Revista Internacional de Investigación en Educación* [Magis. International Journal of Research in Education] 4, no. 7: 201–10.

Dirik, Dilar. 2015. "The Women's Revolution in Rojava: Defeating Fascism by Constructing an Alternative Society." In *A Small Key Can Open a Large Door: The Rojava Revolution*, edited by Strangers in a Tangled Wilderness, 52–64. Combustion Books.

Emergency Committee for Rojava (ECR). 2020. "Reading Group: Kurdish Women's Movement." https://www.defendrojava.org/events/ecr-reading-group-kurdish-womens-movement.

Escobar, Arturo. 2008. *Territories of Difference: Place, Movements, Life, Redes.* Durham, NC: Duke University Press.

Espinoza, Elisa Boyle. 2019. "Fighting with Pens in Rojava's 'War of Education.'" ROAR Mag. https://roarmag.org/essays/fighting-with-pens-in-rojavas-war-of-education/.

Fanon, Frantz. 1963. *The Wretched of the Earth.* 18th ed. New York: Grove Press.

Feminist Africa. 2008. *Researching for Life: Paradigms and Power.* Cape Town: UCT Press.

Foley, Griff. 1999. *Learning in Social Action: A Contribution to Understanding Informal Education.* London: Zed.

———. 2001. "Radical Adult Education and Learning." *International Journal of Lifelong Education* 20, nos. 1/2: 71–88. https://doi.org/10.1080/02601370010008264.

Forte, Tiago. 2018. "Emergent Strategy: Organizing for Social Justice." Forte Labs. https://fortelabs.co/blog/emergent-strategy-organizing-for-social-justice/.

Foucault, Michel. 1980. *Power/Knowledge: Selected Interviews and Other Writings, 1972–1977.* Hassocks, UK: Harvester Press.

Freire, Paulo. 1972. *Pedagogy of the Oppressed.* New York: Continuum.

FRIDA. 2016. "Practicing Individual and Collective Self-Care at FRIDA." https://youngfeministfund.org/practising-individual-and-collective-self-care-at-frida/.

Hill-Collins, Patricia. 1991. *Black Feminist Thought: Knowledge, Consciousness and the Politics of Empowerment*. New York: Routledge.

Holloway, John. 2002. *Change the World without Taking Power*. London: Pluto.

Hope, Anne, and Sally Timmel. 1984. *Training for Transformation: A Community Handbook*. Zimbabwe: Mambo Press.

hooks, bell. 2003. *Teaching Community: Pedagogy of Hope*. London: Routledge.

JASS. n.d. "Que es la Escuela de Alquimia" (internal document).

JASS and Fund for Global Human Rights (FGHR). 2017. "Power and Protection Platform." https://www.jass-fghr.org/power-and-protection.

Kapoor, Dip, and Aziz Choudry. 2010. *Learning from the Ground Up: Global Perspectives on Social Movements and Knowledge Production*. New York: Palgrave Macmillan.

Kilgore, Deborah W. 1999. "Understanding Learning in Social Movements: A Theory of Collective Learning." *International Journal of Lifelong Education* 18, no. 3: 191–202. https://doi.org/10.1080/026013799293784.

Lorde, Audre. 2007. *Sister Outsider: Essays and Speeches*. New York: Crossing Press.

Lugones, María. 2010. "Towards a Decolonial Feminism." *Hypatia* 25, no. 5: 742–59.

Mama, Amina. 2001. "Challenging Subjects: Gender and Power in African Contexts." *African Sociological Review* 5, no. 2: 9–18. doi:10.4314/asr.v5i2.23191.

Melero, Hector S. 2018. "Espacios y prácticas de participación ciudadana. Análisis y propuestas desde un enfoque intercultural" [Citizen participation spaces and practices. Analysis and proposals from an intercultural approach]. PhD diss., Universidad Nacional de Educación a Distancia, Spain.

Miller, Valerie. 2006. "Making Change Happen: Power." Just Associates (JASS). https://www.justassociates.org/sites/justassociates.org/files/mch3_2011_final_0.pdf.

Miller, Valerie, and Lisa VeneKlasen. 2016. "Feminist Popular Education." Just Associates (JASS). https://www.justassociates.org/sites/justassociates.org/files/feminist-popular-education-movement-building-miller-veneklasen.pdf.

Moraes, María C., and Saturnino de la Torre. 2002. "Sentipensar bajo la mirada autopoiética o cómo reencantar creativamente la educación." *Creatividad y Sociedad*, no. 2: 41–56. http://www.waldorfcolombia.org/seccns/Reencantando.pdf.

Motta, Sara C., and Ana M. Esteves. 2014. "The Pedagogical Practices of Social Movements: Reinventing Emancipation in the 21st Century." *Interface: a journal for and about social movements* 6, no. 1: 1–24.

Okech, Awino. 2020. "African Feminist Epistemic Communities and Decoloniality." *Critical African Studies* 12, no. 3: 313–29. https://www.tandfonline.com/doi/full/10.1080/21681392.2020.1810086.

Pithouse, Richard. 2008. "A Politics of the Poor: Shack Dwellers' Struggles in Durban." *Journal of Asian and African Studies* 43, no. 1: 63–94.

Salazar, Juan F. 2015. "Buen Vivir: South America's Rethinking of the Future We Want." *The Conversation*, July 23, 2015. https://theconversation.com/buen-vivir-south-americas-rethinking-of-the-future-we-want-44507.

Sitrin, Marina. 2003. "The Power of the Piqueteros." In *We Are Everywhere: The Irresistible Rise of Global Anti-Capitalism*, edited by Notes from Nowhere, 82–90. London: Verso.

Tamale, Sylvia. 2013. "Confronting the Politics of Non-Conforming Sexualities in Africa." *Africa Studies Review* 56, no. 2: 31–45.

Urgent Action Fund Latin America (UAFLA). 2018. "Care at the Centre: An Ethical and Political Commitment." https://fondoaccionurgente.org.co/site/assets/files/1433/care_at_the_center_web.pdf.

Walters, Shirley, and Linzi Manicom. 1996. *Gender in Popular Education: Methods for Empowerment*. London: Zed Books.

We Rise. 2016. "Feminist Popular Education Tools by and for Movement Builders." Just Associates (JASS). https://werise-toolkit.org/.

PART III. **MEMORY AND COMMEMORATION**

Movement Renewal and Attachments to the Past: The Commemorative Reception of the Feminist Novel *L'Euguélionne* in Québec

Marie-Lise Drapeau-Bisson

Abstract: How might we conceptualize speech acts that commemorate a novel, not in a physical site nor championed by the state or social movement organizations, but rather in various media outlets by audiences of a movement's artistic productions? Using the case of the commemoration of the Québec feminist novel *L'Euguélionne* in newspapers, I introduce the concept of *commemorative reception* and find three claims shaped by different attachments to the novel and the era during which it was published: *extending claims* shaped by dissatisfaction and discouragement; *specific claims* shaped by disappointment and frustration; and *enacting claims* shaped by fear and mourning. These show that avenues for movement renewal were publicly constructed based on feminists' individual affective attachments to the movements' cultural production, which make commemorative reception a useful concept for scholars interested in intergenerational dynamics and the study of abeyance. **Keywords:** commemoration; unusual archives; intergenerational dynamics; movement continuity; abeyance; books; Québec studies

Political books often come to encapsulate an era's political consciousness and thus can come to symbolize a movement's wave of protest. Friedan's *Feminine Mystique* and de Beauvoir's *Le Deuxième Sexe* are examples of such books. While these books may be reviewed harshly by traditional literary critics or collect dust on activists' shelves, they contribute to the transmission of progressive ideas and can be picked up again by contemporary activists wanting to resuscitate such ideas.

This is the case for the Québec feminist novel *L'Euguélionne*. Published in 1976, *L'Euguélionne* is the debut novel of Lucille Durand, more commonly known under her pen name, Louky Bersianik. Because of its parody of

WSQ: Women's Studies Quarterly 50: 3 & 4 (Fall/Winter 2022) © 2022 by Marie-Lise Drapeau-Bisson.
All rights reserved.

Catholic texts as well as its considerable size—a hefty four hundred pages—the novel has been qualified as "the bible of Québec feminism"[1] and was lauded for encapsulating the zeitgeist of Québec's political mobilizations of the 1970s (Basile 1976; Martel 1976). Over the years, the enthusiasm shared by feminist activists and critics faded; while it was a critically acclaimed and best-selling book in the late seventies, Bersianik's debut novel was never anthologized and rarely taught, and it became a forgotten classic, known only among small reception communities. At the time of her death in 2001, Louky Bersianik had lost the popularity she once had. However, as of 2006, various efforts to commemorate *L'Euguélionne* have emerged in the media, such as journalist Josée Boileau's call for a reissuing of *L'Euguélionne* "to save it from oblivion" (*Le Devoir*, December 6, 2011). Pieces such as Boileau's retrieve the novel in a way that is under the radar, different from the plaques or statues that traditionally characterize public commemorations.

How might we conceptualize speech acts that commemorate a novel, neither at a physical site nor championed by the state or social movement organisations, but rather in various media outlets by audiences of a movement's artistic productions? I review the literature on commemoration to show that, while developments in the field have theoretically moved beyond traditional Durkheimian approaches by studying difficult pasts, their focus on physical landmark sites continues to emphasize the conquering narratives and extraordinary events associated with such sites. I turn to Queer and feminist approaches to archiving in order to intervene methodologically in the field of public commemorations. Researching alternative archives opens up possibilities for the study of public commemorations, as it casts individuals in their daily lives, collecting mundane objects and cultural artifacts, and motivated by an affective attachment to the history they document. Inspired by their work, I introduce the concept of *commemorative reception* to define cultural reception as an unusual site of public commemoration characterized by the diffuse character of cultural reception and driven by readers. The concept offers a critical alternative to the typical understanding of memory work commissioned by states or initiated by interest groups and social movement organizations. Instead, commemorative reception is motivated by personal attachment to the work and by audiences' feelings about its trajectory.

Using *L'Euguélionne* as a case study for the development of commemorative reception, I ask: How do feminists understand and emotionally reckon with the legacy of *L'Euguélionne*? How does their attachment to the book shape the claims they make through its commemoration? What do feminists convey about contemporary issues and future avenues for the movement through their commemoration? I answer these questions by analyzing cultural interventions about the novel in the public sphere from a data set of feminist speech acts between 2006 and 2016 in Québec. I find three types of claims made through the commemorative reception of *L'Euguélionne*, each shaped by feminist readers' affective experience of the novel and its legacy. In the first type, commemorative reception displays dissatisfaction and discouragement about the repetition of history and makes claims that extend Bersianik's fate to contemporary issues. In the second type, commemorative reception displays disappointment and frustration about the lack of recognition of Bersianik, as well as women in other fields, denouncing systems that yield such erasure, making specific claims for the recognition of *L'Euguélionne* by literary institutions. Finally, in the third type, commemorative reception deals with the absence of *L'Euguélionne* from the canon and showcases more fear and mourning than disappointment and anger, making claims that enact Bersianik's heritage, thus prefiguring the kind of recognition they wish feminist figures to receive. These three different affective attachments to the book and its legacy shape the way feminists attempt to renew the movement through their claims.

The analysis of feminists' cultural interventions in Québec about a book that became a forgotten classic has theoretical and methodological implications for feminist scholarship beyond this case. The concept of commemorative reception owes its critical lens to Queer and feminist epistemologies that shed light on the analytical richness of affect and the power of history as a resource. These two aspects make commemorative reception useful for future scholars interested in intergenerational dynamics and the study of abeyance.

Literature Review
Commemorating Difficult Pasts

Innovative work in the field of commemoration has focused on difficult pasts and the way agents of memory grapple with the contradictions that come with remembering traumatic events like genocides, wars, and political assassinations. Through a thematic focus on conflict and ambivalence, these studies have theoretically moved away from the Durkheimian understanding of memory work as bringing resolution and reassurance (Vinitzky-Seroussi

2002, 48). Scholars do so by building on the powerful question posed by Wagner-Pacifici and Schwartz: "How is commemoration without consensus, or without pride, possible?" (1991, 379). In doing so, they found that commemoration may be multivocal (Wagner-Pacifici and Schwartz 1991), propose ambivalent interpretations of the past (Pearce 2011), voice suffering and reveal disputes (Hite and Jara 2020), and be fragmented to reach different audiences (Vinitzky-Seroussi 2002).

While theoretically moving away from consensual understandings of commemoration, scholars studying the commemoration of difficult pasts have continued to focus empirically on landmark sites—what Nora has called physical "lieux de mémoire" (Vinitzky-Seroussi 2002, 40)—such as plaques, monuments, or gravesites commissioned by families, organizations, or the state. In doing so, these studies reproduce the narratives that such sites typically channel, and they amplify the voices of political actors who have access to the realms of power that regulate and fund such sites. This methodological focus reproduces conquering narratives of the past and amplifies extraordinary events, even when what is remembered are histories of struggle. I suggest that turning to feminist and Queer approaches on intimate memory work enables researchers to shift our attention to unusual commemorative sites.

From Unusual Archives to Unusual Commemorations
There is a burgeoning literature in critical archival studies that highlights how archives are on the move, moving in loci but also moving affectively (Morra 2020). The idea of moving archives (Morra 2020) builds on Ann Cvetkovich's (2003) influential contribution about archives of feelings and their capacity to capture ephemeral and affective experiences that are not documented by conventional archives.

The erasure, marginalization, and trauma that often characterize gay and lesbian lives reveal the importance of the nontraditional types of archives known as ephemera, the "occasional publications and paper documents, material objects, and items that fall into the miscellaneous category" (Cvetkovich 2003, 243). These unusual archives constitute archives of feelings, "both material and immaterial, at once incorporating objects that might not ordinarily be considered archival, and at the same time, resisting documentation because sex and feelings are too personal or ephemeral to leave records" (Cvetkovich 2003, 244). Examples of archives of feelings include documentary films (Cvetkovich 2003, 244) and graphic novels (Cvetkovich

2008, 119). Similarly, other feminist scholars have studied artistic productions' capacity to capture immaterial experience, for instance artistic displays that document grief and loss following traumatic political killings (Bennett 2002) or photography that serves as a witness to the work of mourning (Phelan 2002). These sites therefore also suggest different selection criteria for materials, showing how, as Ann Cvetkovich writes, "affects [...] make a document significant" (2003, 243–44).

While culture and the arts can document affective and traumatic experiences, archiving sites may include more intimate spaces such as bedside tables (Sheffield 2014). By considering the nightstand as a "repository of artifacts" (115), Sheffield expands the definition of archival materials to include mundane objects that would be judged inappropriate or insignificant in traditional archives, such as lotion, earplugs, and clock radios, as well as lube, neck massagers, and lesbian erotica books. This shifts our focus from the victorious moments of mobilization to the more difficult, ephemeral, and intimate experiences, thus avoiding the archival exceptionalism that privileges the extraordinary moments of activism (114–15). Focusing on trauma and affective experiences, as captured by unusual archives in nontraditional archiving sites, also means considering the involvement in memory work of actors different than social movement organizations and states, a theme I turn to next.

Queer and feminist approaches to archiving cast a variety of individuals involved in documenting the past and their motivations to do so. These include photographers, visual artists and filmmakers as in the above examples, but also "friends, colleagues, lovers, companions and wives" (Micir 2019, 3). Studying modernist women writers facing erasure from literary history, Micir explores the biographical acts women writers used to write themselves into history (2019, 10). In doing so, Micir defines archiving as a "passion project" motivated by attachment rather than financial gain or professional recognition (2019, 14). In casting different people involved in memory work, Micir's work also sheds light on the "implicitly pedagogical, future-oriented impulse" for documenting the past (2019, 7). This recalls Rosenberg's (2000) feminist approach to commemoration as pedagogy, in which there is "an infrangible connection between remembrance and learning" (Simon and Rosenberg 2005, 83). Such learning, however, as Micir reminds us, is not always redemptive (2019, 51)—offering an intergenerational happy ending, for example—and sometimes results in failed or unfinished projects that never reach an audience.

By situating archiving in unusual sites, from artistic productions to bedside tables, and done by a variety of actors, from artists to lovers, Queer and feminist approaches to archiving invite us to think of public commemoration not just as the result of organizational or state initiative but also as done through culture by individuals in their everyday lives. Micir's analysis of friends, lovers, and partners' biographical projects as driven by a "protective empathy" (2019, 5) tempers the entrepreneurial character found in much of the literature on public commemoration. Instead of casting memory entrepreneurs pursuing a business agenda or memory agents pursuing a political mission (Conway 2010), Queer and feminist approaches present actors involved in remembering the past as individuals who are personally and emotionally invested in the realities they document.

I draw from feminist and Queer approaches to unusual archives to conceptualize Québec feminists' memory work of *L'Euguélionne* in alternative sites such as newspapers and magazines as commemorative reception. Conceptualizing cultural reception as a commemorative site enhances our understanding of feminist public memory work. It captures the commemoration of the movement's cultural production, rather than a movement leader or event, as well as a type of commemoration characterized by the diffuseness of cultural reception rather than circumscribed physical landmark sites like statues, plaques, monuments, or gravesites. It also implies defining memory agents as audiences—readers, viewers, and listeners—who interpret, evaluate, and select cultural products they are attached to and wish to see live on.

Case Selection, Methods, and Data

How do scholars go about studying commemoration without a site? To palliate the absence of a physical commemorative site for the novel, I constructed a qualitative data set comprised of cultural interventions by feminists such as intellectuals, community organizers, and other actors in the Québec cultural field who, since late 2006, have taken up the task to retrieve *L'Euguélionne*. I present below the sources of the data I constructed to capture the novel's cultural legacy. Building on Pia Lara's work (1988) on the importance of interventions in the public sphere, I first searched Québec's two most important newspapers by using the search term "*L'Euguélionne*." This led me to map out the central actors involved in the novel's commemoration: France Théoret, who was Bersianik's friend and colleague,

TABLE 1: SUMMARY OF DATA SOURCES

DATA TYPE	DATE	SOURCE	TYPE OF SPEECH ACT	QUANTITY
Newspaper articles	2006–2020	*Le Devoir* *La Presse*	Written	11 articles and opinion columns
Literary magazines	2006–2020	*Nuit Blanche* *Liberté*	Written	2 articles
Interviews	2016–2017	France Théoret Two members of the bookstore collective	Oral	4 in-depth interviews

and a feminist collective who borrowed the title *L'Euguélionne* to name their new bookstore. I then contacted them for interviews to learn more about the motivations behind their specific memory projects, and these interviews are included in the data set.

Commemorative reception is read as speech acts, that is, narratives in the public sphere that consist of "instances of social action" (Atkinson and Coffey 2002). This is in line with Pia Lara's exploration of illocutionary force, which understands narratives as the vehicle for the construction of collective and individual identities (Pia Lara 1988, 36). Speech acts were analyzed by asking the following questions: What are the claims made through the commemoration of *L'Euguélionne*? What is the emotional undertone of the commemoration? How do feminists describe and situate themselves vis-à-vis the era of mobilization during which the book was published? This inductive approach to data collection led to the identification of disappointment, discouragement, frustration, and mourning in parallel to revival efforts, thus leading to this paper's exploration of the affective character of claims in commemorative reception. Finding patterns in the speech acts' moods and claims, I identified three types of claims shaped by feminists' attachments to the novel.

Findings

Close analysis of feminists' commemorative reception reveals three types of claims, each shaped by their affective attachment to the novel and its legacy. First, feminists' dissatisfaction and discouragement have led to claims that extend from *L'Euguélionne* to other contemporary issues. Second, in disappointment and frustration about Bersianik's erasure from the canon, feminists have denounced the systems that reproduce these inequalities in literature and beyond by making specific claims about Bersianik's recognition. Finally, fear and mourning are expressed in commemorative reception that deals with the absence of *L'Euguélionne* through claims that enact Bersianik's legacy.

Extending Bersianik's Fate: Dissatisfaction and Discouragement with the Repetition of History

For some feminists, the commemoration of *L'Euguélionne* is done in parallel to the assertion of a deplorable lack of progress on feminist issues. By making a variety of claims about their current context through their commemoration of the book, feminists expose the continuity of gender oppression rather than making specific claims about *L'Euguélionne* to literary institutions. This type of commemoration is prefaced by an explanation to the contemporary audience of how feminist mobilization was "back then": how vibrant the movement was and the importance of the hard-fought battles. This praise for 1970s feminism is paired with the identification of ongoing contemporary issues, such as violence against women, and expresses discouragement with the repetition of history.

Discouragement is mixed with sadness in the opinion piece by the famous Québec feminist and former politician Lise Payette, who grieves her recently deceased friend, Louky Bersianik: "She was a friend, the kind of friend we love dearly and that we practically never see because our routes separated a long time ago and that we regret not having gotten back in touch with while there was still time" (*Le Devoir*, December 9, 2011). The sadness and regret expressed here are not unique to feminists, as grievers often feel a myriad of emotions related to the deceased. What is unique here is that those feelings are put in parallel to the political identity Payette and Bersianik shared, expressed by connecting her death with those of the anti-feminist shooting at the Montréal Polytechnique engineering school.[2] She dedicated her piece to "the sweet memory of the feminists who disappeared" and writes: "We recently commemorated the death of Polytechnique's young women for the 22nd time. In spite of the years that passed, the pain never disappeared.... While in Ottawa the conservative majority is about to destroy the firearm registry that represented the victory of the assassinated women over this world armed to its teeth, Louky Bersianik also died" (*Le Devoir*, December 9, 2011). Payette connects these two tragic moments to a common phenomenon: women who die in a "world armed to its teeth"

(*Le Devoir*, December 9, 2011). Grief here is both personal and collective, as the pain she refers to stems from the repetition of history: women passing away and precarious gains having to be fought for anew.

In that same newspaper column, the recounting of how Payette first met Bersianik illuminates this personal and collective experience further, linking the loss of both her friend and an era marked by the excitement of the discovery of feminism. Payette tells the story of when they first met in Paris, where they both lived at the age of thirty, a critical time in their adult lives. Payette reminisces about living under the same roof as a turning point in their lives: "Louky and I discovered feminism. . . . For us, the world had just changed. We would never be the same. Feminists, and proud to be" (*Le Devoir*, December 9, 2011). The piece conveys the feeling of empowerment they shared, as feminists "and proud to be."

Payette concludes her piece by extending the violence experienced by the women at Polytechnique and the symbolic violence experienced by Bersianik to other types of violence women experience around the world—from forced marriage to population control—and concludes by assigning blame for the continuation of violence against women: "We say that women have progressed a lot in the past 50 years. We have made it a long way, so it seems. So . . . who is it that did not progress?" (*Le Devoir*, December 9, 2011) Her friend's death and the forgotten book thus mark time, which leads Payette to assess their past shared hopes. This assessment, along with its extension to contemporary issues, is shaped by her discouragement with what she identifies as the repetition of history: women continue to die in oblivion.

Being discouraged about the lack of progress on feminist issues is not solely reserved for the feminists who mobilized in the 1970s. It also comes up in commemoration that draws upon academic expertise to remind contemporary readers of the impact of *L'Euguélionne* for Québec feminist literature. This is what feminist literature expert Isabelle Boisclair does when interviewed by Stéphane Baillargeon, columnist at *Le Devoir*. Baillargeon reports on statistics recently released by the organization Women in Literary Arts on the occasion of International Women's Day. He writes that "the numbers are not very good" (*Le Devoir*, March 8, 2014) and mentions *L'Euguélionne* to signal the lack of progress in the literary scene since the late 1970s. He goes on to explain that the beginning of the Quiet Revolution[3] and the publication of *L'Euguélionne* were two turning points in terms of feminist writing in Québec. As Boisclair points out, however, "Since then? Since then nothing. . . . There have been indeed no other turning points, even if the transformation more or less continues" (*Le Devoir*, March 8, 2014). Boisclair's discouragement about these numbers appears when she criticizes women's representation in *Le Devoir*, the newspaper in which she is being interviewed: "I am obsessed with numbers, but I look forward to the moment when I no longer need to count. Only a few weeks ago in *Le Devoir*, I noted two women for eighteen men in the *Books* section of the paper" (*Le Devoir*, March 8, 2014). While Boisclair does not share a generational affiliation with Bersianik, her interview reveals a similar dissatisfaction and discouragement with the lack of progress in women's presence in the literary scene since the 1970s to Payette's about violence against women.

Denouncing Bersianik's Erasure: Disappointment and Frustration in Claims for Recognition

In contrast with the previous type of claim, which extended from the book to contemporary issues, this second type of claim remains closely connected to the book and its author. Central to claims of this kind are a reevaluation of *L'Euguélionne* for the purpose of denouncing the lack of recognition Bersianik received for her work. Claims for the book's recognition are often made by feminists who experienced the 1970s context as audiences rather than participants. Their disappointment is grounded in *L'Euguélionne*'s lack of recognition *in spite of* the laudatory reviews it received at the time of publication, and their frustration accompanies a critique of the institutions that are at fault. Feminists who make a case for the recognition of Bersianik and her oeuvre frame her fate as yet another case of women's underappreciation.

While claims for recognition are not always openly angry, they nonetheless evoke the frustration of seeing an impactful feminist moment like the publication of *L'Euguélionne* be forgotten by literary and political history. This is the case for feminist columnist Josée Boileau, who, in an homage to Bersianik, evokes her attachment to the book. She reminds the contemporary reader of the book's quality and importance and describes the exhilarating experience readers of *L'Euguélionne* shared at its publication: "It was pleasurable and terribly inspiring" (*Le Devoir*, December 6, 2011). *L'Euguélionne*, according to Boileau, is a work of universal importance as well as powerful piece of writing that disappointingly lost its significance in the literary world: "This unsettling, magnificent and massive literary work that Louky Bersianik published in 1976 no longer has its place in libraries." Even her death is overlooked, as Boileau explains, showing how, in spite of her talent, she did not escape the common lot: "She died Saturday, and her death has gone unnoticed even though she is one of the great names of our literature."

Boileau's reevaluation of *L'Euguélionne* and praise for Bersianik enable rediscovery of the book but also provide an example of the reality that many women face: "All this talent has not prevented Mme. Bersianik to be forgotten, a very feminine reality." There is disappointment in Boileau's comment: even talent and a best-selling novel were not enough for Bersianik to gain lasting recognition. Boileau goes on to show that this remains true for women in various fields, as she rhetorically asks: "How many women are there amongst the 11 laureates of this year's Prix du Québec? Only one. How many state funerals for women? None. And the young generation that we celebrate, be they engineers, producers, orchestra directors or chefs, still is masculine." Boileau's disappointment fuels her critique of other institutions that do not recognize women's contributions. She concludes by making a specific claim that *L'Euguélionne* should be reissued, which, according to her, would help to "repair the omission."

In a more castigating call for recognition than Boileau's, Andrée Ferretti denounces Bersianik's exclusion from an anthology of Québec's twenti-eth-century intellectual monuments. In her opinion piece, she powerfully advocates for Bersianik's recognition as a monument by analyzing her books, including *L'Euguélionne*, and the relevance of her work for Québec intel-lectual thought. Her frustration lies in the lack of recognition Bersianik's word received from the literature institution: "Her essential contribution, until now underevaluated, has been eclipsed by the patriarchy" (*Le Devoir*, August 24, 2006). She connects Bersianik's fate to that of other women as she rhetorically asks: "Would it be because, in this early twenty-first century, like all previous centuries, a woman who reflects on the world as a woman is necessarily occulted? Would it be because women can think and their thinking be recognized, yesterday and today, on the *sine qua non* condition that they situate their work within the patriarchal vision of world and life?" This constitutes the most openly disappointed stance found in the data, as she opens with: "I was extremely disappointed by the absence, in the choice of 'their monuments,' of the immense body of work by Louky Bersianik." Her disappointment is therefore tied to frustration at the patriarchal insti-tutions responsible for the exclusion from the canon other feminist writers and thinkers face.

In another piece by Ferretti, this time in the Québec literary magazine

Nuit Blanche, I find a mix of the disappointment and frustration that characterize the denouncing claims. Ferretti states that talking about Louky Bersianik and her legacy is troublesome because doing so means having to palliate the "spoken and unspoken words that underestimate and obscure an essential contribution to contemporary philosophical thought" (*Nuit Blanche* 44). While in this piece the claim for recognition is more implicit than in her previous newspaper column, the impetus for writing is again the lack of recognition Bersianik received by the literary institution and the need to redress that injustice. Forgetting, in Ferretti's piece, is framed as a threat that justifies the urgency to engage with Bersianik's work and change the systems that have wronged her. She concludes the piece with suggestions for how to engage with Bersianik's oeuvre, which are educational but tinted with accusations: "The reader who is hurried or lazy, or frightened by a prolonged contact with a feminist thought that is philosophically more universal than the recognized philosophies [. . .] can get an overview of this thought by reading *L'Archéologie du future* (Sisyphe 2007), an anthology prepared by Bersianik herself" (46). Ferretti's instructions on how to revisit the work of Bersianik resemble the enacting claims I will explicate in the next section. However, the implicit critique of the literary institution found in her piece shows that claims for recognition aim at challenging what has been said about Bersianik and the systems that led to her erasure, rather than dealing with the absence itself.

Enacting Feminist Heritage: Fearing and Mourning Absence

The third type of claims found in the data enacts rather than asks for *L'Euguélionne*'s recognition. While these claims also deplore the absence of women in collective memory, they are different from the previous types because they do not make specific claims about *L'Euguélionne*. Rather, they aim at rebuilding what is lost, using the book to embody the recognition of feminists' contributions. Their feelings about the book and its legacy are also different in that, instead of discouragement or disappointment, enacting claims come from a fear of missing out on what has been and a sadness for what is lost.

In an opinion piece in *Le Devoir*, feminists highlight how toponyms play an undeniable historical role in Québec and argue that part of that history remains hidden because it does not "[honour] women's memory" (*Le Devoir*, March 5, 2016). They take the opportunity of International Women's Day to ask municipalities to address this issue by adopting toponymic parity, and they provide *L'Euguélionne* Street as an example. They conclude by arguing that, "without such measures [to insure women's representation in cities' toponymies], women from Québec will be relegated to the role of "alibi women," in other words, a cop-out to avoid engaging meaningfully with women's heritage. This claim is thus shaped by absence, expressing the necessity to avoid women's superficial acknowledgment and erasure.

The theme of absence is also found in a 2019 piece in the literary magazine *Liberté*, where the author and editor Valérie Lefebvre-Faucher signals the "weird presence" of Bersianik in her life. She writes that, while discussions of Bersianik often focus on lack—"lack of recognition, lack of memory, lack of openness, and privation" (77)—she nevertheless finds herself haunted by the ghost of Bersianik, who gave her a sense of belonging to a feminist literary tradition (78). Lefrebvre-Faucher provides guidance to potential readers on how to approach Bersianik's oeuvre, and states rather than claims her work's status as a literary classic. She writes: "Her presence in transformation, that is what makes it a classic to me. (Even though I do not expect the specialists to agree with this definition)" (79). Unlike in the second type of claims where feminists asked traditional literary institutions to recognize Bersianik's oeuvre and *L'Euguélionne*'s status as a classic, Lefrebvre-Faucher enacts that recognition without expecting change from literary institutions.

Absence and mourning together shape enacting claims, as shown by the bookstore collective's experience of borrowing the title of the book to name their new feminist space, a gesture friends of Bersianik were touched by. As one interviewee, Camille, explained to me in 2017: "Many people that were friends of Bersianik came and told us *Wow*—they were really touched that we chose this name. . . . So people would come and . . . it was like an opportunity to mourn her" (pers. comm., 2017). The librarians were not mourning their friend through their commemoration of *L'Euguélionne*, but they bore witness to the grief of Bersianik's friends as they created a feminist space that honors the movement's heritage.

Honouring and mourning coexist in claims that deal with the absence of *L'Euguélionne* in the literary canon. For the collective, using a forgotten feminist classic was their way to honour those that came before them. Camille explained how this is especially important for the new generations of feminists: in the current context of a feminist revival, she noted, there is a danger as a young feminist "to position yourself as 'the new feminists.'" The collective's way to avoid that trap, Camille went on to say, is "to perpetuate a history and a tradition that is not perpetuated enough, according to us. That was also the idea: to follow their footsteps" (pers. comm., 2017). A tradition that is "not perpetuated enough" needs rediscovery, which explains the choice of *L'Euguélionne* as the name of the bookstore, rather than another, better-known feminist classic. As Nicolas explained during a 2017 interview: "To choose *L'Euguélionne* instead of *Les Fées ont soifs*, well you. . . . Everyone knows *Les Fées ont soifs*, everyone studies it, it's your token women's theater piece, whereas *L'Euguélionne*, everyone had forgotten it, so we allow for its rediscovery" (pers. comm., 2017).

Therefore, the collective chose *L'Euguélionne* in spite of the fact that, as Nicolas jokingly remarked, it is a name that "half the people cannot pronounce" (pers. comm., 2017). As Stéphanie Dufresne, cofounder of L'Euguélionne, explained to a journalist, it was chosen "to reinstate it" (*Le Devoir*, March 8, 2016). For the collective, rediscovering what they know to be lost enables the perpetuation of feminist history.

Much like the first type of claims, which extend the fate of *L'Euguélionne* to contemporary issues, the enacting claims reveal disappointment about the lack of progress. However, the tone is different. Instead of using *L'Euguélionne* to express discouragement about past unmet hopes, enacting claims express a desire to "keep going" through the rediscovery of forgotten histories. As Nicolas put it: "There were black feminist collectives in Québec, and we've lost that history, women's histories. For sure, there are different dynamics that explain these losses, but these are being rediscovered, and just the fact that we are putting words on it . . . it allows to keep going, to recognise it."

Feminist heritage thus brings to the fore the idea of progress, or lack thereof, and how the rediscovery of alternative histories can palliate that. Prefiguring Bersianik's heritage thus resolves a paralyzing tension for this last group of activists: how to "keep going" knowing it might be forgotten.

Discussion and Conclusion

The commemoration of *L'Euguélionne* in media outlets by Québec feminists is unusual. It is unusual because of the commemorative material, a novel rather than a movement leader or event; because of its site, cultural reception rather than a plaque or statue; and because of the actors involved, friends and readers instead of social movement organizations or state actors. To conceptualize this unusual commemoration, I turned to Queer and feminist approaches to the study of intimate sites and the affective charge of archival material. Inspired by their work, I developed the concept of commemorative reception to better understand sites of public commemoration characterized by the diffuse character of cultural reception and driven by individuals' attachment to a movement's cultural production.

Contemporary conversations about public commemorations have urged us to rethink the way we engage with the past. Defacing of statues and calls to rename streets and institutions by Indigenous and anti-racist movements have brought into question conquering narratives of commemoration that often unequivocally glorify white and masculine historical figures. I suggest that the analysis of commemorative reception presents an opportunity to take up this challenge in our scholarly work. By mapping commemoration outside of traditional physical sites, as undertaken by a variety of actors outside the state and driven by affective attachments to cultural productions, the concept of commemorative reception avoids the archival exceptionalism and conquering undertone that often characterize the commemoration of spectacular historical moments, even those from difficult pasts, such as wars and political assassinations. As an analytical tool rooted in Queer and feminist epistemologies, the concept thus permits not only a theoretical move away from commemoration as resolution but also a methodological consideration of commemoration beyond static and permanent forms like statues, plaques, and monuments. I propose that taking up this challenge by using and applying the concept of commemorative reception in our study of feminist activism has implications for how the story of feminism is told and how we come to understand movement continuity.

The findings suggest that tracing the cultural trajectory of a book through the concept of commemorative reception can be taken up by scholars interested in intergenerational dynamics. Applying the concept of commemorative reception tells the story of three groups, more or less delimited along generations, who feel differently about the book and its legacy, which in turn shapes the way they publicly attempt to renew the movement. First, feminists who deal with what they identify as a lack of progress since the publication of *L'Euguélionne* extend Bersianik's fate to other contemporary issues such as violence against women. These extending claims were more often made by feminists who were participants of the era during which the novel was published. They used the book not to discount what has been achieved since then, but rather as a pedagogical device to mark time and identify ongoing issues that need redress (see, for example, Simon and

Rosenberg 2005). Second, when expressing disappointment and frustration with Bersianik's lack of recognition in spite of her great talent, feminists made specific claims about *L'Euguélionne* paired with a critique of the institutions that led to Bersianik's erasure. These claims were more often made by actors who were audiences to the book during the era in which it was published. Finally, whether it is Lefebvre-Faucher's discussion of Bersianik's "weird presence" in her life or the bookstore collective's rediscovery of lost women's histories, feminists who are inheritors of Bersianik and her era of mobilization deal with the absence of *L'Euguélionne* in the canon through enacting claims. While the data does not permit generalizations about feminism and its waves, future scholars could put the concept of commemorative reception in conversation with scholars' work on the inheritance of anti-racist and gender-radical symbols (Hammer 2020) or of neglected feminist figures (Aronson 2020). This work could produce alternative chronologies of feminism and its intergenerational dynamics through the cultural trajectory of its symbols.

Finally, the case of *L'Euguélionne* in Québec exposed how avenues for movement renewal were publicly constructed through commemoration based on feminists' individual affective attachments to the movement's cultural productions. This extends the work of feminist scholars who have shown how women keep up subversive challenges by doing work behind the scenes in between waves of protest, what are termed "periods of abeyance" in Taylor's (1989) influential work. Service work and commemoration are commonly identified as key tactics that help the movement survive during such periods (Grey and Sawer 2008). This work has a tendency to present commemoration as a way to conserve and hold on to what was until better opportunities come up, whereas the concept of commemorative reception presents a more generative take on commemoration as a way movements renew themselves. This contribution invites scholars studying abeyance to explore how activists' affective attachments to the past fuel future activism.

Marie-Lise Drapeau-Bisson is a PhD candidate at the University of Toronto (Canada). She studies culture, activism, and gender. Her current project explores how feminists use books to animate their political work through the case study of Québec feminist literary classic *L'Euguélionne* by Louky Bersianik. She can be reached at ml.drapeau.bisson@mail.utoronto.ca.

Notes

1. Citations of French Québec newspapers have been translated into English by the author.
2. The Polytechnique anti-feminist shooting happened in Montreal on December 6, 1989. Fourteen women were killed and thirteen people were hurt by the shooter, Marc Lépine. This shooting is a pivotal moment in Canadian feminism, and its commemoration has been central to the movement.
3. The term "Quiet Revolution" refers to a decade of fundamental political and social change in Québec, starting in 1960 with the fall of the Union Nationale populist government and the election of the provincial liberals of Jean Lesage. During this decade emerged three major political projects that would come to define contemporary Québec society: the nationalization of hydroelectricity, the secularization of education, and the emergence of a left-leaning nationalist movement.

Works Cited

Aronson, Amy. 2020. "Recovering the 'Most Neglected Feminist Leader of the Twentieth Century': Crystal Eastman, Historical Memory, and the Bequest of an Intersectional Inheritance." *Women's Studies Quarterly* 48, no. 1: 149–64.

Atkinson, Paul, and Amanda Coffey. 2002. "Revisiting the Relationship between Participant Observation and Interviewing." In *Handbook of Interview Research: Context and Method*, edited by Jaber F. Gubrium and James A. Holstein, 801–14. Thousand Oaks, CA: SAGE Publications.

Baillargeon, Stéphane. 2014. "Où sont les femmes? Littérature, sexisme et medias." *Le Devoir*, March 8, 2014. https://www.ledevoir.com/culture/medias/401909/ou-sont-les-femmes.

Basile, Jean. 1976. "L'Euguélionne de Louky Bersianik, La moitié des hommes sont une femme." *Le Devoir*, March 6, 1976, Cahier 2, 13 & 16.

Beaudin, Évelyne, Geneviève Béliveau, and Gabriel Martin. 2016. "Controns l'invisibilité toponymique des femmes." *Le Devoir*, March 5, 2016. https://www.ledevoir.com/opinion/idees/464684/journee-du-8-mars-controns-l-invisibilite-toponymique-des-femmes.

Bennett, Jill. 2002. "Art, Affect, and the 'Bad Death': Strategies for Communicating the Sense Memory of Loss." *Signs: Journal of Women in Culture and Society* 28, no. 1: 333–51.

Bersianik, Louky. 2012 [1976]. *L'Euguélionne*. Montréal: Éditions TYPO.

Boileau, Josée. 2011. "Louky Bersianik, sortir de l'oubli." *Le Devoir*, December 6, 2011, A6.

Conway, Brian. 2010. "New Directions in the Sociology of Collective Memory and Commemoration." *Sociology Compass* 4, no. 7: 442–53.

Cvetkovich, Ann. 2003. *An Archive of Feelings.* Durham, NC: Duke University Press.

———. 2008. "Drawing the Archive in Alison Bechdel's 'Fun Home.'" *Women's Studies Quarterly* 36, nos. 1/2: 111–28.

Ferretti, Andrée. 2006. "'Monuments,' dites-vous?" *Le Devoir*, August 24, 2006, A6.

———. 2011. "L'oeuvre de louky Bersianik: Un secret bien gardé." *Nuit Blanche*, no. 122, Spring 2011, 44–46.

Grey, Sandra, and Marian Sawer. 2008. *Women's Movements: Flourishing or in Abeyance?* Abingdon, UK: Routledge.

Hammer, Allison K. 2020. "'Doing Josephine': The Radical Legacy of Josephine Baker's Banana Dance." *Women's Studies Quarterly* 48, nos. 1/2: 165–81.

Hite, Katherine, and Daniela Jara. 2020. "Presenting Unwieldy Pasts." *Memory Studies* 13, no. 3: 245–52.

Lalonde, Catherine. 2016. "L'Euguélionne, future librairie féministe à Montréal." *Le Devoir*, March 8, 2016. https://www.ledevoir.com/lire/464891/livres-l-euguelionne-future-librairie-feministe-a-montreal.

Lefebvre-Faucher, Valérie. 2019. "Le terrible fantôme de Louky Bersianik" *Liberté*, no. 324, Summer 2019, 77–79.

Marshall, Daniel, Kevin P. Murphy, and Zeb Tortorici. 2015. "Queering Archives: Intimate Tracings." *Radical History Review 15*, no. 2 (122), 1–10.

Martel, Réginald. 1976. "Quand femme varie" *La Presse*, March 20, 1976, D3.

Micir, Melanie. 2019. *The Passion Projects: Modernist Women, Intimate Archives, Unfinished Lives.* Princeton, NJ: Princeton University Press.

Morra, Linda M. 2020. *Moving Archives.* Waterloo, ON: Wilfrid Laurier University Press.

Payette, Lise. 2011. "La place des femmes." *Le Devoir*, December 9, 2011, A9.

Pearce, Susan C. 2011. "Delete, Restart, or Rewind? Post-1989 Public Memory Work in East-Central Europe." *Sociology Compass* 5, no. 4: 17.

Phelan, Peggy. 2002. "Francesca Woodman's Photography: Death and the Image One More Time." *Signs: Journal of Women in Culture and Society* 27, no. 4: 26.

Pia Lara, Maria. 1988. *Moral Textures: Feminist Narratives in the Public Sphere.* Cambridge: Polity Press.

Rosenberg, Sharon. 2000. "Standing in a Circle of Stone: Rupturing the Binds of Emblematic Memory." In *Between Hope and Despair: Pedagogy and the Remembrance of Historical Trauma*, edited by Roger I. Simon, Sharon Rosenberg, and Claudia Eppert, 78–91. Lanham, MD: Rowman & Littlefield.

Sheffield, Rebecka Taves. 2014. "The Bedside Table Archives: Archive Intervention and Lesbian Intimate Domestic Culture." *Radical History Review* Fall, no. 120: 108–20.

Simon, Roger I., and Sharon Rosenberg. 2005. "Beyond the Logic of Emblematization: Remembering and Learning from the Montréal Massacre." In *The Touch of the Past: Remembrance, Learning, and Ethics,* edited by Roger Simon, 65–86. New York: Palgrave Macmillan.

Taylor, Verta. 1989. "Social Movement Continuity: The Women's Movement in Abeyance." *American Sociological Review* 54, no. 5: 761–75.

Vinitzky-Seroussi, Vered. 2002. "Commemorating a Difficult Past: Yitzhak Rabin's Memorials." *American Sociological Review* 67, no. 1: 30–51.

Wagner-Pacifici, Robin, and Barry Schwartz. 1991. "The Vietnam Veterans Memorial: Commemorating a Difficult Past." *American Journal of Sociology* 97, no. 2: 376–420.

Mourning Sarah Hegazi: Grief and the Cultivation of Queer Arabness

Sophie Chamas and Sabiha Allouche

Abstract: In this article, we engage in a discursive analysis and affective reading of written and recorded responses to the suicide of Sarah Hegazi, an Egyptian queer feminist communist who took her own life in exile in Canada in the summer of 2020. In the aftermath of Hegazi's suicide, queer Arabs across the Middle East and North Africa, as well their diaspora, publicly mourned her death in an unprecedented way through an abundance of social media posts, blogs, articles, Twitter and Instagram hashtags, and vigils. Some mourned her as a friend and comrade, but most did not know Hegazi personally. In what follows, we explore what it was about Hegazi's life and death that inspired such a response from queer Arabs and what this collective mourning was productive of. **Keywords**: queer; grief; Middle East; suicide; mourning; militancy

"The sky is sweeter than the earth; I want the sky and not the earth."
—Sarah Hegazi, June 13, 2020

With these words, posted to her Instagram page a day before her suicide, Sarah Hegazi bid farewell to a world she described as too cruel to bear and survive. In her parting letter, she asked forgiveness of her loved ones, and she forgave the earth its cruelty as she turned toward the sky. The photo that accompanied her message shows her lying in the grass, squinting as the sun shined on her, turned toward the camera with eyes closed and a smile spread across her face.

It is best to describe Hegazi in her own words. As expressed on her Instagram profile, she was "super communist, super gay and feminist" (Hegazi

WSQ: Women's Studies Quarterly **50**: 3 & 4 (Fall/Winter 2022) © 2022 by Sophie Chamas and Sabiha Allouche.
All rights reserved.

2020). Hegazi became known to queer and nonqueer Arabs across the Middle East and North Africa (MENA) and their diaspora when, in 2017, she was arrested for raising a rainbow flag at a Mashrou' Leila concert in her native Cairo.

Mashrou' Leila, a popular Lebanese alternative rock band with an openly queer lead singer, Hamed Sinno, was playing to a crowd of around thirty-five thousand that evening. Sinno (2020) describes the atmosphere as "thick with love and abandon." Amidst the euphoria, two members of the audience scaled their friends' shoulders and unfurled rainbow flags. The crowd, Sinno tells us, cheered: "That part is often left out of the story, the cheering. For the rest of the night, we all feel safe. We are all seen. We are loved." That night, Sinno writes, belonged to those two members of the audience, Sarah Hegazi and Ahmed Alaa: "For one night, Cairo is theirs. The queers have won the Arab Spring." Hegazi was photographed draped in the flag, smiling jubilantly.

In the aftermath of the concert, she was arrested alongside approximately seventy-five others. Her photo had been making the rounds on Egyptian social media, and commentators on television and in print began calling for her and others to be arrested. They were accused of promoting perversion, and they were said to have threatened Egypt's moral fabric and, by extension, its national sovereignty, with homosexuality framed as an instrument of foreign intervention. Hegazi was charged with inciting debauchery. She spent three months in jail, where she was routinely tortured and sexually abused by prison guards and inmates. She was eventually released on bail and granted political asylum in Canada, where she would take her own life on June 14, 2020 (El Sirgany 2020).

In the aftermath of Hegazi's suicide, queer Arabs across the MENA and its diaspora publicly mourned her death through an abundance of social media posts, blogs, articles, Twitter and Instagram hashtags, and vigils. The public response to her death from queer Arab communities was unprecedented. Some mourned her as a friend and comrade, but most did not know Hegazi personally. In what follows, we explore why Hegazi's death inspired such a response from queer Arabs, and what this collective mourning was productive of. We examine how this response affected Hegazi's afterlife on earth while she rested in kinder skies, and how these acts of mourning worked to chip away at the cruelty that killed her, in order to make the earth sweeter for queers who are still bound to it.

Queer Arabs insisted that Hegazi was driven to suicide by the actions of the Egyptian state and the alienation of exile, and that the violence and estrangement she experienced both at home and abroad was a product not only of her queerness but her political identity and commitments. We argue that this framing was generative of a politics of countermemorialization that challenged nationalist commemorative practices and the politics they serve both in the MENA and in the West. This politics of countermemorialization reframed the ideal subject of both queerness and Arabness, destabilizing and reconceptualizing both identity categories via an insistence on the possibilities of their dialectical intertwinement in the face of Western and Middle Eastern discourses adamant about their irreconcilability. We theorize the potentiality of queer Arabness as a mode of both making sense of and being in the world that can subvert, on the one hand, nationalisms, and on the other hand, the pathologization and individualization of queer suicide. We think with a manifestation of queer Arab politics, as a practice of making evident the structural and transnational dimensions of queer suffering and their entanglement with other modes of oppression and marginalization, in ways that encourage a rethinking of queer advocacy and queer politics in the MENA and beyond it.

We have come together in this special issue to celebrate the fiftieth anniversary of *WSQ*. In thinking with the collective mourning that Hegazi's death inspired, and the ways in which queer Arabs made sense of her death, articulated her legacy, and imagined a politics in service of it, we contribute to this issue's call to conceptualize feminist and queer commemoration and its counterhegemonic potentiality. We draw on previous issues of *WSQ*, including *Survival* (Spring/Summer 2016) and *Queer Methods* (Fall/Winter 2016), placing scholarly theorizing around queer continuity in conversation with reflections on the subject by queer Arab activists, as a means of highlighting the generative potential of entangling the journal's past contributions with knowledge produced beyond the academy and beyond the Global North. The call for this special issue asked, how can commemoration "resist reproducing master narratives through feminist and queer reorientations of historical artifacts?" In what follows, we attempt to address this question by examining the ways in which queer Arabs commemorated Hegazi in a manner that pushed against hegemonic conceptualizations of Egyptian and, more broadly, Arab nationalism, the exclusions they are premised on, and the violence they mask, while simultaneously challenging Western narratives both about the causes of queer suicide more generally and the conditions of possibility for queer suffering in the non-Western

world. We ask how queer Arab suffering can be addressed without reproducing hegemonic narratives in the West that exceptionalize and pathologize
Arab queerphobia and weaponise it in the service of political and economic
imperialism.

This article is based on a discursive analysis and affective reading of written and recorded responses to Hegazi's death by queer Arabs. As scholars
of gender and sexuality in the MENA who are also from the region and
embedded within regional and diasporic queer Arab networks, we came
across these responses in the immediate aftermath of Hegazi's death as they
were circulated on our social media feeds, as well as through friendship
and professional circles.[1] What we present here, then, was not selected but
organically discovered by virtue of the spaces we occupy personally and
professionally. The reflections analyzed in this article traveled in significant ways, featuring again and again via shares on a diversity of queer Arab
platforms, from personal social media pages to the accounts of collectives.
The reflections we reference were for the most part written or delivered in
English, and where we reference material originally written in Arabic, we
work with and cite published English translations. We recognize the limitations of engaging material written in a language inaccessible to many in the
MENA. We work, in what follows, with what was available to us, but we
also insist on the theoretical and political purchase of the interventions in
question, and we insist that what we present here circulates in the languages
of the MENA in less formal and less public manners on an everyday basis.
In this article, we offer up a sample of interventions that are occurring in
multiple languages, spaces, and modes in the region and its diaspora, and
of which the material analyzed is but a microcosm.

We focus on reflections that circulated in virtual spaces, rather than
vigils that took place in "real life." With the exception of Lebanon, all public
in-person gatherings in honor of Hegazi took place in diasporic contexts.
Our choice to focus on the virtual derives from our desire to highlight those
modes of remembering, raging, and reflecting that reached as broad a queer
Arab audience as possible and that drew it together as a collectivity across
borders and despite access privileges, rather than atomizing it based on territory and ability to venture into public spaces marked as queer.

We seek to highlight the virtual's potential for creating room for queer
Arabs who are not publicly out, or who move between out-ness and in-ness,
to express and cultivate their identities and connect with others. We are
interested in the space and opportunity offered up by the virtual for the

cultivation of queer Arab identity and belonging by circumventing the dangers and limitations of accessing and cultivating queer life in public spaces in the MENA.[2]

We read the texts presented in this article *as* queer theory, following the likes of Judith Butler, who understands queer theoretical production as a means of making "life liveable" (as cited in Brim and Ghaziani 2016, 18), and as a product of "the desire to persist in the face of precarity" (Luciano and Chen 2015, 193). If a queer orientation toward the past and toward death is a means of staving off the forces that routinely work to eliminate "the present and future of queer experiences, relationships, and feelings" (Brim and Ghaziani 2016, 22–23), we examine what might be learned from the ways in which queer Arabs have made sense of the why and how of queer precarity and imagined modes of challenging it. We are invested in how queer Arabs themselves theorize queerness, Arabness, and queer Arabness; in how they understand state and society and these entities' investment in snuffing out queer life; and in their attentiveness to the political economy of queer abandonment and its consequences.

Furthermore, we are invested in a practice of scholarly care when it comes to the study of queer Arab pain, one that is attentive to the dangers involved in centering the West when studying queer Arab life and in fixating on the ways in which LGBT rights have been weaponized as tools of empire at the expense of addressing the investment that Middle Eastern states have in queer disposability and punishment as tools of political legitimacy. What follows is an attempt at demonstrating what could happen if we turn our gaze away from the West, its assumptions, and its instruments of power and think through the material, rather than cultural, reasons why Arab states harass and kill queers. How, we ask, can an attentiveness to these material conditions reveal Arab and Western states to be two faces of the same monster?

We have paid tribute to Hegazi elsewhere, outside of the confines and restrictions of academic journals. It is not our intention in this work to appropriate her queer death, to codify it, scientize it, or make it a "thing" by cementing it firmly in an institutionalized space (this journal proper). We actively encourage our readers to "de-authorize" (Hemmings 2011, 23) us by not minding our names when disseminating this work, and to think with the material we put forward as "stories that matter" given their potential for "being politically transformative" (Hemmings 2011, 2–3).

Halberstam (2000) has previously cautioned us to mind "the ethics of biography" when relating the afterlives of nonnormative bodies and argues that "all must be read and remembered according to the narratives they meticulously circulated about themselves when they were alive" (62). We not only center Hegazi's life in this work but we also strive to showcase her impact, so apparent in the multitude of mourning voices that responded to her passing.

The Many Deaths of Sarah Hegazi

Sinno (2020) writes that while "many a queer Arab has lost lovers, chosen family, friends and comrades," Hegazi's death "cut differently." Her death "cut differently" because it was obvious to all that she had been driven to suicide by the Egyptian state; that she had, in fact, already been killed by the state prior to fleeing to Canada, where she took her own life.

Moroccan queer feminist Rita Slaoui (2020) explains that "Sarah's death feels particularly violent and personal as she could have been any of us. Many of us can see ourselves and our friends in her. Her death reminds us of the proximity of danger, which, while deluded by optimism, some of us can sometimes forget" (5). Hegazi's gesture at that fateful concert attracted the wrath of a state that saw an opportunity to relegitimize and sediment its own precarious authority by punishing a so-called deviant act. A moment of hope for queer Arabs became an opportunity for the authoritarian state. This revealed that queer emancipation would remain an impossibility so long as state power continued to depend on the production and punishment of deviance (Amar 2013), and the anxieties wrought by geopolitics and neoliberalism continued to be displaced onto those constructed as deviants and framed, as a result, as threats to sovereignty and security. The feelings of "love and abandon" (Sinno 2020) that permeated the Mashrou' Leila concert were quickly replaced by anger, fear, and intense anxiety following Hegazi's death.

On his Instagram page, the novelist Saleem Haddad (2020) spoke of the haunting nature of the photo snapped of Hegazi at the concert—the way it transformed after her arrest and subsequent death from a symbol of possibility to a warning of the consequences awaiting queer Arabs who dared to be queer Arabs in public. Hegazi told the world, in her own words, that prison killed her (Arraf 2018). In the aftermath of her death, queer Arabs insisted that she had been murdered because the pain and trauma that drove her to suicide was the product of routine structural violence, as well as the state-sanctioned moral panics that regularly target queer Arabs and which they live in constant anticipation of (Sinno 2020).

Reflecting on Hegazi's death and the clampdown on personal liberties in contemporary Egypt, Sinno (2020) writes of that fateful concert and frames it as a temporal rupture during which, for an instant, the queers had "won the Arab Spring." In so doing, he sheds light on the investment that the state had in cracking down on the potentiality of that moment through a response that we can understand not only as authoritarian but *counterrevolutionary*. Tareq Baconi (2020) poignantly remarks that "there is nothing more frightening than threatened insecurity. Arab nations, in all their might, trembling in the face of a happy young woman."

In the postcolonial period, Middle Eastern states, including Egypt, have relied for their endurance and legitimacy on a narrative of "permanent emergency" productive of hypersecuritization, and on summoning deviance-as-security-threat to distract from and displace blame for the anxieties that particular neoliberal and geopolitical configurations have been productive of. In the aftermath of the Egyptian revolution and the counterrevolution that followed it, the military's permeation into all facets of Egyptian life heightened this logic of security, which relies on the production of a deviant citizenry. In Hegazi's case, we see the fusing of two pathologies: queer desire and communist aspirations. Communism and queerness become interchangeable. The communist, an ideological deviant, becomes also a sexual deviant, and vice versa. As Slaoui (2020) explains as she reflects on why Hegazi's death affected her so intensely: "Once more, I was face to face with the violence of police-states and societies who target us, the queers, the feminists, the communists, the revolutionaries."

Following Hegazi's death, social media posts demonizing her by citing her queerness and communist beliefs were common in Egypt and the wider region. We understand these violent articulations as a reflection of contemporary sociopolitical and economic anxieties in Egypt and the scapegoating through which the state is spared blame for them. Baconi (2020) writes: "Comment after comment of vile anger, and I could not make out what most rattled these commentators, her queerness, her atheism, her communism or her feminism." Communism is frequently depicted as blasphemous and therefore un-Egyptian, through the equation of its proponents' secular beliefs (the separation of religion from state) with atheist (negation of God's existence) ones. Similarly, the Egyptian state has historically reinforced its sovereignty by criminalizing and punishing queer sexuality, framing it as an instrument of Western imperialism (Pratt 2007). Hegazi's arrest provided the Egyptian state an opportunity to draw on hegemonic notions of proper "Egyptianness" and their entanglement with the protection of national sovereignty in order to relegitimize its own authority.

By not killing Hegazi, the Egyptian state let her live. It relegated her to a slow death, which it framed as a product of her own making, first by disabling her from expressing her whole sense of self and living her queer Arabness openly and fully, then by imprisoning and torturing her for daring to push against this obstruction, and finally by thrusting her into exile where, unable to heal and be whole, she ended her life and thus the state succeeded in finally killing her. Under such circumstances, then, "suicide might represent an escape from slow death" (Puar 2017, 152). Hegazi's arrest and subsequent suicide pointed to and warned of other slow deaths—past, present, and future. Writing for the London-based queer Arab collective Pride of Arabia, GHM (2020) tells of a life characterized by "treading water," as she reflects on the effect that Hegazi's death had on her. "I've become adept at treading," she writes, "but will is never enough, and so I have learned to surround myself with ways to stay afloat. Like people I am going to send your letter to."

Hegazi's relocation to Canada, away from direct state violence, did little to alleviate her trauma. To think of Canada as a guarantor of queer happiness, to use Ahmed's terms (2010), is to turn a blind eye to the webs of censorship and discipline that asylum seekers often find themselves entangled in (Allouche 2017; Greatrick 2019). On this note, and in addition to holding the Egyptian state responsible for Hegazi's death, Arab Queers on stolen Tkaronto and Tiohtià:ke land also held "the Canadian government accountable for its lacklustre support of refugees and their role in internal wars" (Arab Queers 2020). The labor involved in living with and against the traumas that the Egyptian state inflicted upon her, alongside the absence of the intimate attachments of home as well as the alienating nature of life in Canada for a queer communist migrant, gradually depleted Hegazi. As an anonymous post on the Cairo-based Wordpress blog *Queers Who Can't Grief in Public* (QCGP) reminds: "We encounter exile in our very homes, our balconies, our beds. . . . We are already exiled from our bodies" (QCGP 2020a). And so, for queer Arabs, Hegazi's suicide was framed as a murder, and this framing affected the ways in which they mourned as well as enabling the militant nature of their mourning.

In responding to Hegazi's death in the immediate aftermath of her suicide, Haddad (2020) expressed that "if there is one positive thing that has come out of Sarah's death and the tragedy of Sarah's story, it's the fact that I guess for the last week I've been feeling this very strong sense of community as we, the queer Arab community around the world, in the Middle East and those of us living abroad, have been mourning together because we understand, even in our silence, the power of her story, and that her story is all of our stories as well." In other words, the weight of queer melancholia is paradoxically productive. What followed Hegazi's death, in terms of responses from queer Arabs, points to the potentiality of queer melancholia, defined by Prasad (2020) as an "invitation into [queer] kinship" (115). Prasad reminds us that "grief is shared not just in the moment of mourning, but deeply felt as a lasting melancholic bond forged under shared duress." Elegies for Hegazi point to a shared experience that recognizes in a single suicide a collective call for transformative praxis. In the section that follows, we think through this recognition and its potentiality.

Militant Mourning

In their introduction to *WSQ*'s special issue *Survival*, Black, Glasberg, and Bartkowski (2016) ask, "How does queer collectivity change over time—how does it survive?—when death's finality had been its galvanising force?" (17).

In the previous section, we explored why Hegazi's death had such a profound impact on queer Arabs across the MENA and its diaspora, and why they felt compelled to publicly grieve her. In this section, we explore what such public mourning was politically productive of. How did queer Arabs politically harness "the excess" that was Hegazi's afterlife, the trace she left behind (Snorton and Haritaworn 2013, 69), and to what ends?

Building off the work of Judith Butler, Myles and Lewis (2019) argue that "grief is not solely about emotional containment or coping mechanisms; rather, it can sustain important acts of resistance that aim to make death politically productive" (25). Mourners not only transformed Hegazi into a symbol for queer Arabs, but they used her to construct a counterdiscourse around the nation and its values by celebrating her as a queer feminist Arab communist, not merely a queer subject. Hegazi, we are told, had a radical vision for Egypt, rooted in her queer feminism and her communism, and she labored her entire adult life toward cultivating an Egypt for all those who had been expelled from the national imaginary—not only queers and feminists but also the working classes; migrants; religious, racial, and ethnic minorities; the disabled; and the politically progressive, radical, and revolutionary (Zaatari 2020). As Zeina Zaatari (2020) writes, a common thread across the statements made in honor of Hegazi was "the insistence on her intersectionality. . . . Her struggle was not one of identity but for a larger political project for social justice and liberation."

Rand (2007) writes that "the presumption of shared values and identities of the 'nation' is rhetorically built, in part, through the construction and consumption of public memorials" (657). By memorializing not only Hegazi's person but also her politics and her vision for Egypt and the MENA, queer Arabs reimagined the region and projected an alternative future for it characterized by the values that she lived her life committed to. As Slaoui (2020) writes on behalf of the MENA-based queer feminist journal *Kohl*: "*Kohl* is mourning Sarah Hegazi's death. We are also celebrating her life of queer, feminist, communist, leftist, anti-classist, and anti-capitalist activism."

Hegazi became a martyr of an Egypt and a MENA that was yet to come, a country and region from the "then and there" constructed in opposition to the Egypt and MENA of the "here and now" (Muñoz 2009), which killed her and so many others—not only queers but communists, revolutionaries, and other agitators. Hegazi, we are told, was a threat not merely because of her queerness but because of her revolutionary politics. By highlighting this entanglement, those who mourned her pushed against the traditional left in the region, which focuses on class at the expense of all else and is therefore unable to see the link between class struggle and sexual liberation in contexts where moral panics serve to distract from disastrous economic policies. They also pushed against liberal readings of Hegazi that understood her purely through the lens of her sexuality and could not see the political, rather than the cultural or religious, underpinning of her death (Zaatari 2020).

In mourning Hegazi, queer Arabs broadcasted her political vision, making her a martyr for an intersectional cause, rather than merely a lone tragic death. A post by QCGP titled "Sarah's Magic Spell" reads: "Sarah wants us to hold compassion, she wants us to foresee where hate and violence comes from. In her final act, she follows through with her vision, she wants us to be transformed" (2020b). Another post on the blog reads: "I want you to know that I feel and see the change happening in our societies. I feel the anger building up, I feel the people becoming more conscious, not taking the bullshit in the mainstream news anymore, wanting to talk about the uncomfortable things, calling out the homophobes, the racists, the sexists, the capitalists, the police brutality that occurs every single day, the sexual harassment, and all the other human rights violations" (2020c). If "public memorials work politically or deliberatively, acting as 'registers of present and future political concern,' and instructing visitors in national values" (Rand 2007, 657), we can think of the public modes of mourning Hegazi as a practice of countermemorialization that works against the grain of nationalist commemoration to rethink the ideal subject of the nation and region who embodies their values and concerns, and by extension, to rethink who counts as Egyptian and as Arab more generally.

In death, Hegazi reminded queer Arabs who remained that, in the words of Audre Lorde, they were "never meant to survive." In so doing, she made the necropolitics (Mbembe 2011) on which Egypt and other states rely for the reproduction of their power substantially evident. This was, paradoxically, productive of a desire to live on and, importantly, against this necropolitics in her memory and to eschew identity politics for an intersectional approach to queer liberation. Commemorating Hegazi was not only about the important political act of framing her as deserving of being grieved but also about locating and activating the political potentiality of grief by transforming her into a symbol of injustice and the basis for what Myles and Lewis call a politically galvanizing "injustice memory" (2019, 26). Icons, they write, "allow for the characterisation of the deceased as something larger than themselves. . . . In turn, this enables activists to make collective claims in their names and to act upon those claims" (26). Such acts push against the state's claiming of the production of iconicity as its purview, insisting on a practice of counter-iconography as a means of questioning which political deaths should serve as the means for producing the values to which the nation should commit itself.

In *Feeling Backward*, Love (2007) discusses the potentiality of a queer "archive of feeling" that documents the "corporeal and psychic costs of homophobia" (4). She writes of the struggle that confronts "groups constituted by historical injury," who must find a way to "engage with the past without being destroyed by it" (1). In the aftermath of Hegazi's death, queer Arabs embraced a complex mode of engaging their trauma, rage, and hopelessness—of grappling with the horror of realizing that any one of them could have been in her position—in ways that were productive of a desire to fight, live on, and "win the world," as Sinno (2020) writes. In the responses to Hegazi's death, there was an implicit acknowledgment that hope could not be cultivated "at the expense of the past" (Love 2007, 29) and that the future could not be imagined and worked toward without an orientation backward toward those queers who had been injured, killed, and erased by the forces of heteronormativity. Their deaths, and the events leading up to them, revealed the scaffolding holding up particular forms of structural violence and the purpose these structures serve. Feeling backward, in this case, did not only involve remembering and celebrating Hegazi, but offering up a genealogy of her death that de-pathologized her suicide.

By choosing to "stubbornly attach" to a lost subject like Hegazi (Love 2007, 7), a desire for futurity was cultivated, one that cannot be made sense of without an attunement to the collective and transnational nature of the mourning that centered around her. It reminds of the power of standing together in public, of bodies gathered in space, be it digital or material, forcing those who refuse to see these bodies to count them, and allowing these bodies to see themselves as part of something bigger and incapable of being wholly snuffed out (Butler and Athanasiou 2013)—as something capable of "winning the world" (Sinno 2020).

The melancholic attachment to Hegazi is productive rather than destructive and hindering, and in framing it as such, we follow Eng and Kazanjian's (2003) call to "de-pathologize" such relationships to lost objects. Mourning, they tell us, locates the lost object firmly in a past that is no longer; it allows for the lost object to die and remain dead and for the survivor to detach and move on, whereas melancholia not only holds the past in the present but revives it, allowing the dead to not only live on but live anew via those who remain and allow themselves to be possessed and therefore animated differently by lost ones. To return to Love (2007), it is important to recognize not only the political potentiality of communing and becoming with the dead but also the necessity of such an embrace of haunting to the production of queer futurity. Hegazi's death was productive of mourning as militancy, to borrow from the late AIDS activist Douglas Crimp (1944–2019), and her ghost lives on in the affective registers of queer Arabs who have mobilized the sorrow, fear, and anxiety produced by her death into a "militant affect" (Eng and Kazanjian 2003, 10).

In the aftermath of Hegazi's death, what Cvetkovich (2003) calls a trauma culture was formed: a counter–public sphere formed "in and around trauma" (9). Hegazi's death was framed as a collective wound in ways that were productive of politically generative, rather than debilitating, affective responses. In particular, seeing what exile did to her was productive of a desire not to be made to choose between queerness and Arabness, between home and safety. Writing from London, Baconi (2020) asserted: "We're not going anywhere, and we refuse for our love of the region to be made contingent on an impossible self-denial. As we came together by text and phone this past week, there was joy in our communal sisterhood and brotherhood. The same space where Sarah first let her guard down, in that concert, surrounded by friends and allies, recreated itself and held us in our estrangement." Similarly, Sinno (2020) writes, "We spend the first part of our lives demanding air in our homelands, and then we leave to countries where we are promised air, only to find out we were robbed of our lungs." There is much to unpack here. On the one hand is an aspect of queer Arab exile that is often overlooked in the celebratory narratives that pepper the mainstream Western press when it reports on queer asylum recipients and migrants in Europe and North America. What such narratives belie is the fracturing, the fragmentation of the self, that queer Arabs who leave home are subjected to. To be safe one must give up a part of oneself, not merely a variety of important attachments but the very possibility of queer Arabness. Hegazi was killed, Baconi (2020) tells us, "by our society's smallness and its incapacity to make room for the breadth of her humanity." Commentators like Baconi and Sinno point out the pain of having to live with being robbed of the potential of "happiness and freedom at home" (Baconi 2020). Baconi writes: "Conform or vanish. This is the persistent message that is unwittingly or maliciously drummed into us."

In death, Hegazi breathed life into a queer Arabness that had been denied. In doing so, she forced many to reflect on the impossible choice they had to make between an incomplete life at home and an incomplete life abroad, both of which are made more precarious by varying degrees of political and economic oppression. Being queer at home might be unsafe, but so is being Arab, being migrant, being Muslim, and being financially underprivileged, queer, and of color abroad. In the responses to Hegazi's death, we saw the demystification of the West as a queer paradise as mourners reflected on her inability to survive and thrive in Canada. She, as a queer feminist communist deeply attuned to the workings of oppression and the weaponization of liberation for the few as a means of covering over necropolitical regimes that relegate to slow or immediate death the majority of queer people, saw Canada for what it was.

In a sense, Hegazi is framed as having died twice. First, she was killed by the state and then by exile. Haddad (2020) says of queer Arabs in the diaspora:

We leave the Middle East because we want a better life, because we think who we are cannot fit in with what society wants us to be . . . But when you leave there is a haunting . . . It's as if your body splits into these two possibilities, the possibility of staying and the possibility of leaving, and you're always haunted by the what ifs—what if I had stayed? Who would I be if I had stayed? Would I be a more complete person by staying? Because in exile you're always walking around like a bit of a ghost, having lost this part of you that you can't really articulate or describe, and this part of you that never really existed, in a way. Sarah's death, I think, brought home to me and I think brought home to a few of my friends who are also living outside of the Middle East this sadness and this fear, that there is no happy ending, there is no going back, and maybe for a lot of us we will live and die away from our home and away from our families; and that is something that is very difficult to accept.

Elsewhere, Rasha Younes (2020) asks, "What does it mean to arrive to 'safety' in a foreign country, to sit alone with trauma and grief, robbed of any lifeline, and connected only through a computer screen?"

We want, writes Salem (2021), "a safe space that's here and not abroad." In death, Hegazi reignited a desire for a life beyond the binary of "conform or vanish." Baconi (2020) tells us that "faced with that choice, I, as many of us do, absented a part of myself. . . . I built a home elsewhere, in London. Many others, too many, have chosen lives outside the Middle East. Steeped in our privilege, we carry immense guilt at being able to flee, along with much homesickness." Baconi writes of the realization that he could not rid himself of home when in exile, making exile and migration a space and experience of what he calls estrangement, echoing Haddad's comments about the queer Arab ghost in the diaspora. At home, then, the queer Arab is estranged, as they are forced to hide, blend in, or be killed and told they are not of the nation or the culture; and in the diaspora, they are also estranged, forced to give up a fundamental aspect of themselves to survive if privilege allows, as we know not all queers can survive asylum and migration, which sometimes facilitate new processes of slow death (Shakhsari 2014).

Baconi (2020) writes, "We have yet to collectively acknowledge the violence inherent in being told, explicitly or otherwise, that we are not welcome in our homes." Hegazi's death made evident the impossibility of ridding oneself of such a trauma and inspired an anger at the impossible choice queer Arabs were being made to make if they could, as well as the half-lives they were being forced to live and the danger they were being exposed to regardless of whether they stayed or left. Brewer Ball writes that

244 Mourning Sarah Hegazi: Grief and the Cultivation of Queer Arabness

"to escape . . . means saving your skin and leaving a fake skin in the captor's clutches" (quoted in Black, Glasberg, and Bartkowski 2016, 16). If this is the case, what does it *actually* mean to have survived, and what of the skin left behind? Was it in fact fake and discardable, or if leaving it behind did not *immediately* kill you, does that mean you can live without it?

Concluding Remarks

Mainstream approaches to queer suicide in the West tend to put the onus on queer people to push past and transcend the forces oppressing them, rather than placing blame for their deaths on structural violence. This is demonstrated by initiatives like gay journalist Dan Savage's It Gets Better (IGB), a social media campaign founded in the United States in 2010 that gathers and disseminates stories aimed at offering "hope and encouragement to young LGBTQ+ people" (It Gets Better n.d.). Savage initiated what would become the It Gets Better campaign in the aftermath of the suicide of Tyler Clementi, a student at Rutgers University, who took his own life after videos of him having sexual intercourse with another man were disseminated by his roommate and another student (Puar 2012, 150). The viral campaign would come to be composed of DIY videos produced by prominent LGBT individuals and allies in an effort to assure LGBT youth that life will "get better," as a suicide prevention measure.

As Grzanka and Mann (2014) write, "IGB works to compel queer youth to respond to heterosexist violence with a psycho-social refashioning of pain, depression, anxiety and, indeed, suicide into inactive hope, introspective resilience, personal fantasy, and political complacency that locates the 'problem'—and solution—of suicide in the imagined young queer subject of the early 21st century" (372). These types of initiatives demand that queer youth "tough it out through the horrors and violence of bullying . . . in the interest of a 'better' futurity" (Grzanka and Mann 2014, 378). In so doing, they normalize heteronormativity as a natural and unchangeable order that queer youth have to either figure out how to navigate or fold themselves into by becoming ideal homonormative subjects, ignoring the fact that such an invitation to be folded in is, to begin with, always unstable and, secondly, extended to a privileged few (Puar 2012). Queer suicide comes to be framed as a product of personal weakness or failure, of an inability to endure "the normal, developmentally appropriate challenges of society" (Grzanska and Mann 2014, 378).

By contrast, queer Arabs placed the onus for Hegazi's death firmly on state and society. Queer Arabs wrote of Hegazi as having been forced to locate in death the liberation she worked her whole life toward (Arab Queers 2020). Hegazi, we are told, was worn out; she did not fail to survive. Rather than turning attention to the mechanisms through which she could have picked herself up, they focus on the conditions that depleted her and made it impossible to live on. Rather than framing suicide as pathology, taking one's own life is reimagined as "methodology" (Black, Glasberg, and Bartkowski 2016, 17). Black, Glasberg, and Bartkowski write that "against a backdrop of insane, historically rooted white supremacy, black suicide can be a reasonable and resilient approach" (17). Hegazi's suicide can be figured in similar ways.

This framing is meant not to romanticize suicide but to explain it in a way that highlights the conditions for its possibility and the need to focus on structures that are productive of trauma, rather than fixating, as mainstream discourse does, on the individual and their strength or weakness, failure or success. By highlighting the intersections of class, race, gender, and sexuality, such a framing also forces us to question discourses around endurance that reduce queer suicide to a matter of sexuality and fail to recognize the multiple forms of violence that queers of color, migrants, the working classes, and trans folks are being asked to endure by the likes of Dan Savage for the promise of a future that is not only reserved for a privileged few but relies on the making disposable of the majority of queer subjects.

Harnessing the digital as a means of developing a transnational community, queer Arabs were able to come together across borders to reflect on what had been done to them and to make manifest the collective nature of their struggle. The process of mourning together was productive of a politically generative solidarity. The transformation of Hegazi into a memetic symbol with a digital afterlife worked against the Egyptian state and mainstream media's attempts to devalue her life and by extension all queer Arab life. By making her grievable and circulating their grief transnationally via the digital realm, queer Arabs asserted the value of their own lives and those who would follow them (Myles and Lewis 2019, 26), insisting that they are still here and are not going anywhere.

Mourning Hegazi was not only a means of honoring her legacy but also of practicing care toward those queers who remained in the intolerable present, whose own vulnerability and proximity to death was inflated in the aftermath of her arrest and subsequent suicide. Hegazi's death reminded of the impossibility of escaping the wounds that society inflicts, and of the inadequacy of exile and migration, of what gets left behind after the escape and the difficulty of living without that which had to be abandoned for survival, in ways that enlivened the desire to work against the order of things back home and abroad, particularly for those with the privilege to do so.

Sophie Chamas is a lecturer in gender studies at SOAS, University of London. Their work explores the life, death, and afterlife of the radical political imagination in the Middle East and its diaspora. They can be reached at sc118@soas.ac.uk.

Sabiha Allouche is a lecturer in politics at the University of Exeter. She is interested in the workings of gender and sexuality on state and society in the MENA. She is a member of the advisory board of the journal *Kohl: A Journal for Body and Gender Research*. She can be reached at s.allouche@exeter.ac.uk.

Notes

1. Like the actors who feature in this article, we too found ourselves possessed by grief and rage in the aftermath of Hegazi's suicide. Part of what unfolds within these pages is our own grappling with the effect that this individual, who we did not know personally, had on us and so many others from or linked to the MENA and its queer lifeworlds. With the passing of time, as the rage waned and the grief lingered, we noticed an afterlife that, despite the tragedy that ushered it in, appeared to bear a political potentiality that we felt it necessary to excavate.

2. While it is beyond the scope of this article to grapple with this in depth, we hope that our argument might inspire future research on the relationship between the virtual and the production of a transnational queer Arab identity that works against the exclusions of not only state-based MENA nationalisms but of pan-Arabism as well. Might, then, there be a future for Arab nationalism that, by virtue of its entanglement with queerness, abandons the essentialisms and the boundaries that historically defined and demarcated this regional identity?

Works Cited

Ahmed, Sara. 2010. *The Promise of Happiness*. Durham, NC: Duke University Press.

Allouche, Sabiha. 2017. "(Dis)-Intersecting Intersectionality in the Time of Queer Syrian-Refugee-ness in Lebanon." *Kohl* 3, no. 1: 59–77.

Amar, Paul. 2013. *The Security Archipelago*. Durham, NC: Duke University Press.

Arab Queers on Stolen Tkaronto and Tiohtià:ke. 2020. "Grieving Sarah Hegazy: A Statement of Love, Loss, and Liberation." *Pikara*, June 24, 2020. https://www.pikaramagazine.com/2020/06/grieving-sarah-hegazy-statement-of-love-loss-and-liberation/.

Arraf, Jane. 2018. "After Crackdown, Egypt's LGBT Community Contemplates 'Dark Future.'" *NPR*, June 18, 2018. https://www.npr.org/2018/06/18/620110576/after-crackdown-egypts-lgbt-community-contemplates-dark-future.

Baconi, Tareq. 2020. "Our Lives Are Not Conditional: On Sarah Hegazy and Estrangement." *Mada Masr*, June 24, 2020. https://www.madamasr.com/en/2020/06/23/opinion/u/our-lives-are-not-conditional-on-sarah-hegazy-and-estrangement/.

Black, Taylor, Elena Glasberg, and Frances Bartkowski. 2016. "Introduction: Survival, from the Other End of the Telescope." *WSQ* 44, nos. 1/2: 14–29.

Brim, Matt, and Amin Ghazian. 2017. "Introduction: Queer Methods." *WSQ* 44, nos. 3/4: 14–27.

Butler, Judith, and Athena Athanasiou. 2013. *Dispossession: The Performative in the Political*. Cambridge, MA: Polity Press.

Cvetkovich, Ann. 2003. *An Archive of Feelings: Trauma, Sexuality, and Lesbian Public Cultures*. Durham, NC: Duke University Press.

El Sirgany, Sarah. 2020. "How One Gay Egyptian Woman Stood Up to Homophobia and Paid the Ultimate Price." *CNN*, June 17, 2020. https://edition.cnn.com/2020/06/17/middleeast/sarah-hegazi-egypt-intl/index.html.

Eng, David L., and David Kazanjian. 2003. "Introduction: Mourning Remains." In *Loss: The Politics of Mourning*, edited by David L. Eng and David Kazanjian, 1–26. Berkeley, CA: University of California Press.

GHM. 2020. "A Letter to Sarah." Pride of Arabia. June 14, 2020. https://prideofarabia.com/A-letter-to-Sarah.

Greatrick, Aydan. 2019. "'Coaching' Queer: Hospitality and the Categorical Imperative of LGBTQ Asylum Seeking in Lebanon and Turkey." *Migration and Society* 2, no. 1: 98–106.

Grzanka, Patrick R., and Emily S. Mann. 2014. "Queer Youth Suicide and the Psychopolitics of 'It Gets Better.'" *Sexualities* 17, no. 4: 369–93.

Haddad, Saleem (@salhad). 2020. "A few thoughts on the death of Sarah Hegazy #sarahhegazy #sarahegazy." Instagram, June 20, 2020. https://www.instagram.com/tv/CBqBgWHjHwl/?hl=en.

Hegazi, Sarah (@sarahhegazi89). 2020. https://www.instagram.com/sarahhegazi89/?hl=en.

Halberstam, Judith. 2000. "Telling Tales: Brandon Teena, Billy Tipton, and Transgender Biography." *a/b: Auto/Biography Studies* 15, no. 1: 62–81.

Hemmings, Clare. 2011. *Why Stories Matter: The Political Grammar of Feminist Theory*. Durham, NC: Duke University Press.

It Gets Better. n.d. Accessed March 14, 2022. https://itgetsbetter.org/.

Love, Heather. 2007. *Feeling Backward: Loss and the Politics of Queer History*. Cambridge, MA: Harvard University Press.

Luciano, Dana, and Mel Y. Chen. 2015. "Introduction: Has the Queer Ever Been Human?" *GLQ: A Journal of Lesbian and Gay Studies* 21, nos. 2/3: 183–207.

Mbembe, Achilles. 2001. *Necropolitics*. Durham, NC: Duke University Press.

Muñoz, Jose Esteban. 2009. *Cruising Utopia: The Then and There of Queer Futurity*. New York: New York University Press.

Myles, David, and Kelly Lewis. 2019. "Constructing Injustice Symbols in Contemporary Trans Rights Activisms." *Women, Gender & Research* 28, nos. 3/4: 24–42.

Prasad, Pavathria. 2020. "In a Minor Key: Queer Kinship in Times of Grief." *QED: A Journal in GLBTQ Worldmaking* 7, no. 1: 113–19.

Pratt, Nicola. 2007. "The Queen Boat Case in Egypt: Sexuality, National Security and State Sovereignty." *Review of International Studies* 33, no. 1: 129–44.

Puar, Jasbir. 2017. *The Right to Maim: Debility, Capacity, Disability*. Durham, NC: Duke University Press.

———. 2012. "Coda: The Cost of Getting Better: Suicide, Sensation, Switchpoints." *GLQ* 18, no. 1: 149–58.

Queers Who Can't Grief in Public (QCGP). 2020a. "انوائر." June 20, 2020. https://queerswhocantgriefinpublic.wordpress.com/2020/06/20/%d8%b1%d8%ab%d8%a7%d8%a4%d9%86%d8%a7/.

———. 2020b. "Sarah's Magic Spell." July 11, 2020. https://queerswhocantgriefinpublic.wordpress.com/2020/07/11/sarahs-magic-spell/.

———. 2020c. "Dear Sarah." June 18, 2020. https://queerswhocantgriefinpublic.wordpress.com/2020/06/18/dear-sarah/.

Rand, Erin J. 2007. "Repeated Remembrance: Commemorating the AIDS Quilt and Resuscitating the Mourned Subject." *Rhetoric and Public Affairs* 10, no. 4: 655–80.

Salem. 2021. "Queer Quarantines." Mada Masr. June 27, 2021. https://www.madamasr.com/en/2021/06/27/feature/society/queer-quarantines/.

Shakhsari, Sima. 2014. "Killing Me Softly with Your Rights." In *Queer Necropolitics*, edited by Jin Haritaworn, Adi Kuntsman, and Silvia Posocco, 93–110. London: Routledge.

Sinno, Hamed. 2020. "Hamed Sinno on Pride and Mourning in the Middle East." *Frieze*, June 26, 2020. https://www.frieze.com/article/hamed-sinno-pride-and-mourning-middle-east.

Slaoui, Rita. 2020. "Mourning Sarah Hegazy." *Kohl* 6, no. 1: 4–6.

Snorton, C. Riley, and Jin Haritaworn. 2013. "Trans Necropolitics." In *The Transgender Studies Reader*, edited by Aren Aizura and Susan Stryker, 66–76. New York: Routledge.

Younes, Rasha. 2020. "For Sarah Hegazi: In Rage, in Grief, in Exhaustion." *The New Arab*, June 16, 2020. https://www.hrw.org/news/2020/06/16/sarah-hegazy-rage-grief-exhaustion.

Zaatari, Zeina. 2020. "Sarah Hegazi and the Struggle for Freedom." *MERIP*, September 22, 2020. https://merip.org/2020/09/sarah-hegazy-and-the-struggle-for-freedom/.

Beverly Smith's "Notes on This Mess": The Affective Politics of the Lesbian Feminist Killjoy in Queer Progress Narratives

Wendy Mallette

Abstract: This article theorizes the lesbian feminist killjoy's negativity in order to elucidate the temporal, affective, and redemptive politics found within feminist and queer collective memory by bringing *Conditions: Five* and Beverly Smith's "The Wedding" into conversation with Lisa Duggan and Nan Hunter's *Sex Wars*. I show how progress narratives presume the unattractiveness of lesbian feminism while investing queerness with the capacity to overcome lesbian feminism's racial and class exclusions. To counter the way progress narratives' division between good and bad subjects endows contemporary scholarship with a fantasy of innocence, I consider how the lesbian feminist killjoy might be attractive enough to provoke alternative desires. **Keywords:** lesbian feminism; Black feminism; sex wars; affect; feminist publishing; collective memory

In 1976 Barbara Smith published an article in *Women's Studies Newsletter* (which became *Women's Studies Quarterly*, hereafter *WSQ*), which challenged Black studies and women's studies to engage Black women authors and provided *WSQ*'s readership with a bibliography of scholarship on Black women. In the Black Lesbian Writers section, which named Audre Lorde, Pat Parker, and Ann Allen Shockley, Smith writes, "The experience of women-identified black women is almost totally unavailable in fiction and poetry as well as in the social sciences" (1976, 5).

With the publication of the 1979 special issue of the feminist magazine *Conditions*, Barbara Smith and coeditor Lorraine Bethel sought to address these concerns. In their introduction to *Conditions: Five*, "The Black Women's Issue," they note the volume's "herstoric place in women's publishing" due to its collection of the writings of thirty-five Black women, including many who

WSQ: Women's Studies Quarterly 50: 3 & 4 (Fall/Winter 2022) © 2022 by Wendy Mallette. All rights reserved.

had never published before (Bethel and Smith 1979, 13). From 1979 into the mid-1980s, this issue of *Conditions* was widely advertised and discussed in feminist and lesbian publishing efforts, including *WSQ, off our backs, Feminist Studies, Big Mama Rag, The Radical Teacher, Amazon, Sojourner,* and *Gay Community News. Conditions: Five* was the magazine's largest printing: the first run of five thousand copies was shortly followed by a second run of five thousand more (Smith 2000, l–li).[1] In 1983, the issue was expanded into Smith's anthology, *Home Girls,* which was first published by Kitchen Table Press (Smith 1989, 11–12; 2000, xix).

Revisiting *Conditions: Five* allows me to elucidate the affective, temporal, and redemptive politics surrounding lesbian feminism within the stories that feminist and queer studies tell about their pasts and futures. In these stories, the lesbian feminist appears as an outdated, angry, essentialist killjoy with a deterministic view of sex. Moreover, lesbian feminism is made responsible for a range of problems that haunt the disciplines of feminist and queer studies, for example, racial and class exclusions and essentialism. These negative associations exemplify what I call the lesbian feminist killjoy's figural negativity, or, the negative set of images, feelings, and stories—often contradictory—that circulate around and attach to lesbian feminists. This figural negativity is intensified when placed in a narrative of progress.

Before turning to my argument, let me briefly clarify what I mean by the redemptive politics of progress narratives and their relationship to the lesbian feminist killjoy. As Clare Hemmings has shown, the prototypical queer progress narrative goes something like this: in the 1970s, lesbian feminists criticized sex as patriarchal, but this decade was marked by racist, classist, and essentialist exclusions. In the 1980s, or at least *after* lesbian feminism, as the story goes, Black feminists and other feminists of color arrived on the scene and introduced intersectional approaches that challenged the "established" whiteness of lesbian feminism. In this story's triumphant ending, feminism came to realize its true potential in poststructural queerness in the 1990s and beyond (Hemmings 2011, 52–57). These stories of progress carry a redemptive arc: one disavows complicity with the failures of the past and invests the future with the promise to overcome past limitations. The redemptive logic of progress narratives imbues contemporary scholarship with a fantasy of innocence by imagining racism or classism as a remnant of the past. By attending to the negativity of the lesbian feminist killjoy, I challenge such appeals to the innocence of our scholarly projects and instead articulate a pervasive, but uneven, noninnocence that marks sex and sociality.

In the first section, I examine one contribution to *Conditions: Five*, "The Wedding," which was an early publication of Beverly Smith, the twin sister of Barbara Smith. This piece elucidates the dense affective negativity of the feminist killjoy that marks Smith's lesbian feminism and Black feminist consciousness (Ahmed 2010, 50–87; 2017, 251–68).[2] This is not to say that the complex range of emotions, desires, practices, and politics found in Smith's biomythograpic essay are reducible to negativity.[3] Rather, "The Wedding" displays the dynamic character of the lesbian feminist killjoy's negativity, especially its relation to humor, pleasure, and desire.

In the second section, I focus on one predominant narrative within feminist and queer studies—the progress narrative—in which the lesbian feminist killjoy features prominently. I use Lisa Duggan and Nan Hunter's *Sex Wars* to examine the dynamics by which queerness overcomes the failures of lesbian feminism. Drawing out the temporal, racial, and redemptive politics embedded within their narrative, I show how their progress narrative relies on a division between good and bad subjects that invests contemporary scholarship with a powerful innocence that grounds our justice-seeking efforts. I take up the queer progress narrative of *Sex Wars*, not because it is unique in its production of the figure of the lesbian feminist killjoy, but rather because of its accessibility, familiarity, and influence in feminist and queer studies over the last two and a half decades.

In the concluding section, I examine the relationship between the lesbian feminist killjoy's negativity and desirability seen in Smith's essay. The close relationship between negativity and desire is something that tends to go unnoticed in feminist and queer collective memory, where lesbian feminism appears as wholly unattractive. The relationship between pessimism and desirability presses me to ask: What does the lesbian feminist killjoy's negativity tell us, as contemporary scholars, about ourselves and how we think and feel about sex? And how might the lesbian feminist killjoy's negativity unsettle our attachments to the narratives of progress and fantasies of innocence that shape our fields and methods?

Affective Negativity and the Violences of a Happy Sociality

"The Wedding" is composed of a series of journal entries that were written while Beverly Smith was attending the wedding of a friend, who she calls J– – –. Smith tells readers that she and J– – – became best friends during her first year at graduate school in public health, where they were "the only two

Afro-American women" in their year (1979, 103). J– – –'s wedding occurs less than a year after Smith's divorce in 1974. Smith situates the entries by noting that they were written only "a few months after I began to consciously realize myself as a lesbian" but prior to any involvement "in a lesbian sexual relationship" (103). She tells readers that journaling had been "a survival tool" that now revealed much to her "about the juxtapositions of living as a Black woman who is both lesbian and feminist" (103).

While at this friend's wedding, Smith passes the time by escaping to the bathroom to journal. She writes on available scraps of paper, such as the back of the wedding program. Her first entry begins: "I'm in the bathroom trying to get down some notes on this mess. . . . I feel so cynical, so frustrated, almost hysterical and bored" (103; Smith's ellipses). Smith loathes the expectation that she must "masquerad[e] as a nice, straight, middle-class Black 'girl,'" rather than a dyke (104). Her journal entries are saturated with negative affects: she feels nauseated, upset, sick, tired, out-of-place, dislocated, frustrated, and skeptical.

Smith notes that happiness is what she is supposed to feel at the wedding. She should be happy for her friend who has achieved "the supreme goal of any 'real woman,'" finding a Harvard Law grad to marry (106). But instead, she is sickened to witness H– – –, the fiancé of J– – –, reprimand and interrupt J– – – as if she were "a child or a dog" (105). Smith knows that this is precisely what marriage will make of J– – –; she will become, "in short, his wife" (105). Smith notes that weddings are "deadly" celebrations of men's proprietorial relations to women (104). For her friend's sake, she hopes that J– – –'s marriage might turn out to be a "rare, good marriage," but she remains skeptical (106).

Smith mourns the wedding as the irretrievable loss of her friend. The possessive norms of heterosexual marriage, which Smith knows all too well, will almost certainly mean the end of their friendship. Smith's lesbianism has made her an "anathema" to J– – –, who does not support homosexuality (105). Smith's misery at the wedding is exacerbated by a dream she had about J– – –'s desire for her, causing Smith to realize—tragically, for the first time—her own desire for J– – –.

Smith feels out-of-place, not only due to the wedding's ostentatious display of heterosexuality but also its bourgeois extravagance. She writes, "I abhor these tight, proper, nasty-nice people" (104). The display of wealth at the wedding causes her to gravitate toward the catering staff, rather than socializing with the wedding guests. These habits mark her as "anti-social"

(106). Despite her frequent trips to the bathroom, Smith is unsuccessful at avoiding the other guests entirely. She finds herself in an unfortunately long conversation with a man named Art. The groom introduced them because, as Smith explains, "I committed the horrible sin of sitting by myself, not talking with anyone" (107). Now, stuck in a conversation with Art, Smith cannot help but get into an argument. Art claims that politics organized around gender, sexual, or racial concerns are counterproductive to broader political movements. Smith writes, "I totally disagree," and explains that "the larger women's movement and Black feminism" remain necessary because the "net result" of the "broader, supposedly comprehensive movements . . . was to fuck women over" (107).

As the crowd thins, Smith begins to plot her escape from the wedding. Eager for a reason to exit the wedding, she catches a train to make it to an organizing meeting in New York City to form the Gay Caucus of the American Public Health Association. She closes her final journal entry by asking, "So who is going to fight for our lives but us?" (107).

Smith's account of "The Wedding" elucidates how the figural negativity of the lesbian feminist killjoy relates to the promissory character of happiness (see Ahmed 2010). Marriage is imagined as the proper object of desire for middle-class-aspiring women like Smith and J– – –. Marriage orients their desires and is supposed to bring them happiness, but Smith's distance from marriage—her recent divorce, developing lesbianism, and Black feminist consciousness—alienates her from the happy sociality of the wedding party. This shows the violent and disciplinary character of the fantasy of a happy sociality that makes Smith so miserable at the wedding.

Yet Smith's negativity can be considered from a second direction: the negativity of her behaviors and her pessimistic evaluations of objects that others find promising (see Ahmed 2010, 65–66; 2014b, 2). Instead of distancing herself from the lesbian feminist killjoy's threatening negativity, Smith reappropriates that negativity. At the wedding, she performs boredom, apathy, irritation, and aloofness, which she dramatically restages for the readers of *Conditions: Five*. Her journals reflect on marriage's relation to capitalism and the importance of Black feminism. And these refusals to reproduce the violence of the wedding's happy sociality hardly go unnoticed by the other guests, with whom she simply cannot get along. While saturated with negativity, Smith's journaling is not devoid of humor: she writes, for example, "I am so overwhelmed by the fact that heterosexuality is so omnipotent and omnipresent (though certainly not omniscient!)" (106).

Through this negativity and humor, Smith strives to draw out something pleasurable from her unfortunate situation. On the pages of *Conditions: Five,* she performs and cultivates an affective negativity that she hopes might be attractive enough to provoke others' desires.

Disciplinary Politics and Erasures in Queer Progress Narratives

While the figural negativity of Smith's lesbian feminism is generated by ideals around marriage, race, sexuality, and class circulating in the wedding's sociality, this negativity also emerges within the stories that feminist and queer studies tell about how their disciplines came to be. Typical sex wars narratives are largely stories of queer progress in which the lesbian feminist killjoy features prominently. Lisa Duggan and Nan Hunter's influential book, *Sex Wars,* offers a progress narrative about the defeat of puritanical lesbian feminism by queerness. First published in 1995, with revisions and a new introduction for the tenth-anniversary edition in 2006, *Sex Wars* continues to be invoked to establish queer scholarship's proper relationship to sex and politics. The book is composed of a series of essays and talks authored or coauthored by Duggan and Hunter, most of which were first published between 1984 and 1995 in gay, lesbian, and feminist periodicals, both academic and popular.

Sex Wars evidences the fraught temporal politics traced by scholarship on disciplinarity in feminist and queer studies (see, for example, Holland 1996; Wiegman 2000, 2012; Springer 2005; Freeman 2010; Hames-García 2011; Hesford 2013; Del Rio 2015; Musser 2015, 2018; Enke 2018). Duggan and Hunter's progress narrative reproduces the lesbian feminist as white, antisex, and old-fashioned in service of investing queerness with the potential to overcome her failures. They use the term antiporn feminists to describe the subjects of their criticism, though this category embraces lesbian feminists and radical feminists, even as pornography is also divisive among these strands of feminism.[4] The unwieldiness of these categories— antiporn feminism, lesbian feminism, and radical feminism—allows the antiporn feminism of Duggan and Hunter's narrative to translate easily into lesbian feminism in their own narrative, as well as other narratives of the sex wars (e.g., Halberstam 2018, 113, 121–22, 135–36).

In the 1995 introduction to *Sex Wars,* Duggan periodizes the sex wars as follows: "During the decade from 1980 to 1990, a series of bitter political and cultural battles over issues of sexuality convulsed the nation—battles over the regulation of pornography, the scope of legal protections for gay people, the funding of allegedly 'obscene' art, the content of safe-sex education, the scope of reproductive freedom for women, the extent of sexual abuse of children in day care centers, the sexual content of public school curricula, and more" (1). Duggan places the height of the sex wars in the mid-1980s. Hunter's time line in "Contextualizing the Sexuality Debates" similarly centers the sex wars in the 1980s, while also providing a broader history spanning from 1966 to 1994 (and later expanded to 2005) (16). On the one hand, Duggan and Hunter aspire for a multi-issue approach to the sex wars. They name pornography, funding for the arts, civil protections for gays and lesbians, sexual and reproductive health care, HIV/AIDS research, sexual education, and the regulation of music lyrics. Duggan cautions against "narrow identity-based, single-issue politics" as well as "universalizing utopian projects" (3). Duggan and Hunter both contrast their book's contextual approach to the totalizing political vision of feminists who organized against pornography (3–7, 16).

On the other hand, Duggan and Hunter's framing of the sex wars reduces the varied political positions on sex to what Duggan refers to as "the porn wars" (5). Duggan divides the period of debate into two sides: the antiporners and the anti-antiporn position. She positions herself and Hunter on "the anti-antiporn 'side'" (5). She describes the careful attempts of anti-antiporn activists to raise questions that the antiporners neglected, and she narrates the anti-antiporn side's surprise when they were met with rhetorical charges borrowed "from Cold War anticommunists" (5). Duggan writes: "We were ultimately shocked to find ourselves defending our activist communities—of sex workers, of butch-fem dykes, of lesbian sadomasochists—against political attacks, launched *by feminists*. . . . We are talking about sponsorship of state suppression of our livelihoods, our publications, our art work, our political/sexual expression" (5; Duggan's italics). While Duggan may avoid the most obvious binary of prosex and antisex, this framing nevertheless demarcates two clear sides: antiporn and anti-antiporn. The anti-antiporn side is figured heroically as standing up for the sexually marginalized, while the antiporn side is granted a great deal of causal agency for making possible a range of violent actions by state and economic actors. This is not to say that feminists and the alliances they formed are not complicit in troubling economic and political dynamics (see Jakobsen 1995). Nonetheless, the depiction of antiporn villainy and anti-antiporn heroism ends up flattening the multiple strategies that motivated various feminist positions on pornography. Despite Duggan and Hunter's efforts to attend to the complexities of the sex wars, their narrative gives pornography center stage and thus remains within the terms of the debate that they find so monolithic.

While lesbian feminists and radical feminists debated, among other things, various facets of sex, Duggan and Hunter's framing focuses almost exclusively on pornography, especially Catharine MacKinnon's and Andrea Dworkin's relation to antipornography legislation.[5] Duggan describes Dworkin's and MacKinnon's efforts around this legislation as fueling "a moral crusade" (39). Dworkin was the sensationalizing rallier of affect with her "revival-style speeches, not to mention her overalls and unruly appearance" (33). Duggan speculates that, while crowds of feminists were receptive to Dworkin's style in Minneapolis, this would not have worked well in the more conservative Indianapolis, where MacKinnon was brought to consult. Duggan describes MacKinnon—with her "tailored suits," "gold jewelry," and "hair . . . neatly pulled back in a bun"—as "the legal brains" who could articulate the theory behind the law in a less abrasive and more professional manner than Dworkin (33).

Duggan asserts that this piece of legislation—like the literature of antiporn feminists—holds a simplistic, totalizing view of porn "as a unified (patriarchal) discourse with a singular (misogynistic) impact" (6). Furthermore, she is concerned about the way that antiporn frameworks depend on "melodramatic narratives of female innocence and male villainy" that rely on a rigid gender binary (7). In search for an answer to how feminists and right-wing politicians could join in alliance around the Antipornography Civil Rights Ordinance, Duggan hypothesizes that they shared a flat understanding of sex—one that imagines women's sexuality as victimized and without agency or pleasure—and a belief in the threatening power of sexual representation (38). While the troubling dynamics of Dworkin's and MacKinnon's alliances around this legislation cannot be denied, Duggan and Hunter collapse radical feminism's and lesbian feminism's political commitments to those of MacKinnon's and Dworkin's views on sex, and they reduce MacKinnon's and Dworkin's views on sex to the politics of their antipornography ordinance.

Duggan and Hunter's narrative exemplifies the contradictory figural negativity of the lesbian feminist killjoy, including the alignment of lesbian feminism with heterosexuality or a traumatic obsession with men. They frame the antiporn feminist side of the debate as a dangerous alliance between heterosexual feminists and lesbian feminists who are not particularly lesbian. Duggan foregrounds the heterosexuality and hetero-attachments of antiporn feminists: "Antiporners construct a wacky feminist world in which heterosexual monogamous marriage (the kind that Catharine MacKinnon's reported engagement to Jeffrey Masson has prepared her to enter), is not suspect as 'patriarchal,' but lesbian sex is ... because it's 'male!'" (9–10; Duggan's ellipses). It should be noted that MacKinnon never makes such a claim about marriage, and Duggan's leveraging of MacKinnon's engagement to Masson seems oddly personal, given Duggan's concerns about the "personal and vituperative" nature of critique from the antiporn side (5). Although the engagement of an imagined man-hater, MacKinnon, with a famed womanizer, Masson, was an object of fascination across U.S. and U.K. periodicals (see Allen 1993; Kimball 1993; Smith 1993; Jeffries 2006), the two ended their relationship. This is something that Duggan does not revise for the tenth-anniversary edition. Thus, the "wacky feminist world" of antiporn feminists that Duggan associates with Dworkin and MacKinnon seems more to reflect the contradictory negative associations of lesbian feminism rather than to illuminate anything about Dworkin's and MacKinnon's views on sex, marriage, or lesbianism.

While MacKinnon's hetero-relationality is foregrounded, Dworkin's identification as a lesbian goes unmentioned by Duggan and Hunter (see Dworkin 1981, 73–75; 1983, 33, 120; 1989, 62, 111). Moreover, Duggan's description of antiporn feminists—lesbian and heterosexual—as homophobic further marks lesbian feminism as aligned with heteronormativity. Without providing citations, Duggan describes the homophobia of antiporn feminists: "This homophobia was projected onto gay *male* sexuality, allowing 'nice' lesbians to feel normalized by their distance from 'disgusting' male sexuality and promiscuity. This move required that 'bad' lesbian sex be attacked as male-identified—butch-fem dykes and Samois activists were cut off from the normalizing feminine, and cast into the vile male 'outside' envisioned by antiporn feminism" (9; Duggan's italics). Here, lesbian feminism is positioned as uniquely homophobic, at odds with gay politics, and in dangerous alliance with the decency of heterosexual women rather than deviant gays, lesbians, and queers.

Sex Wars underscores the limitations of antiporn feminism—framed as lesbian feminist and radical feminist—in order to invest queerness with the potential to overcome these failures. Duggan situates the final section of *Sex Wars* as an examination of "the political and theoretical significance of a shift from 'lesbian and gay' to 'queer' identifications," noting that this is "a shift I generally advocate" (12). Duggan qualifies that she does not seek to "completely displace" the strategies of gay and lesbian organizing (149). Nevertheless, she frames queer theory as a means to supersede the essentialist failures of "the liberal assimilationist and the militant nationalist strands of gay politics" (154). Furthermore, she proposes that "the elaboration of" the position of queer "within feminist theory could work a radical magic similar to that of the category 'women of color'" (161).

Duggan's queer progress narrative performs what Robyn Wiegman theorizes as "refused identification," which seeks to mark the disciplinary politics of queerness as noncomplicit with the exclusions that marked earlier theorizations of sex (Wiegman 2012, 222). Duggan's temporal framing of queerness's ascendancy over the failures of earlier generations of feminists turns racism into "a symbol of this out of time-ness," as Amber Jamilla Musser notes (2015, 30). For example, Duggan highlights the capaciousness of the term queer and defends it from criticisms that queerness erases the gender specificity of lesbianism. She writes, "But 'queer' has a girl-history too," and she goes on to explain that "during the porn wars, many lesbians who were alienated by lesbian-feminists' homogenizing, white, middle-class, anti-gay-male, antisex discourses, refused the category 'lesbian,' and adopted 'queer' as a mark of separation from such politics. . . . Such uses of 'queer' constructed alliances with gay men, and sometimes privileged them over a feminist 'sisterhood'" (12). To substantiate these claims, Duggan footnotes—without any discussion—Cherríe Moraga's description of herself as queer in a conversation with Amber Hollibaugh.

This conversation between Hollibaugh and Moraga in "What We're Rollin' Around in Bed With" was first published in *Heresies* 12, the "Sex Issue," in 1981. Hollibaugh and Moraga introduce their conversation by explaining: "Our racial and class backgrounds have a huge effect in determining how we perceive ourselves sexually" (1992, 253). Duggan's description of Moraga's refusal of the term lesbian in favor of queer ignores the ways that Moraga, in this essay and other works, positions herself within various feminist conversations around the meanings of lesbianism, lesbian feminism, queer, butch, and femme in relation to her working-class, Chicana positionality (see Moraga 2000, 44, 49; 2011, 4–6; 2015, xxxvi–xxxvii, xxxix). Duggan, however, fails to note that both Moraga and Hollibaugh identify themselves as feminists and lesbians in this essay, even as they also challenge the failure of feminist movements to organize effectively around the sexual politics of working-class and Third World women.

These crucial elements of Hollibaugh and Moraga's conversation are erased when Duggan invokes queer as a more capacious term of alliance over and against the racial and class exclusions of a lesbian feminist past. This move exemplifies Sharon Holland's diagnosis of the disciplinary formation of lesbian and queer studies in relation to lesbians of color. Duggan's queer progress narrative performs a constitutive invocation of lesbian of color reality by footnoting a Chicana lesbian feminist text, but this citation simultaneously erases the very specificity of Chicana lesbianism by using it to ground queerness's potential to inclusively expand (Holland 1996, 251–53; see also Garber 2001, 167–70).

When framed as a narrative of progress in which queerness overcomes the failures of a monolithically white, middle-class lesbian feminist movement, the early contributions of gay, lesbian, queer, and trans scholars of color like Moraga and the Black lesbian feminist contributors to *Conditions: Five* are erased. This narrative then reproduces lesbian feminism as white, antisex, and old-fashioned, investing queerness with a powerful fantasy of innocence. Because progress narratives offer a satisfyingly redemptive story that frames contemporary scholars as bearers of justice over and against the failed subjects of the past, there is a strong compulsion to repeat them. Thus, despite much criticism of the progressive arc of sex wars narratives (see Rich 1986; Goldsby 1993; Schulman 1993), Duggan and Hunter's treatment of the sex wars continues to be cited in genealogical glosses of queer studies (e.g., Jagose 1996, 76–77; McRuer 1997, 15, 217–18n13; 2006, 216n2; Gould 2009, 77; Love 2011, 4, 12n6; Brim and Ghaziani 2016, 25n3).

Desiring the Lesbian Feminist Killjoy

Having traced the lesbian feminist killjoy through the arcs of progress in Duggan and Hunter's redemptive story, I now want to return to the questions that I posed in the introduction: What do queer progress narratives about the lesbian feminist killjoy tell us, as feminist and queer scholars, about ourselves and how we think and feel about sex? And how might the lesbian feminist killjoy's negativity unsettle our attachments to the narratives of progress and fantasies of innocence that shape our fields and methods? Smith's essay, and its relation to the feminist publishing efforts of *Conditions: Five*, offers some answers.

As we have seen, progress narratives rely on a division between good and bad subjects—between the scholar-activist who is sufficiently queer, or at least anti-antisex, and the lesbian feminist whose essentialism, middle-class whiteness, and pessimistic relation to sex is the root of what has gone wrong in feminism.[6] Such narratives inadvertently produce the very limitations of feminism that they seek to counter by reproducing lesbian feminism as monolithically white. As the editors of *Conditions: Five* explain, claims about a lack of Black (lesbian) feminist writers have long functioned as a myth to excuse the "all-whiteness" of feminist publications and, I might add, queer ones (Bethel and Smith 1979, 11). Bethel and Smith go on to argue that *Conditions: Five* "clearly disproves the 'non-existence' of Black feminist and Black lesbian writers and challenges forever our invisibility" (11).

What concerns me about narratives about the middle-class whiteness of lesbian feminism is that they function to erase the thirty-five Black feminist and lesbian contributors to this volume. Moreover, such narratives disavow queerness's complicity in racism and classism by projecting it onto the passé lesbian feminist, as Musser has argued, which generates a powerful fantasy of innocence (2018, 56). Progress narratives can be deeply satisfying in that their division between good and bad subjects sets the stage for contemporary scholars to frame the redemptive promise of our work and our justice-seeking projects. The way that their moralizing plots can secure the value of our scholarship, or even our selfhood, makes us want to repeat them.

As contemporary scholars, we may feel reassured in our knowledge that the lesbian feminist is naive, essentialist, humorless, and unsexy. Even as we attempt to theorize the very incoherence of desire, we know, at least, that our desires are far more sophisticated, complex, and queer than hers. Yet rather than rest in this confidence about the undesirability of lesbian feminist thinking on sex, we might instead ask, what was attractive about their criticisms of the gendered, capitalist, and colonialist logics of sex and marriage? As Ahmed notes, "The killjoy is appealing not despite what she brings up but because of [it]" (2017, 267). Crucially, Smith's essay shows the relationship between the lesbian feminist's negativity and her desirability—something that is frequently erased in queer narratives about the lesbian feminist as an antisex killjoy. Smith's performances of negativity in "The Wedding" are attentive to the killjoy's appeal. She concludes her essay with a provocative desire: "One hope I have is that after reading this other women, especially Black women, will be enspirited to tell their own essential stories" (1979, 108).

Contrary to the assumptions of queer progress narratives that lesbian feminism is unattractive, Smith's essay performs lesbian feminist negativity in order to attract and provoke alternative desires, especially Black lesbian feminist desires. As Smith's journaling indicates, the disciplinary character of marriage and compulsory heterosexuality that is generated by the promise of happiness is difficult to depart from. During the second year of Smith's marriage, she had to burn all of her journals, as she explains, "partly because I felt I had no safe place for them away from my husband and partly because one of my duties in that marriage was to forget who I had been before it" (103). Given the disciplinary character of marriage and heterosexuality, something must have been attractive about such lesbian feminist negativity given that lesbian feminists, including Andrea Dworkin, Jill Johnston, Audre Lorde, Kate Millett, Pat Parker, and Beverly Smith, were all once- (or twice-) divorced lesbians.

Rather than assuming, against all evidence to the contrary, that lesbian feminism was unattractive, perhaps scholars should ask: What about lesbian feminism was powerful enough to provoke such exoduses from marriage and compulsory heterosexuality? Smith tells readers that in the last month of her marriage she returned to her killjoy practice of journaling: "I literally wrote my way out of the marriage" (103). Smith's journaling brings together emotions—like anger, disaffection, grief, and unhappiness—with political analysis in order to mobilize desires for something otherwise. In this, her work joins lesbian feminist and Black feminist literature, including the manifestos, books, collective statements, and musical albums found throughout the archives of lesbian public cultures. This points to what Ahmed describes as "the pull" of lesbian desire that demonstrates sexuality's contingency to histories of contact (2006, 94; see also Freeman 2010, 62–63). Rather than framing queerness as progress, lesbian feminism's capacity to provoke desires demonstrates the contingency of queerness: queerness as "the moment you realize what you did not"—and, I might add, do not—"have to be" (Ahmed 2017, 265).

Rather than claiming innocence or disavowing the negativity that marks lesbian feminism, these killjoys reappropriated and retooled antifeminist figures. Refusing redemptive futurities, lesbian feminist killjoys perform an affective negativity powerful enough to provoke desires that depart from the stifling conditions of the present. Beverly Smith's "notes on this mess" unsettle familiar narratives of progress and challenge us to grapple with the contingency and noninnocence of our desires.

Acknowledgments
Many thanks for the wonderful feedback and conversations about this essay with Emilie Casey, Laulie Eckeberger, Amanda Griffin, Lucia Hulsether, Willie Jennings, Drake Konow, Calli Micale, Rebecca Potts, Kathryn Tanner, Linn Tonstad, and Shatavia Wynn.

Wendy Mallette is an assistant professor of religious studies at the University of Oklahoma. She is currently working on a book manuscript that draws on the archives of lesbian feminist public cultures of the 1960s through 1980s to intervene in conversations around negativity, sin, temporality, and affect in queer studies and religious studies. She can be reached at wendy.mallette@ou.edu.

Notes
1. For further discussion of *Conditions*, see Parkerson (1984, 10–12, 26); Clarke (1999, 20, 22n6); Enszer (2015); and Enszer and Beins (2018).
2. For Ahmed's discussion of the "angry woman of colour," see *The Promise of Happiness* (2010, 67–68) and *The Cultural Politics of Emotion* (2014a, 224–25). For the lesbian feminist as killjoy, see *Queer Phenomenology* (2006, 194n30, 194–95n35).
3. On biomythography, see Audre Lorde's *Zami* (2006). I thank an anonymous reviewer for suggesting the term.
4. The term lesbian feminist figures negatively in Duggan's "Introduction" (12), "Feminist Historians and Antipornography Campaigns" (65), and "Making It Perfectly Queer" (156). Radical feminism also figures negatively in Duggan's "Censorship in the Name of Feminism" (29, 31, 33, 36–37), Duggan, Hunter, and Vance's "False Promises" (43), and Duggan's "Making It Perfectly Queer" (153). Duggan uses lesbian feminism descriptively in "History's Gay Ghetto" (138, 140, 144–45).
5. See Duggan's "Introduction" (5–9), Hunter's "Contextualizing the Sexuality Debates" (16, 23), Duggan's "Censorship in the Name of Feminism" (29–33, 37–39), and Duggan, Hunter, and Vance's "False Promises" (43–45).
6. For a compelling argument examining the production of good and bad objects within feminism, see Nash and Pinto (2021).

Works Cited
Ahmed, Sara. 2006. *Queer Phenomenology: Orientations, Objects, Others*. Durham, NC: Duke University Press.
———. 2010. *The Promise of Happiness*. Durham, NC: Duke University Press.

———. 2014a. *The Cultural Politics of Emotion*. 2nd ed. Edinburgh: Edinburgh University Press.

———. 2014b. *Willful Subjects*. Durham, NC: Duke University Press.

———. 2017. *Living a Feminist Life*. Durham, NC: Duke University Press.

Allen, Charlotte. 1993. "Penthouse Pest." *Washington Post*, November 28, 1993. https://www.washingtonpost.com/archive/opinions/1993/11/28/penthouse-pest/45ed3221-767a-4865-99ee-c53a0d40c960/.

Bethel, Lorraine, and Barbara Smith. 1979. "Introduction." *Conditions* 5, no. 2: 11–15.

Brim, Matt, and Amin Ghaziani. 2016. "Introduction: Queer Methods." *WSQ* 44, nos. 3/4: 14–27.

Clarke, Cheryl. 1999. "Goat Child and Cowboy: Pat Parker as Queer Trickster." In *Movement in Black*, 15–22. Expanded ed. Ithaca, NY: Firebrand Books.

Del Rio, Chelsea. 2015. "Voicing Gay Women's Liberation: Judy Grahn and the Shaping of Lesbian Feminism." *Journal of Lesbian Studies* 19, no. 3: 357–66.

Duggan, Lisa, and Nan D. Hunter. 2006. *Sex Wars: Sexual Dissent and Political Culture*. 10th-anniversary ed. New York: Routledge.

Dworkin, Andrea. 1981. *Our Blood: Prophecies and Discourses on Sexual Politics*. New York: Perigee Books.

———. 1983. *Right-Wing Women*. New York: Perigee Books.

———. 1989. *Letters from a War Zone: Writings 1979–1989*. New York: E. P. Dutton.

Enke, Finn. 2018. "Collective Memory and the Transfeminist 1970s: Toward a Less Plausible History." *TSQ* 5, no. 1: 9–29.

Enszer, Julie R. 2015. "'Fighting to Create and Maintain Our Own Black Women's Culture': *Conditions* Magazine, 1977–1990." *American Periodicals* 25, no. 2: 160–76.

Enszer, Julie R., and Agatha Beins. 2018. "Inter- and Transnational Feminist Theory and Practice in *Triple Jeopardy* and *Conditions*." *Women's Studies* 47, no. 1: 21–43.

Freeman, Elizabeth. 2010. *Time Binds: Queer Temporalities, Queer Histories*. Durham, NC: Duke University Press.

Garber, Linda. 2001. *Identity Poetics: Race, Class, and the Lesbian-Feminist Roots of Queer Theory*. New York: Columbia University Press.

Goldsby, Jackie. 1993. "Queen for 307 Days: Looking B(l)ack at Vanessa Williams and the Sex Wars." In *Sisters, Sexperts, Queers: Beyond the Lesbian Nation*, edited by Arlene Stein, 110–28. New York: Plume.

Gould, Deborah B. 2009. *Moving Politics: Emotion and ACT UP's Fight against AIDS*. Chicago: University of Chicago Press.

Halberstam, Jack. 2018. *Female Masculinity*. 20th-anniversary ed. Durham, NC: Duke University Press.

Hames-García, Michael. 2011. "Queer Theory Revisited." In *Gay Latino Studies: A Critical Reader*, edited by Michael Hames-García and Ernesto Javier Martínez, 19–45. Durham, NC: Duke University Press.

Hemmings, Clare. 2011. *Why Stories Matter: The Political Grammar of Feminist Theory*. Durham, NC: Duke University Press.

Hesford, Victoria. 2013. *Feeling Women's Liberation*. Durham, NC: Duke University Press.

Holland, Sharon P. 1996. "(White) Lesbian Studies." In *The New Lesbian Studies: Into the Twenty-First Century*, edited by Bonnie Zimmerman and Toni A. H. McNaron, 247–55. New York: Feminist Press.

Hollibaugh, Amber, and Cherríe Moraga. 1992. "What We're Rollin' Around in Bed With: Sexual Silences in Feminism—A Conversation Toward Ending Them." In *The Persistent Desire: A Femme-Butch Reader*, edited by Joan Nestle, 243–53. 1st ed. Boston, MA: Alyson Publications.

Jagose, Annamarie. 1996. *Queer Theory: An Introduction*. New York: New York University Press.

Jakobsen, Janet R. 1995. "Agency and Alliance in Public Discourses about Sexualities." *Hypatia* 10, no. 1: 133–54.

Jeffries, Stuart. 2006. "Are Women Human?" *The Guardian*, April 12, 2006. http://www.theguardian.com/world/2006/apr/12/gender. politicsphilosophyandsociety.

Kimball, Roger. 1993. "Sex in the Twilight Zone: Catharine MacKinnon's Crusade." *New Criterion* 12, no. 2: 11–16.

Lorde, Audre. 2006. *Zami, A New Spelling of My Name*. Berkeley, CA: Crossing Press.

Love, Heather. 2011. "Introduction." *GLQ* 17, no. 1: 1–14.

McRuer, Robert. 1997. *The Queer Renaissance: Contemporary American Literature and the Reinvention of Lesbian and Gay Identities*. New York: NYU Press.

———. 2006. *Crip Theory: Cultural Signs of Queerness and Disability*. New York: New York University Press.

Moraga, Cherríe. 2000. *Loving in the War Years: Lo que nunca pasó por sus labios*. Cambridge, MA: South End Press.

———. 2011. *A Xicana Codex of Changing Consciousness: Writings, 2000–2010*. Durham, NC: Duke University Press.

———. 2015. "La jornada: Preface, 1981." In *This Bridge Called My Back: Writings by Radical Women of Color*, edited by Cherríe Moraga and Gloria Anzaldúa, xxxv–xli. 4th ed. Albany, NY: SUNY Press.

Musser, Amber Jamilla. 2015. "Lesbians, Tea, and the Vernacular of Fluids." *Women & Performance* 25, no. 1: 23–40.

———. 2018. *Sensual Excess: Queer Femininity and Brown Jouissance*. New York: NYU Press.

Nash, Jennifer C., and Samantha Pinto. 2021. "A New Genealogy of 'Intelligent Rage,' or Other Ways to Think about White Women in Feminism." *Signs* 46, no. 4: 883–910.

Parkerson, Michelle. 1984. "Some Place That's Our Own: An Interview with Barbara Smith." *off our backs* 14, no. 4: 10–12, 26.

Rich, B. Ruby. 1986. "Feminism and Sexuality in the 1980s." *Feminist Studies* 12, no. 3: 525–61.

Schulman, Sarah. 1993. "Revisiting the Sex Wars." *Lambda Book Report* 3, no. 11: 24.

Smith, Barbara. 1976. "Doing Research on Black American Women." *Women's Studies Newsletter* 4, no. 2: 4–5, 7.

———. 1989. "A Press of Our Own Kitchen Table: Women of Color Press." *Frontiers* 10, no. 3: 11–13.

———. 2000. "Introduction." In *Home Girls: A Black Feminist Anthology*, edited by Barbara Smith, xxi–lviii. New Brunswick, NJ: Rutgers University Press.

Smith, Beverly. 1979. "The Wedding." *Conditions* 5, no. 2: 101–8.

Smith, Dinitia. 1993. "Love Is Strange: The Crusading Feminist and the Repentant Womanizer." *New York Magazine*, March 22, 1993.

Springer, Kimberly. 2005. *Living for the Revolution: Black Feminist Organizations, 1968–1980*. Durham, NC: Duke University Press.

Wiegman, Robyn. 2000. "Feminism's Apocalyptic Futures." *New Literary History* 31, no. 4: 805–25.

———. 2012. *Object Lessons*. Durham, NC: Duke University Press.

PART IV. **BOOK REVIEWS**

Feminist Family Album:
Review of *Feminisms: A Global History*

Tracey Jean Boisseau

Lucy Delap's *Feminisms: A Global History*, Chicago, IL: University of Chicago Press, 2020

This is not a book one summarizes. Constantly fluctuating between the macrolevel themes that form her unorthodox chapter titles (*dreams, ideas, spaces, objects, looks, feelings, actions, songs*) and the microlevel examples she enticingly dangles before us, Lucy Delap keeps us at the edge of our seats, waiting for the next treat, confident that it is likely to be just as tasty and intriguing as the last. Reading this book is a bit like sunbathing on the beach chair next to your most erudite and well-traveled feminist aunt, who scarcely lets ten minutes pass without offering up a "did you know that in the nineteenth century, women . . . ," making everyone else drop their sunglasses down to their nose with a "no way . . . !" and "say that again?" That is not to say that this is not a very serious book of history, about a very serious subject. Still, it is the packaging that is Delap's contribution, rather than the unearthing or even the interpretation. It is as if that favorite, knowledgeable aunt took all the most interesting, unusual, bewitching gems of feminist history that she has been jotting down on notebooks for decades and finally gathered them up, wrapped them in brightly colored categories (*dreams, looks, feelings* . . .), and gifted us each our own copy. Delap's gift resembles not so much a book as a family album—one that allows us to see ourselves in so many guises, across such a span of time, and to glimpse so many relatives we barely remember or never met at all, but in whom we perceive a common legacy and to whom we owe, if not celebration, at least remembrance.

This book is a jumbled parade. However thematically paced, it is still a jumble. Delap's chapters follow no routine chronology nor attempt to find overarching metanarratives. They read as though they were speeches given over the past thirty years, perhaps to mark International Women's Day or some other anniversary meant to remind us that feminism has a history,

WSQ: Women's Studies Quarterly 50: 3 & 4 (Fall/Winter 2022) © 2022 by Tracey Jean Boisseau.
All rights reserved.

that that history is long and star-studded with bold acts, brilliant ideas, and deeply felt emotions, as well as terrible missteps and regrettable retreats. Or maybe this book reads like a women's studies prelim exam—the one that, by the end of writing it, the degree candidate suspects should have been (could become?) a first book. Sometimes we get the feeling that, like that candidate, Delay is just showing off: "Remember this? And, that? I bet you didn't know . . . the other . . . !" She crowds us with memories and shadows and fleetingly glimpsed figures, as if to say: "We have done so much!" And, yes, Virginia, there is a "we"—even if it is not the "global sisterhood" blindly proffered in the 1970s, as if all the systems of oppressions and hierarchies that differentiate women's experiences and make them oppressors as much as oppressed could remain suppressed, hidden, or forgotten. Delap claims there is a shared history, even if we all figure dramatically divergently within it.

Is this book "good"? For whom, and how? If I did not know the cast of characters already, would I understand their significance from reading about them in this book? Do their names stand out to me, and are they real only because I *am* the aunt, discussing the book with the other aunts and older cousins and long-time friends? But what if I were the young niece? Forced to sit silently in the corner and listen to the old women of the family, careful to not make a move or interrupt lest I be told to "go wash something." What do I get from these conversations I am eavesdropping on? Do the names blur into a parade of nothingness, inspire hasty Google searches and shrugged shoulders? Or, do I come away with a sense of all the other aunts and some uncles, and grandparents, and distant cousins whose ghosts surround me, even if I never remember who's who, who did what, or how we are related?

I think it's the latter. I think the intended reader is the niece, the niece who needs this book and others like it, books that commemorate and celebrate, process and evaluate, above all remember and learn from. Delap's book is good.

But like the tale of feminism she tells, Delap's book is not perfect. Unlike other books purporting to be global in scope, Delap does an admirable job of citing examples to shore up her observations and insights, which are drawn from a truly global range of women's experiences and feminist struggles. In the end, unfortunately, this also results in a distinctly ping-ponging, even flattening, effect. People, ideas, and instances can come across as shoehorned to fit a chapter's thematic motif, and historiographical foremothers also sometimes appear thrown-in, almost willy-nilly even. Examples abound of the flattening, or hollowing-out, consequences of her writing strategy. Just to explain, I will pick one three-sentence sequence to elaborate. In her chapter, "Looks," Delap right away raises the issue of the "male gaze," vaguely attributing the insights regarding "women's objectification" in "art, culture, and social life" to (a never specified group of) "1970s activists" (180). That exceedingly broadly phrased sentence is followed up with neither an allusion to the feminist psychoanalytic film theorist Laura Mulvey, nor to the explosive debates about women's cinematic spectatorship that changed our understanding of modern visual culture forever, nor even to a quick recapitulation of the idea that women have internalized their own "to-be-looked-at-ness" so much that they have a tendency to self-surveil and thus inevitably are forced to view themselves as sexual objects (or failures of that proscription). Instead, the next sentence references Chandra Talpade Mohanty's watershed essay, "Under Western Eyes," but to virtually no real effect. Delap actually obscures the link between Mohanty's work, postcolonial analysis, and looking relations, commenting only that Mohanty's essay is a "powerful critique of the failure of 'Western' feminism to understand and respond to the power inequalities faced by Third World women" (180). Shifting colonized women to the center of the analysis of the politics of looking relations is a very fine decision, but how does this throwaway sentence convey or do justice to Mohanty's "powerful critique" or add anything to our understanding of "the gaze," or of colonialism even? The paragraph ends there with a third, and the blandest, sentence of all: "The idea of 'a look' can thus take many forms and touches on some critical elements to feminist thinking and practice" (180). Hmmm. What exactly did we learn from Mohanty or from this paragraph?

To be fair, at other points in the same chapter, Delap's global and chronological ping-ponging strategy works quite well to provide a balanced, rational, analytic approach to the way fashion and body politics have always, everywhere been variously and ambiguously embraced, contested, resisted, interpreted, and subjected to race, colonial, and class politics and contexts. After briefly discussing the #NiUnaMenos (Not One Less) hashtag-led protest (inspiring the contestants of the 2017 Miss Peru contest to replace their "stats" revealing their body measurements with statistics of femicides, violent assaults, and domestic crime as reported in each contestant's home city), Delap insightfully concludes the chapter on "Looks" with a succinct encapsulation of not only her chapter's main point, but perhaps the kernel of wisdom that structures the book overall:

> This gruesome list of assaults was controversial. . . . But it is the very juxta-position, and the voices of the often mute or disregarded models, that give this action force. It provides a striking reminder that feminism can adopt many different platforms and voices, and a "feminist look" can span the beauty contest tiara, the headscarf, and the "freedom suit." (222)

The greatest contribution of this book to our understanding of not just feminist history but of feminism itself is probably Delap's ability to demon-strate what Elsa Barkley Brown often termed the truth of "both/and," and by that she meant the conundrums and paradoxes that historians should not try too hard to rationalize or smooth out of existence in our quest to make the past (whether a system like patriarchy or expressions of feminism) make perfect logical sense. Delap seems to live in the sphere of the both/and. Her book reminds us "of the malleability and context-dependency of feminist ideologies" (246). She refuses "to see feminism only as a textual affair" and insists on the "multi-sensory elements of feminism." She succeeds in countering what she calls the "hard-to-shake European and North Amer-ican dominance of many existing accounts" (334). Delap reports being "struck" (as many readers might also be) by the "borrowing, cross-border influence and sharings," noting that these are not the exceptions but the rule over the last three centuries of women's protest and interventions in patriarchal society. Delap's hope is that "a recognition that feminists have not agreed on a single programme in the past" will "help reduce the toxic-ity of today's disputes" (344). She goes on to insist that

> it is normal, and productive, for any social movement to have many goals and strategies and to mean different things to different people. My account pluralizes feminisms in order to expand the possible and inspire new femi-nist dreams. . . . Others will have very different dreams of the past, and their own dreams, songs, and actions to put forward. This useable history offers inspiration and talking points; not all will agree with my choices, and this dissent is welcomed. There is no definitive selection, and feminism remains an evolving, politically relevant politics. (344)

If you cannot tell, I found Delap's approach refreshing and invigorating, even if the material sometimes felt like a cacophony, even if the author does not have much to impart in the way of interpretation or analysis—instead, she modeled how to get out of the way and let her material occupy center stage. I may not have learned anything for the first time, but she helped me remember the excitement I felt when I first read Charlotte Perkins Gilman,

Audre Lorde, Harriet Taylor Mill, Kate Millett, bell hooks, and Adrienne Rich and when I first read about Mary Wollstonecraft, Maria Stewart, Huda Sha'arawi, Rosika Schwimmer, George Sand, Flora Tristan, Emmeline Pankhurst, Margaret Fuller, Lucretia Mott, Angela Davis, Alexandra Kollontai, Kishida Toshiko, and Ida B. Wells. At one point, that they had existed was enough. Now I want more from them than that they existed. I sometimes want them to have been perfect and perfectly successful. Delap puts me back in conversation with them and with a feminist past that is dizzyingly kaleidoscopic in its imperfections and dazzling nonetheless. *Feminisms: A Global History* is not going to change my life. But it reminds me of when and how my life was changed by feminism.

Tracey Jean Boisseau is a historian of U.S. and transnational feminism and associate professor of women's, gender, and sexuality studies at Purdue University in West Lafayette, Indiana. She is coeditor of *Gendering the Fair* and *Feminist Legal History*, and author of *White Queen*, as well as over two dozen journal articles and book chapters on the history of feminist identity. She can be reached at tjboisseau@purdue.edu.

Review of *We Will Not Cancel Us: And Other Dreams of Transformative Justice*

Ki'Amber Thompson

adrienne maree brown's *We Will Not Cancel Us: And Other Dreams of Transformative Justice*, Chico, CA: AK Press, 2020

If abolition argues that no one is disposable, then how do we hold each other when conflict, harm, or abuse occurs? This question has been heavy on my heart and mind as I move through conflict and hurt in personal and work relationships. While writing this, I have felt incapacitated by grief and rage over the violence and harm that my family and community in San Antonio recently experienced. I have also felt inspired and determined to keep an open heart about the possibilities of abolition. I write this with trust that we are being guided in our abolitionist practices and collective process toward healing and liberation.

I am a survivor of childhood sexual abuse and a survivor of growing up in the hood with regular experiences of police and gun violence. Everything I have experienced is why I am an abolitionist. I have been a student of abolition since, in my second year of undergrad, I fortuitously walked into a talk on abolition by Dylan Rodríguez. The talk was hosted by the Women's Union, a space at Pomona College that provides a gathering place for folks who identify as women and other marginalized genders to learn, study, and organize together. I went to this event for the pizza and serendipitously stumbled upon abolition. This talk inspired and shaped the trajectory of my organizing and academic research. When Rodríguez broke down what prison abolition was all about, it made complete sense to me. Abolition felt like a full-body YES! I became obsessed with abolition. I pondered it daily and committed to deepening my study of abolition, starting a prison abolition club on campus.

Now, I am a PhD student studying how we can bridge abolitionist and decolonial praxes to emerge more socially and environmentally just worlds. I also direct the Charles Roundtree Bloom Project, an outdoor healing justice

WSQ: Women's Studies Quarterly 50: 3 & 4 (Fall/Winter 2022) © 2022 by Ki'Amber Thompson. All rights reserved.

program for youth impacted by incarceration in San Antonio. Abolition still feels like a full-body YES to me. At the same time, practicing abolition is not easy when we have become accustomed to carceral logics of punishment and disposability. adrienne maree brown's *We Will Not Cancel Us: And Other Dreams of Transformative Justice* invites us to grow our capacities to be in conflict and prevent and respond to harm and abuse in ways that depart from these carceral and capitalist logics. The book is a loving critique of calling each other out on social media and offers abolitionist and transformative justice–aligned alternatives.

We Will Not Cancel Us is a six-by-four-inch, eighty-eight-page text closer to a pamphlet or booklet that one can easily carry around. Inspired by her mentor Grace Lee Boggs, brown wanted to create something that people could easily hold and use to have conversations about its radical content. brown opens the book by grounding us in the understanding that abolition means "everything must change, including us" (1). Abolition requires that we be critical not only of systems and institutions that oppress us but of the ways we have internalized those harmful systems in our ways of being with each other. *We Will Not Cancel Us* is concerned with *how we be in relation* with one another in movements, especially abolitionist and Black movement spaces. It is a collective call-in to figure out how we can lean into being in conflict and responding to harm and abuse without punishing each other or perpetuating cycles of harm. Drawing from her experience with and observations of how movement spaces handle conflict, harm, and abuse, brown wrote this book to intervene in the predominant practice of callouts and cancellations.

brown is challenging us, herself included, to move away from reproducing the carceral and capitalist logics of disposability and toward healing, care, and satisfying accountability. She points to the punitive nature of calling each other out and the potential harm it puts community members in when callouts are public. brown emphasizes how public callouts benefit the state and those who want to see our movements fail. She contends that callouts can put community members and our movements at risk as the state continues to surveil and infiltrate movements. brown clarifies that the context in which callouts might be useful is when those with less power need to demand accountability to stop harm or abuse.

We Will Not Cancel Us builds upon brown's *Emergent Strategy* (2017) and *Pleasure Activism* (2019). brown describes emergence as noticing how small actions and critical connections create complex systems that become ecosystems and societies (2017, 3). In *We Will Not Cancel Us*, brown argues that we must practice abolition at the small scale so that abolition and transformative justice are more possible at a large scale. Our everyday practices and how we respond to harm in our relationships and movements are the ground from which we can make large-scale impact. *We Will Not Cancel Us* reminds us that "movements need to become the practice ground for what we are healing towards, co-creating" (57).

In *Pleasure Activism*, brown argues that pleasure is "the force that helps us move beyond the constant struggle, that helps us live and generate futures beyond this dystopic present, futures worthy of our miraculous lives" (2019, 437). For brown, pleasure *is* freedom and propels us to co-create the world. In *We Will Not Cancel Us*, brown grapples with the pleasure that we get from punishing each other. brown asks, "Why does it feel like we are committed to punishment, and enjoying it?" (44). While punishing the people who hurt us might give us some pleasure, it does not heal the pain. How do we unlearn the pleasure we get from punishing each other? How can we invest in the pleasures that heal us rather than the pleasures that create more harm? Perhaps if we can experience more satisfaction from holding each other through generative conflict, healing the root causes of harm, and being in survivor-centered processes of accountability, then we might outgrow the pleasure of punishment.

brown also focuses on fear as a significant affective state to learn from and find discernment within. She encourages us to discern between the fear intended to save our lives and the fear intended to end our lives (38). She wants us "to see what we are afraid of, in others and in ourselves, and discern a path that actually addresses the root of our justified fears" (52). Understanding the affective states that keep us stuck in perpetuating patterns of harm and abuse is crucial to unlearning practices that uphold the same systems we want to dismantle and leaping into alternative practices that align with the kind of world we want to live in. What feelings do we need to tune into more deeply to grow abolition? Audre Lorde's work on the uses of the erotic and anger teaches us that our emotions hold wisdom, and we can leverage them to create change. Working with the Bloom Project and Black Outside, I find that Black youth experiencing joy in outdoor spaces energizes me. Reclaiming pleasure for ourselves by connecting with the land, ourselves, and each other increases my desire and capacity for life. Pleasure can drive and sustain the abolitionist work of growing the worlds we long for.

This text lovingly challenges us to take our own healing and transformation seriously. It is easier to be critical of external forces than look inward. While it is necessary to remain vigilant and resist state violence, making demands of the state is limiting and, frankly, not enough. We also build power through growing our capacities to heal, be in generative conflict, and cultivate interdependence. Our collective healing is at stake.

Healing is not easy. I have been in conversations with a colleague to address conflict and harm that has occurred in our work. Although uncomfortable, we are committed to learning, growing, healing, loving, and being in generative conflict with one another. With each open, honest, and intentional conversation, trust is rebuilt and we gain deeper insights about ourselves and each other, the histories that are underneath the conflict and harm, and what we need to feel good doing this work together. *What do you need?* My cousin asked this question during a family conflict, and I think it can be valuable for anyone practicing abolition. What do you need to heal? What do you need to get your shit together? What do you need to feel loved, cared for, valued, seen, heard? What kind of support do you need to transform into a more healed, less harmful version of yourself? *What do you need?* This question can open doors to figuring out how we grow loving, supportive, healing communities.

Ki'Amber Thompson is a creator, abolitionist environmental justice educator, healing justice practitioner, and doctoral student in sociology at the University of California, Santa Cruz. Ki'Amber is the founder and director of the Charles Roundtree Bloom Project, an outdoor healing justice program for youth impacted by incarceration in their hometown, Yanguana/San Antonio, Texas. Their work is invested in how we heal our relationships with ourselves, each other, and the more-than-human world. Their current research explores how we might bridge abolitionist and environmental justice praxes to emerge socially and environmentally just worlds. They can be reached at kthomps7@ucsc.edu.

Works Cited

brown, adrienne maree. 2017. *Emergent Strategy: Shaping Change, Changing Worlds*. Chico, CA: AK Press.

———. 2019. *Pleasure Activism: The Politics of Feeling Good*. Chico, CA: AK Press.

Review of *Holy Science: The Biopolitics of Hindu Nationalism*

Sunhay You

Banu Subramaniam's *Holy Science: The Biopolitics of Hindu Nationalism*,
Seattle: University of Washington Press, 2019

Building on the insights of feminist, queer, postcolonial, science and technology, and religion studies, *Holy Science* deconstructs the binary between
science and religion to reveal their entangled formations and uneven
effects—the consequences of colonial legacies that privilege science over
religion as a universally objective mode of knowledge production. In pres-
ent-day postcolonial India, Hindu nationalism takes shape through the
rhetoric of science to consolidate and integrate India's past with its future
destiny. The five case studies and chapters that make up the book present
thick descriptions delineating how the rhetoric of science and religion come
together to both clarify and amplify the *hindutva* of Hindu nationalism, an
ideology that naturalizes "a great and grand Hindu past where science, technology, and philosophy thrived" (7). In this imaginary, Hinduism coheres
with modern capitalism, neoliberalism, Western science, and technology to
beckon a return to India's prosperous past in the present. Offering analyses of
scientific studies that undergird and extend the goals of Hindu nationalism,
Subramaniam engages in an "experimental humanities," a methodological
approach that brings together the "empiricism and analytic conventions of
experiments from the sciences and the rhetorical and contextual analyses
from the humanities" (34).

For instance, in her fourth chapter, "Biocitizenship in Neoliberal Times,"
Subramaniam delineates how state investments in Indigenous medical
systems (IMS) such as Ayurveda seek to establish the scientific basis of
India's ancient spiritual healing practices. Advances in Western science are
to affirm what has already been discovered and intuited in India through
more spiritual means of inquiry. Notably, using science to legitimize India's
cultural and historical authority has contradictory effects. While disrupting

***WSQ: Women's Studies Quarterly* 50: 3 & 4 (Fall/Winter 2022)** © 2022 by Sunhay You. All rights reserved.

colonial hierarchies of knowledge, the medicalization of Ayurveda also fortifies a vision of a unified Indian people with shared genetic origins and health concerns. Hindu nationalism ends up reinforcing the disenfranchising structures of the neoliberal and bionational governance that propounds the biological basis of nationhood and individuated citizenship. In this manner, studies in genomics and IMS can amplify essentialist politics of difference that buttress hierarchies of caste and sex in biological terms.

India's Vedic tradition, upon which Hinduism and Indigenous medical systems are based, valorizes India's origins and serves as the basis of what Subramaniam terms "archaic modernity." The "archaic" becomes synonymous with "modernity" as the past becomes the way of the future. The first chapter, "Home and the World: The Modern Lives of the Vedic Sciences," reviews how the Hindu nationalist Bharatiya Janata Party (BJP) mobilized archaic modernity to gain state control and majority support at the dawn of the new millennium. However, this revamped image of Hinduism as synonymous with scientific and technological advancement reinvests in an essentialist gender hierarchy. These competing forces collide in the revival of Vaastushastra, an ancient Indian science for harmonizing living spaces in accordance with the five elements (water, earth, fire, air, and space). Subramaniam notes that this architectural science and style, marketed toward women, has gained much traction as a status symbol. As a gendered site of neoliberal consumerism, Vaastushastra redomesticates women as the bearers of tradition within the home and nation.

In chapter 2, "Colonial Legacies, Postcolonial Biologies: The Queer Politics of (Un)Natural Sex," Subramaniam delves into the Judeo-Christian roots of the biological sciences, especially those that dictate the organic basis of sexual difference and heteronormative sexual reproduction. This legacy lives on in the Indian Penal Code 377 (IPC 377), which identifies any form of "unnatural" intercourse as a criminal offense. Despite its colonial roots, the IPC 377 has garnered the support of Hindu nationalists, who align with its historical investments in eugenics and in identifying and penalizing "undesirable" citizen subjects along the lines of caste, religion, and class. Hindu nationalist lawyers have gone on to defend the code in court, describing nonheteronormative sex acts as abject markers of British and Muslim degeneracy, complicity, and anti-nationalism. While the code has changed to permit consensual gay sex and acknowledge a third gender for transgender people, it sustains the religious-scientific language of the "unnatural" as a critical governing tool.

The following case study, "Return of the Native: Nation, Nature, and Postcolonial Environmentalism," examines how Hindu nationalists co-opt the environmental sciences to nurture nativist investments in preserving the natural order of a pristine past. This nationalist attachment to nativism erupts against the Setusamudram Shipping Canal Project (SSCP). The project was intended to build a passage for commercial ships to travel between India and Sri Lanka, the Arabian Sea, Gulf of Mannar, and Bay of Bengal. However, Hindu nationalists protested the SSCP because it would destroy underwater structures believed to be the remnants of Rama Setu, a mythical bridge that Lord Hanuman built to help Lord Rama rescue his wife Sita. Meanwhile, environmentalists spoke of conservation in terms of the sacred, the need to protect an environment given its associations with particular deities and local religions. This strain of nostalgic nativism has gone so far as to justify the caste system as a self-regulating social system that leads to the sustainable use and circulation of earth's resources and labor. These reverberations of a religious environmental nationalism rely on narratives of "return and rescue" that fail to fully contend with the entanglements between science and religion, nature and culture, and the ways India's pristine environments have been dramatically shaped by colonial powers.

In the last chapter, "Conceiving a Hindu Nation: (Re)Making the Indian Womb," Subramaniam traces the effects of medical tourism in India, particularly around gestational surrogacy. Concerns over the exploitation of Indian surrogate mothers led to the complete commercial ban of gestational surrogacy except for "altruistic surrogacy" (193). A woman can volunteer to be a surrogate as a demonstration of her spiritual virtue. Religious ideologies around women's reproductive duties informed these measures to protect Indian women's wombs. However, given the economic opportunities surrogacy offers women of the lowest socioeconomic means, there have also developed gods of surrogacy that grant these opportunities as divine blessings. Meanwhile, the ancient Indian tradition of *garb sanskat*, "education in the womb," has grown in popularity to endow mothers with the power to shape their children's genetic makeup, including their beauty and intelligence, by following rather puritanical prohibitions against what the mother can eat and enjoy (200). Again, science and religion merge to at once enlist women to further the productivity of neoliberal capital and the consolidation of a Hindu-Indian race.

Holy Science goes a step beyond its case studies to further upset the division between science and religion by challenging disciplinary knowledge formations. Subramaniam engages in a "helical (spiraling) thigmotropic storytelling," most clearly manifest in the science fiction stories that make up the "Avatars of Lost Dreams" included at the end of every chapter (10). These avatars, reincarnations of divine beings based in Hindu mythology, elaborate on the creative potential of the human DNA and carbon-based life (among other scientific phenomena). Subramaniam endeavors to tell stories of her own in which science delivers profound lessons in change and human evolution. She elaborates, "At the heart of avatars is a disassembling of identity and form, and its subsequent assembling into another. Avatars are an expression of a general condition of entanglement and highlight the entanglement of the divine with earthly life" (43). The avatar offers a template for navigating ourselves out of oppositional thinking and into an embrace of "impure politics" (229). Given the ambitious and thorough scope of her other chapters and the limits of the monograph, these mythological accounts of science might read as underdeveloped or, at times, didactic. Nonetheless, the avatars contain the heart of Subramaniam's thesis that the utility of science extends to the stories it enables us to tell about the past and future, which go on to shape what is possible in the present. The avatars entertain other threads of scientific discourse that privilege more networked animacies and contagions. They preach about the joys of surprise and entanglement that eschew any predictable model of development for humans and nations.

Sunhay You is an assistant professor of literary arts and studies at the Rhode Island School of Design. Her current research project examines cultural representations of Asian and Asian American women's erotic sexuality in the wake of U.S. Empire, especially as they coalesce around revenge fantasies, spiritual martyrdom, and posthuman intimacies. She can be reached at syou@risd.edu.

Stretching and Strategizing: Refashioning Queer Studies from the Outside In

Lindsay G. Davis

Matt Brim's *Poor Queer Studies: Confronting Elitism in the University*, Durham, NC: Duke University Press, 2020

In *Poor Queer Studies: Confronting Elitism in the University*, Matt Brim offers a critique of and a wish for Queer Studies. Drawing on his role as a professor of Queer Studies at the College of Staten Island (CSI), "one of the queerest colleges" he knows, Brim lays out a necessary and new direction for Queer Studies, emphasizing the need to inject a multifaceted class and status critique and for "mak[ing] the field stretchy enough to accommodate and respond to its many class locations" (27, 26). Brim demonstrates this adherence to stretchiness by playing with academic form, identifying untold and unsaid weaknesses in the discipline of Queer Studies, and utilizing a diversity of source materials to reconstruct the field from the outside in and anoint a hidden (but not new) field: Poor Queer Studies.

In the introduction, Brim distinguishes between "Poor Queer Studies" and "Rich Queer Studies," arguing that Rich Queer Studies has served as the silent default of the field. Rich Queer Studies is shaped by "choosiness," pedigree, and inability or unwillingness (or some combination thereof) to recognize and grapple with class and status as constitutive factors of queerness. Further, the field "claims radicality" while uplifting varying allegiances to elitism (38). To define Poor Queer Studies, Brim deploys "poor" strategically, dissecting the stigma of the term and maintaining that "because 'poor' cannot be precisely defined, I am able . . . to use the term in a much more inclusive way than a strict definition permits" (25). He asks,

> What if we connected our queer ideas and pedagogies to the material realities of their production (our research budgets and our college websites, our course loads and our commutes, our embodiments and our built environments, our leave time and our overwork, our library holdings and our

WSQ: Women's Studies Quarterly 50: 3 & 4 (Fall/Winter 2022) © 2022 by Lindsay G. Davis. All rights reserved.

bathroom gender policies, our raced work sites and our service work, our salaries and our second jobs) in order to understand those ideas and pedagogies as class- and status-based knowledges that cannot be universalized? (17)

Using his CSI classroom as a site of inquiry, Brim proceeds to answer this question (and many others) over the course of five chapters to rework and nuance the field of Queer Studies.

Brim also gently plays with the form of the monograph as a mode of scholarly production. For example, in chapter 1, he pauses to include a bibliography of queer CSI work, including traditional publications, media exhibitions, novels, plays, and films. He explains that the inclusion of these sources "do[es] not interrupt our ability to learn the story of Poor Queer Studies. Rather, they are the listy evidence of the existence of such a story" (46). Indeed, the list did not disrupt my reading experience. I slowed my pace, taking time to trail the list with my index finger and note specific texts to return to later. Brim's inclusion of this mid-chapter list resonates with Sara Ahmed's understanding of citation as "a rather successful reproductive technology, a way of reproducing the world around certain bodies" by emphasizing previously unnoticed bodies of work (Ahmed 2013). Moreover, his "listy evidence" represents a "conscientious citational practice," defined by historian Andrea Eidinger (who was in turn inspired by colleagues Joanna L. Pearce and Krista McCracken) as "a political practice that academic disciplines used to establish and uphold legitimacy and authority. Regardless of field, this authority tends to attach itself overwhelmingly to white, male scholars" (Eidinger 2019). While Eidinger and McCracken emphasize the roles that race, gender, and status play in the politics of citation, Brim's analysis pushes this practice into more nuanced territory to suggest ways for scholars to think critically about who and why we cite and how a conscious practice might reshape a discipline.

In chapter 2, Brim invites the reader on an unconventional college tour, introducing us to his classroom and the Black, Brown, White, queer, trans, poor, working-class, and first-generation people who number among his students. The journey includes a view into the (crumbling) campus of CSI, where Brim "and his colleagues must understand the tall weeds, the pooled water, the stifling classes, the dirty restrooms, together, in order to do our work" (88). He weaves these conditions around the realities of the neoliberal university and the experience of the student-worker, recognizing as mutually constitutive a shift toward austerity measures, an emphasis on "training," and the weakening of tenure. To further elucidate the bifurcation of Queer Studies, Brim moves beyond New York City by tracing the ways in which Rich Queer Studies functions and manifests at elite institutions, including Yale, UC Santa Cruz, and Harvard. The tour is not merely set in the present but moves around in time, reflecting on the very real effects of the "prestige pipeline" in (Rich) Queer Studies (81–84). This work stretches across the text, reminding the reader of the ways in which Rich and Poor Queer Studies take shape, adopt different questions, and expect to produce different types of students and scholarship.

Chapter 3 explores multiple dimensions of the "queer career," attending to experiences of queer "intellectual laborers," queer student workers, and queer unions. Brim disrupts the increasing emphasis on traditionally "practical" approaches to college (e.g., majoring in business administration or mechanical engineering) and insists on the utility of Poor Queer Studies and its applications to the future employment of his students, offering a list of topics for a course in Applied Queer Studies. Again, I allowed my finger to skim down the page and made note of how I might take up his call. How might I teach a gender studies course that examines "coming out as a workplace issue?" Can I find ways to "train" my students—primarily engineering majors—to respond to "the overlapping and distinct LGBTQ and GNC (gender-nonconforming) issues that arise at work" once they enter the lab, the field, or graduate school (107)? The beauty of *Poor Queer Studies* lies in Brim's insistence on pedagogical reinvention.

Chapters 4 and 5 zoom in on more specific examples, first on the stories of "Poor Queer Studies Mothers" and then on John Keene's 2015 collection, *Counternarratives*, as an example of a Black queer reader. Both chapters are an effort to tell unheard stories and offer concrete "slow and deliberate" pedagogical methods that extend well beyond the CSI classroom to the dinner table, the office copy machine, the commute home (150–52). In chapter 4, Brim argues that "it's not that mothers are missing from our most prominent stories of higher education; it's that poor and working-class mothers are missing from prominent stories of higher education" (148). It is a deft application of "the personal is political," revealing the ways in which "poor mothers' phenomenal and imaginative presences drive concrete pedagogical innovation and praxis" (136). Using *Counternarratives*, chapter 5 offers a road map for reading Black queer literature. Brim takes the reader through the problems his class explored, the support texts they needed to read, and the questions they dared to ask. He enacts this approach to address feelings of "illiteracy" in regard to the Black queer literary tradition as well as to allow his "class to key into particular black queer reading practices," again performing conscious methods of citation (163). Furthermore, by situating Keene's writing as a gateway to "fugitive pedagogies," he thus demonstrates the academic and pedagogical work that Poor Queer Studies can achieve—a disruption of hierarchy and a stretching of what it means to do Queer Studies.

In the epilogue, Brim uses "queer ferrying" as a final way of cultivating, practicing, and teaching Poor Queer Studies. He reminds the reader, "I have come to the point of arguing for cross-class Queer Studies collective action by piecing together the details of my queer work life. *I have wanted to show where my ideas come from*" (197, my emphasis). This is the most striking element of *Poor Queer Studies*. Brim's ideas—and questions and stories and bulleted lists—come from so many places. He works against a traditional, pedigreed hierarchy of knowledge by insisting on class and status as central to Queer Studies. As a humanities professor at a (Rich) STEM-oriented school, I do not face the same obstacles as Brim, but his vision in *Poor Queer Studies* has already propelled my teaching in new and exciting directions.

Lindsay G. Davis is an assistant professor of teaching and codirector of the Gender, Sexuality, and Women's Studies program at Worcester Polytechnic Institute. Her research focuses on the intersections of feminist praxis and pedagogies, race, social media, and the law. She can be reached at lgdavis@wpi.edu.

Works Cited

Ahmed, Sara. 2013. "Making Feminist Points." *feministkilljoys* (blog), September 11, 2013. https://feministkilljoys.com/2013/09/11/making-feminist-points/.

Eidinger, Andrea. 2019. "Cultivating a Conscientious Citation Practice." *Unwritten Histories* (blog), May 7, 2019. https://www.unwrittenhistories.com/cultivating-a-conscientious-citation-practice/.

McCracken, Krista. 2019. "Citation Politics." *Historical Reminiscents* (podcast), May 8, 2019. https://kristamccracken.ca/?p=2385.

PART V. **CLASSICS REVISITED**

An Interview with Brianne Waychoff and Red Washburn, General Editors, *WSQ*

Heather Rellihan, Brianne Waychoff, and Red Washburn

Heather Rellihan: Each issue of *WSQ* features a section entitled "Classics Revisited" whereby contributors reflect on classic texts related to the theme of the issue. For *50!*, the special issue devoted to the fiftieth anniversary of *WSQ* and a half-century of social justice activism within and outside the academy, we are inviting the editors of feminist publications to select an issue of their own journal that they see as a "classic." Thinking about both the issues you've worked on, as well as the issues before your time, what stands out to you as a classic issue of *WSQ* and why?

Red Washburn: In its fifty years thus far, *WSQ* has produced many key issues. Some recent issues that are striking to me are *Queer Methods, Citizenship, Trans-,* and *Women, Crime, and the Criminal Justice System*. I am passionate about scholarship that addresses LGBTQ issues, transnationalism and citizenship rights, and prison abolition. I am very excited about the forthcoming *Nonbinary* issue, as well. It is building and expanding upon the wonderful work of the *Trans-* issue, and *Nonbinary* will engage gender in the field in compelling and interesting ways. In addition, I have a deep value for issues that archive field formation like *Women's Studies Then and Now* and *Curricular and Institutional Change*. I believe we must know our history, show gratitude for our intellectual ancestors, and preserve the field, especially during this critical moment when so many women's, gender, and sexuality studies programs, departments, journals, and conferences, etc., are being defunded.

Brianne Waychoff: I'm not sure that I can identify a classic issue of *WSQ*. One thing that I love about women's, gender, and sexuality studies in

WSQ: Women's Studies Quarterly 50: 3 & 4 (Fall/Winter 2022) © 2022 by Heather Rellihan, Brianne Waychoff, and Red Washburn. All rights reserved.

general, and this journal specifically, is the interdisciplinary work we do. I think sometimes interdisciplinarity defies classification and thus finding a "classic" depends on your orientation. There are people doing great work in many disciplines, but I like the mixed methods that WGSS and many feminist journals highlight because they aren't easily defined. What is a classic for me, coming from a communication and performance studies background, might be completely different from what is classic for someone who identifies as a historian. Or they might be the same. That's what I find interesting about this work. And working with guest editors, who usually have different orientations on our themed issues, is such a treat. I love seeing how people think and the language they use. And I love seeing how that work translates to others.

HR: What makes an issue of a journal a "classic"? Is it its popularity at the time of publication? Its reach? Its ability to resonate over time? A particular kind of prescience that marks it as ahead of its time? Or maybe the ability to capture key debates with nuance and complexity? How much it gets cited? Its teachability? Or, perhaps something else entirely? How would you measure a "classic"?

RW: I think it is imperative to reimagine what a "classic" is and how to revisit it. *WSQ* is part of a feminist tradition of questioning knowledge and power, but like many historical classifications to which feminist historians have spoken, academic journals are not removed from reproducing canonical knowledge systems and hierarchal power. I recall asking my students in Classics in Feminist Theory this question the first day of classes a few years ago, and us thinking about the spectrum of difference, erasure, and marginalization in high art, the hard sciences, and mainstream (white and Western) social movements. Alternately, I like to think about "important" issues that have shaped ways of knowing. Oftentimes, a good marker is characterized not by academic fashionalism, citational popularity, scholarly rockstars, or neoliberalism's problematic tokenism of scholars of color in the name of multiculturalism, but rather by how well it situates concepts and debates in a historical moment, how well it represents people and ideas often marginalized, how well it has shaped critical consciousness, and how well it impacts social change. The latter point is crucial, a "classic" as a revolution of sorts.

BW: I guess I'm not really concerned with what a classic *is*, though I understand why you ask the question. Something that resonates across time, something that introduces a new take on an old idea, something that anticipates the future, or something that gets cited a lot, gets a lot of hits in the databases. I think it could be a combination of any of these things. And I think that could be different for lots of people. For me, there are a few articles that were really helpful when creating the Gender and Women's Studies degree program at BMCC [Borough of Manhattan Community College]. "Building a Home for Feminist Pedagogy" by Christa Baida and Stephanie Jenson-Moulton from the 2007 fall/winter issue and "Women's Studies without a Women's Studies Program: The Case of Hostos Commmunity College" by Jerilyn Fisher in the fall/winter 2002 issue are two pieces that informed my thinking when creating a program and which I reflect on now, five years after our program officially began. A lot of my reading has been in performance studies journals.

I am excited about the issues we have worked on. *Solidão* was produced through a collective agreement with organizations in Brazil and features international collaborators, as well as pieces published in a variety of languages—some translated into English and some not. It was a new undertaking that we were not fully prepared for, but from which we learned a lot about the possibilities and restraints that come from working with an academic journal that is published by a nonprofit press. *Black Love* is a beautiful issue that is both timely and long overdue. It could easily become a classic. And this issue, *50!*, is so exciting, and I look forward to the range of pieces you all as guest editors have brought to us. I am particularly excited about our upcoming fall 2023 issue, *Nonbinary*. I think it will be formative for what we hope is the budding field of nonbinary studies, and will include scholarly and creative work WGSS needs as we continue to interrogate gender and binary ways of thinking.

HR: Thinking about the work of Clare Hemmings and others, what might we learn about ourselves and our field from an understanding of classic issues?

RW: Learning should not promote academic hegemony, cultural capital, or imperial arrogance. I think any critical understanding of "classic" issues will be informed by each person and what resonates with them as a key text in their life at a particular moment, and that could shift—for example, Marx was many different Marxists, though not a very feminist and anti-racist one, during all of his ideological shifts. We gain an understanding of the life of ideas in any text, and that is a very unique experience for each person. To have an archive, a foundation, and a history helps us contextualize meaning across time and space for whenever and wherever we are and what makes sense for us at different moments of living, thinking, reading, and writing.

BW: I completely agree with Red on this. The archive and the history of ideas is important to understand so that we can build upon them—and for me, most importantly, *use* them—to think through our lives, our times, our experiences. I think that sometimes, as academics, we lament the ways in which "classic" ideas make their way into the public imaginary and are distorted or "not right." I think of classic concepts like intersectionality (which Jennifer Nash has written about beautifully) or performativity, which have taken on a popular meaning almost completely opposite their academic meanings. There is this desire to take it back, to own it. I think there is a lot of value in retracing roots, especially as a way to see how the concepts' meanings change. That's why I really like the Classics Revisited section of *WSQ*. It is a space devoted to that type of work.

HR: When you think about *other* feminist journals, are there particular issues that have been formative to your work or to the field? What makes them stand out in your mind?

RW: I am deeply indebted to other feminist journals, including but not limited to *Feminist Studies, Signs, Gender & Society, Meridians, GLQ, Radical History Review,* the *Journal of Lesbian Studies, Social Text,* the *Journal for the Study of Radicalism,* and *Transgender Studies Quarterly,* among countless others. I have been very impressed with *TSQ.* Since its inception, its founding editors, Paisley Currah and Susan Stryker, have pushed trans studies so much in such a short (yet long overdue) time—and this work continues now past their tenure too. Some of the issues that have informed my thought in robust ways are *Trans/Feminisms, Archives and Archiving Now,* and *Trans Futures.* I have used *Trans/Feminisms,* in particular, in much of my work; it is such a stunning issue for addressing the intersections between trans and feminist communities. I recently taught the first issue, *Postposttranssexual: Key Concepts for a Twenty-First-Century Transgender Studies* in my graduate course Feminist Texts and Theories. It was part of a unit on feminist publishing to demystify scholarship for our next generation of feminist scholars. It was truly a delight to brainstorm terms, define them, and redefine them with students.

Brianne Waychoff is an interdisciplinary artist, scholar, activist, and associate professor at CUNY Borough of Manhattan Community College, where they led the creation of BMCC's Gender and Women's Studies Program. Dr. Waychoff is coeditor of *Women's Studies Quarterly*. Their scholarly performance work has been published in a range of journals and presented at venues and festivals throughout the United States and abroad. After this issue was completed, Dr. Brianne Waychoff passed away from 9/11-related kidney cancer on July 25, 2022.

Red Washburn is professor of English, director of Women's, Gender, and Sexuality Studies at Kingsborough Community College, and affiliate faculty of Women's and Gender Studies at the Graduate Center, CUNY. Their articles appear in *Journal for the Study of Radicalism*, *Women's Studies: An Interdisciplinary Journal*, and *Journal of Lesbian Studies*. Their essays are in several anthologies, including *Theory and Praxis: Women's and Gender Studies at Community Colleges*, *Introduction to Women's, Gender & Sexuality Studies: Interdisciplinary and Intersectional Approaches*, and *Trans Bodies, Trans Selves: A Resource for the Transgender Community*. They are the coeditor of Sinister Wisdom's *Dump Trump: Legacies of Resistance*, *Forty-Five Years: A Tribute to the Lesbian Herstory Archives*, and *Trans/Feminisms*. Finishing Line Press published their poetry collections *Crestview Tree Woman* and *Birch Philosopher X*. Their academic book *Irish Women's Prison Writing: Mother Ireland's Rebels, 1960–2010s* is forthcoming from Routledge.

Heather Rellihan is a professor of gender and sexuality studies and chair of Interdisciplinary Studies at Anne Arundel Community College (AACC). She also serves as codirector of the Curriculum Transformation Project at AACC. She is coeditor of *Introduction to Women's, Gender, and Sexuality Studies: Interdisciplinary and Intersectional Approaches* and *Theory and Praxis: Women's and Gender Studies at Community College*. She can be reached at hrellihan@aacc.edu.

An Interview with Ashwini Tambe, Editorial Director, *Feminist Studies*

Heather Rellihan and Ashwini Tambe

Heather Rellihan: Each issue of *WSQ* features a section entitled "Classics Revisited" whereby contributors reflect on classic texts related to the theme of the issue. For *50!*, the special issue devoted to the fiftieth anniversary of *WSQ* and a half-century of social justice activism within and outside the academy, we are inviting the editors of feminist publications to select an issue of their own journal that they see as a "classic." Thinking about both the issues you've worked on, as well as the issues before your time, what stands out to you as a classic issue of *Feminist Studies* and why?

Ashwini Tambe: Congratulations to *WSQ*! Yours is such an interesting question, especially because we're in a dynamic field that has deliberately resisted canonization. There's a constant effervescence and a strong aversion to upholding particular pieces as timeless, which is what the term "classic" usually implies. Given the overall tendency in our field to emphasize movement and change, I would say that classic pieces are those that I return to because they speak in new ways to me. It's not so much that they have content that manages to resist changing interpretations. It's the fact that new interpretations are possible at new political moments.

Now there are individual articles I can think of that are particularly rich in this sense. But since your question is about entire issues, I'll focus on the reach and impact of particular special issues. I think one set of *Feminist Studies* special issues that are classics are those focused on field formation and the institutionalization of WGSS—in particular, the issues focused on the rise of a doctoral degree, the setting up of departments, and the identification of women's studies or women's, gender, and sexuality studies as a

WSQ: Women's Studies Quarterly 50: 3 & 4 (Fall/Winter 2022) © 2022 by Heather Rellihan and Ashwini Tambe. All rights reserved.

field in its own right. These are topics that I think *Feminist Studies* as a journal has really addressed well. For instance, there is the 1998 issue (vol. 24, no. 2) that was about disciplinarity and interdisciplinarity in feminist scholarship; and a forum in 2001 (vol. 27, no. 2) that also revisited that same question; and then a second forum in 2003 (vol. 29, no. 2) on the place of women's studies in the academy. These three classic issues came out around the time when several new doctoral programs were being set up. They were enormously important for our field. They continue to get taught today when students are asked to think about the history of WGSS. They spur new engagement, and we frequently get new submissions that cite them or build on them.

Most recently, the journal revisited the status of the doctoral degree by publishing work by a generation of scholars who were produced by those very doctoral programs that were started in the early 2000s. For our 2018 special issue, *Doctoral Degrees in W/G/S/F Studies: Taking Stock* (vol. 44, no. 2), we invited scholars who had received PhDs in WGSS to come forward and reflect on their experiences in terms of their training, job prospects, and career mobility. Our question was: What does a WGSS degree equip you to do that other academic paths wouldn't have? Perhaps the most contentious topic discussed in the issue was the job market and the fact that there had not been an expressed preference for applicants with doctoral degrees in WGSS in job announcements. I think that discussion about how we should be thinking about our job searches actually had quite an impact—it seemed to have reached a lot of readers, and I know that it was discussed at several faculty retreats. Since then, more job searches stress having a doctoral degree in WGSS, and I think the journal facilitated that shift by providing not only an intellectual argument for it but also an impassioned engagement with the data that we got from NWSA [National Women's Studies Association]. So . . . I'd say the *Feminist Studies* issues that have dealt with field formation are classics.

HR: You talked about being able to revisit the same topic in ways where the meaning might shift depending on the time period in which one is reading. This might be one definition of a classic issue. What other things might make an issue of a journal a classic? Is it its popularity at the time of publication? Its reach? Its ability to resonate over time? A particular kind of prescience that marks it as ahead of its time? Or maybe the ability to capture key debates with nuance and complexity? How much it gets cited? Its teachability? Or, perhaps something else entirely? How else would you measure a classic?

AT: I would say that in addition to asking that an article stand the test of time by speaking to different audiences over time, a piece that represents a moment but yet manages to be rich in its interdisciplinary scope can be a classic. Let me give you an example: Priti Ramamurthy's 2004 article "Why Is Buying a 'Madras' Cotton Shirt a Political Act? A Feminist Commodity Chain Analysis" (vol. 30, no. 3) is one I consider a classic. I teach it frequently. It engages with feminist political economy as well as feminist cultural studies—it analyzes the conditions under which people grow cotton, market cotton products, and consume them in geographically dispersed settings. I've assigned it in courses in South Asian studies, feminist theory, transnational feminisms, and methodology. What makes that article a classic for me is the fact that it speaks readily to different kinds of scholars. And I always find that when I read it afresh, I see new things that I didn't the first time I read it.

HR: Thinking about the work of Clare Hemmings and others, what might we learn about ourselves and our field from an understanding of classic issues?

AT: Claire Hemmings's work is particularly compelling on this question, because she asks us to think hard about the kinds of narratives we use to mark the history of our field. Are we imagining change as linear and progressive, always an improvement? Or are we attached to a narrative of decline? Or are we imagining, perhaps, a nonlinear and even cyclical orientation to the way things change and develop? Your question about how we define a classic actually pushes us to identify our own orientation toward our past. When naming classics, if we only turn to pieces written, say, thirty years ago, we might be participating in a narrative of decline, saying, "Those were the good old days when feminism was done the way it should be done." On the other hand, I think there's a danger, and also sort of an audacity, in saying that something that was published this year or last year is a classic, because it implies that our field has always been just getting better and better. So that's how I'm hearing your question—is that how you intended it?

HR: Yes, and thinking about the issues that you selected from *Feminist*

Studies, I wonder to what extent that your idea of them as classics is shared. And if so, I wonder what that might tell us about our understandings of the field.

AT: Honestly, when you first asked me to pick a classic issue of *Feminist Studies,* I was stumped—I felt like a parent of multiple children asked to declare a favorite child. But there are special issues that I'm particularly proud of because they were ahead of their time. There's the *Race and Transgender Studies* issue (vol. 37, no. 2), which came out in 2011 when race and trans were not frequently studied in conjunction. There's the issue staging a dialogue between postcolonial and decolonial feminists (vol. 43, no. 3), which again was farsighted and pushed people to think hard about what they mean when they say "decolonial." There's our 2020 issue *Feminist Analyses of COVID-19* (vol. 26, no. 3), which we brought out with a very short turnaround time; it spoke in a very timely way to concerns that were on everyone's mind, asking, How do we think about this historic moment that we're living through from a feminist angle? There's also a special issue that we published on reconfiguring African studies (vol. 41, no. 1). That, too, was very provocative, because it asked people to imagine Africa in registers that weren't about development and despair, and placed emphasis on cultural expression, art, and literature. I honestly could go on and on about issues with enormous impact and reach that I've been excited about, but I think the term "classic" again sort of pushes me to think also about what our journal does. I have to say that I think that one thing *Feminist Studies* does especially well is account for our field's formation, growth, and future.

HR: When you think about *other* feminist journals, are there particular issues that have been formative to your work, or to the field? What makes them stand out in your mind?

AT: So I want to say happy birthday to *WSQ* and pick a *WSQ* issue. The special issue titled *Viral* that came out in 2012 (vol. 40, no. 1/2) was wonderful. I thought of that issue because the call for papers from editors Patricia Clough and Jasbir Puar was a really provocative way to ask how we think about virality. That was a time when people were starting to use the word "viral" in a much more colloquial way. When the issue came out, I thought it really exceeded the terms of the call for papers. I really appreciated the number of book reviews that captured various nodes of scholarship in that moment. There was a book review essay that was about biopolitics. There was that cluster of articles about the cyborg, positioning Donna Haraway's "Cyborg Manifesto" as viral for its time, which was a really neat way to frame Haraway's impact. There was an interesting article on social media and advertising, and how to think about virality in that context, and a more creative take by Una Chung that starts with Hitchcock's film *The Birds*, saying those birds are a conceptualization of virality. I just thought it was a really exciting example of a special issue exceeding its call for papers. I don't know as much about its circulation and impact, and in fact, that's a really interesting question that I'd love to chat about a little bit more.

When we talk about classics, how much do we take into account the number of downloads that a particular issue has had? When I looked at our figures for downloads, I found that the numbers did not offer much by way of thematic coherence. Usually, it was just one or two articles in an issue that happened to have been downloaded a lot, not an entire special issue. When we look at the most downloaded articles for *Feminist Studies* (*FS*), what we see is the importance of teachability. Many of these articles were "News and Views"—these are short articles reflecting on particular events that are in the news, offering a feminist spin and a conceptual take that moves beyond the journalistic. So they are intended for professors who want to use a news event to anchor a conversation around a concept. We've run "News and Views" pieces about Slutwalk, Ferguson, the Arab Spring, Occupy Wall Street. They capture activist energy in a way that instructors can use—that's why these are so popular. Interestingly, the fact that these sorts of articles are so heavily downloaded tells me how much our teaching draws from conversation students are having outside the classroom on social media. Instructors are acknowledging it, saying, This is what's on their minds, what can I give them that helps them understand it or unpack it better? *Feminist Studies* has been in a really good position to offer such articles because we handle our production process in-house, and so we can publish very timely pieces in a short turnaround time. For instance, after Trump's election we had a poetry forum that came out within two months of the election—which is an interesting thing for a scholarly journal to do, because we're not technically about responding to the news, right? But we've been able to also do that surprisingly well.

Ashwini Tambe is professor and director of Women's, Gender, and Sexuality Studies at George Washington University. She is the editorial director of *Feminist Studies*, the oldest journal of interdisciplinary feminist scholarship in the United States. Her scholarship on transnational South Asian history focuses on the relationship between law, gender, and sexuality. Her 2009 book *Codes of Misconduct: Regulating Prostitution in Late Colonial Bombay* traces how law-making and law-enforcement practices shaped the rise of the city's red light district. Her 2019 book *Defining Girlhood in India: A Transnational Approach to Sexual Maturity Laws*, supported by SSHRC and NEH grants, examines the legal paradoxes in age standards for girls' sexual consent in India. Both books examine the direction and flow of transnational influences. Her most recent book *Transnational Feminist Itineraries* (coedited with Millie Thayer) features essays by leading gender studies scholars confronting authoritarianism and religious and economic fundamentalism. She can be reached at tambe@gwu.edu.

Heather Rellihan is a professor of gender and sexuality studies and chair of Interdisciplinary Studies at Anne Arundel Community College (AACC). She also serves as codirector of the Curriculum Transformation Project at AACC. She is coeditor of *Introduction to Women's, Gender, and Sexuality Studies: Interdisciplinary and Intersectional Approaches* and *Theory and Praxis: Women's and Gender Studies at Community College*. She can be reached at hrellihan@aacc.edu.

An Interview with Barbara Ransby, Editor, *Souls: A Critical Journal of Black Politics, Culture, and Society*

Charlene A. Carruthers and Barbara Ransby

Charlene A. Carruthers: This special issue is devoted to the fiftieth anniversary of *WSQ*, and a half-century of social justice activism within and outside the academy. We are inviting editors of feminist publications to select the issue of their own journal that they see as a classic. Though *Souls: A Critical Journal of Black Politics, Culture, and Society* foregrounds Black studies, it also exists within a genealogy of feminist publications. This is well reflected through your leadership and the journal's history. Let's begin with you: How did you become the journal's editor?

Barbara Ransby: I'm a historian of feminism, Black feminist, writer, and activist of many years. I was not looking to edit a journal per se; I had worked with an editorial academic advisory group to *Ms.* Magazine, but really had not administered a journal. But my dear friend, Manning Marable, who was then at Columbia, started *Souls*, which I had written for and been a supporter of for a number of years. It was started in 1999 and was envisioned as a journal that would capture the diaspora but also engage with audiences around the politics and the organizing going on in communities. The journal also engaged audiences beyond the university, so that was what I thought was really some of its strength. Manning, who I considered a feminist—he considered himself a feminist, but that wasn't primarily how he was identified—he wrote about the Black Freedom Movement, a very important article called "Groundings with My Sisters: Patriarchy and the Exploitation of Black Women" in 1983, several decades before he died. And for many of us, that was a really important intervention in the very male-centric political and intellectual discourse in the Black community. I always saw him as an ally of Black feminists and LGBTQ folks. He tragically died of

WSQ: Women's Studies Quarterly 50: 3 & 4 (Fall/Winter 2022) © 2022 by Charlene A. Carruthers and Barbara Ransby. All rights reserved.

an illness in 2011. The journal was still based then at Columbia University, but no one was poised to take over the editorship of the journal. Manning's wife, Leith Mullins, who was a friend, comrade, and cofounder of the Black Radical Congress, asked me if I would take over as editor in chief. I saw it as a temporary stopgap measure until someone else was going to be able to do it. I've ended up doing it for ten years. It moved to University of Illinois at Chicago, which was quite a move because it was at an East Coast Ivy League institution with many more resources than we have. It came to our humble public Midwestern university. There were adjustments to be made. We didn't have all of the institutional resources that Columbia had. But I'm proud of what we've done the last ten years. My initial editorial statement was that I saw this as foregrounding Black feminism, and that that was the contribution that I would bring to the journal as its new editor, and I hope that I kept true to that.

CAC: Why Black feminism for this journal?

BR: Black feminism comes with me wherever I go. If I'm going to be the editor of a journal, it is going to be influenced by Black feminist politics. That said, I also think that a journal committed to the diaspora and a journal committed to Black liberation has to center Black feminism, because that's the only way we're going to get there. I have tried to include Black feminist issues and topics and themes and writers and editors. That's been important to me.

CAC: What stands out to you as a classic issue of *Souls* and why?

BR: We did a *Combahee at 40* special issue. It was in 2017, volume 19, issue 3. I coedited it with Barbara Smith and Margo Okazawa-Rey, who are two of the original members of the Combahee River Collective. It also coincided with the National Women's Studies Association Conference, which I was president of at the time, what I think was a wonderful conference, which you participated in and many others, celebrating the Black feminist political and intellectual tradition of the Combahee River Collective. I think that is a classic issue. It was an exciting issue to put together. I was so honored to coedit with Barbara and Margo. We had an article on women in the Black Panther Party. We had an article by Loretta Ross on reproductive justice; we had an article on Black women's activism by Treva Lindsay. Terrion

Williamson did really important work with coining this term. I don't know if she coined it, but the sterilization of Black death, talking about the Boston murders of Black women as the catalyst for the formation of the Combahee River Collective. We had an article by Charisse Burden-Stelly, on antiradicalism and anti-Blackness in the McCarthy era. It really covered the gamut and included some voices, writers, scholars, and activists who have played a really important role.

CAC: What makes an issue of a journal a classic? Would you say its popularity at the time of the publication or how the issue resonates over time? Is there a particular kind of impression that marks it as ahead of its time? Is it its ability to capture key debates, how much it gets cited? Its teachability? Or is it something else entirely?

BR: I would say its reach, its relevance over time, and if it captures the essence of a period, or a trend or set of ideas. In most cases, that will mean that it's taught widely and read widely. It captures the essence of something, such that the voices that have been the most influential are featured, that the debates are centered, that were critical, that proved to be critical debates over time. The classic suggests that the relevance of it is beyond the moment at which it's produced. The Combahee River Collective statement in 1977 has become this enduring Black feminist manifesto. It has become an enduring document that captured the spirit of Black feminism and has a much further reach and much greater relevance than any of the people involved in writing it could have imagined at the time. The fact that we focused on that document, and saw the importance of that document, helps to make that issue a classic issue—even though the issue is only five years old.

CAC: Are there particular issues of other Black feminist or feminist journals that have been formative to your work or to the field?

BR: The journal *Meridians* has been formative to my work. There is an issue of *Meridians* on African feminisms—not African American, not diasporic, but African feminism. It was titled that, and that issue was very important and foregrounded the work and writings and ideas of women from the African continent in ways that most other journals, feminist or not, have not. I have taught, referenced, and gone back to that issue in my own international solidarity work around South Africa.

CAC: What is it about that particular issue, that it's still on your mind?

BR: In a lot of discussions about Black diasporic and international politics, there was, in my generation, a lot of Black nationalism in the United States that was homophobic and patriarchal. Part of the argument was that feminism was Eurocentric and that in Africa, Black people had their own kind of gender and familial relations that are not patriarchal, that transcended that. This issue is a classic, because it intervened in that debate and put to rest the idea that there wasn't an authentic African feminist voice. Those women were very powerful, compelling, and savvy writers. There were people from Zimbabwe, Ghana, Nairobi, Morocco, and other parts of North Africa and the Continent.

CAC: As we look to the next fifty years of *WSQ,* and even more broadly, feminist journals, what would you like to see? What sorts of intellectual and or political interventions might we want to consider?

BR: You asked about *Souls* and why I thought *Souls* should be considered a Black feminist journal—or, how did I envision it that way? People might say, "Well, some of those articles are not what you would primarily describe as feminist." But I would say this—a Black feminist sensibility, a transnational feminist sensibility, should run throughout everything we do, discuss, research, and write. And it's not like a political position. It is an approach and a sensibility. So you're always asking certain kinds of questions. What were, what *are* we taking for granted, etcetera. I would love to see *WSQ* take on a variety of issues around justice and peace and affirming our humanity in the world in a very comprehensive way, and seeing what does a feminist voice and perspective look like when applied to, for example, to the war that's unfolding and raging in Ukraine right now? What are the Black feminist questions? Because then we make sure that race is included as one of the variables. But how do we ask the kinds of questions that a Black feminist perspective would inform, about issues that don't seem on the surface to many people to be primarily about Black feminism or Black women? How has colonialism played out? What were the models of colonialism that Putin is now putting in place? What is happening to some of the most vulnerable people? What does it mean to say: women and children leave and men should stay and fight? There are a lot of gender and gender justice questions. In situations all over the world, climate for example, you can bring a Black feminist lens to it in terms of the places in the world and the people who are less able to run away from the crisis. Those who are most impacted and abandoned when the crises occur. I'm one of the people who are looking out of necessity for some of the most, the boldest and most creative solutions. I would like to see *WSQ* be very expansive in the subjects and very focused in the kind of perspectives and questions that are brought to bear by its editors and writers.

CAC: In the next fifty years, what sort of impact would you like to see *Souls* have in the world?

BR: The future of print publishing is a big question overall. I would like for *Souls* to have much more of an online presence; it would reach people quicker and would be able to intervene in cutting-edge debates in a more timely fashion. That said, it's not a magazine; it is a journal. It's more meditative. It's more thoughtful in dealing with issues over time, as opposed to the immediacy of what's happening in the moment. I would like to see art much more prominent in *Souls*. While we are a literary and verbal culture, we are also a visual culture. And increasingly, this generation of young people are watching, viewing, dissecting what they see. Manning imagined it, and I embraced it, as a journal that created a forum for us to talk about how to get free and how to change the world. I hope that that stays front and center, because no matter what happens, the next generation, when I retire and am long gone, will still be asking the question: How do we get free, and how do we change the world? Because it's not a destination. It's a process. I hope a journal like *Souls* can make some sort of contribution into that liberatory process.

Barbara Ransby is the John D. MacArthur Chair, and Distinguished Professor, in the departments of Black Studies, Gender and Women's Studies, and History at the University of Illinois at Chicago. She also directs the campus-wide Social Justice Initiative, a project that promotes connections between academics and community organizers doing work on social justice. She can be reached at bransby@uic.edu.

Charlene A. Carruthers (she/her) is a writer, filmmaker, and Black studies PhD student at Northwestern University. A practitioner of telling more complete stories, her work interrogates historical conjunctures of Black freedom-making post-emancipation and decolonial revolution, Black governance, and Black feminist abolitionist geographies. She is author of *Unapologetic: A Black, Queer and Feminist Mandate for Radical Movements*. She can be reached at charlenecarruthers@northwestern.edu.

PART VI. **POETRY AND CREATIVE WORKS**

They

Cathleen Calbert

I was pretty, certain, and au courant (thought I),
dusted with yellow (yes, chalk, yes, blackboard),

giving my "he or she" lectures. Oh, I taught 'em
all right. *"He" can't subsume "She."* MLA, baby!

Also, you were straight or gay. (Bi possibly.)
Male or female nonetheless. Even "trannies."

Feminist or foe. Intersectionality not on the map.
Before this, Hellman's mayo or Miracle Whip,

which I preferred (I didn't always have good taste).
Bologna or cotto salami in our home. Whole milk

or nothing—except this white dust slimming
ladies poured into water. Binaries weren't false

and "slippery slope" a rhetorical fallacy.
Nescafe or Folgers. Cheerios or Wheaties.

Phone calls tied you to one spot, so you sat
and listened. If you weren't home, you missed it.

For me, briefly, garter belts until the beauty
of pantyhose. I know taupe was never pleasing

but bare legs coupled with Spanx? This is better?
I remember my mother's talcumed girdle,

WSQ: Women's Studies Quarterly 50: 3 & 4 (Fall/Winter 2022) © 2022 by Cathleen Calbert. All rights reserved.

that plastic, bathroom smell, followed by my hip
electric blue brassiere before I set myself free.

Only strippers had fake boobs, carnies tattoos,
as far as I knew anyway (which wasn't much).

Now what would my lesson be? With cis, ze, hir,
a plethora of genders and sexualities? Sure,

"they" still sounds plural for old sticklers like us.
But we were fucked up too, bud. I don't even

want to write the words we used in our youth.
Let the kids try and teach us something new.

Cathleen Calbert's writing has appeared in *Ms.*, *The Nation*, the *New York Times*, the *Paris Review*, *Poetry*, and elsewhere. She is the author of four books of poems: *Lessons in Space*, *Bad Judgment*, *Sleeping with a Famous Poet*, and *The Afflicted Girls*. Her awards include the 92nd Street Y Discovery Poetry Prize, a Pushcart Prize, the Sheila Motton Book Prize, and the Mary Tucker Thorp Professorship at Rhode Island College. She can be reached at cathleen.calbert@gmail.com.

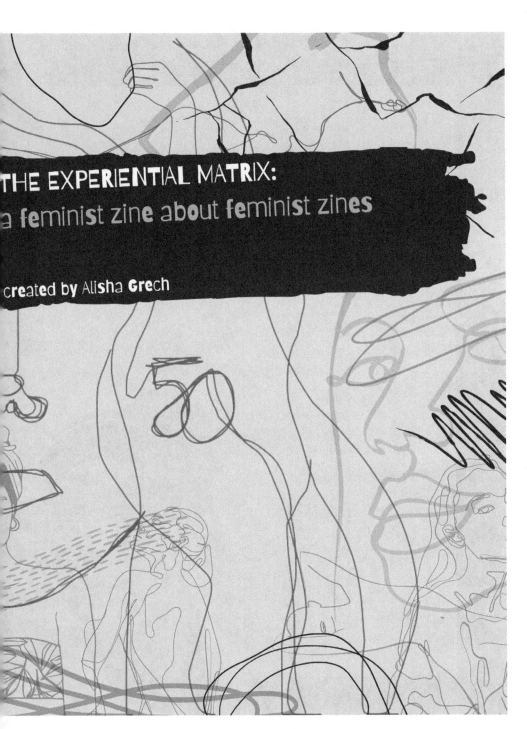

THE EXPERIENTIAL MATRIX:
a feminist zine about feminist zines

created by Alisha Grech

WSQ: Women's Studies Quarterly 50: 3 & 4 (Fall/Winter 2022) © 2022 by Alisha Grech. All rights reserved.

A NOTE FROM THE CREATOR

I first came across a call for WSQ's 50th issue in June of 2021. At the time, I was just dipping my toes into the world of zines—specifically, local Canadian feminist zines. Now, I come to you several months into the future, happily immersed, enthralled and perhaps a bit perplexed by feminist zines.

For the past 50 years (and arguably longer), zines have been provoking and supporting BIPOC, queer, and women-centred communities in ways that prominent magazine publications cannot—in this, connecting persons of different sizes, ages, geographical locations, race, ethnicity, and identity through their shared interest of being one thing: a fan.

In this hybridized art piece-feminist-zine-about-feminist-zines, I will examine other women-produced zines and the history of the zine itself. I also hope to explore the future of the women-produced zines that have been emerging in a COVID-19 setting.

Special thanks to Victoria Law, my pug and my partner for helping me in this creative endeavour.

Cheers to you WSQ on the past 50 issues.

WITH LOVE,
ALISHA

310

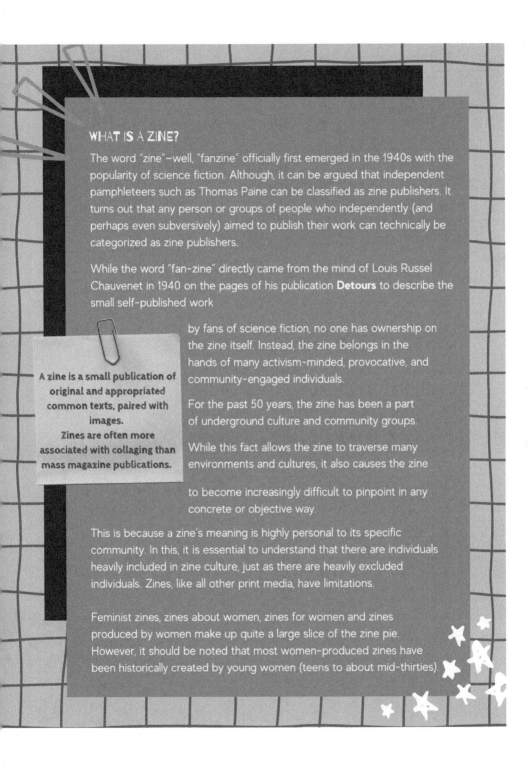

WHAT IS A ZINE?

The word "zine"—well, "fanzine" officially first emerged in the 1940s with the popularity of science fiction. Although, it can be argued that independent pamphleteers such as Thomas Paine can be classified as zine publishers. It turns out that any person or groups of people who independently (and perhaps even subversively) aimed to publish their work can technically be categorized as zine publishers.

While the word "fan-zine" directly came from the mind of Louis Russel Chauvenet in 1940 on the pages of his publication **Detours** to describe the small self-published work by fans of science fiction, no one has ownership on the zine itself. Instead, the zine belongs in the hands of many activism-minded, provocative, and community-engaged individuals.

A zine is a small publication of original and appropriated common texts, paired with images.
Zines are often more associated with collaging than mass magazine publications.

For the past 50 years, the zine has been a part of underground culture and community groups.

While this fact allows the zine to traverse many environments and cultures, it also causes the zine to become increasingly difficult to pinpoint in any concrete or objective way.

This is because a zine's meaning is highly personal to its specific community. In this, it is essential to understand that there are individuals heavily included in zine culture, just as there are heavily excluded individuals. Zines, like all other print media, have limitations.

Feminist zines, zines about women, zines for women and zines produced by women make up quite a large slice of the zine pie. However, it should be noted that most women-produced zines have been historically created by young women (teens to about mid-thirties).

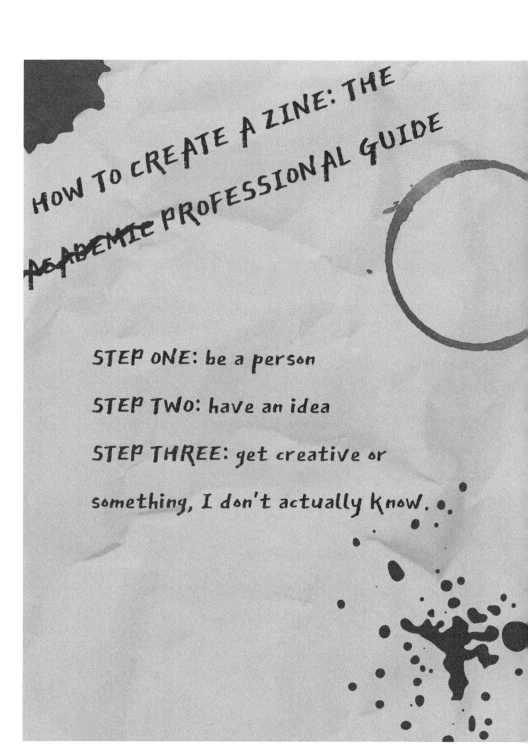

HOW TO CREATE A ZINE: THE ~~ACADEMIC~~ PROFESSIONAL GUIDE

STEP ONE: be a person

STEP TWO: have an idea

STEP THREE: get creative or something, I don't actually know.

ZINES: HERE, THERE, EVERYWHERE

1940's - 1970's

The "fanzine" picks up particular attention and with it, a new way for communities to gather over their interests manifests. The first fanzines allowed people to establish unique creative networks.

The rise of counterculture in the 1950's saw with it the growth of underground publications with a focus on issues such as racism, inequality and women's rights. During this time, zines gave groups of people such as BIPOC, LGBTQIA+ and women a voice outside of the scope of the mainstream.

1970's - 1990's

During this time, many zines were printed cheaply and spread through small, localized networks. In these publications, art, politics, culture pieces and activism articles were combined into a single issue at a time. This redefined the possibility of what publications could be - spaces for thought, creativity and radical communication.

In the 1980's the punk music scene exploded into the self publishing world, representing a powerful subculture for mass cultural revolt.

1990's - 2000's

In the 1990's the world saw the subversive, the superbly powerful riot grrrl movement. Growing from similar punk subculture, this zine movement focused primarily on feminism, sex and gender-identity. Largely, the riot grrrl movement in its rebellion against American patriarchal norms, greatly influenced the rise of third wave feminism. Like many other zines before them, the riot grrrl movement emphasized the importance of personal experience, utilizing the zine as a feminist tool for community-building.

Detours by L.R Chauvenet - 1940

The Femizine by the Fanettes - 1950

Bad Day at Lime Rock by Lee Hoffman - 1950

International Times by Barry Mike and John Hopkins - 1966

Girda, by Mike Murase, Dinora Gil and Laura Lib - 1969

Punk by John Holmstrom, Ged Dunn and Legs McNeil - 1976

Sniffin Glue by Mark Perry and Danny Baker - 1976

JD's by GB Jones and Bruce LaBruce - 1985

Homocore by Deke Nihilison - 1988

Jigsaw by Tobi Vail - 1988

Chainsaw by Donna Dresch - 1990

Fat Girl by April Miller - 1990

Girl Germs by Allison Wolfe and Molly Newman - 1991

Bikini Kill by Kathleen Hanna, Tobi Vail and Kathy Wilcox - 1991

Rollerderby by Lisa Carver - 1992

Bust by Debbie Stoller - 1993

Bitch by Andi Zeisler - 1996

B*TCHES WHO BITE BACK

ITS TIME TO RIOT (GRRRL)

Here's a bold statement: not all women-produced zines are created equal.

Since I'm flexing my non-academic-subversive-cool-kid muscles, I'm allowed to be bold. Right. So...

While any woman can arguably participate in zine creation or zine communities, specific women-produced zines are understood to have influenced zine culture and (on a larger scale) feminism entirely.

Once upon a time, in the year nineteen-ninety-something, Kathleen Hanna was studying at Evergreen State College in Olympia, Washington. To Kathleen and her bandmates, punk rock often felt like a space for boys and boys only. And this sentiment wasn't just being expressed by them. It was resonating out over the airwaves of other feminist-focused groups. Then, like a beautiful punk-rock phoenix, a movement of rioting women rose from the ashes of punk-rock sexism.

And thus, the Riot Grrrl movement was born.

And like the most prominent zine culture at the time, Riot Grrrl was made up of white, middle class, cis-gender women.

Bikini Kill, Bratmobile, Babes in Toyland, 7 Year Bitch, Calamity Jane, Excuse IT, Heavens to Betsy

Though the Riot Grrrl movement is commonly thought of as the golden age of zine culture and feminist centred zines, politically motivated zines have existed long before in communities of colour.

What is Riot Grrrl: a social movement, primarily based in the good old USA, focused on female-punk-rock bands and alternative, political writings on sexism in creative industries.

From La Catrina Cavalera cartoons created by José Guadalupe Posada in the 1900s to Black Panther Party handouts in the 1960s, zines transcend their punk-rock-popularity.

315

Zines establish Feminist Pedagogy in three ways
1) participatory learning
2) validation of personal experience
3) development of critical thinking
– Kimberly Creasap, "Zine-Making as Feminist Pedagogy"

"Zines are sites of feminist memory work in which the personal and political are fused."
– Red Chidgey, "Reassess Your Weapons: the making of feminist memory in young women's zines"

"Like scrapbooks and pamphlets, zines have allowed girls and women to write about issues that were not written about anywhere else."
– Kimberly Creasap, "Zine-Making as Feminist Pedagogy"

RAD (W)RIGHTINGS: SCHOLARLY EXCERPTS ON FEMINIST ZINES

"the most important characteristic of zines for feminism is their ability to make women and girls cultural producers. Women-produced zines provide an alternative to mainstream culture, and their existence demonstrates to other girls and women that they can also produce culture rather than consume it"
– Brandi Leigh-Ann Bell, "Riding the third wave: women-produced zines and feminisms"

"By creating their own cultural products, women and girls are creating their own space."
– Brandi Leigh-Ann Bell, "Riding the third wave: women-produced zines and feminisms"

ZINES DEAL WITH PEOPLE AND COMMUNITIES. Zines "should not be viewed merely as part of a research itinerary to be ticked off one by one, transcribed and analysed, and never considered again."
–Michelle Kempson, "'My Version of Feminism': Subjectivity, DIY and the Feminist Zine"

Zines are not just the place through which feminist ideas are shared, Zines are also the place through which feminist memory is PRESERVED
–Red Chidgey, "Reassess Your Weapons: the making of feminist memory in young women's zines"

WHOSE ZINE IS IT ANYWAY: A CONVERSATION WITH VICTORIA LAW

On a grey Toronto afternoon in July, I picked up the phone to talk to Victoria Law.

As the line rang, I sat in silence, watching the rain dribble down the window. Then, finally, the warmth of her voice came through with a simple "hello?" From 2003 to 2020, Victoria Law has served as an outside publisher and co-editor for the zine Tenacious: Art and Writings by Women in Prison in addition to her career as a journalist and writer, exploring the United States prison system. Tenacious (if you haven't heard of it) is a compilation of articles, thought pieces, diary entries, poetry and works of art by incarcerated women across the United States. In over 30 issues, Tenacious has covered subject matter such as foster care, motherhood, addiction, racism in the United States prison system, education, and sexual harassment by prison staff.

For Victoria Law and those she worked with, women-produced zines hold special power, especially for incarcerated women:

> In 2001... I wasn't hearing anything about what women in prisons were doing to resist and organize, and at the time in the United States, there were over ninety-thousand women in jails and prisons. And through that, I realized that women were organizing around a different set of issues in prison, and many were mothers to young children...

> ...Women in prison reached out to me and said, we're not seeing our own experiences represented in the media. We aren't seeing anything about what it's like to be a woman in prison, a mother in prison. We're not seeing anyone write about that... In the early 2000s, people weren't thinking about women in prison—when you thought of prison back then, you think of men."

WHOSE ZINE IS IT ANYWAY: A CONVERSATION WITH VICTORIA LAW

Editing and curating Tenacious was about establishing a form of community that has been challengingly out of reach for incarcerated women. As Victoria explains:

"Publishing submissions from women in prison can be challenging because you were getting a handwritten piece of paper—transcribing it in itself was challenging...And, despite technological advances, it's become more difficult to send information back and forth. I know one prison states that it must be white paper only into a binding. Another prison says, no greeting cards. One prison in Pennsylvania has all prisoner mail sent to a private company in Florida that prints all of the mail, and prisoners get scanned copies—so you never get the physical copy of the card or the drawing that your kid made."

Unlike the Riot Grrrls of the past or the COVID-creators of today, incarcerated women do not have the same access to zine-creation.

There are no resources for photocopying, editing, or even submitting a piece of work freely in prison. When talking to Victoria Law about the many restrictions female inmates face, I asked her what her goals were as an editor:

"I wanted to get the story out there, you know? Even though Tenacious never had a wide circulation outside of prison, like people were interested and would ask for it...

...But I wanted to get the stories out there so people could read about what's happening to women in prison. People could read about what was happening in different prisons, from someone in Illinois, reading about someone in prison in Oregon... All I ask of people creating zines now is to consider women in the prison system."

318

GENERATION Z(INE): HONORABLE MENTIONS FOR THE ZINES OF TODAY

HOAX, a US bi-annual queer, feminist and compilation zine.

GIRLS GET BUSY, more so a creative platform than actual zine, but hey it works.

CRYBABY, a gen-z online and print zine featuring independent artists.

MUCHACHA FANZINE, a radical, intersectional and decolonial Xicana feminist zine.

PLASMA DOLPHIN, an arts and culture zine that is women produced and women founded.

SHOTGUN SEAMSTRESS, a Black, punk, queer and women focused zine.

F WORD, a montreal-based intersectional feminist zine.

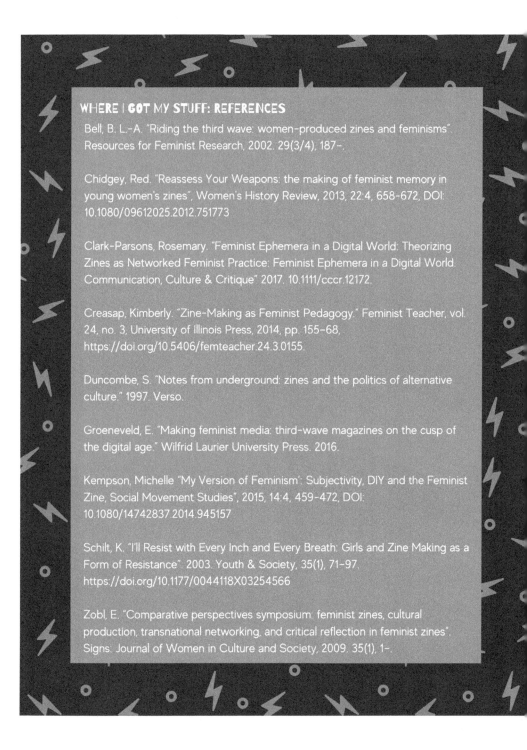

WHERE I GOT MY STUFF: REFERENCES

Bell, B. L.-A. "Riding the third wave: women-produced zines and feminisms". Resources for Feminist Research, 2002. 29(3/4), 187-.

Chidgey, Red. "Reassess Your Weapons: the making of feminist memory in young women's zines", Women's History Review, 2013, 22:4, 658-672, DOI: 10.1080/09612025.2012.751773

Clark-Parsons, Rosemary. "Feminist Ephemera in a Digital World: Theorizing Zines as Networked Feminist Practice: Feminist Ephemera in a Digital World. Communication, Culture & Critique" 2017. 10.1111/cccr.12172.

Creasap, Kimberly. "Zine-Making as Feminist Pedagogy." Feminist Teacher, vol. 24, no. 3, University of Illinois Press, 2014, pp. 155–68, https://doi.org/10.5406/femteacher.24.3.0155.

Duncombe, S. "Notes from underground: zines and the politics of alternative culture." 1997. Verso.

Groeneveld, E. "Making feminist media: third-wave magazines on the cusp of the digital age." Wilfrid Laurier University Press. 2016.

Kempson, Michelle "My Version of Feminism': Subjectivity, DIY and the Feminist Zine, Social Movement Studies", 2015, 14:4, 459-472, DOI: 10.1080/14742837.2014.945157

Schilt, K. "I'll Resist with Every Inch and Every Breath: Girls and Zine Making as a Form of Resistance". 2003. Youth & Society, 35(1), 71-97. https://doi.org/10.1177/0044118X03254566

Zobl, E. "Comparative perspectives symposium: feminist zines, cultural production, transnational networking, and critical reflection in feminist zines". Signs: Journal of Women in Culture and Society, 2009. 35(1), 1-.

Alisha Grech is a writer and multidisciplinary creative artist and scholar based out of Tkaronto, Toronto, Canada. Currently, Alisha is a doctoral student at the University of Toronto, where her research centers around mainstream North American feminism, whiteness, and gender-based violence. Her work has been featured in magazines such as *Purple Glow*, *Intermission*, *Raani Creative*, and *Blank Magazine*. She can be reached at alisha@alishagrech.com.

PART VII. **ALERTS AND PROVOCATIONS**

Dobbs and the Politics of Reproduction

Premilla Nadasen

When I first heard the news that *Roe v. Wade* had been overturned by the Supreme Court in the *Dobbs v. Jackson Women's Health Organization* decision, one week before this article was due, my heart sank. I knew it was coming, but that didn't soften the blow. I scrapped an earlier draft of this piece and shifted my focus. So, what does this landmark decision mean for feminist political struggle? For the field of women's, gender, and sexuality studies (WGSS)?

The overturning of *Roe* has implications for a whole host of issues regarding privacy, sexuality, and protection of individual rights, in addition to reproductive justice. Sexual autonomy and freedom, not only for cisgender women, are under threat, as Justice Clarence Thomas made clear in his concurring opinion that the court should also reconsider previous rulings regarding contraception and same-sex marriage. *Dobbs* paves the way to undo same-sex marriage, in vitro fertilization, interracial marriage, contraception, and transgender rights. At the same time, it is stunning that abortion has been declared illegal in many parts of the country at a moment when sexual assault is both widespread and very much in public discourse—when it is being paraded and defended by the likes of Brett Kavanaugh and Donald Trump. Especially because there is no exception for rape, the decision seems to disregard the pervasiveness of sexual assault and create a scenario where the victims must pay the price for the sins of the assailant.

As important as the legal right to abortion is, reproductive justice encompasses a much wider set of issues. As articulated by women of color scholars and activists, reproductive justice is a framework that incorporates the right to terminate a pregnancy, access to contraception, an end to coerced sterilizations, and social and economic support for mothers and

WSQ: Women's Studies Quarterly 50: 3 & 4 (Fall/Winter 2022) © 2022 by Premilla Nadasen. All rights reserved.

children (Roberts 1997; Ross et al. 2017). Reproductive justice entails both bodily autonomy and guarantees that people have the freedom to decide if and when they want to have children.

Since the 1960s, feminists such as welfare rights activists fought for mothers to have the economic resources to ensure reproductive justice (Nadasen 2005). The welfare rights movement's demands for both sexual autonomy and state financial assistance to raise their children illustrate how reproductive justice is inextricably bound up with mothering, care work, and financial stability. The right to an abortion is one building block in a larger structure that has served as a foundation to ensure women's political and economic freedom.

Over time, these rights have slowly eroded. In 1977, Congress passed the Hyde Amendment, which prohibited federal funding for abortion, making abortion less accessible to poor women. Despite measures put in place to protect women from coerced sterilizations, as recently as 2010 women in California prisons were sterilized, often under pressure, without state approval (Chappel 2013). In 1996 the transformation of welfare from a cash entitlement program to block grants to states led to a precipitous decline in the number of single parents on public assistance. And because of pervasive and systemic racism and discrimination, Black women have much worse maternal health outcomes (Davis 2019). No federal policies in the U.S. provide the kind of comprehensive support that families require to raise and care for children. According to the Department of Labor, only 56 percent of American workers qualify for the Family Medical Leave Act, and many of those don't get paid leave (Brown, Herr, Roy, and Klerman 2020). *Dobbs* is just one in a long line of assaults on reproductive justice.

It is ironic that the Mississippi-based Jackson Women's Health Organization is at the center of the *Dobbs* decision. It is a clinic I am familiar with because of my visits to the state where I have worked with the Mississippi Low-Income Child Care Initiative (MLICCI), an advocacy organization for poor mothers and struggling childcare providers. MLICCI has spent the past twenty years lobbying the state of Mississippi to release (not allocate) money designated for childcare for low-income mothers—which the state has not done. Mississippi is one of the stingiest states when it comes to supporting poor single mothers, giving a family of three only $260 a month and assisting only 5 percent of needy families (Zane 2021). Even more appalling, a state audit in 2020 revealed that a vast majority of welfare funds was being diverted to friends of the head of the state welfare department (Wolfe 2020). So, it is puzzling that in a state with such concern about the lives of fetuses, there is so little concern about the lives of babies and children.

The pro-life movement has rarely sought to protect babies. While it demands state action to revoke the fundamental right of women to make decisions about their own bodies, purportedly in the name of the fetus, it has not demanded expanded state welfare assistance or programs to feed women, infants, and children. It doesn't address questions of forced sterilization, the lack of access to women's reproductive health, quality prenatal care, or affordable childcare.

The *Dobbs* decision came down amid one of the biggest care crises in the country's history. A care crisis has been brewing in mainstream America for the past thirty years. As more and more middle-class white women have entered the labor market, families have grappled with the question of who would care for the children, clean the house, and cook the meals. People who could afford it filled the "care deficit"—as Arlie Hochschild (2002) named it—by purchasing consumer goods to ease household chores and outsourcing work to companies or private household workers, most of whom are poor women of color.

Poor and working-class families, particularly families of color, have struggled with a care crisis for much longer, since women's employment rates for these groups were higher and they didn't have the resources to outsource care work. But during the pandemic, when all families were hit hard by the shutdown of schools and day cares, the care crisis came to a head.

During my term as president of the National Women's Studies Association (NWSA), I initiated a survey of WGSS programs impacted by COVID-19. I was interested in tracking how people were coping and how their institutions were addressing the crisis. With the help of the NWSA staff, we launched a survey and wrote a report about COVID and care work. We found, unsurprisingly, that WGSS programs faced furloughs and budget cuts, women faculty and service workers were disproportionately burdened with childcare, universities did not provide the support that women employees needed, and professional demands escalated in tandem with home responsibilities (Nadasen, Ash, and Jones 2020).

The pandemic foregrounded the crisis of care and amplified ideas germinated in WGSS about the essential nature of this labor. The labors of biological and social reproduction have historically been sites of exploitation. The gendered division of labor and the labor of social reproduction, both paid and unpaid, are foundational to capitalism. Feminist scholars have written for decades about the need for high-quality day care and social supports for women because this work is critical. Those ideas were embraced during the pandemic, although in watered-down form. Despite the urgency of the moment and robust rationale, the proposals for an expanded infrastructure to support care work that were on the table failed, and no long-term substantive solutions to the care crisis have been instituted. The *Dobbs* decision is even more threatening to women's personal autonomy and success in the labor market and families' economic security in the context of an unresolved care crisis. It creates a situation of forced biological reproduction, and for those who don't have an option, forced and unpaid motherhood and care work.

The *Dobbs* decision is part of a longer battle waged by conservatives against reproductive rights, LGBTQ rights, racial equality, and gender equality. In September 2020 Donald Trump issued an "Executive Order on Combating Race and Sex Stereotyping," which President Biden reversed a few months later upon taking office. Despite the progressive-sounding name of Trump's order, it essentially banned the federal government and contractors from offering what he called "divisive" diversity training that had a critical approach to race and gender or grappled seriously with racism and sexism. The order was issued, not coincidentally, in a context of nationwide Black Lives Matter protests that escalated in response to a series of killings of unarmed Black people. The Executive Order also ignited local initiatives.

In 2021 Iowa passed a law that prohibited the teaching of several things in state-funded schools, including topics around race or sex that result in "discomfort, guilt, anguish or any other form of psychological distress" (Richardson 2021). The idea that banning educational topics because it makes children uncomfortable is ridiculous. Children get uncomfortable when they are in physics class and gym. It is unthinkable to say that those subjects cannot be taught because children may be uncomfortable. The law also bans teaching that either the United States or the state of Iowa is fundamentally racist or sexist. This clause is especially perplexing because the bill itself is evidence of the systemic racism and sexism of the state of Iowa. And one could only hope that in passing it, Iowa lawmakers feel discomfort, guilt, and anguish.

Iowa is only one of many battlegrounds across the country and the world where right-wing attacks seek to muddle the truth, deny the facts, and rewrite the historical and contemporary narrative in order to construct a white supremacist, heteropatriarchal, religiously fanatical society. They are not proposing a total ban on teaching race and gender. Rather, they are peddling a specific, inaccurate version of race and gender, one that erases incontrovertible facts and decades of solid historical research. It is part of an orchestrated attempt to silence progressive voices and is a first step toward demagoguery that could lead us down a path to fascism.

One charge by those on the right is that WGSS and critical race theory promote activism. One would hope so. Part of the mission of a liberal arts education is to cultivate engaged citizens. The pedagogical framework developed in these fields is not to feed students information but to give them the tools to develop a critical perspective, examine facts, and come to their own conclusions. This does and should enable them to shape the world around them. All academic work influences ideas or policy. Political scientists analyze elections and highlight what they understand as the core political issues. Economists make predictions and offer recommendations about economic growth and recession. Academic research, writing, and teaching has an impact on our understanding of the world, which influences future policy proposals. That's a good thing. Decisions should be made from a place of knowledge rather than ignorance.

WGSS and critical race theory are under attack because of their very success. Africana, Indigenous, ethnic, and women's, gender, and sexuality studies have demonstrated that race and gender, as well as racism and sexism, are foundational to U.S. society and a necessary component of any education. This now conventional wisdom is evidence of the analytical power of the field and its commitment to democratic engagement.

Fifty years ago, WGSS was born out of a democratic impulse, and it continues to represent not elite academics, but most people. The power and influence of WGSS is evident all around us—the discussions about reproductive justice, the care crisis, labor organizing, women's equality, gay and trans rights, racial justice, the climate crisis, and more. It is simply not possible to discuss any issue today without bringing into the fold questions of gender, race, class, and sexuality. Many of the rights people take for granted have emerged directly from social movements. The U.S. Supreme Court, in contrast, is out of touch and squarely at odds with the vast majority of Americans who support individual privacy and personal autonomy.

Although progressive academics have made unprecedented inroads, there is still much work to be done. The progressive future is at a crossroads. Judicial war is being waged on freedom of speech and people's ability to govern themselves and their communities. Violent armed struggle is being waged on social movements, schools, houses of worship, people of African descent, immigrants, Indigenous communities, and transgender people. An intellectual war is being waged on our very right to speak and teach what we know is true at a time when what we say matters more than ever.

WGSS got its start in the streets. It was seeded, fertilized, and nurtured in defense of women's rights. It gained traction with its theoretical contributions, insight into social organization, analyses of operations of power, and public policy impact. As it made its way into the institution, it also became institutionalized. And many, but not all, programs lost their radical edge. That connection to burgeoning social movements is being forged once again.

Over the past fifteen years there has been renewed mass organizing—campaigns such as #MeToo and #TimesUp around sexual assault, immigration marches, labor organizing led by teachers, nurses, and domestic workers, the Movement for Black Lives and racial justice organizing, and Occupy Wall Street and other grassroots struggles for economic justice. There has never been more need for the scholarship and voice of women's and gender studies and feminist activism.

WGSS is at its strongest when it encounters challenges. It was born in a context marked by inequity, discrimination, and ongoing assaults on women and gender-nonconforming people. At a time when women didn't have access to reproductive support and some women were routinely forcibly sterilized, when there was little acknowledgment of the serial murders of Black and Indigenous women, when there were no services for survivors of domestic violence, when "don't say gay" was more common than not, when poor mothers didn't have adequate economic assistance.

WGSS must continue to demonstrate its relevance not only to academic study—it has been very successful at that—but also to people outside of academia. It turned the tide once. It can do so again.

Premilla Nadasen is a professor of history at Barnard College, director of the Barnard Center for Research on Women, and past president of the National Women's Studies Association. She is most interested in the activism and visions of liberation of poor and working-class women of color and is the author of two award-winning books *Welfare Warriors: The Welfare Rights Movement in the United States* and *Household Workers Unite: The Untold Story of African American Women Who Built a Movement*. Her forthcoming book on the care economy is due out in 2023 (Haymarket). She can be reached at pnadasen@barnard.edu.

Works Cited

Brown, Scott, Jane Herr, Radha Roy, and Jacob Alex Klerman. 2020. "Employee and Worksite Perspectives of the Family and Medical Leave Act: Results from the 2018 Surveys." July 2020. Rockville, MD: Abt Associates.

Chappel, Bill. 2013. "California's Prison Sterilizations Reportedly Echo Eugenics Era." *NPR*, July 9, 2013. https://www.npr.org/sections/thetwo-way/2013/07/09/200444613/californias-prison-sterilizations-reportedly-echoes-eugenics-era.

Davis, Dána-Ain. 2019. *Reproductive Injustice: Racism, Pregnancy and Premature Birth*. New York: NYU Press.

Hochschild, Arlie. 2002. "Love and Gold." In *Global Woman: Nannies, Maids, and Sex Workers in the New Economy*, edited by Arlie Russell Hochschild and Barbara Ehrenreich, 15–30. New York: Henry Holt & Company.

Nadasen, Premilla. 2005. *Welfare Warriors: The Welfare Rights Movements in the United States*. New York: Routledge.

Nadasen, Premilla, Jen Ash, and Briona Jones. 2020. "WGSS Programs during COVID: A Data Brief from NWSA." National Women's Studies Association, October 7, 2020. https://cdn.ymaws.com/www.nwsa.org/resource/resmgr/budget_cuts_and_covid_data_b.pdf.

Richardson, Ian. 2021. "Iowa Gov. Kim Reynolds Signs Law Targeting Critical Race Theory, Saying She's Against 'Discriminatory Indoctrination.'" *Des Moines Register*, June 8, 2021. https://www.desmoinesregister.com/story/news/politics/2021/06/08/governor-kim-reynolds-signs-law-targeting-critical-race-theory-iowa-schools-diversity-training/7489896002/.

Roberts, Dorothy. 1997. *Killing the Black Body: Race, Reproduction, and the Meaning of Liberty*. New York: Pantheon.

Ross, Loretta, Lynn Roberts, Erica Derkas, Whitney Peoples, and Pamela Bridgewater Toure, eds. 2017. *Radical Reproductive Justice: Foundations, Theory, Practices, Critique*. New York: Feminist Press.

Wolfe, Anna. 2020. "Report: Fewer Mississippians Received Cash Assistance in 2020, Even during a Pandemic." *Clarion Ledger*, November 14, 2020. https://www.clarionledger.com/story/news/politics/2020/11/14/tanf-report-fewer-mississippi-residents-got-cash-assistance-2020/6286660002/.

Zane, Ali. 2021. "Mississippi Raises TANF Benefits but More Improvements Needed, Especially in South." Center on Budget and Policy Priorities (website), May 4, 2021. https://www.cbpp.org/blog/mississippi-raises-tanf-benefits-but-more-improvements-needed-especially-in-south.

Community Tributes to Brianne Waychoff

It is with a heavy heart that I write to share that my dear friend and colleague, Dr. Brianne Waychoff, passed away from 9/11-related kidney cancer on Monday, July 25, 2022. She was forty-three. Dr. Waychoff was a brilliant professor, colleague, scholar, artist, performer, and activist, an interdisciplinary powerhouse, and all-around incredible changemaker in the world.

Dr. Brianne Waychoff was associate professor of communication and the co-coordinator of Gender, Women's, and Sexuality Studies at the Borough of Manhattan Community College of the City University of New York (BMCC). Her BA was in theatre and her MA was in women's and gender studies from the University of Northern Iowa. She earned a PhD in communication studies with an emphasis in performance studies and minor in women's and gender studies from Louisiana State University. Dr. Waychoff published in a range of scholarly journals, including *Text and Performance Quarterly*, *The Journal of Pacific Affairs*, and *Liminalities: A Journal of Performance Studies*. They were coeditor of *Women's Studies Quarterly*, published by the Feminist Press. She also was chair of the Community College Caucus of the National Women's Studies Association, chair of the nominating committee for the Performance Studies Division of the National Communication Association, and a member of the Organization for the Study of Communication, Language, and Gender. They served on the editorial boards of *Text and Performance Quarterly*, *Liminalities: A Journal of Performance Studies*, and *Women and Language*. Her research interests were women's studies, speech, social justice issues, queer theory, performance studies, media studies, gender studies, gender and sexuality studies, feminist theory, disability studies, cultural diversity, and communication studies. Dr. Waychoff also cocreated the Gender, Women's, and Sexuality Studies program and major at BMCC, where they taught Introduction to Gender and Women's Studies, Gender and Communication, Gender and Women's Studies Capstone,

Fundamentals of Public Speaking, Oral Interpretation, and Mass Media, among other courses. She presented performance work at professional venues and festivals throughout the United States, was invited guest artist at several institutions in the US and abroad, and won grants and other awards for her scholarly and creative work. Dr. Waychoff's commitment to gender justice was acknowledged nationally when she was invited by the White House to participate in the United State of Women Summit in 2016, celebrating the accomplishments of women and girls and making plans for the future.

Besides Dr. Waychoff's impressive professional work, they were a kind, compassionate, empathetic, and deeply loving person. I met her at the panel I organized to bring Women's, Gender, and Sexuality Studies chairs, directors, and coordinators together across the CUNY campuses to celebrate the twenty-fifth anniversary of the WGSS program at Kingsborough Community College in 2019. She was a vibrant part of the panel, along with Dr. Antonio (Jay) Pastrana, Prof. Jen Gaboury, Dr. Mobina Hashmi, Dr. JV Fuqua, Dr. Laura Westengard, Dr. Jerilyn Fisher, Dr. Allia Abdullah-Matta, Dr. Jacqueline Jones, and me. Even that day, Brianne offered to help blow up balloons with the students and me to set up. I met them again the next semester over juice and dressed down in T-shirts and overalls with Dr. Martens and tattoos out in order to discuss building a pipeline for WGSS students from the AA to MA level with the hope of a PhD in the future. The following semester they were one of four CUNY faculty, along with Dr. Paisley Currah, Dr. Yaari Felber-Seligman, and me, to testify at the City Council's hearing on trans and nonbinary rights and funding for students and faculty at CUNY. Doing this work together, we decided we wanted to keep doing feminist and LGBTQ scholarship together. We applied to be the next editors of *WSQ*. When Brianne and I started working for *WSQ* in September 2020, my beloved mother died unexpectedly from a heart attack, just three weeks into my tenure. I will never forget how Brianne gave me permission to take off time, to go slower, to grieve. They just got it. I also will never forget how they offered to come to my mother's graveside service upstate to be by my side, along with my close friends, family, and wife, and allow me to pay respects to my mother. She would text me to check in and send me pictures of her French feminist theorist cats, Luce and Jules, when I was deep in grief from losing my mom, then uncle, and then dog all within a year. Their kindness and empathy just helped everything. While we had not known each other that long, we talked very regularly for the journal, as well as about our lives, and she showed up so hard for the journal, students, faculty, and me. It pulled me back up. I gave back to them when they were down—when their parents' house was destroyed, when their grandmother died, when they were diagnosed with cancer after driving cross-country to help a mutual friend Dr. JV Fuqua move, and when they were in and out of the hospital. My hand was out ready and steady to pull them up, too. I sent them gifts, picked up their work, encouraged them to rest, checked in over calls, texts, memes, and animal pictures, and sent them a stuffed animal cat when no flowers and no visitors were allowed due to COVID. It was our critical friendship and language of care. I really wish I could have done more for them. I really wish life were not so unfair to such a generous, thoughtful, and sweet person. However, while I am very sad she passed far too young, I am relieved she is at peace, not in pain. I will always remember the down-to-earth conversations we had about liking to mow the lawn, rest as resistance, weird feminist art shares, cats on doors and in strange places, riot grrrl faves, the costumes they made for their nibling, and dancing into work meetings with "Staying Alive" in our heads.

Dr. Waychoff opened doors for CUNY students and faculty to do feminist, LGBTQIA+, and social justice work. I am honored I could work with them over the past two years to coedit *WSQ*. Even during a pandemic and with advanced cancer, Brianne was an intellectual rock star. She worked so hard and with so much love for the sake of feminist scholarship, even when she was so sick and doing Zoom meetings at Sloan Kettering. I will always remember their vision for a better world, commitment to creativity and art, their encouragement of community college students and faculty, remarkable diligence and devotion to scholarship and the field of Women's, Gender, and Sexuality Studies, and practice of diversity, inclusion, and equity. It is unfortunate that WGSS graduate students at the Graduate Center will not be able to take Feminist Texts and Theories with Dr. Waychoff, but Dr. Dána-Ain Davis and Dr. JV Fuqua will keep them alive in spirit at the Graduate Center this year. We will be doing several tributes for them, including in the *Nonbinary* issue we were supposed edit together with Dr. JV Fuqua and Dr. Marquis Bey.

My heart goes out to all of Dr. Waychoff's loved ones, including family, partner Dr. Ben Powell, friends, colleagues, and students. Rest in Power, Breezo, with much, much love, respect, and gratitude! —**Red Washburn**

Though I knew Brianne only for a short time at *WSQ,* I feel the loss for the *WSQ* and CUNY community. As an incoming graduate student with no experience in publishing, I at times felt like a burden at the journal. I know Brianne will remain one of the best "bosses" that I've ever had for never making me feel that way. You could tell that Brianne was an educator at heart. They were so patient, and always willing to get on a phone or Zoom call if I needed help. I felt guided and protected by Brianne in our work environment which I think is so rare.

I am positive Brianne touched many people's lives in far greater ways, as an artist, performer, teacher, and family member. I remember when she showed us this amazing Halloween costume she made for her nephew. Thank you, Brianne, for being such a positive light. You leave behind a great legacy that will not be forgotten. —**Amy Iafrate**

Brianne was an amazing light for everyone they touched. I am so grateful to have known them. They left a mark on the world, and everyone they knew. Thank you for existing, and thank you for being an example to me. —**Ivy Bryan**

Brianne was a beautifully positive light of energy that brought joy and ease to working with them. They were a kind and supportive mentor, and my time at *WSQ* was made all that better through having them as coeditor. They brought love and light to all of those who had the chance to have them in their lives, regardless of how short or long the time was. They will be so missed by me, and their entire community. —**Alex Stamson**

Brianne was a brilliant, passionate, and deeply kind person. In the brief time I was lucky enough to know them, I was inspired by the excitement and commitment they brought to their work at *WSQ* and to the broader project of feminist scholarship and activism. They showed up for this cause, even under trying circumstances. Their influence on *WSQ* will be long-lasting. Despite ongoing health struggles, Brianne was extraordinarily generous with their time and energy, with me and with the many others she mentored or collaborated with. They were patient and supportive, they often sent words of encouragement during stressful or trying moments. I can only imagine what a joy it would have been to have them as a professor, and my heart goes out to their students, past and present. *WSQ* has lost a brilliant coeditor and

CUNY has lost a remarkable scholar, artist, activist and educator. They are missed. —**Googie Karrass**

Brianne had a smart heart or a loving mind, I'm not sure which, but in the brief and deep time I shared with them they integrated intellectual integrity and community care with rare skill. Brianne brought creativity, rigor, kindness, ferocity, and care into our shared institutional spaces. In doing so, they changed those spaces, they supercharged them with a kind of transformative presence and intentionality. Perhaps it was their theater and performance background, but they knew how to bring their whole being into the room or to the task at hand. It's hard to describe. Here is someone, I thought to myself the first time I met with Drs. Waychoff and Red Washburn about their collaborative efforts to create a sustainable home for *WSQ* at CUNY, here are two people, actually, who I want to learn with and lean on as we plan and agitate for progressive, feminist institutional change. We hoped CUNY, the people's university, a deeply pluralistic university full of possibilities, would integrate *WSQ* more holistically into its mission, nurturing future generations of just-now emerging feminists by honoring the generations of radical feminist forbears who preceded us: writers, educators, and publishers who transformed CUNY from within—from Audre Lorde to Mina Shaughnessy to June Jordan to Florence Howe. We drew power and sought guidance from their legacy. Now Brianne is among them, their powerful legacies entwined.

Brianne made other ways of being and modes of working possible through her everyday practice of showing up. They showed up again and again for us: we, their colleagues, their students, their friends. They showed up to get the work done and to remind us of why the work mattered. As their illness advanced, they helped us draft job descriptions and plan interviews. They created workflow docs and publication schedules. They organized our files on Dropbox and opened an account to accept submissions via Submittable. The care-filled, justice-fueled respect with which she approached all aspects of the work inspired others to respect all aspects of their work and themselves more fully. At our last meeting, she said, "I think I can say this now, I'm not going to get better." Why show up to do the work when the future is not assured? These questions are called into stark relief when facing a terminal illness or a global health crisis, but it's also an existential reality we all face in our own ways.

I am frankly astonished by the bravery and generosity of her belief that our shared vision of a future CUNY reorganized around just, ethical, and equitable feminist values was worth her time and labor, even when she knew she might not be with us to enjoy its fruition. Her capacity to lead us so intelligently toward shared goals while mired in the disheartening traffic of everyday difficulties exacerbated by a terminal illness, a global pandemic, and regressive democracy starving its institutions of higher education is an inspiration and a call to action.

With every encounter, she edged my thinking closer toward the big picture, the better, gentler, and more just world we longed and fought for at CUNY. She reminded me it's nearer than we know, it's present in our collective efforts to bring it into being. Perhaps most powerfully, Brianne acted every day "as if" the institutional future we envisioned was already real. Their belief in that future strengthened my own resolve to live it "as if" even as we pursue it at CUNY. Belief can travel between people like that, braiding us together into a more equitable future. We have seen the power unexamined belief has to override critical thinking, but a deeply held critical belief in the immanence of a better world is a beautiful, motivating thing to find in a CUNY colleague. —**Kendra Sullivan**

I met Brianne through Red Washburn, and I remember Brianne's calm as we talked about her teaching the Feminist Texts and Theories course. What I remember most though, is that she believed in possibility. Even when there was uncertainty in her own life, she assumed that possibility was always waiting. That, to me, is the sign of a person who is committed and generous. Brianne's generous spirit along with her calm contributed to my own ability to think about futures and capacious giving. I am so honored to have been in her orbit although just for a short time. Who she was, is reminder, that possibility is ever there for us. We just have to see it and reach for it. Thank you my friend. —**Dána-Ain Davis**

I was one of Brianne's colleagues at BMCC. I was a union comrade. A feminist compa. And, we were also neighbors. These past few weeks, I have been thinking about these different positions. We got along so well. We shared many interests. I always thought that, in the end, we would become pals, BFFs. I admired them deeply. I liked when they shared ideas at meetings, when they talked about their students, and also liked their style—and I know Brianne liked mine (I'm not bragging, we used to compliment each other's outfits). We kept making plans to hang out in Washington Heights, where we both lived, but it didn't happen much—the hanging out. Although time passed, it really didn't matter, because we both knew, or thought, we would always have another opportunity. We did succeed once. Brianne came to my place. This was in March 2018—so long ago! There was this action idea, decided on by the BMCC-PSC chapter, to do a march to the President's Office to demand more reassigned hours. Someone suggested a motif: we would be workload creeps. Brianne and I were both at the meeting. Right there and then, we decided to form the BMCC-PSC art committee. We invited others to join, but nobody did. We didn't care. We met on a Saturday evening to create a workload creep. We built a Frankenstein of sorts, from scratch. We also talked a lot. About writers we both liked, about our research, about fun things we could do together here in Washington Heights—go for a walk, work together at a coffee shop. We said we would hang out again, but we didn't. When I learned that Brianne had passed away, I felt the loss of a friendship in the making. The loss of time. I also thought

about this evening we spent together, and searched for the photo of the workload creep, until I found it on my Instagram. I do feel a bit silly sharing all of this here—Brianne was involved in meaningful projects, important collabs—but, what can I say, I cherish this memory, this form of collaboration. —**Ángeles Donoso Macaya**

Brianne was quite a force. She'll be remembered by many as someone who was committed to fairness and inclusion, who communicated with acuity her refreshing beliefs and points of view, someone talented who laughed easily and was welcoming to all. I am so, so sorry to learn that Brianne has left us, but if she is free from pain now, that's a blessing that can be consoling. Brianne made indelible impressions that I want to keep alive by motivating me to deliberately speak and act righteously as one way to honor her memory. —**Jerilyn Fisher**

Brianne was, first, my neighbor. Brianne was that in the biggest sense of the term. I met Ben and Brianne in 2014 when I moved into "The 509" in Hamilton Heights. I thought Brianne was the coolest. Over the years and in different contexts as part of the CUNY-verse, we became colleagues and our friendship grew. I loved Brianne's energy, their smarts, and their ability to always find strategies to battle the ever-increasing BS of daily life as queer, gender nonconforming folks. Brianne was a deep friend. Brianne was hilarious. Sometimes, they would bust out dancing in convenience stores or on the sidewalk. During the early months of Covid lockdown, The 509 became a fortress with its occupants helping each other in ways that, in other times, may have seemed trivial. However, from piggybacking on each other's FreshDirect orders (with Ben staying up all night just to get a delivery slot) out of an abundance of caution and just downright fear to taking masked walks with my German shepherd, Sylvie, Brianne saved my mental health as I struggled to shift to an online teaching mode. In May, I wanted to go fly fishing on the Neversink River. I asked Brianne if they wanted to ride up to Katrina Falls with me. They declined. The thought of riding with another person in a metal container—if it was not absolutely necessary—was untenable, and reasonably so. A few weeks later, Brianne and I drove up to the Neversink Unique Area and hiked to a beautiful spot. We took Sylvie with us; we packed food and beverages. Brianne went swimming and watched Sylvie while I fished a few yards away. We talked a lot on those outings. Brianne and I brainstormed about organizing a queers-on-the-trail hiking group. We talked a lot about "Reel Out for Trout," a fly-fishing group that I, thanks to Brianne, am determined to create. They took great photos of Sylvie and me that day. Brianne was dear to me in so many ways. When it came time for me to move out of The 509, Brianne drove my car with Sylvie and Raymond (my kitty) all the way from NYC to New Mexico during February and early March 2021. I drove a twenty-four-foot truck, "Patty LePenske," with my belongings. Little did we know that Brianne was already quite ill. After we got to my house, Brianne enjoyed the bright, New Mexico winter sun. They sat in my yard, in the sun, looking at the mountains, reading, and thinking those Brianne thoughts. I miss Brianne. When I think of Brianne, I see them in the sun, framed by the mountains. —**JV Fuqua**

We are so saddened by Brianne's passing, but will remember them always, with fondness in our hearts. Anyone who has worked or participated in interdisciplinary fields like women's, gender, and sexuality studies, or in nonprofit publishing, will know just how much tenacity and spirit it takes to sustain this work, to keep pushing boundaries and amplifying marginalized and critical perspectives at all times. Brianne possessed this tenacity in spades. Their energy and vision were invaluable to sustaining *WSQ* throughout the years of the pandemic, when everything about the future was uncertain. Brianne showed up, tirelessly—and kept going, kept pushing. They are an inspiration, and their legacy will live on, always, in this work and in the hearts of those whose lives they touched. —**Margot Atwell, Lauren Hook, Nick Whitney, and the Feminist Press team**

CONTEMPORARY BLACK BRITISH WOMEN WRITERS

TULSA STUDIES IN WOMEN'S LITERATURE

FALL 2022, VOL. 41, NO. 2